Vegetables

Natural Pests and Diseases Control

Authorised in organic farming

Rudolphe Lemmens

2026

Vegetables. Natural Pests and Diseases Control © 2026 by Rudolphe Lemmens.

Book and Cover design by Rudolphe Lemmens

This book is available as a smartphone and tablet app from:

Édition : BoD · Books on Demand, 31 avenue Saint-Rémy, 57600 Forbach, bod@bod.fr
Impression : Libri Plureos GmbH, Friedensallee 273, 22763 Hambourg (Allemagne)
ISBN: 978-2-3226-1354-0

Dépôt légal : Avril 2025

Table of content

4

Introduction

Introduction to organic gardening principles

Organic gardening is a holistic system that sustain the health of soils, environment and humans. It depends on ecological processes, biodiversity, and life-cycles rather than the use of chemical inputs. It combines tradition, innovation, science, feeling to benefit the environment and promote fair relationship and good quality of life. The whole garden is considered as an organism with closed nutrient and energy cycle system. It relies on farming practises preserving the long term sustainability of the soil and its habitants and reducing nonrenewable resources.

Organic gardeners use the fundamental components and natural processes of ecosystems, such as soil organism activities, nutrient cycling, and species distribution and competition, directly and indirectly as garden management tools to prevent pests from reaching damage levels. Soil fertility and and crop nutrients are managed through tillage and cultivation practices, crop rotations, cover, and companion crops and supplemented with manure, composts, crop waste material, and others.

The rules of organic agriculture allow the use of unregistered products such as decoctions, infusions and macerations of plants, which can be prepared on the farm or shared among farmers.

Plant protection products authorised for use in organic farming differ among countries depending on the differences in crops, pests, and cropping systems, as well as regulations and standards adopted by these countries. Check with your certification organism if you are a registered organic farmer before any doubt in using a product.

Introduction to the book

Identification of crop pests is important but sometimes very difficult in the garden, luckily to overcome this, damage by pests and symptoms of plant diseases are mostly specific to a vegetable and therefor more easily be distinguished in the garden. The regular (daily) inspection of the garden for pests, to determine their presence, their abundance and damage serves as information for decision making regarding control methods. Pests can be detected by visual observation, or also pheromone and trapping techniques.

Vegetables

Vegetables, the most common vegetables grown in a family garden are selected and described. Symptoms and damage to the plant parts as leaves, stems, flowers and roots are linked to the pests attacking the specific vegetable. E.g. Yellow leaves on tomato indicate early blight. Yellow leaves on beetroot indicate boron deficiency.

Pests

Pests, are selected for their commonness on the cultivated vegetables. They are short described and attention is paid to the damage and symptoms to identify them. Control methods are proposed in two remedies systems: Immediate action or proactive action.

Remedies

All the remedies proposed are described in detail, how to use, on what to use and eventually how to prepare them yourself.

Some definitions

Proactive management of pests includes the use of cultural control methods biological methods and starts with crop rotation, selection of crop plant varieties, timing of planting and harvesting, irrigation management, mulching, weeding, sanitation, removal of debris and crop residues, promoting beneficial insects and use of trap crops and companion plants.

Cultural control methods also include such methods as handpicking insects, mowing, hoeing, flaming, soil solarisation, biofumigation, tilling, washing, row covers, protective nets, sticky paper collars, water pressure sprays, insect vacuums and many others.

Biological methods are the use of beneficial organisms that can be introduced or attracted to the garden to reduce insect pest populations. It exist of introducing pest's natural enemies to the garden or glasshouse where they do not occur naturally, or even smarter boosting the naturally occurring natural enemies population by providing a favourable environment to them.

Biopesticides are characterised by having minimal or no risk to the environment, natural enemies, and non target organisms due to their mode of action, rapid degradation, and the small amounts applied to control pests. They are slow acting, have a relatively critical application times, and suppress rather than eliminate a pest population.

Biopesticides can be defined as bio-based substances, derived from bacteria, entomopathogenic fungi, plants, nematodes, and viruses, acting against crop pests with different mechanisms of action. Biopesticides, compared to synthetic pesticides, have advantages such as being environmentally benign and free of harmful residues, not provoking chemical resistance development in pests, having low-cost production, and being easy to use. Biopesticides coupled withorganic proactive pest management can be employed to maintain your garden in good health and produce safe vegetables.

How to use the book

Checking vegetables allow you to discover symptoms or damages on leaves, stems, fruits or roots on a specific crop. In the book you consult the specific vegetables and then you look for the symptoms on leaves or other parts of the plant. For ease of use the symtoms are classified by fungi, bacteria or insects. E.g. You grow lettuce and find out the leaves have irregular holes or perforations, by experience you know only insects can provoke this type of damage. The book propose one or more pests who are provoking this damage.

Lettuce Symptomes on: Leaves Insects. Leaves with perforations ⋯▸ Slug and Snail.

Then you consult the pest section of the book, to confirm your firsts diagnoses. In this section the pest are described in more detail and if the characteristics of the pest are not covering what you have seen in the garden you shall have to search for other candidates. It is also possible that the same symptoms on the plant are provoked by more than one pest. Once the pest identified a list of remedies are proposed.

Slugs and snails. Symptoms: Leaves with perforations, Traces of trash. ⋯▸ List of proactive and immediate actions. Make your choice.

Following the gravity of pest infection or damage caused, in between the remedies you can select immediate action or proactive actions. Some remedies can be bought in garden centres others can be home made. Follow carefully the recipes provided. Always handle products with care even homemade sprays.

Legumes

Artichoke

Botanical name
Cyanara cardunculus var. scolymus

Family
Asteraceae

English name
Globe artichoke, French artichoke, Green artichoke.

Names in other languages
Artichaut (FR), Artischocke (DE), Artisjok (NL), Articiococo (IT), Alcachofra (PO), Alcachofa (SP).

Related plants
Cardoon (*Cyanara cardunculus var. altilis*) selected for edible leaf stems.

Description
The globe artichoke also known by the names French artichoke and green artichoke in the U.S., is a variety of a species of thistle cultivated as a food. The edible portion of the plant consists of the flower buds before the flowers come into bloom. The budding artichoke flower-head is a cluster of many budding small flowers (an inflorescence), together with many bracts, on an edible base. Once the buds bloom, the structure changes to a coarse, barely edible form. Another variety of the same species is the cardoon, a perennial plant native to the Mediterranean region. Both wild forms and cultivated varieties (cultivars) exist.

Pests
African Cotton Leafworm, Artichoke Moth, Artichoke Pear-shaped Weevil, Artichoke Plume Moth, Artichoke Root Aphid, Ascochyta Rot, Bean Aphids, Black Dolphin Aphids, Black Rot, Botrytis Blight, Collar rot, Cotton Worm, Cucumber Mosaic Virus, Daisy-root Aphid, Frosted Orange Moth, Gray Mold, Green Artichoke Aphid, Green Leaf Beetle, Green Tortoise Beetle, Grey Mould, Leaf Spot, Lettuce Root Aphid, Powdery Mildew, Ramularia Bract Spot, Ramularia Leaf Spot, Red Spider Mite, Sclerotinia Wilt, Thistle Aphid, Two-spotted Mite, Verticillium Wilt, White Mold, White Rot, Xanthomonas Disease of Artichoke.

Symptons on:
Flowers
Galleries

◇ Capitules and bracts (flowers) with galleries in which various caterpillars can be found ⋯▸ Artichoke Moth. Artichoke Plume Moth: Noctuids several species, mainly Hydraecia xanthenes (Artichoke moth) and Gortyna flavago.

◇ Galleries in flowerheads ⋯▸ Frosted Orange Moth. Artichoke Moth: The damage is caused by the caterpillars climbing up the stems bearing the developed flower heads.

Spots

◇ Brown or black spots, extending from the tips of the bracts ⋯▸ Ascochyta Rot. Black Rot. Leaf Spot: Spots covered with speckles distributed in brownish or blackish concentric circles appear on the leaves or the outer bracts of the flower heads. These spots can reach 1 to 2 cm long.

◇ Grayish colored soft, mushy spots on flowers ⋯▸ Gray Mold. Grey Mould. Botrytis Blight: Regardless of the organs affected, the dying tissues become covered with a very characteristic dense gray mold, consisting of the conidiophores and conidia of the fungus.

◇ Blackish-brown spots, which may become covered with grayish mold ⋯▸ Gray Mold. Grey Mould. Botrytis Blight: Blackish-brown spots, extending from the base of the bracts, which may become covered with grayish mold (fruiting bodies). Sometimes, sclerotia are present. This disease develops secondarily following an injury or other disease.

◇ Translucent, oily-looking spots that turn brown ⋯▸ Xanthomonas Disease of Artichoke: Damage to artichokes appears in spring, on the bracts of the flower heads which have small translucent spots.

Leaves
Damage
◇ Leaf eaten (irregular holes) ⋯→ Cotton Worm. African Cotton Leafworm: The damage caused by caterpillars, which vary in color from gray to reddish or yellowish, is recognizable by the large bites on the leaves.

Deformation
◇ Leaves curled or shrivelled ⋯→ Bean Aphids. Black Dolphin Aphids: Presence of black aphids on the leaves, on the flower stems and the flower heads. As soon as they appear, deformation of the attacked leaves and development of sooty mold.

◇ Leaves curled and deformed ⋯→ Green Artichoke Aphid

Discoloring
◇ Grayish, brown leaves, completely dried out ⋯→ Ramularia Leaf and Bract Spot: Complete drying of the leaf. This disease develops on older plants after harvest.

◇ Leaves turn yellow and wilt ⋯→ Artichoke Pear-shaped Weevil; The leaves turn yellow and decay, especially those at the base of the plant.

◇ Leaves discoulouring bronzed or silvery ⋯→ Red Spider Mite. Two-spotted Mite: They damage the plant by piercing its cells to feed on them. The leaves turn pale and become stained yellow. To protect themselves and improve their microclimate, they weave a web around the leaf. A strong attack of mites leads to the leaves rolling and drying out, then falling off.

Galleries
◇ Leaf and petiole with gallery dug by a white larva ⋯→ Artichoke Pear-shaped Weevil: Yellowing of the leaves and galleries dug in the petioles by a white, curved, legless larva, which can reach 3 mm.

Presence
◇ Presence of aphids. Deformed leaf ⋯→ Thistle Aphid, Plum - thistle aphid: Aphids whose color varies from yellow to brown located on the underside of the leaves and at the base of the flower heads. Aphids feed on the contents of the cells of the epidermis of the leaves by biting and sucking the sap.

◇ Gnawed, planed sheet with treatments on the upper surface ⋯→ Green Leaf Beetle, Green Tortoise Beetle: Leaves eaten by adults and larvae. Leaf tissues are not pierced.

◇ Presence of black aphids ⋯→ Bean Aphids. Black Dolphin Aphids: Presence of black aphids on the leaves, on the flower stems and capitals. As soon as they appear, deformation of the attacked leaves and development of sooty mold.

◇ Presence of yellowish-green aphids ⋯→ Thistle Aphid, Plum - thistle aphid: Presence of yellowish-green aphids, located exclusively on the lower surface of the leaves. They are never found on the flower heads and do not cause any deformation of the leaves.

◇ Presence of aphids ⋯→ Green Artichoke Aphid: The green artichoke aphid lives on the underside of the leaves, apparently without causing leaf deformation. Artichokes infested with large numbers of aphids are seriously weakened, reducing the size and value of the artichoke heads.

◇ Presence of caterpillars ⋯→ Cotton Worm. African Cotton Leafworm: The Mediterranean noctuid or cotton worm causes damage which is recognizable by the large portions eaten out of the leaves.

◇ Presence of larvae and adult beetles ⋯→ Green Leaf Beetle, Green Tortoise Beetle: Adult artichoke beetles cluster on leaves and shoots, which they attack by riddling them with irregular holes.

Spots
◇ Leaves with of angular, grayish to brown spots ⋯→ Ramularia Leaf and Bract Spot: Appearance of numerous, confluent, angular, yellowish, grayish spots, on which a whitish mold appears. Spots can quickly confluent over the entire leaf blade, causing the leaf to dry out completely.

◇ Irregular blackish brown spots ⋯→ Ascochyta Rot. Black Rot. Leaf Spot: Spots covered with speckles distributed in concentric brownish or blackish circles. Attacks occur in autumn, when the temperature drops and humidity increases.

◇ Translucent, oily-looking spots that turn brown ⋯→ Xanthomonas Disease of Artichoke: The leaves of artichokes are more discreetly affected and the disease can go unnoticed until the flower heads form.

◇ Yellow/brown spots ⋯→ Verticillium Wilt: Marginal drying, sometimes asymmetrical. In the stem, brown lesions at the level of the conductive tissue. Atrophied and deformed capitula.

◇ Yellowish then brown spots on the upper surface of the leaf ⋯→ Powdery Mildew, Oidium: Yellowish then brown spots on the upper surface of the leaf, generally limited by the large veins, whitish felting on the lower surface.

Stunted
◇ Deformation and stunting of plants ⋯→ Cucumber Mosaic Virus. CMV: Artichoke latent virus (ALV, Potyvirus) is transmitted by aphids. Cucumber mosaic virus (CMV) induces deformation and stunting of plants.

Plants whole
Wilting
◇ Wilting of the entire plant -> Verticillium Wilt: The leaves soften and become duller. The leaves begin to yellow, then turn brown as they become necrotic. The characteristic feature is the asymmetry of the symptoms, with many leaves only affected on one half. The disease progresses from the bottom to the top of the plant. Verticillium wilt causes dark streaks under the bark.

◇ Wilted plants ⋯→ Lettuce Root Aphid: Aphids'

bites and nutritional withdrawals from the roots cause the plant to wilt and die.

Roots or tubers
Presence

◇ Presence of colonies of gray aphids on roots ⤳ Lettuce Root Aphid: Presence of very numerous yellowish-white aphids along the roots, these bearing a fairly visible tuft of white wax.

◇ Root with white sooty mold ⤳ Lettuce Root Aphid: Development of very numerous yellowish-white insects along the roots, these carrying a fairly visible tuft of white wax.

◇ Presence of aphid colonies ⤳ Artichoke Root Aphid. Daisy-root Aphid: The artichoke root aphid, which is rather white, is particularly harmful to the artichoke due to the presence of colonies on the roots, causing a significant reduction in the development of the plant and the size of the flower heads.

Stems
Galleries

◇ Stems with galleries in which various caterpillars can be found ⤳ Artichoke Moth. Artichoke Plume Moth: Noctuids several species, mainly Hydraecia xanthenes (Artichoke moth) and Gortyna flavago.

◇ Stems with galleries and presence of waste deposits, sawdust ⤳ Frosted Orange Moth. Artichoke Moth: Infested plants show ventilation holes along their stems for galleries, as well as evacuation holes, through which abundant blackish droppings are discharged.

Lesions

◇ Reddish and brown lesions ⤳ Black Scurf. Rhizoctonia Canker. Stem Canker. Crater spot; Presence of reddish and brown lesion at the collar.

◇ Stems with brownish canker lesions ⤳ Rhizoctonia collar rot; Rhizoctonia brown rot also produces cankers located at the base (at the collar) of young plants or more developed plants, grown in certain humid and heavily contaminated soils. These cankerous alterations have a reddish-brown color.

Presence

◇ White mold on the stem and collar ⤳ White Rot. White Mold. Sclerotinia Wilt: Black or dark brown sclerotia form inside the stems. This uncommon disease can sometimes lead to the death of the plant.

Asparagus

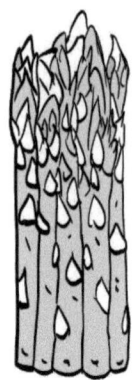

Botanical name
Asparagus officinalis

Family
Liliaceae/Asparagaceae

English name
Asparagus, Garden asparagus, White asparagus, Green asparagus

Names in other languages
Asperge (FR), Tuin Asperge (NL), Gemüse-Spargel (DE), Asparago comune (IT), Espargos (PO), Espárrago verano (SP).

Description
Asparagus (*Asparagus officinalis*) is an herbaceous perennial plant in the family Asparagaceae which is grown for its young shoots, or spears, which are eaten as a vegetable. The asparagus plant is tall with scale like leaves emerging from the underground stem (rhizome) and has stout stems and feathery foliage. The flowers are bell shaped and occur alone or in pairs. They are green-white to yellow in color. After flowering, a round red berry is formed with 1 to 6 black seeds. Asparagus can live for 20 or more years and can attain a height between 100–150 cm (39.4–59.1 in).

Pests
Asparagus Aphid, Asparagus Beetle, Twelve-spotted Asparagus Beetle, Asparagus Fly, Asparagus Maggot, Asparagus Moth, Beet Armyworm, Bright-line Brown-eyes Moth, Cercosporosa Leaf Spot, Click Beetle, Striped Elaterid Beetle, Wireworms, Fusarium Root Rot, Fusarium Wilt, Glasshouse Whitefly. Greenhouse Whitefly, Phoma, Rust, Violet Root-rot of Asparagus

Symptoms on:
Leaves
Damage

◇ Leaves with irregular holes ⋯→ Armyworms, Beet Armyworm: Older Spodoptera exigua caterpillars migrate to the apex of the plants where they feed mainly on thegrowing areas. They make large holes in the leaves and sometimes leave only the veins behind. The damage caused considerably affects the growth of the plants. In heavy infestations, the damage can extend to the stems and, in the worst cases, to the fruits, which the caterpillars consume entirely from the inside.

Defoliation

◇ Plants defoliated ⋯→ Asparagus Beetle. Twelve-spotted Asparagus Beetle: The larvae of the leaf beetle feed on all the foliage until the plant is exhausted.

Presence

◇ Yellow-green to black pustules on leaves ⋯→ Rust: On the upper side of the leaves, you will see tiny white, orange or even brown spots appear depending on the species. If you turn these leaves over, you will see that these spots correspond to tiny pustules of the same color. The lesions are generally yellow, brown or red, but can be dark brown or black at the end of the season.

◇ Presence of caterpillars ⋯→ Bright-line Brown-eyes Moth: The damage caused by this moth on cabbage and beet leaves is generally not very significant.

◇ Presence of caterpillars ⋯→ Armyworms, Beet Armyworm: Older Spodoptera exigua caterpillars migrate to the apex of the plants where they feed mainly on the growing areas. They make large holes in the leaves and sometimes leave only the veins behind. The damage caused considerably affects the growth of the plants. In heavy infestations, the damage can extend to the stems and, in the worst cases, to the fruits, which the caterpillars consume entirely from the inside.

Spots

◇ White, slightly raised spots on leaves ⸱⸱⸱→ Rust: On the upper side of the leaves, you will see tiny white, orange or even brown spots appear depending on the species. If you turn these leaves over, you will see that these spots correspond to tiny pustules of the same color.

◇ Reddish-orange spots on leaves ⸱⸱⸱→ Rust: On the upper side of the leaves, you will see tiny white, orange or even brown spots appear depending on the species. If you turn these leaves over, you will see that these spots correspond to tiny pustules of the same color. The lesions are generally yellow, brown or red, but can be dark brown or black at the end of the season.

◇ Leaf spots with brown-reddish margins ⸱⸱⸱→ Cercosporosa Leaf Spot, Cercosporia blight: Cercospora blight initially causes small, oval, gray to tan lesions with red borders. Severe infections may cause entire ferns to turn yellow or brown. Cercospora blight may cause reduced vigor and yield of spears the next spring.

Stunted

◇ Stunted leaves ⸱⸱⸱→ Glasshouse Whitefly. Greenhouse Whitefly: The numerous bites and feeding suctions of whiteflies on the foliage, just like those of aphids, cause a slowdown in plant development.

Plants whole
Dieback

◇ Plant slowly desiccates ⸱⸱⸱→ Asparagus Moth: The larva attacks the root system, devours the buds and hollows out the roots. It causes the disappearance of the plants which dry out during the summer; young plantations are particularly vulnerable.

Discoloring

◇ Deformed plant, yellow leaf ⸱⸱⸱→ Rust: Discoloration and die-back of foliage and plants.

Presence

◇ Presence of larvae and adult beetles ⸱⸱⸱→ Asparagus Beetle. Twelve-spotted Asparagus Beetle: The main damage is due to the larvae which eat away and destroy all the green branches of the shoots, considerably or totally reducing any possibility of chlorophyll assimilation.

Stunted

◇ Plants stunted ⸱⸱⸱→ Fusarium Root Rot: Diseased plants wilt to a greater or lesser extent during the hottest times of the day; this wilting is sometimes reversible. In the most serious cases, the plants eventually dry out completely.

Roots or tubers
Decay

◇ Rotting of roots ⸱⸱⸱→ Fusarium Root Rot: The cause of these wiltings is to be found at the level of the collar of the feet. At this location, a wet lesion has developed, a rot that has gradually spread to the lower part of the stem and the taproot, but also to the upper part of the root system. At the collar, the altered tissues are wet and show a dark to brownish tint. This lesion ends up girdling the stem for several centimeters. The roots located in the

◇ same layer of soil are also affected. Their cortex turns yellow, brown and decomposes.

Galleries

◇ Galleries in roots ⸱⸱⸱→ Click Beetle. Striped Elaterid Beetle. Wireworms: As larvae development takes up to four years, in an infected soil we can find larvae of different ages. They live at different depths, depending on the moment of the year, as they are highly sensitive to heat and dryness. They eat or pierce the underground organs of the plant: roots, crowns, bud leaves and turions.

Stems
Deformation

◇ Deformed turions ⸱⸱⸱→ Asparagus Fly, Asparagus Maggot: The asparagus fly larva feeds by digging galleries inside young buds (turions) during its growth period. These injuries will prevent the sap from circulating and therefore weaken the claw until it dries out.

Discoloring

◇ Purple to light-brown stems ⸱⸱⸱→ Violet Root-rot of Asparagus: This illness leads to the production of small turions with a tendency to branch out; subsequently, the plants start to dry up. The infection occurs in the rhyzome and the collar of the stem; its clearest symptom is the appearance of a pink layer that will then turn purple.

Necrosis

◇ Necrotic stems ⸱⸱⸱→ Fusarium Wilt: An affected plant has a yellowing, stunted, wilted appearance, sometimes with gummosis on the stem. Discoloration and vascular browning of the collar progressing towards the stem and roots, and developing into cortical rot.Sort

Presence

◇ Presence of aphids ⸱⸱⸱→ Asparagus Aphid: Brachycorynella asparagi is a serious pest of asparagus. Feeding of the aphid causes a characteristic distortion of the terminal bud termed 'rosetting' (=witches brooms) of asparagus, with the internodes being shortened and the leaves being both shortened and turned blue green. Strong aphid infestation can cause dieback of seedlings. Affected stems of mature plants develop imperfectly, become stunted and broom-like, with plants growing in the shape of a bush.

Beetroot. Beet

Botanical name
Beta vulgaris

Family
Chenopodiaceae - Amaranthaceae

English name
Beetroot. Red beet.

Names in other languages
Betterave potagère. Betterave rouge (FR), Rode biet (NL), Rote Bete. Rote Rübe (DE), Barbabietola rossa (IT), Beterraba (PO), Remolacha (SP).

Description
Beets (*Beta vulgaris*) are herbaceous biennial root vegetables in the family Chenopodiaceae grown for their edible root. The plant is usually erect with a long main root and a rosette of leaves growing on stems. The leaves are oval in shape, arranged alternately on the stem and grow 20–40 cm (7.9–15.7 in) in length. The roots are usually red in color. The plant produces sessile green flowers and can reach 1–2 m (3.3–6.6 ft) in height when in flower.

Pests
Bean Aphids, Black Dolphin Aphids, Beet Armyworm, Beet Curly Top Virus, BCTV, Beet Fly, Mangold Fly, Beet Moth, Boron Deficiency, Brightline Brown-eyes Moth, Cabbage Stem Flea Beetle, Cercosporosa Leaf Spot, Click Beetle, Striped Elaterid Beetle, Wireworms, Dark Swordgrass Moth, Black cutworm, Greasy cutworm, Fusarium Wilt, Garden Dart Moth, June Beetles, May Beetles, Potato Aphid, Powdery Mildew, Slug and Snail, Garden Slug, Loach, Little Grey Slug, Vine Snail, White Garden Snail, Violet Rot,White Rot, White Mold, Sclerotinia Wilt.

Symptoms on:
Leaves
Damage

◇ Leaves with perforations ⋯→ Dark Sword-grass Moth. Black cutworm. Greasy cutworm: Early larval stages feed on the leaves and create small holes with irregular contours. Later stages attack the stem, often during sowing, and consequently cut the seedlings at ground level.

◇ Perforated leaves ⋯→ Cabbage Stem Flea Beetle: It is difficult to monitor the activity of the adult of the large rapeseed flea beetle: it occurs at night. Its damage, on the other hand, is easily recognizable because the insect bites the cotyledons and young leaves in a circular fashion. Perforations can also be observed.

◇ Leaves with perforations ⋯→ Slug and Snail. Garden Slug. Loach. Little Grey Slug. Vine Snail. White Garden Snail: The slug consumes the leaves of plants between the veins, which gives them a serrated appearance. It digs small holes in the tubers. When the attack is serious, the stems are cut and consumed, the plants disappear.

◇ Leaves with irregular holes ⋯→ Armyworms, Beet Armyworm: Older Spodoptera exigua caterpillars migrate to the apex of the plants where they feed mainly on the growing areas. They make large holes in the leaves and sometimes leave only the veins behind. The damage caused considerably affects the growth of the plants. In heavy infestations, the damage can extend to the stems and, in the worst cases, to the fruits, which the caterpillars consume entirely from the inside.

Decay

◇ Soft watery rot on lower leaves ⋯→ White Rot. White Mold. Sclerotinia Wilt: Pre and post-emergent damping off, crown rot, and blighting of foliage and petioles. Small, hard, irregular, black structures called sclerotia may be present on or in plant tissue (especially inside stem and petiole tissue).

Deformation

◇ Leaves curled or shrivelled ⋯▸ Bean Aphids. Black Dolphin Aphids: Presence of black aphids on the leaves, on the flower stems and the flower heads. As soon as they appear, deformation of the attacked leaves and development of sooty mold.

Discoloring

◇ Leaves discoulouring yellowish ⋯▸ June Beetles, May Beetles, Chafer beetles: The adults are phyllophagous and the larvae, called "white grubs" are root-eating. They deform the roots and cause the plant to wilt.

◇ Yellow leaves on plants ⋯▸ Boron Deficiency: Symptoms appear on young leaves: wrinkled, fragile leaves, slowed growth. Then wilting of the leaves with the appearance of brown or black spots on the petioles. Young leaves wilt, turn black and dry out.

◇ Leaves turn yellow and wilt ⋯▸ Fusarium Wilt: An affected plant has a yellowing, stunted, wilted appearance, sometimes with gummosis on the stem. Discoloration and vascular browning of the collar progressing towards the stem and roots, and developing into cortical rot.

◇ Leaves turn yellow and wilt ⋯▸ Beet Curly Top Virus. BCTV: Leaf curling and embossing, irregular and prominent veins are observed. Plants are sometimes stunted. Leaves are occasionally rough and eventually turn yellow.

Galleries

◇ Leaves with galleries ⋯▸ Beet Fly. Mangold Fly: The first generation beet fly larvae are the most harmful: they penetrate the leaves, between the two epidermis, and devour part of the tissue responsible for photosynthesis. They then dig galleries: whitish sinuosities can be observed. These galleries cause the leaves to dry out, turn brown, become pierced and lose their photosynthetic capacity.

◇ Leaves with galleries ⋯▸ Beet Moth, Beet worm: The larva, as soon as it hatches, reaches the leaves in the center of the plant in which it digs irregular silky galleries. Its presence is identified by the presence of black excrement on the plants.

Lesions

◇ Brown lesions on leaves ⋯▸ Beet Fly. Mangold Fly: The first generation beet fly larvae are the most harmful: they penetrate the leaves, between the two epidermis, and devour part of the tissue responsible for photosynthesis. They then dig galleries: whitish sinuosities can be observed. These galleries cause the leaves to dry out, turn brown, become pierced and lose their photosynthetic capacity.

Presence

◇ White to gray powder coverage on leaves ⋯▸ Powdery Mildew, Oidium: The heart leaves are covered with purplish-grey spores on the underside. They thicken, curl, and curl up. Older leaves turn yellow on the outside, then blacken and die. Only a few isolated plants or foci are damaged.

◇ Presence of black aphids ⋯▸ Bean Aphids. Black Dolphin Aphids: Presence of black aphids on the leaves, on the flower stems and capitals. As soon as they appear, deformation of the attacked leaves and development of sooty mold.

◇ Presence of aphids ⋯▸ Potato Aphid: The most classic symptoms are a curling of heavily infested leaves and a slowdown in the growth of the plants

◇ Presence of cutworms ⋯▸ Garden Dart Moth. Cutworm: The larvae feed on the roots of plants, cutting them at night.

◇ Presence of caterpillars ⋯▸ Bright-line Brown-eyes Moth: The damage caused by this moth on cabbage and beet leaves is generally not very significant.

◇ Presence of caterpillars ⋯▸ Armyworms, Beet Armyworm: Older Spodoptera exigua caterpillars migrate to the apex of the plants where they feed mainly on the growing areas. They make large holes in the leaves and sometimes leave only the veins behind. The damage caused considerably affects the growth of the plants. In heavy infestations, the damage can extend to the stems and, in the worst cases, to the fruits, which the caterpillars consume entirely from the inside.

Spots

◇ Yellowish then brown spots on the upper surface of the leaf ⋯▸ Powdery Mildew, Oidium: Yellowish then brown spots on the upper surface of the leaf, generally limited by the large veins, whitish felting on the lower surface.

◇ Leaf spots with brown-reddish margins ⋯▸ Cercosporosa Leaf Spot, Cercosporia blight: Cercospora blight initially causes small, oval, gray to tan lesions with red borders. Severe infections may cause entire ferns to turn yellow or brown. Cercospora blight may cause reduced vigor and yield of spears the next spring.

Plantlets
Dieback

◇ Damaged cotyledons ⋯▸ Dark Sword-grass Moth. Black cutworm. Greasy cutworm: Early larval stages feed on the leaves and create small holes with irregular contours. Later stages attack the stem, often during sowing, and consequently cut the seedlings at ground level.

Plants whole
Stunted

◇ Stunted plants ⋯▸ Cabbage Stem Flea Beetle: It is difficult to monitor the activity of the adult of the large rapeseed flea beetle: it occurs at night. Its damage, on the other hand, is easily recognizable because the insect bites the cotyledons and young leaves in a circular fashion. Perforations can also be observed.

Roots or tubers
Decay
◇ Internal brown rot ⋯⋅→ Boron Deficiency: Boron deficiency causes inner tissue to be reddish brown, or brown or gray concentric rings develop inside the roots, it also causes brown heart rot.

Galleries
◇ Galleries in roots ⋯⋅→ Click Beetle. Striped Elaterid Beetle. Wireworms: As larvae development takes up to four years, in an infected soil we can find larvae of different ages. They live at different depths, depending on the moment of the year, as they are highly sensitive to heat and dryness. They eat or pierce the underground organs of the plant: roots, crowns, bud leaves and turions.

Presence
◇ Grubs present in the soil ⋯⋅→ June Beetles, May Beetles, Chafer beetles: The adults are phyllophagous and the larvae burrowd in the soil, called "white grubs", are root-eating. They deform the roots and cause the plant to wilt.

Stems
Dieback
◇ Damaged stems ⋯⋅→ Dark Sword-grass Moth. Black cutworm. Greasy cutworm: Early larval stages feed on the leaves and create small holes with irregular contours. Later stages attack the stem, often during sowing, and consequently cut the seedlings at ground level.

Necrosis
◇ Necrotic stems ⋯⋅→ Fusarium Wilt: An affected plant has a yellowing, stunted, wilted appearance, sometimes with gummosis on the stem. Discoloration and vascular browning of the collar progressing towards the stem and roots, and developing into cortical rot.Sort

Stunted
◇ Stems stunted ⋯⋅→ Beet Moth, Beet worm: The larva, as soon as it hatches, reaches the leaves in the center of the plant in which it digs irregular silky galleries. Its presence is identified by the presence of black excrement on the beets.

Broad-bean

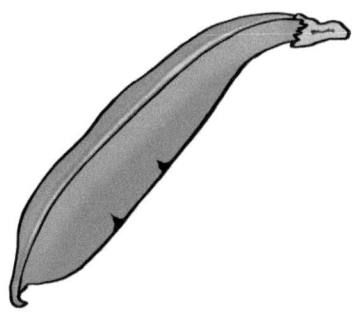

Botanical name
Vicia faba

Family
Fabaceae

English name
Broad-bean, Broadbean

Names in other languages
Fève (FR), Tuinboon (NL), Ackerbohne (DE), Fava (IT), Fava (PO), Haba (SP).

Description
Broad bean (*Vicia faba*) is a leguminous plant in the family Fabaceae primarily grown for its edible beans. Broad bean is a an annual vetch reaching between 0.5–1.8 m (1.6–6 ft) tall. There are often multiple stems originating from the base of the plant and the compound leaves are often broad, oval shaped, and come groups of 6 leaflets to a stem. The flowers are white with purple markings. Between 1 and 4 pods develop from each flower cluster.

Pests
Bean Aphids, Black Dolphin Aphids, Bean Beetle, Pea beetle, Fusarium Root Rot, Pea Root Nematode. Pea Cyst Nematode, Pea Thrips, Pea Weevil, Pea and Bean Weevil, Powdery Mildew, Rust.

Symptoms on:
Pods
Damage

◇ Seeds with holes ⋯→ Bean Bruchid: Presence of holes caused by larvae.

Dieback

◇ Fruit drop early ⋯→ Pea Thrips: Its outbreaks cause the plant to weaken and flowers to abort, leading to crop losses. It is also a vector of different viruses.

Leaves
Damage

◇ Leaf edges eaten ⋯→ Pea Weevil. Pea and Bean Weevil: Notches made by adults on the leaves can limit the density of young seedlings. In addition, attacks by larvae which feed on nodules and roots cause delays in vegetation.

Deformation

◇ Leaves curled or shrivelled ⋯→ Bean Aphids. Black Dolphin Aphids: Presence of black aphids on the leaves, on the flower stems and the flower heads. As soon as they appear, deformation of the attacked leaves and development of sooty mold.

◇ Leaves shrivelled ⋯→ Pea Thrips: Its outbreaks cause the plant to weaken and flowers to abort, leading to crop losses. It is also a vector of different viruses.

Discoloring

◇ Leaves turn yellow and die ⋯→ Pea Root Nematode. Pea Cyst Nematode: The leaves turn yellow and fall prematurely, the plants twist at the base, growth is stopped and the plants remain dwarfed.

Presence

◇ White to gray powder coverage on leaves ⋯→ Powdery Mildew, Oidium: The heart leaves are covered with purplish-grey spores on the underside. They thicken, curl, and curl up. Older leaves turn yellow on the outside, then blacken and die. Only a few isolated plants or foci are damaged.

◇ Presence of black aphids ⇢ Bean Aphids. Black Dolphin Aphids: Presence of black aphids on the leaves, on the flower stems and capitals. As soon as they appear, deformation of the attacked leaves and development of sooty mold.

◇ Presence of honey dew on leaves ⇢ Bean Aphids. Black Dolphin Aphids: Aphids suck large volumes of sap. The excess sugary fluid, honeydew, is secreted by the aphids. It adheres to plants, where it promotes growth of sooty molds.

◇ Presence of sooty mould on leaves ⇢ Bean Aphids. Black Dolphin Aphids: Aphids suck large volumes of sap. The excess sugary fluid, honeydew, is secreted by the aphids. It adheres to plants, where it promotes growth of sooty molds.

Spots

◇ Reddish-orange spots on leaves ⇢ Rust: On the upper side of the leaves, you will see tiny white, orange or even brown spots appear depending on the species. If you turn these leaves over, you will see that these spots correspond to tiny pustules of the same color. The lesions are generally yellow, brown or red, but can be dark brown or black at the end of the season.

◇ Yellowish then brown spots on the upper surface of the leaf ⇢ Powdery Mildew, Oidium: Yellowish then brown spots on the upper surface of the leaf, generally limited by the large veins, whitish felting on the lower surface.

Plants whole
Stunted

◇ Plants stunted ⇢ Fusarium Root Rot: Diseased plants wilt to a greater or lesser extent during the hottest times of the day; this wilting is sometimes reversible. In the most serious cases, the plants eventually dry out completely.

Roots or tubers
Decay

◇ Rotting of roots ⇢ Fusarium Root Rot: The cause of these wiltings is to be found at the level of the collar of the feet. At this location, a wet lesion has developed, a rot that has gradually spread to the lower part of the stem and the taproot, but also to the upper part of the root system. At the collar, the altered tissues are wet and show a dark to brownish tint. This lesion ends up girdling the stem for several centimeters. The roots located in the same layer of soil are also affected. Their cortex turns yellow, brown and decomposes.

Deformation

◇ Roots abnormally increased or swellings ⇢ Pea Root Nematode. Pea Cyst Nematode: The roots are poorly developed and have only a limited number of bacterial nodules; the rootlets are abundant and bear clusters of cysts.

Dieback

◇ Roots damaged ⇢ Pea Weevil. Pea and Bean Weevil: Notches made by adults on the leaves can limit the density of young seedlings. In addition, attacks by larvae which feed on nodules and roots cause delays in vegetation.

Seeds
Damage

◇ Beans with small holes ⇢ Bean Beetle. Pea beetle: The presence of bruchids in beans, peas or beans makes them unfit for consumption, reduces the germination rate of seeds and presents risks of re-infestation of crops. A bean can accommodate 5 to 6 individuals.

Stems
Presence

◇ Presence of colonies of aphids ⇢ Bean Aphids. Black Dolphin Aphids: The black bean aphid is a major pest of sugar beet, bean, and celery crops, with large numbers of aphids cause stunting of the plants. Beans suffer damage to flowers and pods which may not develop properly.

Broccoli

Botanical name
Brassica oleracea var. *italica*

Family
Brassicaceae

English name
Broccoli

Names in other languages
Chou brocoli (FR), Brocoli (NL), Brokkoli (DE), Cavolo broccolo (IT), Bróculos (PO), Brócoli (SP).

Related plants
Winter cauliflower

Description
Broccoli (*Brassica oleracea*) is an herbaceous annual or biennial grown for its edible flower heads which are used as a vegetable. The broccoli plant has a thick green stalk, or stem, which gives rise to thick, leathery, oblong leaves which are gray-blue to green in color. The plant produces large branching green flower heads covered with numerous white or yellow flowers. Broccoli can be annual or biennial depending on the variety and can grow to 1 m (3.3 ft) in height.

Pests
Beet Armyworm, Cabbage Aphid, Cabbage Club Root, Cabbage Maggot, Cabbage Stem Flea Beetle, Cabbageworm, Imported Cabbage Worms, Damping Off, Dark Sword-grass Moth, Black cutworm, Greasy cutworm, Diamond-back Moth, Downy Mildew of Crucifers, Early Blight of Potato/Tomato, Gray Mold. Grey Mould, Botrytis Blight.

Symptoms on:
Leaves
Damage

◇ Perforated leaves ⋯→ Cabbage Stem Flea Beetle: It is difficult to monitor the activity of the adult of the large rapeseed flea beetle: it occurs at night. Its damage, on the other hand, is easily recognizable because the insect bites the cotyledons and young leaves in a circular fashion. Perforations can also be observed.

◇ Leaves with holes ⋯→ Cabbageworm. Imported Cabbage Worms: Caterpillars devour the leaves of cruciferous plants, sometimes leaving only the large veins. In addition, their excrement, diluted by rain or dew, accumulates in the heart of the plant and makes it inedible.

◇ Leaves with irregular holes ⋯→ Armyworms, Beet Armyworm: Older Spodoptera exigua caterpillars migrate to the apex of the plants where they feed mainly on the growing areas. They make large holes in the leaves and sometimes leave only the veins behind. The damage caused considerably affects the growth of the plants. In heavy infestations, the damage can extend to the stems and, in the worst cases, to the fruits, which the caterpillars consume entirely from the inside.

◇ Leaves with holes ⋯→ Diamond-back Moth: The damage is significant on cabbages. The caterpillars first eat the outer leaves and then gradually migrate to the young leaves in the center. They join them together with silk threads and soil them with their excrement.

Deformation

◇ Leaves curled or shrivelled ⋯→ Cabbage Aphid: In the event of an outbreak, the plant can be completely covered by aphids, their honeydew and their exuviae.

Discoloring

◇ Reddening, yellowing of the leaves ⋯→ Cabbage Club Root: Aerial part of the plant: reduced development, especially during early attacks, wilting or even reddening of the foliage.

Lesions

◇ Purple or brown irregular shaped areas on leaves ⋯→ Downy Mildew of Crucifers: It first appears on older leaves, as white, yellow or brownish spots on the upper surfaces and downy grayish mold on the corresponding undersides.

◇ Brownish black lesions on leaves ⋯→ Early Blight of Potato/Tomato: Affected leaves and petioles turn yellow, then brown or black. Leaflets shrivel at the edges, and in severe infections the entire leaf wilts and dies.

Presence

◇ Coating of gray fungus spores on leaves ⋯→ Gray Mold. Grey Mould. Botrytis Blight: Regardless of the organs affected, the dying tissues become covered with a very characteristic dense gray mold, consisting of the conidiophores and conidia of the fungus.

◇ Presence of colonies of aphids ⋯→ Cabbage Aphid: In the event of an outbreak, the plant can be completely covered by aphids, their honeydew and their exuviae.

◇ White to gray, "downy" areas on under leaf surfaces. ⋯→ Downy Mildew of Crucifers: It first appears on older leaves, as white, yellow or brownish spots on the upper surfaces and downy grayish mold on the corresponding undersides.

◇ Presence of caterpillars ⋯→ Cabbageworm. Imported Cabbage Worms: Caterpillars devour the leaves of cruciferous plants, sometimes leaving only the large veins.

◇ Presence of honeydew and sooty moulds on leaves ⋯→ Cabbage Aphid: In the event of an outbreak, the plant can be completely covered by aphids, their honeydew and their exuviae.

◇ Presence of caterpillars ⋯→ Diamond-back Moth: The damage is significant on cabbages. The caterpillars first eat the outer leaves and then gradually migrate to the young leaves in the center. They join them together with silk threads and soil them with their excrement.

◇ Presence of caterpillars ⋯→ Armyworms, Beet Armyworm: Older Spodoptera exigua caterpillars migrate to the apex of the plants where they feed mainly on the growing areas. They make large holes in the leaves and sometimes leave only the veins behind. The damage caused considerably affects the growth of the plants. In heavy infestations, the damage can extend to the stems and, in the worst cases, to the fruits, which the caterpillars consume entirely from the inside.

Plantlets
Dieback

◇ Damaged cotyledons ⋯→ Dark Sword-grass Moth. Black cutworm. Greasy cutworm: Early larval stages feed on the leaves and create small holes with irregular contours. Later stagesattack the stem, often during sowing, and consequently cut the seedlings at ground level.

Wilting

◇ Wilted, collapsed and dead young seedlings ⋯→ Damping Off: Seeds rot and fail to germinate, or even germinate, but seedlings fail to grow. A translucent area completely covers the stem near the soil surface. The affected tissues rot, leading to wilting and collapse of the seedlings.

Plants whole
Stunted

◇ Stunted plants ⋯→ Cabbage Stem Flea Beetle: It is difficult to monitor the activity of the adult of the large rapeseed flea beetle: it occurs at night. Its damage, on the other hand, is easily recognizable because the insect bites the cotyledons and young leaves in a circular fashion. Perforations can also be observed.

Wilting

◇ Wilted plants ⋯→ Cabbage Maggot, Cabbage Fly: Damage is observed in nurseries and at all stages of vegetation. On leafy vegetables, the root part is more or less destroyed. Attacked plants can be recognized by the faded appearance they take on during hot days; the leaves often turn purplish red, turn yellow and sometimes dry out.

◇ Wilted plants ⋯→ Cabbage Club Root: Underground part of the plant: root deformation or presence of galls on the roots. These galls are firm (full interior), whitish then turn brown and rot, leading to the death of the plant.

Roots or tubers
Deformation

◇ Roots abnormally increased or swellings ⋯→ Cabbage Club Root: Underground part of the plant: root deformation or presence of galls on the roots. These galls are firm (full interior), whitish then turn brown and rot, leading to the death of the plant.

Presence

◇ Presence of maggots in roots ⋯→ Cabbage Maggot, Cabbage Fly: The larvae of the cabbage fly penetrate into the fleshy parts and dig galleries. The root part is more or less destroyed. Attacked plants can be recognized by the faded appearance they take on during hot days; the leaves often turn purplish red, turn yellow and sometimes dry out.

Stems
Dieback

◇ Damaged stems ⋯→ Dark Sword-grass Moth. Black cutworm. Greasy cutworm: Early larval stages feed on the leaves and create small holes with irregular contours. Later stages attack the stem, often during sowing, and consequently cut the seedlings at ground level.

Brussels Sprout

Botanical name
Brassica oleracea var. gemmifera

Family
Brassicaceae

English name
Brussels sprouts

Names in other languages
Chou de Bruxelles (FR), Spruit (NL) Rosenkohl (DE), Cavolo di Bruxelles (IT), Couve de Bruxelas (PO), Repollo de Bruselas (SP).

Description
Brussel sprouts (*Brassica oleracea*) are a cultivar of cabbage in the family Brassicaceae grown for their edible small leafy green buds, which resemble miniature cabbages. The plant has long, smooth and leathery leaves which can be green to purple in color and are arranged alternately on the stem. The sprouts form at the base of each leaf, in a long, spiral stem. The edible portion of the crop is the bud, which is a small cabbage-like head. It is a light green to green/blue in color. The plant is biennial but grown as an annual and can reach 0.6–1 m (2–3 ft) in height with a spread of 0.5–0.6 m (1.5–2 ft).

Pests
Cabbage Aphid, Cabbage Club Root, Cabbage Maggot, Cabbage Stem Flea Beetle, Cabbageworm, Imported Cabbage Worms, Damping Off, Dark Sword-grass Moth, Black cutworm, Greasy cutworm, Diamond-back Moth, Downy Mildew of Crucifers, Early Blight of Potato/Tomato, Gray Mold. Grey Mould, Botrytis Blight, Turnip Gall Weevil, Verticillium Wilt.

Symptoms on:
Leaves
Damage

◇ Perforated leaves ⋯→ Cabbage Stem Flea Beetle: It is difficult to monitor the activity of the adult of the large rapeseed flea beetle: it occurs at night. Its damage, on the other hand, is easily recognizable because the insect bites the cotyledons and young leaves in a circular fashion. Perforations can also be observed.

◇ Leaves with holes ⋯→ Cabbageworm. Imported Cabbage Worms: Caterpillars devour the leaves of cruciferous plants, sometimes leaving only the large veins.

◇ Leaves with holes ⋯→ Diamond-back Moth: The damage is significant on cabbages. The caterpillars first eat the outer leaves and then gradually migrate to the young leaves in the center. They join them together with silk threads and soil them with their excrement.Sort

Deformation

◇ Leaves curled or shrivelled ⋯→ Cabbage Aphid: In the event of an outbreak, the plant can be completely covered by aphids, their honeydew and their exuviae.

Discoloring

◇ Reddening, yellowing of the leaves ⋯→ Cabbage Club Root: Aerial part of the plant: reduced development, especially during early attacks, wilting or even reddening of the foliage.

Lesions

◇ Purple or brown irregular shaped areas on leaves ⋯→ Downy Mildew of Crucifers: It first appears on older leaves, as white, yellow or brownish spots on the upper surfaces and downy grayish mold on the corresponding undersides.

◇ Brownish black lesions on leaves ⋯→ Early Blight of Potato/Tomato: Affected leaves and petioles turn yellow, then brown or black. Leaflets shrivel at the edges, and in severe infections the entire leaf wilts and dies.

Presence

◇ Coating of gray fungus spores on leaves ⋯→ Gray Mold. Grey Mould. Botrytis Blight: Regardless of the organs affected, the dying tissues become covered with a very characteristic dense gray mold, consisting of the conidiophores and conidia of the fungus.

◇ Presence of colonies of aphids ⋯→ Cabbage Aphid: In the event of an outbreak, the plant can be completely covered by aphids, their honeydew and their exuviae.

◇ White to gray, "downy" areas on under leaf surfaces. ⋯→ Downy Mildew of Crucifers: It first appears on older leaves, as white, yellow or brownish spots on the upper surfaces and downy grayish mold on the corresponding undersides.

◇ Presence of caterpillars ⋯→ Cabbageworm. Imported Cabbage Worms: Caterpillars devour the leaves of cruciferous plants, sometimes leaving only the large veins.

◇ Presence of honeydew and sooty moulds on leaves ⋯→ Cabbage Aphid: In the event of an outbreak, the plant can be completely covered by aphids, their honeydew and their exuviae.

◇ Presence of caterpillars ⋯→ Diamond-back Moth: The damage is significant on cabbages. The caterpillars first eat the outer leaves and then gradually migrate to the young leaves in the center. They join them together with silk threads and soil them with their excrement.

Spots

◇ Yellow/brown spots ⋯→ Verticillium Wilt: Marginal drying, sometimes asymmetrical. In the stem, brown lesions at the level of the conductive tissue. Atrophied and deformed capitula.

Plantlets
Dieback

◇ Damaged cotyledons ⋯→ Dark Sword-grass Moth. Black cutworm. Greasy cutworm: Early larval stages feed on the leaves and create small holes with irregular contours. Later stages attack the stem, often during sowing, and consequently cut the seedlings at ground level.

Wilting

◇ Wilted, collapsed and dead young seedlings ⋯→ Damping Off: Seeds rot and fail to germinate, or even germinate, but seedlings fail to grow. A translucent area completely covers the stem near the soil surface. The affected tissues rot, leading to wilting and collapse of the seedlings.

Plants whole
Stunted

◇ Stunted plants ⋯→ Cabbage Stem Flea Beetle: It is difficult to monitor the activity of the adult of the large rapeseed flea beetle: it occurs at night. Its damage, on the other hand, is easily recognizable because the insect bites the cotyledons and young leaves in a circular fashion. Perforations can also be observed.

Wilting

◇ Wilting of the entire plant ⋯→ Verticillium Wilt: The leaves soften and become duller. The leaves begin to yellow, then turn brown as they become necrotic. The characteristic feature is the asymmetry of the symptoms, with many leaves only affected on one half. The disease progresses from the bottom to the top of the plant. Verticillium wilt causes dark streaks under the bark.

◇ Wilted plants ⋯→ Cabbage Maggot, Cabbage Fly: Damage is observed in nurseries and at all stages of vegetation. On leafy vegetables, the root part is more or less destroyed. Attacked plants can be recognized by the faded appearance they take on during hot days; the leaves often turn purplish red, turn yellow and sometimes dry out.

◇ Wilted plants ⋯→ Cabbage Club Root: Underground part of the plant: root deformation or presence of galls on the roots. These galls are firm (full interior), whitish then turn brown and rot, leading to the death of the plant.

Roots or tubers
Deformation

◇ Roots abnormally increased or swellings ⋯→ Cabbage Club Root: Underground part of the plant: root deformation or presence of galls on the roots. These galls are firm (full interior), whitish then turn brown and rot, leading to the death of the plant.

◇ Swelling of roots ⋯→ Turnip Gall Weevil: The substances introduced at the time of egg laying and the larval secretions cause an enlargement of the collar or gall, which can reach 2 to 3 cm in diameter in cabbage.

Presence

◇ Presence of maggots in roots ⋯→ Cabbage Maggot, Cabbage Fly: The larvae of the cabbage fly penetrate into the fleshy parts and dig galleries. The root part is more or less destroyed. Attacked plants can be recognized by the faded appearance they take on during hot days; the leaves often turn purplish red, turn yellow and sometimes dry out.

Stems
Dieback

◇ Damaged stems ⋯→ Dark Sword-grass Moth. Black cutworm. Greasy cutworm: Early larval stages feed on the leaves and create small holes with irregular contours. Later stages attack the stem, often during sowing, and consequently cut the seedlings at ground level.

Cabbage

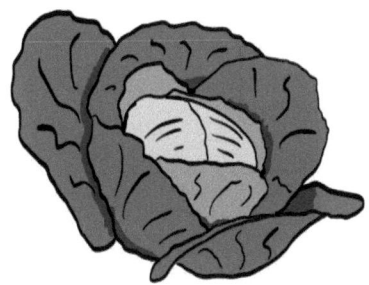

Botanical name
Brassica oleracea var. sabauda

Family
Brassicaceae

English name
Savoy cabbage

Names in other languages
Chou de Milan. Chou de Savoie (FR), Savooiekool (NL), Wirsingkohl (DE), Cavolo verza (IT), Couve crespa (PO), Col de Saboya (SP).

Description
The cabbage plant (*Brassica oleracea*) is an herbaceous annual or biennial vegetable in the family Brassicaceae grown for its edible head. There are many different varieties of cabbage which include the white and red cabbage (*Brassica oleracea var. capitata*) and the savoy cabbage (*Brassica oleracea var. sabauda*). The head of the cabbage is round and forms on a short thick stem. The leaves are thick and alternating with wavy or lobed edges and the roots are are fibrous and shallow. The plant produces large yellow flowers. The densely leaved heads can range in size from 0.5 to 3.6 kg (1-8 lb) depending on variety.

Pests
Beet Armyworm, Black Leg, Crucifer Collar Rot, Black Rot of Cabbage, Bright-line Brown-eyes Moth, Cabbage and Cauliflower Cyst Nematode, Cabbage Aphid, Cabbage Bug, Cabbage Club Root, Cabbage Fly, Cabbage Maggot, Cabbage Stem Flea Beetle, Cabbageworm, Damping Off, Dark Sword-grass Moth, Black cutworm, Diamond-back Moth, Downy Mildew of Crucifers, Early Blight of Potato/Tomato, Garden Dart Moth, Gray Mold, Potato Aphid, Silver-Y moth, South American Miner Fly, Turnip Flea Beetle, Turnip Gall Weevil, Turnip Maggot, Turnip Root Fly.

Symptoms on:
Leaves
Damage

◇ Perforated leaves ⋯→ Cabbage Stem Flea Beetle: It is difficult to monitor the activity of the adult of the large rapeseed flea beetle: it occurs at night. Its damage, on the other hand, is easily recognizable because the insect bites the cotyledons and young leaves in a circular fashion. Perforations can also be observed.

◇ Leaves with holes ⋯→ Cabbageworm. Imported Cabbage Worms: Caterpillars devour the leaves of cruciferous plants, sometimes leaving only the large veins. In addition,their excrement, diluted by rain or dew, accumulates in the heart of the plant and makes it inedible.

◇ Leaves with irregular holes ⋯→ Armyworms, Beet Armyworm: Older Spodoptera exigua caterpillars migrate to the apex of the plants where they feed mainly on the growing areas. They make large holes in the leaves and sometimes leave only the veins behind. The damage caused considerably affects the growth of the plants.

◇ Leaves with irregular holes ⋯→ Turnip Flea Beetle. Large Striped Flea Beetle, Striped Turnip Flea Beetle: When adults resume activity in the spring, they gather on wild and cultivated cruciferous plants and make small bites of 1 to 2 mm in diameter that do not penetrate the entire thickness of the leaf. If there are many flea beetles and the temperature is high, the damage can be significant, particularly on young seedlings that risk being destroyed.

◇ Leaf eaten (irregular holes) ⋯→ Cotton Worm. African Cotton Leafworm: The damage caused by caterpillars, which vary in color from gray to reddish or yellowish, is recognizable by the large bites on the leaves.

◇ Leaves with holes ⋯→ Diamond-back Moth: The damage is significant on cabbages. The caterpillars first eat the outer leaves and then gradually migrate to the young leaves in the center. They join them together with silk threads and soil them with their excrement.

Deformation

◇ Leaves curled or shrivelled ⋯▸ Cabbage Aphid: In the event of an outbreak, the plant can be completely covered by aphids, their honeydew and their exuviae.

Discoloring

◇ Reddening, yellowing of the leaves ⋯▸ Cabbage Club Root: Aerial part of the plant: reduced development, especially during early attacks, wilting or even reddening of the foliage.

◇ Bleached leaves ⋯▸ Cabbage Bug. Rape Bug. Crucifer Shield Bug. Brassica Bug: With their piercing-sucking apparatus, the larvae and adults feed by sucking the sap, which causes the leaves to turn white and slows down the growth of the cabbage. The very large number of punctures on the leaves of young plants can lead to the death of the host plant.

Galleries

◇ Leaves with galleries ⋯▸ South American Miner Fly. South American Leaf Miner: Feeding pits and mined leaves with galleries depreciate the harvest.

Lesions

◇ Purple or brown irregular shaped areas on leaves ⋯▸ Downy Mildew of Crucifers: It first appears on older leaves, as white, yellow or brownish spots on the upper surfaces and downy grayish mold on the corresponding undersides.

◇ Brownish black lesions on leaves ⋯▸ Early Blight of Potato/Tomato: Affected leaves and petioles turn yellow, then brown or black. Leaflets shrivel at the edges, and in severe infections the entire leaf wilts and dies.

◇ Leaves with V-shaped lesions ⋯▸ Black Rot of Cabbage: On leaves: yellowish spots on the edge developing in a "V" shape. The colonized vessels take on a blackish color. The spot evolves by turning brown and the blade tears. At the point of insertion of an attacked and detached leaf, observation of a blackening of the vessels.

Presence

◇ Coating of gray fungus spores on leaves ⋯▸ Gray Mold. Grey Mould. Botrytis Blight: Regardless of the organs affected, the dying tissues become covered with a very characteristic dense gray mold, consisting of the conidiophores and conidia of the fungus.

◇ Presence of colonies of aphids ⋯▸ Cabbage Aphid: In the event of an outbreak, the plant can be completely covered by aphids, their honeydew and their exuviae.

◇ White to gray, "downy" areas on under leaf surfaces. ⋯▸ Downy Mildew of Crucifers: It first appears on older leaves, as white, yellow or brownish spots on the upper surfaces and downy grayish mold on the corresponding undersides.

◇ Presence of aphids ⋯▸ Potato Aphid: The most classic symptoms are a curling of heavily infested leaves and a slowdown in the growth of the plants

◇ Presence of caterpillars ⋯▸ Cabbageworm. Imported Cabbage Worms: Caterpillars devour the leaves of cruciferous plants, sometimes leaving only the large veins. In addition, their excrement, diluted by rain or dew, accumulates in the heart of the plant and makes it inedible.

◇ Presence of honeydew and sooty moulds on leaves ⋯▸ Cabbage Aphid: In the event of an outbreak, the plant can be completely covered by aphids, their honeydew and their exuviae.

◇ Presence of cutworms ⋯▸ Garden Dart Moth. Cutworm: The larvae feed on the roots of plants, cutting them at night.

◇ Presence of caterpillars ⋯▸ Diamond-back Moth: The damage is significant on cabbages. The caterpillars first eat the outer leaves and then gradually migrate to the young leaves in the center. They join them together with silk threads and soil them with their excrement.

◇ Presence of caterpillars ⋯▸ Bright-line Brown-eyes Moth: The damage caused by this moth on cabbage and beet leaves is generally not very significant.

◇ Presence of caterpillars ⋯▸ Cotton Worm. African Cotton Leafworm: The Mediterranean noctuid or cotton worm causes damage which is recognizable by the large portions eaten out of the leaves.

◇ Presence of caterpillars ⋯▸ Armyworms, Beet Armyworm: Older Spodoptera exigua caterpillars migrate to the apex of the plants where they feed mainly on the growing areas. They make large holes in the leaves and sometimes leave only the veins behind. The damage caused considerably affects the growth of the plants.

◇ Leaf with presence of grayish white lesion ⋯▸ Black Leg. Crucifer Collar Rot : This fungus causes white to ash-grey spots measuring 5 to 15 mm in diameter on the cotyledons and on the leaves, on which the pycnidia, characteristic black spots, are distinguished.

◇ Presence of bugs ⋯▸ Cabbage Bug. Rape Bug. Crucifer Shield Bug. Brassica Bug: Presence of the adult insect and larva on leaves. Presence of eggs on the underside of the leaves. Observe the leaves to see the appearance of white spots. Be careful not to confuse these bugs with other red and black bugs such as Pyrrhocoris apterus, better known as the "firebug". These do not cause any damage to cabbage.

Spots

◇ Leaves with yellowish spots which evolve into a blackish coloration ⋯▸ Black Rot of Cabbage: On leaves: yellowish spots on the edge developing in a "V" shape. The colonized vessels take on a blackish color. The spot evolves by turning brown and the blade tears. At the point of insertion of an attacked and detached leaf, observation of a blackening of the vessels.

Plantlets
Dieback

◇ Damaged cotyledons ⋯→ Dark Sword-grass Moth. Black cutworm. Greasy cutworm: Early larval stages feed on the leaves and create small holes with irregular contours. Later stages attack the stem, often during sowing, and consequently cut the seedlings at ground level.

Wilting

◇ Wilted, collapsed and dead young seedlings ⋯→ Damping Off: Seeds rot and fail to germinate, or even germinate, but seedlings fail to grow. A translucent area completely covers the stem near the soil surface. The affected tissues rot, leading to wilting and collapse of the seedlings.

Plants whole
Infested zone

◇ Infested plants form a circular area in the field ⋯→ Cabbage and Cauliflower Cyst Nematode. Brassica Cyst Nematode: In the field, infested plants form a circular area and appear stunted.

Stunted

◇ Stunted plants ⋯→ Cabbage Stem Flea Beetle: It is difficult to monitor the activity of the adult of the large rapeseed flea beetle: it occurs at night. Its damage, on the other hand, is easily recognizable because the insect bites the cotyledons and young leaves in a circular fashion. Perforations can also be observed.

◇ Plants stunted ⋯→ Cabbage and Cauliflower Cyst Nematode. Brassica Cyst Nematode: In the field, infested plants form a circular area and appear stunted.

Wilting

◇ Wilted plants ⋯→ Cabbage Maggot, Cabbage Fly: Damage is observed in nurseries and at all stages of vegetation. On leafy vegetables, the root part is more or less destroyed. Attacked plants can be recognized by the faded appearance they take on during hot days; the leaves often turn purplish red, turn yellow and sometimes dry out.

◇ Wilted plants ⋯→ Cabbage Club Root: Underground part of the plant: root deformation or presence of galls on the roots. These galls are firm (full interior), whitish then turn brown and rot, leading to the death of the plant.

Roots or tubers
Decay

◇ Internal brown rot ⋯→ Boron Deficiency: Boron deficiency causes inner tissue to be reddish brown, or brown or gray concentric rings develop inside the roots, it also causes brown heart rot.

Deformation

◇ Roots abnormally increased or swellings ⋯→ Cabbage Club Root: Underground part of the plant: root deformation or presence of galls on the roots. These galls are firm (full interior),

whitish then turn brown and rot, leading to the death of the plant.

◇ Swelling of roots ⋯→ Turnip Gall Weevil: The substances introduced at the time of egg laying and the larval secretions cause an enlargement of the collar or gall, which can reach 2 to 3 cm in diameter in cabbage.

Dieback

◇ Roots damaged ⋯→ Cabbage and Cauliflower Cyst Nematode. Brassica Cyst Nematode: On roots: formation of an abnormal abundance of fine browned rootlets bearing whitish pinhead-shaped cysts.

Presence

◇ Presence of maggots in roots ⋯→ Cabbage Maggot, Cabbage Fly: The larvae of the cabbage fly penetrate into the fleshy parts and dig galleries. The root part is more or less destroyed. Attacked plants can be recognized by the faded appearance they take on during hot days; the leaves often turn purplish red, turn yellow and sometimes dry out.

◇ Roots with presence of maggots ⋯→ Turnip Maggot. Turnip Root Fly: On root vegetables, the larvae dig galleries that can go up to the petiole of the leaves and make the vegetable unfit for consumption. When the attack is massive, the plants stop growing, take on a leaden color and lack turgidity; little by little, they turn yellow and die.

Stems
Decay

◇ Collar rot ⋯→ Black Leg. Crucifer Collar Rot : This fungus causes white to ash-grey spots measuring 5 to 15 mm in diameter on the cotyledons and leaves, on which the pycnidia, characteristic black spots, are distinguished. After a symptomless winter phase, the necroses of the collar appear when vegetation resumes.

Dieback

◇ Damaged stems ⋯→ Dark Sword-grass Moth. Black cutworm. Greasy cutworm: Early larval stages feed on the leaves and create small holes with irregular contours. Later stages attack the stem, often during sowing, and consequently cut the seedlings at ground level.

Carrot

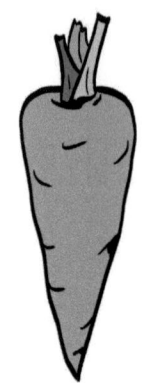

Botanical name
Daucus carota subsp. *sativus*

Family
Apiaceae

English name
Carrot

Names in other languages
Carotte (FR), Wortel (NL), Karotte (DE), Carota (IT), Cenoura (PO), Zanahoria (SP).

Description
Carrot (*Daucus carota*) is an edible, biennial herb in the family Apiaceae grown for its edible root. The carrot plant produces a rosette of 8–12 leaves above ground and a fleshy conical taproot below ground. The plant produces small (2 mm) flowers which are white, red or purple in color. The root can grow to between 5 and 50 cm (2.0–20 in) long and reach 5 cm (2.0 in) in diameter. The foliage of the plant can reach a height of 150 cm (59.1 in) when in flower.

Pests
Bean Aphids, Black Dolphin Aphids, Carrot Fly, Carrot Root Nematode, Carrot Cyst Nematode, Celery Late Blight ,Cercosporosa Leaf Spot, Click Beetle, Striped Elaterid Beetle, Wireworms, Early Blight of Potato/Tomato, Green Peach Aphid, Hawthorn Aphids, Itersonilia Canker, Parsnip Canker, Lettuce Root Aphid, Powdery Mildew, Red Spider Mite, Two-spotted Mite, Rust, Soft rot, White Rot on Carrot, Cottony rot, Violet Root Rot, White Rot, White Mold, Sclerotinia Wilt.

Symptoms on:
Leaves
Decay

◇ Soft watery rot on lower leaves ⋯⋅→ White Rot. White Mold. Sclerotinia Wilt: Pre and post-emergent damping off, crown rot, and blighting of foliage and petioles. Small, hard, irregular, black structures called sclerotia may be present on or in plant tissue (especially inside stem and petiole tissue).

Deformation

◇ Curled leaves ⋯⋅→ Celery Late Blight : The disease first manifests itself by the appearance of small light brown spots on the foliage. In case of severe attacks, the petioles turn yellow, the leaves curl up and dry out.

◇ Leaves curled or shrivelled ⋯⋅→ Bean Aphids. Black Dolphin Aphids: Presence of black aphids on the leaves, on the flower stems and the flower heads. As soon as they appear, deformation of the attacked leaves and development of sooty mold.

◇ Leaves curled or shrivelled ⋯⋅→ Green Peach Aphid: Myzus persicae is very polyphagous and, in summer, it has more than forty different families of host plants. The colonies secrete a honeydew that promotes the installation of sooty mold, a fungus that then slows down the photosynthesis of the covered parts. It is the most important aphid vector of viruses.

Discoloring

◇ Leaves discoulouring bronzed or silvery ⋯⋅→ Red Spider Mite. Two-spotted Mite: They damage the plant by piercing its cells to feed on them. The leaves turn pale and become stained yellow. To protect themselves and improve their microclimate, they weave a web around the leaf. A strong attack of mites leads to the leaves rolling and drying out, then falling off.

◇ Leaves turn yellow ⋯⋅→ Carrot Fly, Carrot Rust Fly: Yellowing or reddening of the foliage of affected plants is often observed.

Lesions

◇ Brownish black lesions on leaves ⤍ Early Blight of Potato/Tomato: Affected leaves and petioles turn yellow, then brown or black. Leaflets shrivel at the edges, and in severe infections the entire leaf wilts and dies.

◇ Orange to brown lesions on leaves ⤍ Itersonilia Canker. Parsnip Canker: On leaves, symptoms occur as small orange to brown lesions with a pale green halo.

◇ Leaves with water-soaked lesions ⤍ Soft rot. White Rot on Carrot, Cottony rot: Symptoms on foliage first appear as water-soaked, dark olive-green lesions associated with collapsed tissues. Lesions expand rapidly over the entire leaf, petiole, and rosette with infected tissues soon becoming covered by abundant cottony, white mycelium.

Presence

◇ White to gray powder coverage on leaves ⤍ Powdery Mildew, Oidium: The heart leaves are covered with purplish-grey spores on the underside. They thicken, curl, and curl up. Older leaves turn yellow on the outside, then blacken and die. Only a few isolated plants or foci are damaged.

◇ Presence of black aphids ⤍ Bean Aphids. Black Dolphin Aphids: Presence of black aphids on the leaves, on the flower stems and capitals. As soon as they appear, deformation of the attacked leaves and development of sooty mold.

◇ Presence of colonies of aphids ⤍ Hawthorn Aphids: Dysaphis apiifolia can damage celery crops by stunting growth, by transmitting celery yellow spot virus and by contaminating the crop with honeydew and debris.

◇ Leaves with fine silk webbing ⤍ Red Spider Mite. Two-spotted Mite: They damage the plant by piercing its cells to feed on them. The leaves turn pale and become stained yellow. To protect themselves and improve their microclimate, they weave a web around the leaf.

◇ Presence of red spider mites, cast skins and egg shells ⤍ Red Spider Mite. Two-spotted Mite: Spider mites always leave behind cast skins and egg shells.

◇ Presence of honeydew and sooty moulds on leaves ⤍ Willow-Carrot Aphid: If aphid infestation is heavy it may cause leaves to yellow and/or distorted, necrotic spots on leaves and/or stunted shoots; aphids secrete a sticky, sugary substance called honeydew which encourages the growth of sooty mold on the plants.

Spots

◇ Leaves with yellow, brown, necrotic and concentric spots ⤍ Early Blight of Potato/ Tomato: Small yellow spots quickly turn brown-black, necrotic, circular and sharply outlined, measuring about 5 mm in diameter, which gradually spread concentrically.

◇ Reddish-orange spots on leaves ⤍ Rust: On the upper side of the leaves, you will see tiny white, orange or even brown spots appear depending on the species. If you turn these leaves over, you will see that these spots correspond to tiny pustules of the same color. The lesions are generally yellow, brown or red, but can be dark brown or black at the end of the season.

◇ Pale brown spots on leaves ⤍ Celery Late Blight : The disease first manifests itself by the appearance on the foliage of small light brown spots, often delimited by the fine veins of the leaves but sometimes with irregular contours, ranging in size from 1 to 4 mm. They gradually turn reddish-brown and have small black dots called pycnidia in their center on the upper surface.

◇ Yellowish then brown spots on the upper surface of the leaf ⤍ Powdery Mildew, Oidium: Yellowish then brown spots on the upper surface of the leaf, generally limited by the large veins, whitish felting on the lower surface.

◇ Leaf spots with brown-reddish margins ⤍ Cercosporosa Leaf Spot, Cercosporia blight: Cercospora blight initially causes small, oval, gray to tan lesions with red borders.

Wilting

◇ Wilting of leaves ⤍ Soft rot. White Rot on Carrot, Cottony rot: Sclerotinia causes infection during any growth stage of the carrot. Extensive root decay will lead to wilt and collapse the aboveground portion of the plant. The "cottony" white mycelium appears on infected tissue, usually at the base of the plant. Inside this mycelium are black, irregular-shaped structures called sclerotia.

Plants whole
Stunted

◇ Plants stunted ⤍ Carrot Fly, Carrot Rust Fly: The roots have slowed growth and the plant can disappear in the event of an early attack.

◇ Stunted plants ⤍ Carrot Root Nematode. Carrot Cyst Nematode: Affected carrots are small. The rootlets, abnormally developed and numerous, give the root system a characteristic hairy appearance.

◇ Stunted plants ⤍ Carrot motley dwarf (CMD) virus, Carrot redeaf virus (CRLV), Carrot mottle virus (CMoV): Yellow and red leaves; stunted plant growth.

Wilting

◇ Wilted plants ⤍ Lettuce Root Aphid: Aphids' bites and nutritional withdrawals from the roots cause the plant to wilt and die.

Roots or tubers
Dieback

◇ Roots damaged ⤍ Carrot Root Nematode. Carrot Cyst Nematode: Affected carrots are small. The rootlets, abnormally developed and numerous, give the root system a characteristic hairy appearance.

Discoloring

◇ Purplish coloration of roots ⋯→ Violet Root Rot: On roots, presence of superficial purple spots in the form of felting of fine filaments, developing from the base of the root and which can develop over the entire root.

Galleries

◇ Galleries in roots ⋯→ Carrot Fly, Carrot Rust Fly: The larvae dig galleries in the roots, especially on the outer layer. Each root can host several larvae (about ten). Attacked carrots have very slow growth and take on a bitter taste.

◇ Galleries in roots ⋯→ Click Beetle. Striped Elaterid Beetle. Wireworms: As larvae development takes up to four years, in an infected soil we can find larvae of different ages. They live at different depths, depending on the moment of the year, as they are highly sensitive to heat and dryness. They eat or pierce the underground organs of the plant.

Lesions

◇ Brown, black or purple black lesions on roots ⋯→ Itersonilia Canker. Parsnip Canker: On roots, cankers form mainly on the crown and shoulder, although lateral roots may be affected. Lesions are superficial and brown, black, or purple black. Secondary decay of cankers can occur.

Presence

◇ Presence of yellow larvae in roots ⋯→ Carrot Fly, Carrot Rust Fly: The larva is a very elongated maggot (6 to 7 mm), shiny yellowish white. It is the larvae that cause the damage by penetrating the roots and digging winding galleries.

◇ Presence of colonies of gray aphids on roots ⋯→ Lettuce Root Aphid: Presence of very numerous yellowish-white aphids along the roots, these bearing a fairly visible tuft of white wax.

◇ Root with white sooty mold ⋯→ Lettuce Root Aphid: Development of very numerous yellowish-white insects along the roots, these carrying a fairly visible tuft of white wax.

Spots

◇ Small white mealy spots ⋯→ Potato Tuber Nematode. Potato Cyst Nematode: The nematode initially causes small white mealy spots just below the surface that are only visible if the skin is removed.

Stems

Presence

◇ Presence of caterpillars ⋯→ Common Swift Moth. Garden Swift Moth: The roots and collars are eaten away, which leads to the gradual drying out of the plant.

Cauliflower

Botanical name
Brassica oleracea var. botrytis

Family
Brassicaceae

English name
Cauliflower

Names in other languages
Chou-fleur (FR), Bloemkool (NL), Blumenkohl (DE), Cavolfiore (IT), Couve-flor ((PO), Coliflor (SP).

Description
Cauliflower (*Brassica oleracea var. botrytis*) is an herbaceous annual or biennial vegetable plant in the family Brassicaceae grown for its edible head. The head is actually a mass of abortive flowers. Cauliflower plants are shallow rooted with a small, thickened stem. The ribbed leaves branch off the top of the stem and are light green in color. The plant can reach a height of 1–1.5 m (3.3–4.9 ft) and is most commonly grown as an annual, harvested between 60 and 100 days after planting.

Pests
Beet Armyworm, Cabbage and Cauliflower Cyst Nematode, Brassica Cyst Nematode, Cabbage Aphid, Cabbage Club Root, Cabbage Maggot, Cabbage Stem Flea Beetle, Cabbageworm, Imported Cabbage Worms, Damping Off, Dark Sword-grass Moth, Black cutworm, Greasy cutworm, Diamond-back Moth, Downy Mildew of Crucifers, Early Blight of Potato/Tomato, Gray Mold, Grey Mould, Botrytis Blight, Molybdenum Deficiency, Whiptail, Turnip Flea Beetle, Large Striped Flea Beetle, Striped Turnip Flea Beetle, Turnip Gall Weevil, Turnip Maggot, Turnip Root Fly.

Symptoms on:
Leaves
Damage

◇ Perforated leaves ⋯→ Cabbage Stem Flea Beetle: It is difficult to monitor the activity of the adult of the large rapeseed flea beetle: it occurs at night. Its damage, on the other hand, is easily recognizable because the insect bites the cotyledons and young leaves in a circular fashion. Perforations can also be observed.

◇ Leaves with holes ⋯→ Cabbageworm. Imported Cabbage Worms: Caterpillars devour the leaves of cruciferous plants, sometimes leaving only the large veins. In addition, their excrement, diluted by rain or dew, accumulates in the heart of the plant and makes it inedible.

◇ Leaves with irregular holes ⋯→ Armyworms, Beet Armyworm: Older Spodoptera exigua caterpillars migrate to the apex of the plants where they feed mainly on the growing areas. They make large holes in the leaves and sometimes leave only the veins behind. Thedamage caused considerably affects the growth of the plants.

◇ Leaves with irregular holes ⋯→ Turnip Flea Beetle. Large Striped Flea Beetle, Striped Turnip Flea Beetle: When adults resume activity in the spring, they gather on wild and cultivated cruciferous plants and make small bites of 1 to 2 mm in diameter that do not penetrate the entire thickness of the leaf. If there are many flea beetles and the temperature is high, the damage can be significant, particularly on youngseedlings that risk being destroyed.

◇ Leaves with holes ⋯→ Diamond-back Moth: The damage is significant on cabbages. The caterpillars first eat the outer leaves and then gradually migrate to the young leaves in the center. They join them together with silk threads and soil them with their excrement.

Deformation

◇ Leaves curled or shrivelled ⋯→ Cabbage Aphid: In the event of an outbreak, the plant can be completely covered by aphids, their honeydew and their exuviae.

◇ Only midrib develops ⋯→ Molybdenum Deficiency. Whiptail: Distorted leaves with reduced leaf area and chlorotic leaf margins. "Whiptail" formation. Symptoms begin at the younger leaves.

Discoloring

◇ Reddening, yellowing of the leaves ⋯→ Cabbage Club Root: Aerial part of the plant: reduced development, especially during early attacks, wilting or even reddening of the foliage.

◇ Leaves turn white ⋯→ Molybdenum Deficiency. Whiptail: Leaf margins show chlorosis and slight necrosis.

Lesions

◇ Purple or brown irregular shaped areas on leaves ⋯→ Downy Mildew of Crucifers: It first appears on older leaves, as white, yellow or brownish spots on the upper surfaces and downy grayish mold on the corresponding undersides.

◇ Brownish black lesions on leaves ⋯→ Early Blight of Potato/Tomato: Affected leaves and petioles turn yellow, then brown or black. Leaflets shrivel at the edges, and in severe infections the entire leaf wilts and dies.

Presence

◇ Coating of gray fungus spores on leaves ⋯→ Gray Mold. Grey Mould. Botrytis Blight: Regardless of the organs affected, the dying tissues become covered with a very characteristic dense gray mold, consisting of the conidiophores and conidia of the fungus.

◇ Presence of colonies of aphids ⋯→ Cabbage Aphid: In the event of an outbreak, the plant can be completely covered by aphids, their honeydew and their exuviae.

◇ White to gray, "downy" areas on under leaf surfaces. ⋯→ Downy Mildew of Crucifers: It first appears on older leaves, as white, yellow or brownish spots on the upper surfaces and downy grayish mold on the corresponding undersides.

◇ Presence of caterpillars ⋯→ Cabbageworm. Imported Cabbage Worms: Caterpillars devour the leaves of cruciferous plants, sometimes leaving only the large veins. In addition, their excrement, diluted by rain or dew, accumulates in the heart of the plant and makes it inedible.

◇ Presence of honeydew and sooty moulds on leaves ⋯→ Cabbage Aphid: In the event of an outbreak, the plant can be completely covered by aphids, their honeydew and their exuviae.

◇ Presence of caterpillars ⋯→ Diamond-back Moth: The damage is significant on cabbages. The caterpillars first eat the outer leaves and then gradually migrate to the young leaves in the center. They join them together with silk threads and soil them with their excrement.

Plantlets
Dieback

◇ Damaged cotyledons ⋯→ Dark Sword-grass Moth. Black cutworm. Greasy cutworm: Early larval stages feed on the leaves and create small holes with irregular contours. Later stages attack the stem, often during sowing, and consequently cut the seedlings at ground level.

Wilting

◇ Wilted, collapsed and dead young seedlings ⋯→ Damping Off: Seeds rot and fail to germinate, or even germinate, but seedlings fail to grow. A translucent area completely covers the stem near the soil surface. The affected tissues rot, leading to wilting and collapse of the seedlings.

Plants whole
Infested zone

◇ Infested plants form a circular area in the field ⋯→ Cabbage and Cauliflower Cyst Nematode. Brassica Cyst Nematode: In the field, infested plants form a circular area and appear stunted.

Stunted

◇ Stunted plants ⋯→ Cabbage Stem Flea Beetle: It is difficult to monitor the activity of the adult of the large rapeseed flea beetle: it occurs at night. Its damage, on the other hand, is easily recognizable because the insect bites the cotyledons and young leaves in a circular fashion. Perforations can also be observed.

◇ Plants stunted ⋯→ Cabbage and Cauliflower Cyst Nematode. Brassica Cyst Nematode: In the field, infested plants form a circular area and appear stunted.

Wilting

◇ Wilted plants ⋯→ Cabbage Maggot, Cabbage Fly: Damage is observed in nurseries and at all stages of vegetation. On leafy vegetables, the root part is more or less destroyed. Attacked plants can be recognized by the faded appearance they take on during hot days; the leaves often turn purplish red, turn yellow and sometimes dry out.

◇ Wilted plants ⋯→ Cabbage Club Root: Underground part of the plant: root deformation or presence of galls on the roots. These galls are firm (full interior), whitish then turn brown and rot, leading to the death of the plant.

Roots or tubers
Deformation

◇ Roots abnormally increased or swellings ⋯→ Cabbage Club Root: Underground part of the plant: root deformation or presence of galls on the roots. These galls are firm (full interior), whitish then turn brown and rot, leading to the death of the plant.

◇ Swelling of roots ⋯→ Turnip Gall Weevil: The substances introduced at the time of egg laying and the larval secretions cause an enlargement of the collar or gall, which can reach 2 to 3 cm in diameter in cabbage.

Dieback

◇ Roots damaged ⋯→ Cabbage and Cauliflower Cyst Nematode. Brassica Cyst Nematode: On roots: formation of an abnormal abundance of fine browned rootlets bearing whitish pinhead-shaped cysts.

Presence

◇ Presence of maggots in roots ⋯→ Cabbage Maggot, Cabbage Fly: The larvae of the cabbage fly penetrate into the fleshy parts and dig galleries. The root part is more or less destroyed. Attacked plants can be recognized by the faded appearance they take on during hot days; the leaves often turn purplish red, turn yellow and sometimes dry out.

◇ Roots with presence of maggots ⋯→ Turnip Maggot. Turnip Root Fly: On root vegetables, the larvae dig galleries that can go up to the petiole of the leaves and make the vegetable unfit for consumption. When the attack is massive, the plants stop growing, take on a leaden color and lack turgidity; little by little, they turn yellow and die.

Stems

Dieback

◇ Damaged stems ⋯→ Dark Sword-grass Moth. Black cutworm. Greasy cutworm: Early larval stages feed on the leaves and create small holes with irregular contours. Later stages attack the stem, often during sowing, and consequently cut the seedlings at ground level.

Celeriac

Botanical name
Apium graveolens var. *rapaceum*

Family
Apiaceae

English name
Celeriac, Celery root, Knob celery

Names in other languages
Céleri rave (FR), Knolselderij (NL), Knollensellerie (DE), Sedano rapa (IT), Aipo-rábano (PO), Apio nabo (SP).

Description
Celeriac (*Apium graveolens* var. *rapaceum*) is an aromatic biennial plant in the family Apiaceae grown primarily for its roots which are used as vegetables.

Pests
Boron Deficiency, Carrot Fly, Celery Fly, Celery Late Blight, Celery Root Rot, Cercosporosa Leaf Spot, Cucumber Mosaic Virus, CMV, Damping Off, Fusarium Root Rot, Hawthorn Aphids, Powdery Mildew, Rust, Slug and Snail, Garden Slug, Loach, Little Grey Slug, Vine Snail, White Garden Snail, White Rot, White Mold, Sclerotinia Wilt.

Symptoms on:
Leaves
Decay

◇ Soft watery rot on lower leaves ⋯→ White Rot. White Mold. Sclerotinia Wilt: Pre and post-emergent damping off, crown rot, and blighting of foliage and petioles. Small, hard, irregular, black structures called sclerotia may be present on or in plant tissue (especially inside stem and petiole tissue).

Deformation

◇ Curled leaves ⋯→ Celery Late Blight: The disease first manifests itself by the appearance of small light brown spots on the foliage. In case of severe attacks, the petioles turn yellow, the leaves curl up and dry out.

◇ Dry out leaves ⋯→ Celery Late Blight: In case of severe attacks, the petioles turn yellow, the leaves curl up and dry out, greatly reducing the growth of the celeriac root and making the foliage of the celeriac branches completely unfit for consumption.

Discoloring

◇ Yellow leaves on plants ⋯→ Boron Deficiency: Symptoms appear on young leaves: wrinkled, fragile leaves, slowed growth. Then wilting of the leaves with the appearance of brown or black spots on the petioles. Young leaves wilt, turn black and dry out.

◇ Leaves turn yellow and wilt ⋯→ Celery Fly: The leaves take on a burnt and dried out appearance. Deprived of a large part of the leaf surface and therefore having reduced photosynthetic activity, celery produces only a puny bulb.

◇ Leaves turn yellow ⋯→ Carrot Fly, Carrot Rust Fly: Yellowing or reddening of the foliage of affected plants is often observed.

Galleries

◇ Galleries in leaves ⋯→ Celery Fly: It is the larvae

that cause damage. The leaves are covered with mines, the collective mines resulting in a large white blister becoming brown. The excrement shines through transparency, between the two epidermis of the leaf.

Presence

◇ Presence of white larvae ⋯▸ Celery Fly: The larva develops in the mines dug during its development.

◇ Presence of colonies of aphids ⋯▸ Hawthorn Aphids: Dysaphis apiifolia can damage celery crops by stunting growth, by transmitting celery yellow spot virus and by contaminating the crop with honeydew and debris.

◇ Slime trails ⋯▸ Slug and Snail. Garden Slug. Loach. Little Grey Slug. Vine Snail. White Garden Snail: Slime trail' that signals their presence.

Spots

◇ Reddish-orange spots on leaves ⋯▸ Rust: On the upper side of the leaves, you will see tiny white, orange or even brown spots appear depending on the species. If you turn these leaves over, you will see that these spots correspond to tiny pustules of the same color. The lesions are generally yellow, brown or red, but can be dark brown or black at the end of the season.

◇ Pale brown spots on leaves ⋯▸ Celery Late Blight : The disease first manifests itself by the appearance on the foliage of small light brown spots, often delimited by the fine veins of the leaves but sometimes with irregular contours, ranging in size from 1 to 4 mm. They gradually turn reddish-brown and have small black dots called pycnidia in their center on the upper surface.

◇ Yellowish then brown spots on the upper surface of the leaf ⋯▸ Powdery Mildew, Oidium: Yellowish then brown spots on the upper surface of the leaf, generally limited by the large veins, whitish felting on the lower surface.

◇ Leaf spots with brown-reddish margins ⋯▸ Cercosporosa Leaf Spot, Cercosporia blight: Cercospora blight initially causes small, oval, gray to tan lesions with red borders. Severe infections may cause entire ferns to turn yellow or brown.

Plantlets
Wilting

◇ Wilted, collapsed and dead young seedlings ⋯▸ Damping Off: Seeds rot and fail to germinate, or even germinate, but seedlings fail to grow. A translucent area completely covers the stem near the soil surface. The affected tissues rot, leading to wilting and collapse of the seedlings.

Plants whole
Stunted

◇ Plants stunted ⋯▸ Carrot Fly, Carrot Rust Fly: The roots have slowed growth and the plant can disappear in the event of an early attack.

◇ Plants stunted ⋯▸ Fusarium Root Rot: Diseased plants wilt to a greater or lesser extent during the hottest times of the day; this wilting is sometimes reversible. In the most serious cases, the plants eventually dry out completely.

◇ Deformation and stunting of plants ⋯▸ Cucumber Mosaic Virus. CMV: Artichoke latent virus (ALV, Potyvirus) is transmitted by aphids. Cucumber mosaic virus (CMV) induces deformation and stunting of plants.

Roots or tubers
Decay

◇ Rotting of roots ⋯▸ Fusarium Root Rot: The cause of these wiltings is to be found at the level of the collar of the feet. At this location, a wet lesion has developed, a rot that has gradually spread to the lower part of the stem and the taproot, but also to the upper part of the root system. At the collar, the altered tissues are wet and show a dark to brownish tint. This lesion ends up girdling the stem for several centimeters. The roots located in the same layer of soil are also affected. Their cortex turns yellow, brown and decomposes.

◇ Internal brown rot ⋯▸ Boron Deficiency: Boron deficiency causes inner tissue to be reddish brown, or brown or gray concentric rings develop inside the roots, it also causes brown heart rot.

Galleries

◇ Galleries in roots ⋯▸ Carrot Fly, Carrot Rust Fly: The larvae dig galleries in the roots, especially on the outer layer. Each root can host several larvae (about ten). Attacked carrots have very slow growth and take on a bitter taste.

Lesions

◇ Brown lesions on tubers ⋯▸ Celery Root Rot, Phoma crown and root rot: Brown spots on the surface of the root, near the collar. Then appearance of cortical crusts which take on a scaly appearance. Wilting of the foliage of the affected plants and rotting of the necrotic areas.

Presence

◇ Presence of yellow larvae in roots ⋯▸ Carrot Fly, Carrot Rust Fly: The larva is a very elongated maggot (6 to 7 mm), shiny yellowish white. It is the larvae that cause the damage by penetrating the roots and digging winding galleries.

Spots

◇ Small white mealy spots ⋯▸ Potato Tuber Nematode. Potato Cyst Nematode: The nematode initially causes small white mealy spots just below the surface that are only visible if the skin is removed.

Celery

Botanical name
Apium graveolens

Family
Apiaceae

English name
Celery, Stalk celery, Pascal.

Names in other languages
Céleri (FR), Selderij (NL), Bleich-Sellerie (DE), Sedano (IT) Aipo (PO), Apio (SP).

Description
Celery (*Apium graveolens*) is an aromatic biennial plant in the family Apiaceae grown primarily for its stalk which are used as vegetables. The rhombic leaves of the celery plant grow in a rosette and are 3–6 cm (1.2–2.4 in) long and 2–4 cm (0.8–1.6 in) broad on a branched central stem which is highly ribbed. The plant produces creamy white flowers in dense umbels (an umbrella of short flower stalks) and produces broad oval seeds 1.5–2 mm (<0.1 in) long and wide.

Pests
American Serpentine Leaf Miner, Beet Armyworm, Boron Deficiency, Celery Fly, Celery Late Blight, Celery Miner Fly, Cercosporosa Leaf Spot, Cucumber Mosaic Virus, CMV, Damping Off, Fusarium Root Rot, Fusarium Wilt, Hawthorn Aphids, Phoma, Powdery Mildew, Rust, Slug and Snail, Garden Slug, Loach, Little Grey Slug, Vine Snail, White Garden Snail, South American Miner Fly, South American Leaf Miner, White Rot, White Mold, Sclerotinia Wilt.

Symptoms on:
Leaves
Damage

◇ Leaves with irregular holes ⋯→ Armyworms, Beet Armyworm: Older Spodoptera exigua caterpillars migrate to the apex of the plants where they feed mainly on the growing areas. They make large holes in the leaves and sometimes leave only the veins behind. The damage caused considerably affects the growth of the plants

Decay

◇ Soft watery rot on lower leaves ⋯→ White Rot. White Mold. Sclerotinia Wilt: Pre and post-emergent damping off, crown rot, and blighting of foliage and petioles. Small, hard, irregular, black structures called sclerotia may be present on or in plant tissue (especially inside stem and petiole tissue).

Deformation

◇ Curled leaves ⋯→ Celery Late Blight: The disease first manifests itself by the appearance of small light brown spots on the foliage. In case of severe attacks, the petioles turn yellow, the leaves curl up and dry out.

◇ Dry out leaves ⋯→ Celery Late Blight: In case of severe attacks, the petioles turn yellow, the leaves curl up and dry out, greatly reducing the growth of the celeriac root and making the foliage of the celeriac branches completely unfit for consumption.

Discoloring

◇ Yellow leaves on plants ⋯→ Boron Deficiency: Symptoms appear on young leaves: wrinkled, fragile leaves, slowed growth. Then wilting of the leaves with the appearance of brown or black spots on the petioles. Young leaves wilt, turn black and dry out.

◇ Leaves turn yellow and wilt ⋯→ Celery Fly: The leaves take on a burnt and dried out appearance. Deprived of a large part of the leaf surface and therefore having reduced photosynthetic activity, celery produces only a puny bulb.

◇ Leaves turn yellow and wilt ⋯→ Fusarium Wilt: An affected plant has a yellowing, stunted, wilted appearance, sometimes with gummosis on the stem. Discoloration and vascular browning of the collar progressing towards the stem and roots, and developing into cortical rot.

◇ Red stripes on roots, shoots and leaves ⋯→ Phoma: Known as a damping off agent, phoma also causes leaf necrosis. The first symptoms are often spots or Pink to wine-red streaks located on the leaves or taproot. These symptoms can progress to black necrosis with often diffuse borders located on leaves and cotyledons.

Galleries

◇ Galleries in leaves ⋯→ Celery Fly: It is the larvae that cause damage. The leaves are covered with mines, the collective mines resulting in a large white blister becoming brown. The excrement shines through transparency, between the two epidermis of the leaf.

◇ Leaves with galleries ⋯→ Celery Miner Fly: Liriomyza bryoniae attacks the cotyledons and terminal leaves. The larvae dig mines between the two epidermis in the thickness of the leaves, along the main vein and on either side of it.

◇ Leaves with galleries ⋯→ South American Miner Fly. South American Leaf Miner: Feeding pits and mined leaves with galleries depreciate the harvest.

◇ Leaves with galleries ⋯→ American Serpentine Leaf Miner: The main damage is due to larvae which mine the leaves. This damage is particularly serious on small plants in nurseries or just transplanted, which can die.

Presence

◇ Presence of white larvae ⋯→ Celery Fly: The larva develops in the mines dug during its development.

◇ Presence of colonies of aphids ⋯→ Hawthorn Aphids: Dysaphis apiifolia can damage celery crops by stunting growth, by transmitting celery yellow spot virus and by contaminating the crop with honeydew and debris.

◇ Slime trails ⋯→ Slug and Snail. Garden Slug. Loach. Little Grey Slug. Vine Snail. White Garden Snail: Slime trail' that signals their presence.

◇ Presence of caterpillars ⋯→ Armyworms, Beet Armyworm: Older Spodoptera exigua caterpillars migrate to the apex of the plants where they feed mainly on the growing areas. They make large holes in the leaves and sometimes leave only the veins behind. The damage caused considerably affects the growth of the plants.

◇ Presence of honeydew and sooty moulds on leaves ⋯→ Willow-Carrot Aphid: If aphid infestation is heavy it may cause leaves to yellow and/or distorted, necrotic spots on

leaves and/or stunted shoots; aphids secrete a sticky, sugary substance called honeydew which encourages the growth of sooty mold on the plants.

Spots

◇ Reddish-orange spots on leaves ⋯→ Rust: On the upper side of the leaves, you will see tiny white, orange or even brown spots appear depending on the species. If you turn these leaves over, you will see that these spots correspond to tiny pustules of the same color. The lesions are generally yellow, brown or red, but can be dark brown or black at the end of the season.

◇ Pale brown spots on leaves ⋯→ Celery Late Blight : The disease first manifests itself by the appearance on the foliage of small light brown spots, often delimited by the fine veins of the leaves but sometimes with irregular contours, ranging in size from 1 to 4 mm. They gradually turn reddish-brown and have small black dots called pycnidia in their center on the upper surface.

◇ Yellowish then brown spots on the upper surface of the leaf ⋯→ Powdery Mildew, Oidium:

◇ Yellowish then brown spots on the upper surface of the leaf, generally limited by the large veins, whitish felting on the lower surface.

◇ Leaf spots with brown-reddish margins ⋯→ Cercosporosa Leaf Spot, Cercosporia blight: Cercospora blight initially causes small, oval, gray to tan lesions with red borders. Severe infections may cause entire ferns to turn yellow or brown. Cercospora blight may cause reduced vigor and yield of spears the next spring.

Wilting

◇ Withered leaves ⋯→ Early Blight of Potato/ Tomato: Leaf Spot of Celery. The initial symptoms were many small, light brown, irregular-shaped spots on the leaves. The lesions gradually enlarged in the later stage of the disease, and multiple lesions coalesced to form large irregular brown spots, and eventually the whole leaves died.

Plantlets
Wilting

◇ Wilted, collapsed and dead young seedlings ⋯→ Damping Off: Seeds rot and fail to germinate, or even germinate, but seedlings fail to grow. A translucent area completely covers the stem near the soil surface. The affected tissues rot, leading to wilting and collapse of the seedlings.

Plants whole
Stunted

◇ Deformation and stunting of plants ⋯→ Cucumber Mosaic Virus. CMV: Artichoke latent virus (ALV, Potyvirus) is transmitted by aphids. Cucumber mosaic virus (CMV) induces deformation and stunting of plants.

◇ Plants stunted ⋯→ Fusarium Root Rot: Diseased plants wilt to a greater or lesser extent during the hottest times of the day; this wilting is sometimes reversible. In the most serious cases, the plants eventually dry out completely.

Roots or tubers
Decay

◇ Rotting of roots ⋯→ Fusarium Root Rot: The cause of these wilting is to be found at the level of the collar of the feet. At this location, a wet lesion has developed, a rot that has gradually spread to the lower part of the stem and the taproot, but also to the upper part of the root system. At the collar, the altered tissues are wet and show a dark to brownish tint. This lesion ends up girdling the stem for several centimetres. The roots located in the same layer of soil are also affected. Their cortex turns yellow, brown and decomposes.

◇ Internal brown rot ⋯→ Boron Deficiency: Boron deficiency causes inner tissue to be reddish brown, or brown or gray concentric rings develop inside the roots, it also causes brown heart rot.

Spots

◇ Small white mealy spots ⋯→ Potato Tuber Nematode. Potato Cyst Nematode: The nematode initially causes small white mealy spots just below the surface that are only visible if the skin is removed.

Stems
Lesions

◇ Reddish and brown lesions ⋯→ Black Scurf. Rhizoctonia Canker. Stem Canker. Crater spot: Presence of reddish and brown lesion at the collar.

Necrosis

◇ Necrotic stems ⋯→ Fusarium Wilt: An affected plant has a yellowing, stunted, wilted appearance, sometimes with gummosis on the stem. Discoloration and vascular browning of the collar progressing towards the stem and roots, and developing into cortical rot.

Chard

Botanical name
Beta vulgaris var. *cicla*

Family
Chenopodiaceae

English name
Chard, Swiss chard

Names in other languages
Blette (FR), Mangold (DE), Warmoes (NL), Bietola (IT), Acelga (PO), Acelgas (SP).

Description
Chard (*Beta vulgaris* var *cicla*) is an herbaceous biennial plant in the family Chenopodiaceae grown for its edible leaves and leaf stalks. The chard plant has an erect growth habit with a basal rosette of leaves with long fleshy petioles which can be red or white in color. The leaves are large and wrinkled with a pronounced midrib and prominent veins. The chard plant can reach 30–60 cm (12–16 in) in height and is usually grown as an annual, harvested after one growing season.

Pests
Bean Aphids, Black Dolphin Aphids, Beet Curly Top Virus, BCTV, Beet Fly, Mangold Fly, Cabbage Stem Flea Beetle, Cercosporosa Leaf Spot, Powdery Mildew, Rust, Slug and Snail, Garden Slug, Loach, Little Grey Slug, Vine Snail, White Garden Snail.

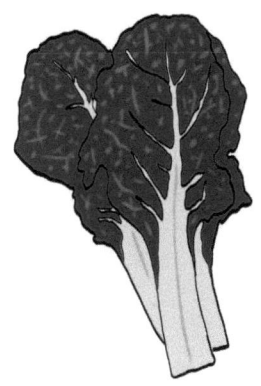

Symptoms on:
Leaves
Damage

◇ Perforated leaves ⋯→ Cabbage Stem Flea Beetle: It is difficult to monitor the activity of the adult of the large rapeseed flea beetle: it occurs at night. Its damage, on the other hand, is easily recognizable because the insect bites the cotyledons and young leaves in a circular fashion. Perforations can also be observed.

◇ Leaves with perforations ⋯→ Slug and Snail. Garden Slug. Loach. Little Grey Slug. Vine Snail. White Garden Snail: The slug consumes the leaves of plants between the veins, which gives them a serrated appearance. It digs small holes in the tubers. When the attack is serious, the stems are cut and consumed, the plants disappear.

Deformation

◇ Leaves curled or shrivelled ⋯→ Bean Aphids. Black Dolphin Aphids: Presence of black aphids on the leaves, on the flower stems and the flower heads. As soon as they appear, deformation of the attacked leaves and development of sooty mold.

Discoloring

◇ Leaves turn yellow and wilt ⋯→ Beet Curly Top Virus. BCTV: Leaf curling and embossing, irregular and prominent veins are observed. Plants are sometimes stunted. Leaves are occasionally rough and eventually turn yellow.

Galleries

◇ Leaves with galleries ⋯→ Beet Fly. Mangold Fly: The first generation beet fly larvae are the most harmful: they penetrate the leaves, between the two epidermis, and devour part of the tissue responsible for photosynthesis. They then dig galleries: whitish sinuosities can be observed. These galleries cause the leaves to dry out, turn brown, become pierced and lose their photosynthetic capacity.

Lesions

◇ Brown lesions on leaves ⋯→ Beet Fly. Mangold Fly: The first generation beet fly larvae are the most harmful: they penetrate the leaves, between the two epidermis, and devour part of the tissue responsible for photosynthesis. They then dig galleries: whitish sinuosities can be observed. These galleries cause the leaves to dry out, turn brown, become pierced and lose their photosynthetic capacity.

Presence

◇ White to gray powder coverage on leaves ⋯→ Powdery Mildew, Oidium: The heart leaves are covered with purplish-grey spores on the underside. They thicken, curl, and curl up. Older leaves turn yellow on the outside, then blacken and die. Only a few isolated plants or foci are damaged.

◇ Presence of black aphids ⋯→ Bean Aphids. Black Dolphin Aphids: Presence of black aphids on the leaves, on the flower stems and capitals. As soon as they appear, deformation of the attacked leaves and development of sooty mold.

Spots

◇ Reddish-orange spots on leaves ⋯→ Rust: On the upper side of the leaves, you will see tiny white, orange or even brown spots appear depending on the species. If you turn these leaves over, you will see that these spots correspond to tiny pustules of the same color. The lesions are generally yellow, brown or red, but can be dark brown or black at the end of the season.

◇ Leaf spots with brown-reddish margins ⋯→ Cercosporosa Leaf Spot, Cercosporia blight: Cercospora blight initially causes small, oval, gray to tan lesions with red borders. Severe infections may cause entire ferns to turn yellow or brown.

Plants whole
Stunted

◇ Stunted plants ⋯→ Cabbage Stem Flea Beetle: It is difficult to monitor the activity of the adult of the large rapeseed flea beetle: it occurs at night. Its damage, on the other hand, is easily recognizable because the insect bites the cotyledons and young leaves in a circular fashion. Perforations can also be observed.

Courgette

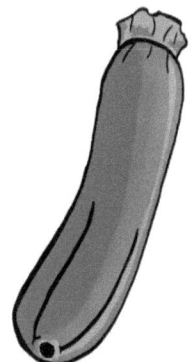

Botanical name
Cucurbita pepo pepo

Family
Cucurbitaceae

English name
Courgette, Zucchini

Names in other languages
Courgette (FR), Zucchini (DE), Courgette (NL), Zucchine (IT), Curgetes (PO), Calabacines (SP).

Related plants
Spaghetti squash, Scallop.

Description
The zucchini or courgette (*Cucurbita pepo pepo*) belongs to the family Cucurbitaceae. It is an annual plantwith a bushy habit and often without tendrils, with alternate distinctly palmately 5–7 lobed leaves. Flowers are male and female and yellow. The fruit is usually harvested when still immature at about 15 to 25 cm (6 to 10 in) long. It can be dark or light green, white, yellow or orange in color.

Pests
Anthracnose Fruit Rot, Celery Late Blight, Cotton Aphid, Cucumber Mosaic Virus, CMV, Damping Off, Early Blight of Potato/Tomato, Fusarium Root Rot, Fusarium Wilt, Gray Mold, Grey Mould, Botrytis Blight, Onion Thrips. Thrips, Powdery Mildew, Red Spider Mite, Two-spotted Mite, Scab of Cucurbits, Verticillium Wilt, White Rot, White Mold, Sclerotinia Wilt.

Symptoms on:
Flowers
Spots

◇ Blackish-brown spots, which may become covered with grayish mold ⇢ Gray Mold. Grey Mould. Botrytis Blight: Blackish-brown spots, extending from the base of the bracts, which may become covered with grayish mold (fruiting bodies). Sometimes, sclerotia are present. This disease develops secondarily following an injury or other disease.

Fruits
Spots

◇ Hollow, brown spot with yellow halo ⇢ Scab of Cucurbits: Small moist lesions appear on the leaves, often the youngest. These lesions gradually expand to form more or less circular spots, turning brown and necrotic as they age. They can sometimes take on a grayish tint and be surrounded by a more or less large yellow halo.

Leaves
Deformation

◇ Curled leaves ⇢ Celery Late Blight : The disease first manifests itself by the appearance of small light brown spots on the foliage. In case of severe attacks, the petioles turn yellow, the leaves curl up and dry out.

◇ Leaves curled or shrivelled ⇢ Cotton Aphid: Aphids, following their nutritional bites, are responsible for chlorotic spots and the deformation of young leaves which tend to roll up and more or less blister.

Discoloring

◇ Leaves turn yellow and wilt ⇢ Fusarium Wilt: An affected plant has a yellowing, stunted, wilted appearance, sometimes with gummosis on the stem. Discoloration and vascular browning of the collar progressing towards the stem and roots, and developing into cortical rot.

◇ Silvery marks on leaves ⋯→ Onion Thrips. Thrips: In a greenhouse, colonies can be very developed and direct damage is often significant. The larvae and adults of the tobacco and onion thrips puncture the contents of the subepidermal cells. The infested leaves are then dotted with numerous silver spots corresponding to groups of emptied cells. This symptom is typically associated with the presence of small piles of black feces.

◇ Leaves discoulouring bronzed or silvery ⋯→ Red Spider Mite. Two-spotted Mite: They damage the plant by piercing its cells to feed on them. The leaves turn pale and become stained yellow. To protect themselves and improve their microclimate, they weave a web around the leaf. A strong attack of mites leads to the leaves rolling and drying out, then falling off.

Lesions

◇ Circular, brown, and necrotic lesions on leaves ⋯→ Early Blight of Potato/Tomato: Small yellow spots rapidly turning black-brown, necrotic, circular and sharply outlined, approximately 5 mm in diameter, which gradually expand concentrically.

◇ Pale yellow or water-soaked regular or irregular lesions on leaves ⋯→ Anthracnose: Depending on the fungus responsible, these brown or black spots can be circular or irregular, they then appear either on the edge of the leaves or along the veins. The necrotic areas extend more or less concentrically, the limit with healthy tissue being very clear.

Presence

◇ Coating of gray fungus spores on leaves ⋯→ Gray Mold. Grey Mould. Botrytis Blight: Regardless of the organs affected, the dying tissues become covered with a very characteristic dense gray mold, consisting of the conidiophores and conidia of the fungus.

◇ White to gray powder coverage on leaves ⋯→ Powdery Mildew, Oidium: The heart leaves are covered with purplish-grey spores on the underside. They thicken, curl, and curl up. Older leaves turn yellow on the outside, then blacken and die. Only a few isolated plants or foci are damaged.

◇ Presence of honey dew on leaves ⋯→ Cotton Aphid: In addition to aphid colonies, we often observe white molts and the presence of honeydew on the surface of the aerial organs of zucchini and other plants.

◇ Presence of sooty mould on leaves ⋯→ Cotton Aphid: In addition to aphid colonies, we often observe white molts and the presence of honeydew on the surface of the aerial organs on which sooty mold develops. Remember that the latter can have several consequences, including a reduction in photosynthesis and leaf respiration and soiling of fruits thus rendered unmarketable.

◇ Leaves with fine silk webbing ⋯→ Red Spider Mite. Two-spotted Mite: They damage the plant by piercing its cells to feed on them. The leaves turn pale and become stained yellow. To protect themselves and improve their microclimate, they weave a web around the leaf. A strong attack of mites leads to the leaves rolling and drying out, then falling off.

◇ Presence of red spider mites, cast skins and egg shells ⋯→ Red Spider Mite. Two-spotted Mite: Spider mites always leave behind cast skins and egg shells.

Spots

◇ Yellow/brown spots ⋯→ Verticillium Wilt: Marginal drying, sometimes asymmetrical. In the stem, brown lesions at the level of the conductive tissue. Atrophied and deformed capitula.

◇ Yellowish then brown spots on the upper surface of the leaf ⋯→ Powdery Mildew, Oidium:

◇ Yellowish then brown spots on the upper surface of the leaf, generally limited by the large veins, whitish felting on the lower surface.

◇ Leaves with angular spots ⋯→ Scab of Cucurbits: Small, necrotic brown spots appear on the leaves. They can also be grayish, brown on the periphery, sometimes angular, surrounded by a yellow halo. Brown nerve necroses also form.

Plantlets
Wilting

◇ Wilted, collapsed and dead young seedlings ⋯→ Damping Off: Seeds rot and fail to germinate, or even germinate, but seedlings fail to grow. A translucent area completely covers the stem near the soil surface. The affected tissues rot, leading to wilting and collapse of the seedlings.

Plants whole
Stunted

◇ Deformation and stunting of plants ⋯→ Cucumber Mosaic Virus. CMV: Artichoke latent virus (ALV, Potyvirus) is transmitted by aphids. Cucumber mosaic virus (CMV) induces deformation and stunting of plants.

◇ Plants stunted ⋯→ Fusarium Root Rot: Diseased plants wilt to a greater or lesser extent during the hottest times of the day; this wilting is sometimes reversible. In the most serious cases, the plants eventually dry out completely

Wilting

◇ Wilting of the entire plant ⋯→ Verticillium Wilt: The leaves soften and become duller. The leaves begin to yellow, then turn brown as they become necrotic. The characteristic feature is the asymmetry of the symptoms, with many leaves only affected on one half. The disease progresses from the bottom to the top of the plant. Verticillium wilt causes dark streaks under the bark.

Roots or tubers
Decay

◇ Rotting of roots ⋯→ Fusarium Root Rot: The cause of these wilting is to be found at the level of the collar of the feet. At this location, a wet lesion has developed, a rot that has gradually spread to the lower part of the stem and the taproot, but also to the upper part of the root system. At the collar, the altered tissues are wet and show a dark to brownish tint. This lesion ends up girdling the stem for several centimetres. The roots located in the same layer of soil are also affected. Their cortex turns yellow, brown and decomposes.

Stems

Lesions

◇ Reddish and brown lesions ⋯→ Black Scurf. Rhizoctonia Canker. Stem Canker. Crater spot: Presence of reddish and brown lesion at the collar.

Necrosis

◇ Necrotic stems ⋯→ Fusarium Wilt: An affected plant has a yellowing, stunted, wilted appearance, sometimes with gummosis on the stem. Discoloration and vascular browning of the collar progressing towards the stem and roots, and developing into cortical rot.

Presence

◇ Coating of gray fungus spores on stems ⋯→ Gray Mold. Grey Mould. Botrytis Blight: Lesions, even cankers, more or less extensive, are visible on the stems, mainly located at the level of pruning and disbudding wounds. Let us add that the lesions are generally covered with a very characteristic grayish to beige mold.

◇ White mold on the stem and collar ⋯→ White Rot. White Mold. Sclerotinia Wilt: Black or dark brown sclerotia form inside the stems. This uncommon disease can sometimes lead to the death of the plant.eter, which gradually expand con

Cucumber

Botanical name
Cucumis sativus

Family
Cucurbitaceae

English name
Cucumber

Names in other languages
Concombre (FR), Komkommer (NL), Gurke (DE), Cetriolo (IT), Pepino (PO), Pepino (SP).

Related plants
Gherkin, Pickling cucumber.

Description
Cucumber (*Cucumis sativus*) is a warm season, vining, annual plant in the family Cucurbitaceae grown for its edible cucumber fruit. The cucumber plant is a sprawling vine with large leaves and curling tendrils. The plant may have 4 or 5 main stems from which the tendrils branch. The leaves of the plant are arranged alternately on the vines, have 3–7 pointed lobes and are hairy. The cucumber plant produces yellow flowers that are 4 cm (1.6 in) in diameter. The cucumber fruit varies in shape but is generally a curved cylinder rounded at both ends that can reach up to 60 cm (24 in) in length 10 cm (3.9 in) in diameter. Cucumber plants are annual plants, surviving only one growing season and the vines can reach up to 5 m (16.4 ft) in length.

Pests
Anthracnose Fruit Rot, Anthracnose of Cucurbits, Cabbage Stem Flea Beetle,Celery Late Blight, Cotton Aphid, CMV, Damping Off, Downy mildew of Cucurbits, Early Blight of Potato/Tomato, Fusarium Root Rot, Fusarium Wilt, Gray Mold. Grey Mould. Botrytis Blight, Onion Thrips. Thrips, Potato Aphid, Powdery Mildew, Red Spider Mite. Two-spotted Mite, Slug and Snail, South American Miner Fly. South American Leaf Miner, Southern Green Stink bug, Verticillium Wilt, White Rot. White Mold. Sclerotinia Wilt.

Symptoms on:
Flowers
Spots

◇ Blackish-brown spots, which may become covered with grayish mold ⸱⸱⸱➤ Gray Mold. Grey Mould. Botrytis Blight: Blackish-brown spots, extending from the base of the bracts, which may become covered with grayish mold (fruiting bodies). Sometimes, sclerotia are present. This disease develops secondarily following an injury or other disease.

Fruits
Lesions

◇ Black circular lesions ⸱⸱⸱➤ Anthracnose of Cucurbits: Circular spots on fruits, dark to blackish in the center, spreading to internal tissues.

Spots

◇ Fruits with white spots ⸱⸱⸱➤ Southern Green Stink Bug: Young fruits have small, punctate spots, with the underlying tissues being lighter in color than the rest.

Leaves
Damage

◇ Perforated leaves ⸱⸱⸱➤ Cabbage Stem Flea Beetle: It is difficult to monitor the activity of the adult of the large rapeseed flea beetle: it occurs at night. Its damage, on the other hand, is easily recognizable because the insect bites the cotyledons and young leaves in a circular fashion. Perforations can also be observed.

◇ Leaves with perforations ⸱⸱⸱➤ Slug and Snail. Garden Slug. Loach. Little Grey Slug. Vine Snail. White Garden Snail: The slug consumes the leaves of plants between the veins, which gives them a serrated appearance. It digs small holes in the tubers. When the attack is serious, the stems are cut and consumed, the plants disappear.

Deformation

◇ Curled leaves ⸱⸱⸱→ Celery Late Blight: The disease first manifests itself by the appearance of small light brown spots on the foliage. In case of severe attacks, the petioles turn yellow, the leaves curl up and dry out.

◇ Leaves curled or shrivelled ⸱⸱⸱→ Cotton Aphid: Aphids, following their nutritional bites, are responsible for chlorotic spots and the deformation of young leaves which tend to roll up and more or less blister.

Discoloring

◇ Leaves turn yellow and wilt ⸱⸱⸱→ Fusarium Wilt: An affected plant has a yellowing, stunted, wilted appearance, sometimes with gummosis on the stem. Discoloration and vascular browning of the collar progressing towards the stem and roots, and developing into cortical rot.

◇ Silvery marks on leaves ⸱⸱⸱→ Onion Thrips. Thrips: In a greenhouse, colonies can be very developed and direct damage is often significant. The larvae and adults of the tobacco and onion thrips puncture the contents of the subepidermal cells. The infested leaves are then dotted with numerous silver spots corresponding to groups of emptied cells. This symptom is typically associated with the presence of small piles of black feces.

◇ Leaves discoulouring bronzed or silvery ⸱⸱⸱→ Red Spider Mite. Two-spotted Mite: They damage the plant by piercing its cells to feed on them. The leaves turn pale and become stained yellow. To protect themselves and improve their microclimate, they weave a web around the leaf. A strong attack of mites leads to the leaves rolling and drying out, then falling off.

Galleries

◇ Leaves with galleries ⸱⸱⸱→ South American Miner Fly. South American Leaf Miner: Feeding pits and mined leaves with galleries depreciate the harvest.

Lesions

◇ Circular, brown, and necrotic lesions on leaves ⸱⸱⸱→ Early Blight of Potato/Tomato: Small yellow spots rapidly turning black-brown, necrotic, circular and sharply outlined, approximately 5 mm in diameter, which gradually expand concentrically.

◇ Pale yellow or water-soaked regular or irregular lesions on leaves ⸱⸱⸱→ Anthracnose: Depending on the fungus responsible, these brown or black spots can be circular or irregular, they then appear either on the edge of the leaves or along the veins. The necrotic areas extend more or less concentrically, the limit with healthy tissue being very clear.

Mosaic pattern

◇ Leaves with mosaic pattern ⸱⸱⸱→ Downy mildew of Cucurbits: Wet, oily leaf spots that turn yellow and quickly become necrotic. The spots are mostly angular in shape because they are delimited by the veins. Eventually, the leaf blade presents a mosaic of yellow and/or brown spots if the lesions are necrotic.

Presence

◇ Coating of gray fungus spores on leaves ⸱⸱⸱→ Gray Mold. Grey Mould. Botrytis Blight: Regardless of the organs affected, the dying tissues become covered with a very characteristic dense gray mold, consisting of the conidiophores and conidia of the fungus.

◇ White to gray powder coverage on leaves ⸱⸱⸱→ Powdery Mildew, Oidium: The heart leaves are covered with purplish-grey spores on the underside. They thicken, curl, and curl up. Older leaves turn yellow on the outside, then blacken and die. Only a few isolated plants or foci are damaged.

◇ Presence of aphids ⸱⸱⸱→ Potato Aphid: The most classic symptoms are a curling of heavily infested leaves and a slowdown in the growth of the plants

◇ Presence of honey dew on leaves ⸱⸱⸱→ Cotton Aphid: In addition to aphid colonies, we often observe white molts and the presence of honeydew on the surface of the aerial organs of zucchini and other plants.

◇ Presence of sooty mould on leaves ⸱⸱⸱→ Cotton Aphid: In addition to aphid colonies, we often observe white molts and the presence of honeydew on the surface of the aerial organs on which sooty mold develops. Remember that the latter can have several consequences, including a reduction in photosynthesis and leaf respiration and soiling of fruits thus rendered unmarketable.

◇ Leaves with fine silk webbing ⸱⸱⸱→ Red Spider Mite. Two-spotted Mite: They damage the plant by piercing its cells to feed on them. The leaves turn pale and become stained yellow. To protect themselves and improve their microclimate, they weave a web around the leaf. A strong attack of mites leads to the leaves rolling and drying out, then falling off.

◇ Slime trails ⸱⸱⸱→ Slug and Snail. Garden Slug. Loach. Little Grey Slug. Vine Snail. White Garden Snail: Slime trail' that signals their presence.

◇ Presence of red spider mites, cast skins and egg shells ⸱⸱⸱→ Red Spider Mite. Two-spotted Mite: Spider mites always leave behind cast skins and egg shells.

◇ Presence of caterpillars ⸱⸱⸱→ Bright-line Brown-eyes Moth: The damage caused by this moth on cabbage and beet leaves is generally not very significant.

◇ Leaves with grey powder ⸱⸱⸱→ Downy mildew of Cucurbits: Presence on the lower face of the blade of felting whose coloring varies from light gray to dark mauve.

Spots

◇ Yellow/brown spots ⸱⸱⸱→ Verticillium Wilt: Marginal drying, sometimes asymmetrical. In the stem, brown lesions at the level of the conductive tissue. Atrophied and deformed capitula.

◇ Yellowish then brown spots on the upper surface of the leaf ⸱⸱⸱→ Powdery Mildew, Oidium:

Yellowish then brown spots on the upper surface of the leaf, generally limited by the large veins, whitish felting on the lower surface.

◇ Leaves with irregular brown spots and a yellowish halo. ⋯→ Anthracnose of Cucurbits: Wet lesion spots, rather circular, gradually turning brown and red before becoming necrotic. Presence of a translucent to yellowish halo around the lesions, the internal tissues can decompose and fall off, giving the leaf blade a riddled appearance. Sometimes significant defoliation.

◇ Leaves with yellow spots ⋯→ Downy mildew of Cucurbits: Wet, oily leaf spots that turn yellow and quickly become necrotic. The spots are mostly angular in shape because they are delimited by the veins. Eventually, the leaf blade presents a mosaic of yellow and/or brown spots if the lesions are necrotic.

Plantlets
Wilting

◇ Wilted, collapsed and dead young seedlings ⋯→ Damping Off: Seeds rot and fail to germinate, or even germinate, but seedlings fail to grow. A translucent area completely covers the stem near the soil surface. The affected tissues rot, leading to wilting and collapse of the seedlings.

Plants whole
Stunted

◇ Deformation and stunting of plants ⋯→ Cucumber Mosaic Virus. CMV: Artichoke latent virus (ALV, Potyvirus) is transmitted by aphids. Cucumber mosaic virus (CMV) induces deformation and stunting of plants.

◇ Stunted plants ⋯→ Cabbage Stem Flea Beetle: It is difficult to monitor the activity of the adult of the large rapeseed flea beetle: it occurs at night. Its damage, on the other hand, is easily recognizable because the insect bites the cotyledons and young leaves in a circular fashion. Perforations can also be observed.

◇ Plants stunted ⋯→ Fusarium Root Rot: Diseased plants wilt to a greater or lesser extent during the hottest times of the day; this wilting is sometimes reversible. In the most serious cases, the plants eventually dry out completely.

◇ Stunted plants with yellow marbling ⋯→ Cucumber Mosaic Virus. CMV: The symptoms expressed by the mosaic virus can be of several types: mosaic or leaf mottling, progressive yellowing of the foliage, necrotic rings, deformation of flowers, fruits and leaves. Transmission occurs through many species of aphids, but the black aphid (Aphis gossypii) is predominant.

Wilting

◇ Wilting of the entire plant ⋯→ Verticillium Wilt: The leaves soften and become duller. The leaves begin to yellow, then turn brown as they become necrotic. The characteristic feature is the asymmetry of the symptoms, with many leaves only affected on one half. The disease progresses from the bottom to the top of the plant. Verticillium wilt causes dark streaks under the bark.

Roots or tubers
Decay

◇ Rotting of roots ⋯→ Fusarium Root Rot: The cause of these wilting is to be found at the level of the collar of the feet. At this location, a wet lesion has developed, a rot that has gradually spread to the lower part of the stem and the taproot, but also to the upper part of the root system. At the collar, the altered tissues are wet and show a dark to brownish tint. This lesion ends up girdling the stem for several centimetres. The roots located in the same layer of soil are also affected. Their cortex turns yellow, brown and decomposes.

Stems
Lesions

◇ Reddish and brown lesions ⋯→ Black Scurf. Rhizoctonia Canker. Stem Canker. Crater spot: Presence of reddish and brown lesion at the collar.

Necrosis

◇ Necrotic stems ⋯→ Fusarium Wilt: An affected plant has a yellowing, stunted, wilted appearance, sometimes with gummosis on the stem. Discoloration and vascular browning of the collar progressing towards the stem and roots, and developing into cortical rot.

Presence

◇ Coating of gray fungus spores on stems ⋯→ Gray Mold. Grey Mould. Botrytis Blight: Lesions, even cankers, more or less extensive, are visible on the stems, mainly located at the level of pruning and disbudding wounds. Let us add that the lesions are generally covered with a very characteristic grayish to beige mold.

◇ White mold on the stem and collar ⋯→ White Rot. White Mold. Sclerotinia Wilt: Black or dark brown sclerotia form inside the stems. This uncommon disease can sometimes lead to the death of the plant.

Eggplant

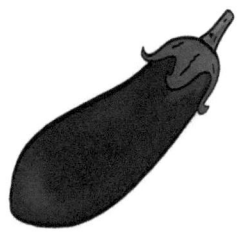

Botanical name
Solanum melongena

Family
Solanaceae

English name
Eggplant, Aubergine

Names in other languages
Aubergine (FR), Aubergine (NL), Aubergine (DE), Melanzana (IT), Beringela (PO), Berenjena (SP).

Description
The eggplant or aubergine (*Solanum melongena*), belongs in the plant family Solanaceae. The eggplant is a much-branched shrub up to 2 metres tall with a long taproot which extends deep into the ground. The stems and leaves are densely covered with star-shaped hairs and sometimes prickles. The leaves are arranged alternately along the stem, each with a petiole. The leaves have hairy margins. The Hermaphrodite flowers are usually solitary and are supported by a 1-3 cm long stalk. Smaller, functionally male flowers appear on the same inflorescence. The fruits is a globose to oblong fleshy berry, 2-35 cm (sometimes longer) and 2-20 cm broad. The fruit is generally smooth and shiny and has many seeds. The colour ranges from white, green or from purple to black.

Pests
Anthracnose Fruit Rot, Bacterial Canker of Tomato, Beet Armyworm, Colorado Potato Beetle, Cotton Aphid, Cotton Whitefly, Tobacco Whitefly, Cucumber Mosaic Virus, CMV, Damping Off, Fusarium Root Rot, Glasshouse Whitefly, Greenhouse Whitefly, Gray Mold, Grey Mould, Botrytis Blight, Onion Thrips, Thrips, Potato Aphid, Powdery Mildew, Red Spider Mite, Two-spotted Mite, Silver-Y moth, Common Silver-Y moth, Cabbage Army Moth, Southern Green Stink bug, Tobacco Mosaic Virus, TMV, Tomato Leaf Miner, Tomato Russet Mite, Verticillium Wilt.

Symptoms on:
Flowers
Discoloring

◇ Leaves turn yellow ⟶ Cotton Whitefly. Tobacco Whitefly: The tobacco whitefly occupies the entire plant. Presence of numerous "white flies" and honeydew, slow growth of plants, development of sooty mold on aerial organs, yellowing and necrosis of the leaf blade.

Spots

◇ Blackish-brown spots, which may become covered with grayish mold ⟶ Gray Mold. Grey Mould. Botrytis Blight: Blackish-brown spots, extending from the base of the bracts, which may become covered with grayish mold (fruiting bodies). Sometimes, sclerotia are present. This disease develops secondarily following an injury or other disease.

Fruits
Spots

◇ Fruits with soft, pasty spots of a grayish tint ⟶ Gray Mold. Grey Mould. Botrytis Blight: Soft, wet rots develop at the stalk scar of fruits, sometimes at the tips. Lesions are usually circular and elongated, pale brown to brown in color; the tissues often collapse. Fruit rot can be observed both during cultivation and after harvest, as well as during storage, transport, and marketing.

◇ Fruits with white spots ⟶ Southern Green Stink Bug: Young fruits have small, punctate spots, with the underlying tissues being lighter in color than the rest.

Leaves
Damage

◇ Leaves with irregular holes ⟶ Colorado Potato Beetle: They are very harmful because of their voracity and the fact that they can consume the entire foliage. The larvae begin to devour the leaves that carry them and then those neighboring up to the top of the plant. Their consumption is very important and rapid.

◇ Leaves with perforations ⟶ Silver-Y moth. Common Silver-Y moth. Cabbage Army Moth.: The caterpillar is active mainly at night, it devours the leaf blades and cuts the petioles. During the day, it remains attached to the underside of the leaves.

◇ Leaves with irregular holes ⟶ Armyworms, Beet Armyworm: Older Spodoptera exigua caterpillars migrate to the apex of the plants where they feed mainly on the growing areas. They make large holes in the leaves and sometimes leave only the veins behind. The damage caused considerably affects the growth of the plants. In heavy infestations, the damage can extend to the stems and, in the worst cases, to the fruits, which the caterpillars consume entirely from the inside.

Deformation

◇ Leaves shrivelled ⟶ Southern Green Stink Bug: Presence of larvae and adults on affected organs. Wilting of apex leaves. Blisters on stems.

◇ Leaves curled or shrivelled ⟶ Cotton Aphid: Aphids, following their nutritional bites, are responsible for chlorotic spots and the deformation of young leaves which tend to roll up and more or less blister.

Discoloring

◇ Leaves turn yellow and wilt ⟶ Fusarium Wilt: An affected plant has a yellowing, stunted, wilted appearance, sometimes with gummosis on the stem. Discoloration and vascular browning of the collar progressing towards the stem and roots, and developing into cortical rot.

◇ Silvery marks on leaves ⟶ Onion Thrips. Thrips: In a greenhouse, colonies can be very developed and direct damage is often significant. The larvae and adults of the tobacco and onion thrips puncture the contents of the subepidermal cells. The infested leaves are then dotted with numerous silver spots corresponding to groups of emptied cells. This symptom is typically associated with the presence of small piles of black feces.

◇ Leaves discoulouring bronzed or silvery ⟶ Red Spider Mite. Two-spotted Mite: They damage the plant by piercing its cells to feed on them. The leaves turn pale and become stained yellow. To protect themselves and improve their microclimate, they weave a web around the leaf. A strong attack of mites leads to the leaves rolling and drying out, then falling off.

Galleries

◇ Leaves with mines or galleries ⟶ Tomato Leaf Miner: Leafminer larvae dig mines and galleries on aerial organs. Leaves become mined with whitish spots that darken and become necrotic.

Lesions

◇ Pale yellow or water-soaked regular or irregular lesions on leaves ⟶ Anthracnose: Depending on the fungus responsible, these brown or black spots can be circular or irregular, they then appear either on the edge of the leaves or along the veins. The necrotic areas extend more or less concentrically, the limit with healthy tissue being very clear.

Mosaic pattern

◇ Leaves with yellowing of leaf edges and mosaic pattern ⟶ Tobacco Mosaic Virus. TMV: Leaves to be mottled light and dark green, they often look like they are variegated. They may also be thickened, puckered, brittle and distorted as well.

Necrosis

◇ Shrivelling and necrosis of leaves ⟶ Tomato Russet Mite: The underside of the leaves or leaflets of the lower part of the plants takes on a greasy or metallic tint. Subsequently, the leaves show a rather bronze coloration from which the name of this disease originates.

Presence

◇ Presence of honey dew on leaves ⟶ Glasshouse Whitefly. Greenhouse Whitefly: We can observe the presence of numerous whiteflies and honeydew, plant growth is slowed, there is sooty mold on the aerial organs, as well as yellowing and necrosis of the leaf blade.

◇ Presence of sooty mould on leaves ⟶ Glasshouse Whitefly. Greenhouse Whitefly: We can observe the presence of numerous whiteflies and honeydew, plant growth is slowed, there is sooty mold on the aerial organs, as well as yellowing and necrosis of the leaf blade.

◇ Coating of gray fungus spores on leaves ⟶ Gray Mold. Grey Mould. Botrytis Blight: Regardless of the organs affected, the dying tissues become covered with a very characteristic dense gray mold, consisting of the conidiophores and conidia of the fungus.

◇ Presence of colonies of whiteflies ⟶ Glasshouse Whitefly. Greenhouse Whitefly: Presence of numerous "whiteflies" and honeydew, slowed plant growth, development of sooty mold on aerial organs, yellowing and necrosis of the leaf blade. Whiteflies are easily detected by moving the leaves.

◇ Presence of larvae and adult beetles ⟶ Colorado Potato Beetle: Check plants every 3-4 days for presence of larvae and adults. It is considered to be the most important insect defoliator of potatoes. It may also cause considerable damage to tomato and aubergine crops with both adults and larvae feeding on the plant's foliage.

◇ White to gray powder coverage on leaves ⟶ Powdery Mildew, Oidium: The heart leaves are covered with purplish-grey spores on the underside. They thicken, curl, and curl up. Older leaves turn yellow on the outside, then blacken and die. Only a few isolated plants or foci are damaged.

◇ Presence of aphids ⟶ Potato Aphid: The most classic symptoms are a curling of heavily infested leaves and a slowdown in the growth of the plants

◇ Presence of honey dew on leaves ⋯▸ Cotton Aphid: In addition to aphid colonies, we often observe white molts and the presence of honeydew on the surface of the aerial organs of zucchini and other plants.

◇ Presence of sooty mould on leaves ⋯▸ Cotton Aphid: In addition to aphid colonies, we often observe white molts and the presence of honeydew on the surface of the aerial organs on which sooty mold develops. Remember that the latter can have several consequences, including a reduction in photosynthesis and leaf respiration and soiling of fruits thus rendered unmarketable.

◇ Leaves with fine silk webbing ⋯▸ Red Spider Mite. Two-spotted Mite: They damage the plant by piercing its cells to feed on them. The leaves turn pale and become stained yellow. To protect themselves and improve their microclimate, they weave a web around the leaf. A strong attack of mites leads to the leaves rolling and drying out, then falling off.

◇ Presence of red spider mites, cast skins and egg shells ⋯▸ Red Spider Mite. Two-spotted Mite: Spider mites always leave behind cast skins and egg shells.

◇ Presence of caterpillars ⋯▸ Silver-Y moth. Common Silver-Y moth. Cabbage Army Moth.: The caterpillar is active mainly at night, it devours the leaf blades and cuts the petioles. During the day, it remains attached to the underside of the leaves.

◇ Presence of honey dew on leaves ⋯▸ Cotton Whitefly. Tobacco Whitefly: The tobacco whitefly occupies the entire plant. Presence of numerous "white flies" and honeydew, slow growth of plants, development of sooty mold on aerial organs, yellowing and necrosis of the leaf blade.

◇ Presence of caterpillars ⋯▸ Armyworms, Beet Armyworm: Older Spodoptera exigua caterpillars migrate to the apex of the plants where they feed mainly on the growing areas. They make large holes in the leaves and sometimes leave only the veins behind. The damage caused considerably affects the growth of the plants. In heavy infestations, the damage can extend to the stems and, in the worst cases, to the fruits, which the caterpillars consume entirely from the inside.

Spots

◇ Leaves with yellow, brown, necrotic and concentric spots ⋯▸ Early Blight of Potato/ Tomato:

◇ Small yellow spots quickly turn brown-black, necrotic, circular and sharply outlined, measuring about 5 mm in diameter, which gradually spread concentrically.

◇ Yellow/brown spots ⋯▸ Verticillium Wilt: Marginal drying, sometimes asymmetrical. In the stem, brown lesions at the level of the conductive tissue. Atrophied and deformed capitula.

◇ Yellowish then brown spots on the upper surface of the leaf ⋯▸ Powdery Mildew, Oidium: Yellowish then brown spots on the upper surface of the leaf, generally limited by the large veins, whitish felting on the lower surface.

◇ Brown spots surrounded by a halo ⋯▸ Late Blight. Potato and Tomato Late Blight: On the upper side of the leaves, small discolored spots are observed that turn brown and are surrounded by a light green to yellow halo. On the underside, in humid conditions, a characteristic white felting appears.

Wilting

◇ Wilting of leaves ⋯▸ Verticillium Wilt: Partial wilting of some lower leaves at the hottest times of the day, reversible during the night. Softening and progressive yellowing of sectors of the leaf blade, often interveinal and in the shape of a "V". The latter eventually turn brown and become necrotic.

Plantlets
Wilting

◇ Wilted, collapsed and dead young seedlings ⋯▸ Damping Off: Seeds rot and fail to germinate, or even germinate, but seedlings fail to grow. A translucent area completely covers the stem near the soil surface. The affected tissues rot, leading to wilting and collapse of the seedlings.

Plants whole
Defoliation

◇ Plants defoliated ⋯▸ Colorado Potato Beetle: Larvae may defoliate potato plants resulting in yield losses up to 100% if the damage occurs prior to tuber formation. Larvae may consume 40 cm2 of potato leaves during the entire larval stage, but adults are capable of consuming 10 cm2 of foliage per day.

Stunted

◇ Deformation and stunting of plants ⋯▸ Cucumber Mosaic Virus. CMV: Artichoke latent virus (ALV, Potyvirus) is transmitted by aphids. Cucumber mosaic virus (CMV) induces deformation and stunting of plants.

◇ Plants stunted ⋯▸ Fusarium Root Rot: Diseased plants wilt to a greater or lesser extent during the hottest times of the day; this wilting is sometimes reversible. In the most serious cases, the plants eventually dry out completely.

Wilting

◇ Wilting of the entire plant ⋯▸ Bacterial Canker of Tomato: Bacterial canker often manifests itself, at least at the beginning of its development, by the appearance on the leaflets of livid interveinal spots which quickly become necrotic. Very often, they are followed by leaf wilting, the leaflets tending in this case to curl downwards. Eventually, the seedlings, like adult plants, can wilt and dry out completely.

◇ Wilting of the entire plant ⋯▸ Verticillium Wilt: The leaves soften and become duller. The leaves begin to yellow, then turn brown as they become necrotic. The characteristic feature is the asymmetry of the symptoms, with many leaves only affected on one half. The disease progresses from the bottom to the top of the plant. Verticillium wilt causes dark streaks under the bark.

Roots or tubers
Decay

◇ Rotting of roots ⇢ Fusarium Root Rot: The cause of these wilting is to be found at the level of the collar of the feet. At this location, a wet lesion has developed, a rot that has gradually spread to the lower part of the stem and the taproot, but also to the upper part of the root system. At the collar, the altered tissues are wet and show a dark to brownish tint. This lesion ends up girdling the stem for several centimetres. The roots located in the same layer of soil are also affected. Their cortex turns yellow, brown and decomposes.

Spots

◇ Small white mealy spots ⇢ Potato Tuber Nematode. Potato Cyst Nematode: The nematode initially causes small white mealy spots just below the surface that are only visible if the skin is removed.

Stems
Lesions

◇ Reddish and brown lesions ⇢ Black Scurf. Rhizoctonia Canker. Stem Canker. Crater spot: Presence of reddish and brown lesion at the collar.

Presence

◇ Coating of gray fungus spores on stems ⇢ Gray Mold. Grey Mould. Botrytis Blight: Lesions, even cankers, more or less extensive, are visible on the stems, mainly located at the level of pruning and disbudding wounds. Let us add that the lesions are generally covered with a very characteristic grayish to beige mold.

Fennel

Botanical name
Foeniculum vulgare

Family
Apiaceae

English name
Fennel

Names in other languages
Fenouil (FR), Fenchel (DE), Venkel (NL), Finocchio (IT), Funcho (PO), Hinojo (SP).

Description
Fennel (*Foeniculum vulgare*) is an herbaceous perennial plant in the family Apiaceae grown for use as a herb or flavoring. The fennel plant is an erect herb with 4–5 hollow stems and distinctly divided feathery foliage. The leaves are simple and linear and are 2–15 cm in length. The plant produces flowers on flat umbels which can be 20 cm (7.9 in) in diameter and possess 20-50 tiny yellow flowers. The plant may reach 2 m (6.6 ft) in height. Fennel is a short-lived plant and is almost always grown as an annual.

Pests
Carrot Fly, Hawthorn Aphids, Powdery Mildew.

Symptoms on:
Leaves
Discoloring

◇ Leaves turn yellow ⋯▸ Carrot Fly, Carrot Rust Fly: Yellowing or reddening of the foliage of affected plants is often observed.

Lesions

◇ Brown black necrotic lesions ⋯▸ Alternaria leaf blight: Small brownish spots with a yellow halo on the edges of older leaves, developing into necrosis.

Presence

◇ Presence of colonies of aphids ⋯▸ Hawthorn Aphids: Dysaphis apiifolia can damage celery crops by stunting growth, by transmitting celery yellow spot virus and by contaminating the crop with honeydew and debris.

Spots

◇ Yellowish then brown spots on the upper surface of the leaf ⋯▸ Powdery Mildew, Oidium: Yellowish then brown spots on the upper surface of the leaf, generally limited by the large veins, whitish felting on the lower surface.

Plants whole
Stunted

◇ Plants stunted ⋯▸ Carrot Fly, Carrot Rust Fly: The roots have slowed growth and the plant can disappear in the event of an early attack.

Garlic

Botanical name
Allium sativum

Family
Liliaceae

English name
Garlic

Names in other languages
Ail (FR), Knoflook (NL), Knoblauch (DE), Aglio comune (IT), Alho (PO), Ajo (SP).

Description
Garlic (*Allium sativum*) is a an herbaceous, annual, bulbous plant in the family Liliaceae grown for its pungent, edible bulb of the same name. The bulb can be up to 7 cm (2.8 in) in diameter and is made up of 1–15 cloves. The stem is very short and flattened and gives way to a pseudostem, The garlic plant can possess 6–12 flat, blade-like leaves which can stretch up to 50 cm (19.7 in) long. The plant can reach 60 cm (23.6 in) in height and is an annual, surviving only one growing season.

Pests
Bacterial Blight of Garlic, Basal Rot, Boron Deficiency, Botrytis Rot, Neckrot, Brachyserus of Garlic, Downy Mildew of Alliums, Early Blight of Potato/Tomato, Leek Moth, Onion Moth, Onion and Leek Rust, Onion Fly, Penicillium Decay, Seed Clove Decay, Bleu Mold, Skin Blotch of Garlic, Stem Nematode, Bulb and Stem Nematode, White Rot, White Mold, Sclerotinia Wilt.

Symptoms on:
Leaves
Decay

◇ Soft watery rot on lower leaves ⋯→ White Rot. White Mold. Sclerotinia Wilt: Pre and post-emergent damping off, crown rot, and blighting of foliage and petioles. Small, hard, irregular, black structures called sclerotia may be present on or in plant tissue (especially inside stem and petiole tissue).

Deformation

◇ Leaves distorted ⋯→ Stem Nematode. Bulb and Stem Nematode: Deformation and swelling of the stem, uncontrolled development and wilting of the leaves. The plant is stocky and is clearly less developed than a healthy plant.

Discoloring

◇ Leaves turn yellow and wilt ⋯→ Onion Fly: On young seedlings: the plant wilts and then dies. A larva can attack several seedlings in succession. If the plant is more developed, it wilts, especially in hot weather, and may die.

◇ Yellow leaves on plants ⋯→ Boron Deficiency: Symptoms appear on young leaves: wrinkled, fragile leaves, slowed growth. Then wilting of the leaves with the appearance of brown or black spots on the petioles. Young leaves wilt, turn black and dry out.

Galleries

◇ Galleries in leaves ⋯→ Leek Moth, Onion Moth: The leaves are mined, perforated, partly consumed, the leaves end up having a lacerated appearance.

Lesions

◇ White lesions on the leaves ⋯→ Bacterial Blight of Garlic: At the start of the attack, oval lesions appear at the top of the leaf sheaths. They develop into brown leaf rot and then into foot rot in wet weather. In dry weather, the development is stopped: the lesion becomes white.

Presence

◇ Leaves with grey powder ⋯→ Downy Mildew of Alliums: At the beginning of vegetation: dwarf plants with chlorotic, deformed leaves, covered with a velvety gray mycelium. During vegetation: presence of elongated spots on leaves and stems of a yellowish appearance and covered with a gray felting.

Spots

◇ Leaves with yellow, brown, necrotic and concentric spots ⋯→ Early Blight of Potato/Tomato: Small yellow spots quickly turn brown-black, necrotic, circular and sharply outlined, measuring about 5 mm in diameter, which gradually spread concentrically.

◇ Bright-orange spots on leaves ⋯→ Onion and Leek Rust: Affected leek, garlic and onion leaves have small pustular lesions that are initially whitish to beige. These spread slightly and give rise to bright orange to brown pustules, with the leaves eventually drying out.

Plants whole
Spots

◇ Leaves with necrotic spots, turn yellow and die ⋯→ Basal Rot: Necrotic spots with dark brown, slightly sunken, irregular lesions on the leaves and stems, leading to wilting.

Stunted

◇ Plants stunted ⋯→ Leek Moth, Onion Moth: The plants age prematurely and the larvae move to the more turgid bulb where they dig galleries.

Roots or tubers
Decay

◇ Rotted bulbs/cloves ⋯→ Basal Rot: In garlic and onion, rot typically initiates in the base of the bulb, then spreads into the bulb.

Dieback

◇ Roots and bulbs decay ⋯→ Onion Fly: Attacks by flies encourage the development of rot, visible only when pulled out, and which attract other saprophagous flies whose maggots are then found in the bulb.

◇ Damaged bulbs ⋯→ Brachyserus of Garlic: Attacked bulbs of Liliaceae are internally hollowed. Damage to garlic can involve one or more cloves. Around the hollowed parts, the external membrane is sunken and soft to the touch and there is often a dark plug present, composed of larval faecal droppings mixed with other debris.

Lesions

◇ Brown or black lesions on bulbs ⋯→ Skin Blotch of Garlic: During storage of garlic, the skins of the bulbs turn black.

Presence

◇ Rotten bulbs with white felting ⋯→ White Rot. White Mold. Sclerotinia Wilt: The mycelium forms a white felt on the surface of the rotten parts, in which black sclerotia can be observed.

◇ Bluish-green or grey areas on cloves ⋯→ Penicillium Decay. Seed Clove Decay. Bleu

Mold: Initial symptoms are seen as water soaked areas on the outer surfaces of scales. This leads to development of the green-blue, powdery mold on the surface of the lesions. When the bulbs are cut, these lesions are seen as tan or grey colored areas.

◇ Presence of white maggots ⋯→ Onion Fly: Maggots are found in the bulb.

◇ Decayed bulbs with gray mould ⋯→ Botrytis Rot. Neckrot: Botrytis bulb rot generally appears during storage, although infection originates in the field. Initial symptoms usually begin at the neck, where affected tissue softens, becomes water-soaked, and turns brown. In storage, a gray mold can be seen on the surface of the bulbs or between the scales. Black sclerotia cluster around the neck and between the scales.

Stems
Presence

◇ White mold on the stem and collar ⋯→ White Rot. White Mold. Sclerotinia Wilt: Black or dark brown sclerotia form inside the stems. This uncommon disease can sometimes lead to the death of the plant.

◇ Stems with larvae ⋯→ Leek Moth, Onion Moth: The plants age prematurely and the larvae move to the more turgid bulb where they dig galleries.

Green Bean.
Common Bean

Botanical name
Phaseolus vulgaris

Family
Fabaceae

English name:
Green Bean. Common Bean. French bean

Names in other languages
Haricots fins (FR) Grüne Bohnen (DE), Sperzie boontjes, Groene bonen (NL), Fagiolini verdi (IT), Feijões verdes (PO), Judías verdes (SP).

Description
The common bean (*Phaseolus vulgaris*) is an herbaceous annual plant in the family Fabaceae which is grown as a pulse and green vegetable. The common bean can be bushy, vine-like or climbing depending on the variety being grown. The leaves grow alternately on the stems, are green or purple in color and are divided into 3 oval leaflets with smooth edges. The leaves can grow 6–15 cm (2.4–5.9 in) long and 3–11 cm (1.2–4.3 in) wide. The common bean produces white, pink, lilac or purple flowers which are approximately 1 cm (0.4 in) in diameter, and bean pods 8–20 cm (3.1–7.9 in) long and 1–1.5 cm (0.4–0.6 in) wide which can range in color from green to yellow or black to purple. Each pod contains 4-6 smooth, kidney-shaped beans. Common bean plants are annual plants and last only one growing season and range greatly in size from the bushy varieties 20–60 cm (7.9–24 in) in height; to vines or runner beans which can reach 2–3 m (6 ft 7 in–9 ft 10 in) in length.

Pests
Anthracnose Fruit Rot, Bacterial Brown Spot, Bean Aphids, Bean Beetle, Pea beetle, BYMV, Cercosporosa Leaf Spot, CMV, Damping Off, Fusarium Root Rot, Fusarium Wilt, Garden Dart Moth, Gray Mold, Lettuce Root Aphid, Onion Thrips, Pea Aphid, Pea Root Nematode, Pea Thrips, Pea Weevil, Powdery Mildew, Red Spider Mite, Rust, Bean Seed Fly, Southern Green Stink bug, Sclerotinia Wilt.

Symptoms on:
Flowers
Spots

◇ Blackish-brown spots, which may become covered with grayish mold ⋯→ Grey Mould. Grey Mould. Botrytis Blight: Blackish-brown spots, extending from the base of the bracts, which may become covered with grayish mold (fruiting bodies). Sometimes, sclerotia are present. This disease develops secondarily following an injury or other disease.

Fruits
Damage

◇ Seeds with holes ⋯→ Bean Bruchid: Presence of holes caused by larvae.

Spots

◇ Fruits with white spots ⋯→ Southern Green Stink Bug: Young fruits have small, punctate spots, with the underlying tissues being lighter in color than the rest.

Leaves
Damage

◇ Leaf edges eaten ⋯→ Pea Weevil. Pea and Bean Weevil: Notches made by adults on the leaves can limit the density of young seedlings. In addition, attacks by larvae which feed on nodules and roots cause delays in vegetation.

Decay

◇ Soft watery rot on lower leaves ⋯→ White Rot. White Mold. Sclerotinia Wilt: Pre and post-emergent damping off, crown rot, and blighting of foliage and petioles. Small, hard, irregular, black structures called sclerotia may be present on or in plant tissue (especially inside stem and petiole tissue).

Deformation

◇ Leaves curled or shrivelled ⋯→ Bean Aphids. Black Dolphin Aphids: Presence of black aphids on the leaves, on the flower stems and the flower heads. As soon as they appear, deformation of the attacked leaves and development of sooty mold.

◇ Leaves shrivelled ⋯→ Pea Thrips: Its outbreaks cause the plant to weaken and flowers to abort, leading to crop losses. It is also a vector of different viruses.

Discoloring

◇ Leaves turn yellow and wilt ⋯→ Fusarium Wilt: An affected plant has a yellowing, stunted, wilted appearance, sometimes with gummosis on the stem. Discoloration and vascular browning of the collar progressing towards the stem and roots, and developing into cortical rot.

◇ Silvery marks on leaves ⋯→ Onion Thrips. Thrips: In a greenhouse, colonies can be very developed and direct damage is often significant. The larvae and adults of the tobacco and onion thrips puncture the contents of the subepidermal cells. The infested leaves are then dotted with numerous silver spots corresponding to groups of emptied cells. This symptom is typically associated with the presence of small piles of black feces.

◇ Leaves discoulouring bronzed or silvery ⋯→ Red Spider Mite. Two-spotted Mite: They damage the plant by piercing its cells to feed on them. The leaves turn pale and become stained yellow. To protect themselves and improve their microclimate, they weave a web around the leaf. A strong attack of mites leads to the leaves rolling and drying out, then falling off.

◇ Leaves turn yellow and die ⋯→ Pea Root Nematode. Pea Cyst Nematode: The leaves turn yellow and fall prematurely, the plants twist at the base, growth is stopped and the plants remain dwarfed.

Lesions

◇ Pale yellow or water-soaked regular or irregular lesions on leaves ⋯→ Anthracnose: Depending on the fungus responsible, these brown or black spots can be circular or irregular, they then appear either on the edge of the leaves or along the veins. The necrotic areas extend more or less concentrically, the limit with healthy tissue being very clear.

◇ Circular, brown, and necrotic lesions on leaves ⋯→ Bacterial Brown Spot : On leaves: small wet necroses that develop to form a large pale green halo giving a well-marked chlorotic appearance to the foliage. Systemically infected plants are light green in color and are often stunted and deformed.

Mosaic pattern

◇ Leaves with mosaic pattern ⋯→ Bean Yellow Mosaic Virus. BYMV: Presence first of dark green to green-yellow mosaic pattern then red-brown to black-brown on leaves causing them to wilt.

Presence

◇ Coating of gray fungus spores on leaves ⋯→ Gray Mold. Grey Mould. Botrytis Blight: Regardless of the organs affected, the dying tissues become covered with a very characteristic dense gray mold, consisting of the conidiophores and conidia of the fungus.

◇ White to gray powder coverage on leaves ⋯→ Powdery Mildew, Oidium: The heart leaves are covered with purplish-grey spores on the underside. They thicken, curl, and curl up. Older leaves turn yellow on the outside, then blacken and die. Only a few isolated plants or foci are damaged.

◇ Presence of black aphids ⋯→ Bean Aphids. Black Dolphin Aphids: Presence of black aphids on the leaves, on the flower stems and capitals. As soon as they appear, deformation of the attacked leaves and development of sooty mold.

◇ Presence of honey dew on leaves ⋯→ Bean Aphids. Black Dolphin Aphids: Aphids suck large volumes of sap. The excess sugary fluid, honeydew, is secreted by the aphids. It adheres to plants, where it promotes growth of sooty molds.

◇ Presence of sooty mould on leaves ⋯→ Bean Aphids. Black Dolphin Aphids: Aphids suck large volumes of sap. The excess sugary fluid, honeydew, is secreted by the aphids. It adheres to plants, where it promotes growth of sooty molds.

◇ Leaves with fine silk webbing ⋯→ Red Spider Mite. Two-spotted Mite: They damage the plant by piercing its cells to feed on them. The leaves turn pale and become stained yellow. To protect themselves and improve their microclimate, they weave a web around the leaf. A strong attack of mites leads to the leaves rolling and drying out, then falling off.

◇ Presence of red spider mites, cast skins and egg shells ⋯→ Red Spider Mite. Two-spotted Mite: Spider mites always leave behind cast skins and egg shells.

◇ Presence of caterpillars ⋯→ Silver-Y moth. Common Silver-Y moth. Cabbage Army Moth.: The caterpillar is active mainly at night, it devours the leaf blades and cuts the petioles. During the day, it remains attached to the underside of the leaves.

◇ Presence of aphids ⋯→ Pea Aphid. Green Pea Louse.: Aphid populations can literally explode and become damaging to crops if not controlled. In growing areas, leaves become deformed and turn yellow. This aphid is the main vector of several viruses.

◇ Presence of cutworms ⋯→ Garden Dart Moth. Cutworm: The larvae feed on the roots of plants, cutting them at night.

◇ Presence of caterpillars ⋯→ Bright-line Brown-eyes Moth: The damage caused by this moth on cabbage and beet leaves is generally not very significant.

Spots

◇ Reddish-orange spots on leaves ⋯→ Rust: On the upper side of the leaves, you will see tiny white, orange or even brown spots appear depending on the species. If you turn these leaves over, you will see that these spots correspond to tiny pustules of the same color.

The lesions are generally yellow, brown or red, but can be dark brown or black at the end of the season.

◇ Yellowish then brown spots on the upper surface of the leaf ⋯▸ Powdery Mildew, Oidium: Yellowish then brown spots on the upper surface of the leaf, generally limited by the large veins, whitish felting on the lower surface.

◇ Leaf spots with brown-reddish margins ⋯▸ Cercosporosa Leaf Spot, Cercosporia blight: Cercospora blight initially causes small, oval, gray to tan lesions with red borders. Severe infections may cause entire ferns to turn yellow or brown.

Plantlets
Dieback

◇ Damaged cotyledons ⋯▸ Seedcorn Maggot. Bean Seed Fly: Fly larvae damage the sprouts of developing seeds and bulbs as well as transplanted plants. They often cause plant rot, leading to the total or partial destruction of seedlings and crops.

Wilting

◇ Wilted, collapsed and dead young seedlings ⋯▸ Damping Off: Seeds rot and fail to germinate, or even germinate, but seedlings fail to grow. A translucent area completely covers the stem near the soil surface. The affected tissues rot, leading to wilting and collapse of the seedlings.

Plants whole
Stunted

◇ Deformation and stunting of plants ⋯▸ Cucumber Mosaic Virus. CMV: Artichoke latent virus (ALV, Potyvirus) is transmitted by aphids. Cucumber mosaic virus (CMV) induces deformation and stunting of plants.

◇ Plants stunted ⋯▸ Fusarium Root Rot: Diseased plants wilt to a greater or lesser extent during the hottest times of the day; this wilting is sometimes reversible. In the most serious cases, the plants eventually dry out completely.

◇ Wilted plants ⋯▸ Lettuce Root Aphid: Aphids' bites and nutritional withdrawals from the roots cause the plant to wilt and die.

Roots or tubers
Decay

◇ Rotting of roots ⋯▸ Fusarium Root Rot: The cause of these wilting is to be found at the level of the collar of the feet. At this location, a wet lesion has developed, a rot that has gradually spread to the lower part of the stem and the taproot, but also to the upper part of the root system. At the collar, the altered tissues are wet and show a dark to brownish tint. This lesion ends up girdling the stem for several centimetres. The roots located in the same layer of soil are also affected. Their cortex turns yellow, brown and decomposes.

Deformation

◇ Roots abnormally increased or swellings ⋯▸ Pea Root Nematode. Pea Cyst Nematode: The roots are poorly developed and have only a limited number of bacterial nodules; the rootlets are abundant and bear clusters of cysts.

Dieback

◇ Roots damaged ⋯▸ Pea Weevil. Pea and Bean Weevil: Notches made by adults on the leaves can limit the density of young seedlings. In addition, attacks by larvae which feed on nodules and roots cause delays in vegetation.

Presence

◇ Presence of colonies of gray aphids on roots ⋯▸ Lettuce Root Aphid: Presence of very numerous yellowish-white aphids along the roots, these bearing a fairly visible tuft of white wax.

◇ Root with white sooty mold ⋯▸ Lettuce Root Aphid: Development of very numerous yellowish-white insects along the roots, these carrying a fairly visible tuft of white wax.

Seeds
Damage

◇ Beans with small holes ⋯▸ Bean Beetle. Pea beetle: The presence of bruchids in beans, peas or beans makes them unfit for consumption, reduces the germination rate of seeds and presents risks of re-infestation of crops. A bean can accommodate 5 to 6 individuals.

Stems
Necrosis

◇ Necrotic stems ⋯▸ Fusarium Wilt: An affected plant has a yellowing, stunted, wilted appearance, sometimes with gummosis on the stem. Discoloration and vascular browning of the collar progressing towards the stem and roots, and developing into cortical rot.

Presence

◇ Coating of gray fungus spores on stems ⋯▸ Gray Mold. Grey Mould. Botrytis Blight: Lesions, even cankers, more or less extensive, are visible on the stems, mainly located at the level of pruning and disbudding wounds. Let us add that the lesions are generally covered with a very characteristic grayish to beige mold.

◇ Presence of colonies of aphids ⋯▸ Bean Aphids. Black Dolphin Aphids: The black bean aphid is a major pest of sugar beet, bean, and celery crops, with large numbers of aphids cause stunting of the plants. Beans suffer damage to flowers and pods which may not develop properly.

Kohlrabi

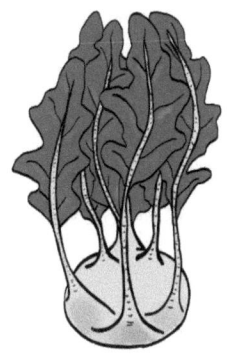

Botanical name
Brassica oleracea var. *gongylodes*

Family
Brassicaceae

English name
Kohlrabi

Names in other languages
Chou-rave (FR), Koolrabi (NL), Kohlrabi (D),
Cavolo rapa (IT), Couve rábano (P), Col rábano,
Colinabo (SP).

Description
Kohlrabi (*Brassica oleracea* var. *gongylodes*) is an
herbaceous biennial grown for its edible stem. The
kohlrabi plant has an erect stem which is swollen
at the bottom, close to the soil. The swelling
resembles a turnip in appearance, can reach up to
10 cm (4 in) in diameter and may be green, white
or purple in color depending on the variety. The
leaves of the plant grow from the stem and have
long petioles and a waxy appearance. Kohlrabi
can grow to a height of 40–50 cm (16–20 in) and
although biennial, is commonly grown as an
annual.

Pests
Cabbage Aphid, Cabbage Bug, Rape Bug,
Crucifer Shield Bug, Brassica Bug, Cabbage Club
Root, Cabbage Maggot, Cabbage Stem Flea
Beetle, Cabbageworm, Imported Cabbage
Worms, Damping Off, Dark Sword-grass Moth,
Black cutworm, Greasy cutworm, Downy Mildew
of Crucifers, Early Blight of Potato/Tomato, Gray
Mold, Grey Mould, Botrytis Blight, Turnip Gall
Weevil.

Symptoms on:
Leaves
Damage

◇ Perforated leaves ⤳ Cabbage Stem Flea
Beetle: It is difficult to monitor the activity of
the adult of the large rapeseed flea beetle: it
occurs at night. Its damage, on the other hand,
is easily recognizable because the insect bites
the cotyledons and young leaves in a circular
fashion. Perforations can also be observed.

◇ Leaves with holes ⤳ Cabbageworm. Imported
Cabbage Worms: Caterpillars devour the
leaves of cruciferous plants, sometimes
leaving only the large veins. In addition, their
excrement, diluted by rain or dew, accumulates
in the heart of the plant and makes it inedible.

Deformation

◇ Leaves curled or shrivelled ⤳ Cabbage Aphid:
In the event of an outbreak, the plant can be
completely covered by aphids, their honeydew
and their exuviae. The cabbages or rapeseeds
thus attacked develop poorly and die.

Discoloring

◇ Reddening, yellowing of the leaves ⤳ Cabbage
Club Root: Aerial part of the plant: reduced
development, especially during early attacks,
wilting or even reddening of the foliage.

◇ Bleached leaves ⤳ Cabbage Bug. Rape Bug.
Crucifer Shield Bug. Brassica Bug: With their
piercing-sucking apparatus, the larvae and
adults feed by sucking the sap, which causes
the leaves to turn white and slows down the
growth of the cabbage. The very large number
of punctures on the leaves of young plants can
lead to the death of the host plant.

Lesions

◇ Purple or brown irregular shaped areas on
leaves ⤳ Downy Mildew of Crucifers: It first
appears on older leaves, as white, yellow or
brownish spots on the upper surfaces and
downy grayish mold on the corresponding
undersides.

◇ Brownish black lesions on leaves ⋯➤ Early Blight of Potato/Tomato: Affected leaves and petioles turn yellow, then brown or black. Leaflets shrivel at the edges, and in severe infections the entire leaf wilts and dies.

Presence

◇ Coating of gray fungus spores on leaves ⋯➤ Gray Mold. Grey Mould. Botrytis Blight: Regardless of the organs affected, the dying tissues become covered with a very characteristic dense gray mold, consisting of the conidiophores and conidia of the fungus.

◇ Presence of colonies of aphids ⋯➤ Cabbage Aphid: In the event of an outbreak, the plant can be completely covered by aphids, their honeydew and their exuviae.

◇ White to gray, "downy" areas on under leaf surfaces. ⋯➤ Downy Mildew of Crucifers: It first appears on older leaves, as white, yellow or brownish spots on the upper surfaces and downy grayish mold on the corresponding undersides.

◇ Presence of caterpillars ⋯➤ Cabbageworm. Imported Cabbage Worms: Caterpillars devour the leaves of cruciferous plants, sometimes leaving only the large veins. In addition, their excrement, diluted by rain or dew, accumulates in the heart of the plant and makes it inedible.

◇ Presence of honeydew and sooty moulds on leaves ⋯➤ Cabbage Aphid:

◇ In the event of an outbreak, the plant can be completely covered by aphids, their honeydew and their exuviae.

◇ Presence of bugs ⋯➤ Cabbage Bug. Rape Bug. Crucifer Shield Bug. Brassica Bug: Presence of the adult insect and larva on leaves. Presence of eggs on the underside of the leaves. Observe the leaves to see the appearance of white spots. Be careful not to confuse these bugs with other red and black bugs such as Pyrrhocoris apterus, better known as the "firebug". These do not cause any damage to cabbage.

Plantlets
Dieback

◇ Damaged cotyledons ⋯➤ Dark Sword-grass Moth. Black cutworm. Greasy cutworm: Early larval stages feed on the leaves and create small holes with irregular contours. Later stages attack the stem, often during sowing, and consequently cut the seedlings at ground level.

Wilting

◇ Wilted, collapsed and dead young seedlings ⋯➤ Damping Off: Seeds rot and fail to germinate, or even germinate, but seedlings fail to grow. A translucent area completely covers the stem near the soil surface. The affected tissues rot, leading to wilting and collapse of the seedlings.

Plants whole
Stunted

◇ Stunted plants ⋯➤ Cabbage Stem Flea Beetle: It is difficult to monitor the activity of the adult of the large rapeseed flea beetle: it occurs at night. Its damage, on the other hand, is easily recognizable because the insect bites the cotyledons and young leaves in a circular fashion. Perforations can also be observed.

Wilting

◇ Wilted plants ⋯➤ Cabbage Maggot, Cabbage Fly: Damage is observed in nurseries and at all stages of vegetation. On leafy vegetables, the root part is more or less destroyed. Attacked plants can be recognized by the faded appearance they take on during hot days; the leaves often turn purplish red, turn yellow and sometimes dry out.

◇ Wilted plants ⋯➤ Cabbage Club Root: Underground part of the plant: root deformation or presence of galls on the roots. These galls are firm (full interior), whitish then turn brown and rot, leading to the death of the plant.

Roots or tubers
Deformation

◇ Roots abnormally increased or swellings ⋯➤ Cabbage Club Root: Underground part of the plant: root deformation or presence of galls on the roots. These galls are firm (full interior), whitish then turn brown and rot, leading to the death of the plant.

◇ Swelling of roots ⋯➤ Turnip Gall Weevil: The substances introduced at the time of egg laying and the larval secretions cause an enlargement of the collar or gall, which can reach 2 to 3 cm in diameter in cabbage.

Presence

◇ Presence of maggots in roots ⋯➤ Cabbage Maggot, Cabbage Fly: The larvae of the cabbage fly penetrate into the fleshy parts and dig galleries. The root part is more or less destroyed. Attacked plants can be recognized by the faded appearance they take on during hot days; the leaves often turn purplish red, turn yellow and sometimes dry out.

Stems
Dieback

◇ Damaged stems ⋯➤ Dark Sword-grass Moth. Black cutworm. Greasy cutworm: Early larval stages feed on the leaves and create small holes with irregular contours. Later stages attack the stem, often during sowing, and consequently cut the seedlings at ground level.

Lamb's Lettuce

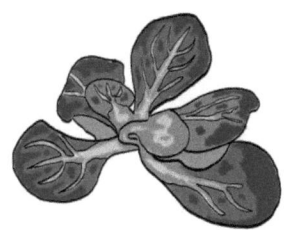

Botanical name
Valeriana locusta

Class
Caprifoliaceae

English name
Lamb's Lettuce, Corn salad, Common consalad.

Names in other languages
Mâche, Doucette (FR), Veldsla (NL), Feldsalat (DE) Agnellino (IT) Alface-de-cordeiro (PO), Canónigo (SP).

Description
Lamb's lettuce (*Valeriana locusta*) is a small annual plant that is eaten as a leaf vegetable. It is also called Corn salad or Common corn salad. It grows in a low rosette with spatulate leaves up to 15.2 cm long.

Pests
Damping Off, Gray Mold, Grey Mould, Botrytis Blight, Phoma, Powdery Mildew, Seedcorn Maggot, Bean Seed Fly.

Symptoms on:
Leaves
Discoloring

◇ Red stripes on roots, shoots and leaves ⋯→ Phoma: Known as a damping off agent, phoma also causes leaf necrosis. The first symptoms are often spots or pink to wine-red streaks located on the leaves or taproot.

Presence

◇ Coating of gray fungus spores on leaves ⋯→ Gray Mold. Grey Mould. Botrytis Blight: Regardless of the organs affected, the dying tissues become covered with a very characteristic dense gray mold, consisting of the conidiophores and conidia of the fungus.

◇ White to gray powder coverage on leaves ⋯→ Powdery Mildew, Oidium: The heart leaves are covered with purplish-grey spores on the underside. They thicken, curl, and curl up. Older leaves turn yellow on the outside, then blacken and die.

Spots

◇ Yellowish then brown spots on the upper surface of the leaf ⋯→ Powdery Mildew, Oidium: Yellowish then brown spots on the upper surface of the leaf, generally limited by the large veins, whitish felting on the lower surface.

Plantlets
Dieback

◇ Damaged cotyledons ⋯→ Seedcorn Maggot. Bean Seed Fly: Fly larvae damage the sprouts of developing seeds and bulbs as well as transplanted plants.

Wilting

◇ Wilted, collapsed and dead young seedlings ⋯→ Damping Off: Seeds rot and fail to germinate, or even germinate, but seedlings fail to grow.

Leek

Botanical name
Allium porrum

Class
Liliaceae

English name
Leek

Names in other languages
Poireau (FR), Prei (NL), Aschlauch (DE), Porro (IT), Alho porro (PO), Puerro (SP).

Related plants
Chives (*Allium schoenoprasum*).

Description
Leek (*Allium porrum*) is a biennial vegetable in the family Liliaceae, grown for its edible bulb and leaves. The plant is a slightly developed bulb attached to a cylindrical stem formed by the overlapping thick, flat leaves. The plant can produce clusters of white, pink or purple flowers and blue-black seeds in the second year. The plant can reach 0.6–0.9 m (2–3 ft) and can be grown as an annual, harvested after one growing season or as a biennial with two growing seasons.

Pests
American Serpentine Leaf Miner, Cercosporosa Leaf Spot, Dark Sword-grass Moth, Black cutworm, Greasy cutworm, Downy Mildew of Alliums, Early Blight of Potato/Tomato, Leek Moth. Onion Moth, Onion and Leek Rust, Onion Fly, Onion Maggot, Onion Thrips. Thrips, Powdery Mildew, White Rot, White Mold, Sclerotinia Wilt.

Symptoms on:
Leaves
Decay

◇ Soft watery rot on lower leaves ⋯→ White Rot. White Mold. Sclerotinia Wilt: Pre and post-emergent damping off, crown rot, and blighting of foliage and petioles. Small, hard, irregular, black structures called sclerotia may be present on or in plant tissue (especially inside stem and petiole tissue).

Discoloring

◇ Leaves turn yellow and wilt ⋯→ Onion Fly: On young seedlings: the plant wilts and then dies. A larva can attack several seedlings in succession. If the plant is more developed, it wilts, especially in hot weather, and may die.

◇ Silvery marks on leaves ⋯→ Onion Thrips. Thrips: In a greenhouse, colonies can be very developed and direct damage is often significant. The larvae and adults of the tobacco and onion thrips puncture the contents of the subepidermal cells. The infested leaves are then dotted with numerous silver spots corresponding to groups of emptied cells. This symptom is typically associated with the presence of small piles of black feces.

Galleries

◇ Galleries in leaves ⋯→ Leek Moth, Onion Moth: The leaves are mined, perforated, partly consumed, the leaves end up having a lacerated appearance.

◇ Leaves with galleries ⋯→ Onion Maggot: In spring, damage occurs after the first flight. The first mines are very small, but leeks in cultivation are then small, and a few maggots are enough to kill a plant. In autumn, leeks are larger and survive even while hosting large populations of larvae. The mines do not rot; in some cases, they have a clean, whitish appearance. Sometimes the color is pinkish-brown, clearly visible on the white basal part of the leaves.

◇ Leaves with galleries ⟶ American Serpentine Leaf Miner: The main damage is due to larvae which mine the leaves. This damage is particularly serious on small plants in nurseries or just transplanted, which can die.

Presence

◇ White to gray powder coverage on leaves ⟶ Powdery Mildew, Oidium: The heart leaves are covered with purplish-grey spores on the underside. They thicken, curl, and curl up. Older leaves turn yellow on the outside, then blacken and die. Only a few isolated plants or foci are damaged.

◇ Presence of maggots in leaves and bulbs ⟶ Onion Maggot: In autumn, the leeks are larger and survive even while hosting large populations of larvae. The mines do not rot, in some cases they have a clean appearance of whitish hue. It also happens that the coloring is pinkish-brown, clearly visible on the white basal part of the leaves.

◇ Leaves with grey powder ⟶ Downy Mildew of Alliums: At the beginning of vegetation: dwarf plants with chlorotic, deformed leaves, covered with a velvety gray mycelium. During vegetation: presence of elongated spots on leaves and stems of a yellowish appearance and covered with a gray felting.

Spots

◇ Leaves with yellow, brown, necrotic and concentric spots ⟶ Early Blight of Potato/ Tomato: Small yellow spots quickly turn brown-black, necrotic, circular and sharply outlined, measuring about 5 mm in diameter, which gradually spread concentrically.

◇ Bright-orange spots on leaves ⟶ Onion and Leek Rust: Affected leek, garlic and onion leaves have small pustular lesions that are initially whitish to beige. These spread slightly and give rise to bright orange to brown pustules, with the leaves eventually drying out.

◇ Yellowish then brown spots on the upper surface of the leaf ⟶ Powdery Mildew, Oidium: Yellowish then brown spots on the upper surface of the leaf, generally limited by the large veins, whitish felting on the lower surface.

◇ Leaf spots with brown-reddish margins ⟶ Cercosporosa Leaf Spot, Cercosporia blight: Cercospora blight initially causes small, oval, gray to tan lesions with red borders. Severe infections may cause entire ferns to turn yellow or brown. Cercospora blight may cause reduced vigor and yield of spears the next spring.

Plants whole
Stunted

◇ Plants stunted ⟶ Leek Moth, Onion Moth: The plants age prematurely and the larvae move to the more turgid bulb where they dig galleries.

Roots or tubers
Dieback

◇ Roots and bulbs decay ⟶ Onion Fly: Attacks by flies encourage the development of rot, visible only when pulled out, and which attract other saprophagous flies whose maggots are then found in the bulb.

Presence

◇ Presence of white maggots ⟶ Onion Fly: Maggots are found in the bulb.

Stems
Dieback

◇ Damaged stems ⟶ Dark Sword-grass Moth. Black cutworm. Greasy cutworm: Early larval stages feed on the leaves and create small holes with irregular contours. Later stages attack the stem, often during sowing, and consequently cut the seedlings at ground level.

Presence

◇ White mold on the stem and collar ⟶ White Rot. White Mold. Sclerotinia Wilt: Black or dark brown sclerotia form inside the stems. This uncommon disease can sometimes lead to the death of the plant.

◇ Stems with larvae ⟶ Leek Moth, Onion Moth: The plants age prematurely and the larvae move to the more turgid bulb where they dig galleries.

Lettuce

Botanical name
Lactuca sativa

Class
Asteraceae

English name
Lettuce

Names in other languages
Laitue (FR), Kropsla (NL), Salat (DE), Lattuga (IT),
Alface-repolhuda (PO), Lechuga (SP).

Related plants
Radicchio, Sugarloaf, Belgian endive.

Description
Lettuce (*Lactuca sativa,*) is a leafy herbaceous
annual or biennial plant in the family Asteraceae
grown for its leaves which are used as a salad
green. The lettuce plant can vary greatly in size,
shape and leaf type but generally, the leaves of the
plant form a dense head or loose rosette. The
stem of the plant is short, with larger leaves
arranged at the bottom and becoming
progressively smaller further up the stem. Leaves
can be smooth or curly and are usually green or
red in color. The lettuce plant can grow to a height
of 30–100 cm (12–40 in) in height and is typically
grown as an annual, harvested after only one
growing season.

Pests
Celery Late Blight, Cercosporosa Leaf Spot, Click
Beetle, Wireworms, Common Swift Moth,
Damping Off, Dark Sword-grass Moth, Greasy
cutworm, Gray Mold, Botrytis Blight, Green Peach
Aphid, June Beetles, Lettuce Aphid, Lettuce
bacterial rot, Lettuce drop, Lettuce mosaic virus,
Lettuce Root Aphid, March Crane Fly, Potato
Aphid, Powdery Mildew, Ring Spot on Lettuce,
Anthracnose, Slug and Snail, South American
Miner Fly.

Symptoms on:
Leaves
Damage

◇ Leaves with perforations ⸱⸱⸱▸ Slug and Snail.
Garden Slug. Loach. Little Grey Slug. Vine
Snail. White Garden Snail: The slug consumes
the leaves of plants between the veins, which
gives them a serrated appearance. It digs
small holes in the tubers. When the attack is
serious, the stems are cut and consumed, the
plants disappear.

Decay

◇ Collar rot ⸱⸱⸱▸ Lettuce drop: Sclerotinia minor only
infects the stems and leaves in contact with the
soil. Once infection takes place, the fungus will
cause a brown, soft decay that eventually
destroys the plant crown tissue. Older leaves
then wilt and later the entire plant will wilt and
collapse

Deformation

◇ Curled leaves ⸱⸱⸱▸ Celery Late Blight: The
disease first manifests itself by the appearance
of small light brown spots on the foliage. In
case of severe attacks, the petioles turn yellow,
the leaves curl up and dry out.

◇ Leaves curled or shrivelled ⸱⸱⸱▸ Green Peach
Aphid: Myzus persicae is very polyphagous
and, in summer, it has more than forty different
families of host plants. The colonies secrete a
honeydew that promotes the installation of
sooty mold, a fungus that then slows down the
photosynthesis of the covered parts. It is the
most important aphid vector of viruses.

Discoloring

◇ Leaves discouvering yellowish ⸱⸱⸱▸ June Beetles,
May Beetles, Chafer beetles: The adults are
phyllophagous and the larvae, called "white
grubs" are root-eating. They deform the roots
and cause the plant to wilt.

Galleries

◇ Leaves with galleries ⸱⸱⸱▸ South American Miner
Fly. South American Leaf Miner: Feeding pits

and mined leaves with galleries depreciate the harvest.

Mosaic pattern

◇ Leaves with mosaic pattern ⋯→ Lettuce mosaic virus: The lettuce mosaic virus, as its name suggests, is primarily responsible for more or less marked marbling and mosaics.

Presence

◇ Coating of gray fungus spores on leaves ⋯→ Gray Mold. Grey Mould. Botrytis Blight: Regardless of the organs affected, the dying tissues become covered with a very characteristic dense gray mold, consisting of the conidiophores and conidia of the fungus.

◇ White to gray powder coverage on leaves ⋯→ Powdery Mildew, Oidium: The heart leaves are covered with purplish-grey spores on the underside. They thicken, curl, and curl up. Older leaves turn yellow on the outside, then blacken and die. Only a few isolated plants or foci are damaged.

◇ Presence of aphids ⋯→ Potato Aphid: The most classic symptoms are a curling of heavily infested leaves and a slowdown in the growth of the plants

◇ Slime trails ⋯→ Slug and Snail. Garden Slug. Loach. Little Grey Slug. Vine Snail. White Garden Snail: Slime trail' that signals their presence.

◇ Presence of caterpillars ⋯→ Silver-Y moth. Common Silver-Y moth. Cabbage Army Moth.: The caterpillar is active mainly at night, it devours the leaf blades and cuts the petioles. During the day, it remains attached to the underside of the leaves.

◇ Presence of aphids ⋯→ Lettuce Aphid. Current-lettuce Aphid: They are sap suckers. In general, direct damage from spoliation is very minor on lettuce. It is the contamination that is serious because a salad full of aphids is inedible. The lettuce aphid is especially dangerous as a virus vector.

Spots

◇ Pale brown spots on leaves ⋯→ Celery Late Blight: The disease first manifests itself by the appearance on the foliage of small light brown spots, often delimited by the fine veins of the leaves but sometimes with irregular contours, ranging in size from 1 to 4 mm. They gradually turn reddish-brown and have small black dots called pycnidia in their center on the upper surface.

◇ Yellowish then brown spots on the upper surface of the leaf ⋯→ Powdery Mildew, Oidium: Yellowish then brown spots on the upper surface of the leaf, generally limited by the large veins, whitish felting on the lower surface.

◇ Leaf spots with brown-reddish margins ⋯→ Cercosporosa Leaf Spot, Cercosporia blight: Cercospora blight initially causes small, oval, gray to tan lesions with red borders. Severe infections may cause entire ferns to turn yellow or brown. Cercospora blight may cause reduced vigor and yield of spears the next spring.

◇ Leaves with brown spots ⋯→ Lettuce bacterial rot: The damage is confined to the main rib, which also takes on a brown to black tint.

◇ Leaves with yellow spots ⋯→ Ring Spot of Lettuce. Anthracnose: This fungus is mainly responsible for spots on all parts of the leaves close to the soil. On the leaf blade, these are initially small and damp. Later, they spread and become rather circular. Their delimitation by the veins can give them an angular appearance. The damaged tissues take on an orange to brown color. They soon lighten as they dry out, split and fall. The leaves are thus riddled.

Wilting

◇ Leaves wilted ⋯→ Lettuce drop: Sclerotinia minor only infects the stems and leaves in contact with the soil. Once infection takes place, the fungus will cause a brown, soft decay that eventually destroys the plant crown tissue. Older leaves then wilt and later the entire plant will wilt and collapse.

Plantlets
Dieback

◇ Damaged cotyledons ⋯→ Dark Sword-grass Moth. Black cutworm. Greasy cutworm: Early larval stages feed on the leaves and create small holes with irregular contours. Later stages attack the stem, often during sowing, and consequently cut the seedlings at ground level.

Wilting

◇ Wilted, collapsed and dead young seedlings ⋯→ Damping Off: Seeds rot and fail to germinate, or even germinate, but seedlings fail to grow. A translucent area completely covers the stem near the soil surface. The affected tissues rot, leading to wilting and **collapse of the seedlings.**

Plants whole
Wilting

◇ Wilted plants ⋯→ Lettuce Root Aphid: **Aphids' bites and nutritional withdrawals from the roots cause the plant to wilt and die.**

◇ Wilted plants ⋯→ March Crane Fly. Leatherjackets: Tipula larvae can cause crop damage by feeding on roots and stems, leading to yellowing, stunted growth, and plant death.

Roots or tubers
Dieback

◇ Roots damaged ⋯→ March Crane Fly. Leatherjackets: Soil-inhabiting larvae of crane flies, leatherjackets feed on the roots and underground parts of the stem on a wide range of crops. Attacks are most common in crops following a grass rotation. Collar and roots eaten away.

Galleries

◇ Galleries in roots ⋯→ Click Beetle. Striped

Elaterid Beetle. Wireworms: As larvae development takes up to four years, in an infected soil we can find larvae of different ages. They live at different depths, depending on the moment of the year, as they are highly sensitive to heat and dryness. They eat or pierce the underground organs of the plant: roots, crowns, bud leaves and turions.

Presence

◇ Grubs present in the soil ⋯⋯→ June Beetles, May Beetles, Chafer beetles: The adults are phyllophagous and the larvae burrow in the soil, called "white grubs", are root-eating. They deform the roots and cause the plant to wilt.

◇ Presence of colonies of gray aphids on roots ⋯⋯→ Lettuce Root Aphid: Presence of very numerous yellowish-white aphids along the roots, these bearing a fairly visible tuft of white wax.

◇ Root with white sooty mold ⋯⋯→ Lettuce Root Aphid: Development of very numerous yellowish-white insects along the roots, these carrying a fairly visible tuft of white wax.

Spots

◇ Small white mealy spots ⋯⋯→ Potato Tuber Nematode. Potato Cyst Nematode: The nematode initially causes small white mealy spots just below the surface that are only visible if the skin is removed.

Stems
Dieback

◇ Damaged stems ⋯⋯→ Dark Sword-grass Moth. Black cutworm. Greasy cutworm: Early larval stages feed on the leaves and create small holes with irregular contours. Later stages attack the stem, often during sowing, and consequently cut the seedlings at ground level.

Presence

◇ Presence of caterpillars ⋯⋯→ Common Swift Moth. Garden Swift Moth: The roots and collars are eaten away, which leads to the gradual drying out of the plant.

Melon

Botanical name
Cucumis melo

Class
Cucurbitaceae

English name
Melon, Muskmelon, Cantaloupe, Canary melon.

Names in other languages
Melon (FR), Melone (DE), Meloen (NL), Melone (IT),
Melone (PO), Melão (SP).

Related plants
Watermelon (*Citrullus lanatus*)

Description
The melon (*Cucumis melo)* belong to the family
Cucurbitaceae. It has typically sweet edible,
fleshy fruits. Many different cultivars have been
produced. It is is an annual trailing vine with
pubescent striated stems, bearing unbranched
tendrils at the base of the long petioles. The
leaves are simple and alternate, nearly round,
basally cordate, and may have 3-7 shallow
palmate lobes. The melon fruit is a fleshy berry
that is round to ellipsoid, hairy during its early
development, and smooth to reticulate at maturity.
Melon fruits are highly variable in color, showing
shades of yellow, green, orange, white, and often
mottled or striped. The flesh is also variable and
usually yellow, orange, pink, white, or green.

Pests
American Serpentine Leaf Miner, Anthracnose
Fruit Rot, Anthracnose of Cucurbits,
Cercosporosa Leaf Spot, Cotton Aphid,
Cucumber Mosaic Virus. CMV, Downy mildew of
Cucurbits, Early Blight of Potato/Tomato,
Fusarium Root Rot, Fusarium Wilt, Gray Mold,
Grey Mould, Botrytis Blight, Green Peach Aphid,
Powdery Mildew, Red Spider Mite, Two-spotted
Mite, Scab of Cucurbits.

Symptoms on:
Flowers
Spots

◇ Blackish-brown spots, which may become
covered with grayish mold ⋯→ Grey Mould. Grey
Mould. Botrytis Blight: Blackish-brown spots,
extending from the base of the bracts, which
may become covered with grayish mold
(fruiting bodies). Sometimes, sclerotia are
present. This disease develops secondarily
following an injury or other disease.

Fruits
Lesions

◇ Black circular lesions ⋯→ Anthracnose of
Cucurbits: Circular spots on fruits, dark to
blackish in the center, spreading to internal
tissues.

Spots

◇ Hollow, brown spot with yellow halo ⋯→ Scab of
Cucurbits: Small moist lesions appear on the
leaves, often the youngest. These lesions
gradually expand to form more or less circular
spots, turning brown and necrotic as they age.
They can sometimes take on a grayish tint and
be surrounded by a more or less large yellow
halo.

Leaves
Deformation

◇ Leaves curled or shrivelled ⋯→ Green Peach
Aphid: Myzus persicae is very polyphagous
and, in summer, it has more than forty different
families of host plants. The colonies secrete a
honeydew that promotes the installation of
sooty mold, a fungus that then slows down the
photosynthesis of the covered parts. It is the
most important aphid vector of viruses.

◇ Leaves curled or shrivelled ⋯→ Cotton Aphid:
Aphids, following their nutritional bites, are
responsible for chlorotic spots and the
deformation of young leaves which tend to roll
up and more or less blister.

Discoloring

◇ Leaves turn yellow and wilt ⋯▸ Fusarium Wilt: An affected plant has a yellowing, stunted, wilted appearance, sometimes with gummosis on the stem. Discoloration and vascular browning of the collar progressing towards the stem and roots, and developing into cortical rot.

◇ Leaves turn white ⋯▸ Molybdenum Deficiency. Whiptail: Leaf margins show chlorosis and slight necrosis.

◇ Leaves discoulouring bronzed or silvery ⋯▸ Red Spider Mite. Two-spotted Mite: They damage the plant by piercing its cells to feed on them. The leaves turn pale and become stained yellow. To protect themselves and improve their microclimate, they weave a web around the leaf. A strong attack of mites leads to the leaves rolling and drying out, then falling off.

Galleries

◇ Leaves with galleries ⋯▸ American Serpentine Leaf Miner: The main damage is due to larvae which mine the leaves. This damage is particularly serious on small plants in nurseries or just transplanted, which can die.

Lesions

◇ Circular, brown, and necrotic lesions on leaves ⋯▸ Early Blight of Potato/Tomato: Small yellow spots rapidly turning black-brown, necrotic, circular and sharply outlined, approximately 5 mm in diameter, which gradually expand concentrically.

◇ Pale yellow or water-soaked regular or irregular lesions on leaves ⋯▸ Anthracnose: Depending on the fungus responsible, these brown or black spots can be circular or irregular, they then appear either on the edge of the leaves or along the veins. The necrotic areas extend more or less concentrically, the limit with healthy tissue being very clear.

Mosaic pattern

◇ Leaves with mosaic pattern ⋯▸ Downy mildew of Cucurbits: Wet, oily leaf spots that turn yellow and quickly become necrotic. The spots are mostly angular in shape because they are delimited by the veins. Eventually, the leaf blade presents a mosaic of yellow and/or brown spots if the lesions are necrotic.

Presence

◇ Coating of gray fungus spores on leaves ⋯▸ Gray Mold. Grey Mould. Botrytis Blight: Regardless of the organs affected, the dying tissues become covered with a very characteristic dense gray mold, consisting of the conidiophores and conidia of the fungus.

◇ White to gray powder coverage on leaves ⋯▸ Powdery Mildew, Oidium: The heart leaves are covered with purplish-grey spores on the underside. They thicken, curl, and curl up. Older leaves turn yellow on the outside, then blacken and die. Only a few isolated plants or foci are damaged.

◇ Presence of honey dew on leaves ⋯▸ Cotton Aphid: In addition to aphid colonies, we often observe white molts and the presence of honeydew on the surface of the aerial organs of zucchini and other plants.

◇ Presence of sooty mould on leaves ⋯▸ Cotton Aphid: In addition to aphid colonies, we often observe white molts and the presence of honeydew on the surface of the aerial organs on which sooty mold develops. Remember that the latter can have several consequences, including a reduction in photosynthesis and leaf respiration and soiling of fruits thus rendered unmarketable.

◇ Leaves with fine silk webbing ⋯▸ Red Spider Mite. Two-spotted Mite: They damage the plant by piercing its cells to feed on them. The leaves turn pale and become stained yellow. To protect themselves and improve their microclimate, they weave a web around the leaf. A strong attack of mites leads to the leaves rolling and drying out, then falling off.

◇ Presence of red spider mites, cast skins and egg shells ⋯▸ Red Spider Mite. Two-spotted Mite: Spider mites always leave behind cast skins and egg shells.

◇ Leaves with grey powder ⋯▸ Downy mildew of Cucurbits: Presence on the lower face of the blade of felting whose coloring varies from light gray to dark mauve.

Spots

◇ Leaves with irregular brown spots and a yellowish halo. ⋯▸ Anthracnose of Cucurbits: Wet lesion spots, rather circular, gradually turning brown and red before becoming necrotic. Presence of a translucent to yellowish halo around the lesions, the internal tissues can decompose and fall off, giving the leaf blade a riddled appearance. Sometimes significant defoliation.

◇ Leaf spots with brown-reddish margins ⋯▸ Cercosporosa Leaf Spot, Cercosporia blight: Cercospora blight initially causes small, oval, gray to tan lesions with red borders. Severe infections may cause entire ferns to turn yellow or brown. Cercospora blight may cause reduced vigor and yield of spears the next spring.

◇ Leaves with yellow spots ⋯▸ Downy mildew of Cucurbits: Wet, oily leaf spots that turn yellow and quickly become necrotic. The spots are mostly angular in shape because they are delimited by the veins. Eventually, the leaf blade presents a mosaic of yellow and/or brown spots if the lesions are necrotic.

◇ Leaves with angular spots ⋯▸ Scab of Cucurbits: Small, necrotic brown spots appear on the leaves. They can also be grayish, brown on the periphery, sometimes angular, surrounded by a yellow halo. Brown nerve necroses also form.

Plants whole
Stunted

◇ Deformation and stunting of plants ⋯▸ Cucumber Mosaic Virus. CMV: Artichoke latent virus (ALV, Potyvirus) is transmitted by aphids. Cucumber mosaic virus (CMV) induces deformation and stunting of plants.

◇ Plants stunted ⋯→ Fusarium Root Rot: Diseased plants wilt to a greater or lesser extent during the hottest times of the day; this wilting is sometimes reversible. In the most serious cases, the plants eventually dry out completely.

◇ Stunted plants with yellow marbling ⋯→ Cucumber Mosaic Virus. CMV: The symptoms expressed by the mosaic virus can be of several types: mosaic or leaf mottling, progressive yellowing of the foliage, necrotic rings, deformation of flowers, fruits and leaves. Transmission occurs through many species of aphids, but the black aphid (Aphis gossypii) is predominant.

Roots or tubers
Decay

◇ Rotting of roots ⋯→ Fusarium Root Rot: The cause of these wilting is to be found at the level of the collar of the feet. At this location, a wet lesion has developed, a rot that has gradually spread to the lower part of the stem and the taproot, but also to the upper part of the root system. At the collar, the altered tissues are wet and show a dark to brownish tint. This lesion ends up girdling the stem for several centimetres. The roots located in the same layer of soil are also affected. Their cortex turns yellow, brown and decomposes.

Stems
Necrosis

◇ Necrotic stems ⋯→ Fusarium Wilt: An affected plant has a yellowing, stunted, wilted appearance, sometimes with gummosis on the stem. Discoloration and vascular browning of the collar progressing towards the stem and roots, and developing into cortical rot.

Presence

◇ Coating of gray fungus spores on stems ⋯→ Gray Mold. Grey Mould. Botrytis Blight: Lesions, even cankers, more or less extensive, are visible on the stems, mainly located at the level of pruning and disbudding wounds. Let us add that the lesions are generally covered with a very characteristic grayish to beige mold.

Napa
Chinese Cabbage

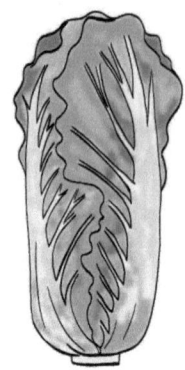

Botanical name
Brassica rapa subsp. pekinensis

Class
Brassicaceae

English name
Napa, Chinese Cabbage, Petsai or Pe-tsai, Chinese leaf.

Names in other languages
Chou de Pékin. Chou de Chine pommé (FR), Chinese kool (NL), Breitblättriger China-Kohl (DE), Cavolo sedano (IT), Couve petsai.(PO), Repollo chino (SP).

Related plants
Pak-choi.

Description
Napa or Chinese cabbage (*Brassica rapa subsp. pekinensis*) belongs to the family Brassicaceae. It occurs in both annual and biennial forms but is cultivated as an annual. It forms an upright head of either tightly overlapping leaves or sometimes a looser head of more separated leaves. Shape and size differ markedly between cultivars and head weight may vary between 1.4 and 4.5 kg. Leaf color in the hearted centers is usually a creamy white, but outer leaves vary from dark to light green.

Pests
Anthracnose Fruit Rot, Cabbage Aphid, Cabbage Club Root, Cabbage Maggot, Cabbage Stem Flea Beetle, Cabbageworm, Imported Cabbage Worms, Damping Off, Dark Sword-grass Moth, Black cutworm, Greasy cutworm, Diamond-back Moth, Downy Mildew of Crucifers, Gray Mold, Grey Mould, Botrytis Blight.

Symptoms on:
Leaves
Damage

◇

◇ Leaves with holes ⋯▸ Cabbageworm. Imported Cabbage Worms: Caterpillars devour the leaves of cruciferous plants, sometimes leaving only the large veins. In addition, their excrement, diluted by rain or dew, accumulates in the heart of the plant and makes it inedible.

◇ Leaves with holes ⋯▸ Diamond-back Moth: The damage is significant on cabbages. The caterpillars first eat the outer leaves and then gradually migrate to the young leaves in the center. They join them together with silk threads and soil them with their excrement.

Deformation

◇ Leaves curled or shrivelled ⋯▸ Cabbage Aphid: In the event of an outbreak, the plant can be completely covered by aphids, their honeydew and their exuviae.

Discoloring

◇ Reddening, yellowing of the leaves ⋯▸ Cabbage Club Root: Aerial part of the plant: reduced development, especially during early attacks, wilting or even reddening of the foliage.

Lesions

◇ Pale yellow or water-soaked regular or irregular lesions on leaves ⋯▸ Anthracnose: Depending on the fungus responsible, these brown or black spots can be circular or irregular, they then appear either on the edge of the leaves or along the veins. The necrotic areas extend more or less concentrically, the limit with healthy tissue being very clear.

◇ Purple or brown irregular shaped areas on leaves ⋯▸ Downy Mildew of Crucifers: It first appears on older leaves, as white, yellow or brownish spots on the upper surfaces and downy grayish mold on the corresponding undersides.

Presence

◇ Coating of gray fungus spores on leaves ⋯→ Gray Mold. Grey Mould. Botrytis Blight: Regardless of the organs affected, the dying tissues become covered with a very characteristic dense gray mold, consisting of the conidiophores and conidia of the fungus.

◇ Presence of colonies of aphids ⋯→ Cabbage Aphid: In the event of an outbreak, the plant can be completely covered by aphids, their honeydew and their exuviae.

◇ White to gray, "downy" areas on under leaf surfaces. ⋯→ Downy Mildew of Crucifers: It first appears on older leaves, as white, yellow or brownish spots on the upper surfaces and downy grayish mold on the corresponding undersides.

◇ Presence of caterpillars ⋯→ Cabbageworm. Imported Cabbage Worms: Caterpillars devour the leaves of cruciferous plants, sometimes leaving only the large veins. In addition, their excrement, diluted by rain or dew, accumulates in the heart of the plant and makes it inedible.

◇ Presence of honeydew and sooty moulds on leaves ⋯→ Cabbage Aphid: In the event of an outbreak, the plant can be completely covered by aphids, their honeydew and their exuviae.

◇ Presence of caterpillars ⋯→ Diamond-back Moth: The damage is significant on cabbages. The caterpillars first eat the outer leaves and then gradually migrate to the young leaves in the center. They join them together with silk threads and soil them with their excrement.

Plantlets
Dieback

◇ Damaged cotyledons ⋯→ Dark Sword-grass Moth. Black cutworm. Greasy cutworm: Early larval stages feed on the leaves and create small holes with irregular contours. Later stages attack the stem, often during sowing, and consequently cut the seedlings at ground level.

Wilting

◇ Wilted, collapsed and dead young seedlings ⋯→ Damping Off: Seeds rot and fail to germinate, or even germinate, but seedlings fail to grow. A translucent area completely covers the stem near the soil surface. The affected tissues rot, leading to wilting and collapse of the seedlings.

Plants whole
Stunted

◇ Stunted plants ⋯→ Cabbage Stem Flea Beetle: It is difficult to monitor the activity of the adult of the large rapeseed flea beetle: it occurs at night. Its damage, on the other hand, is easily recognizable because the insect bites the cotyledons and young leaves in a circular fashion. Perforations can also be observed.

Wilting

◇ Wilted plants ⋯→ Cabbage Maggot, Cabbage Fly: Damage is observed in nurseries and at all stages of vegetation. On leafy vegetables, the root part is more or less destroyed. Attacked plants can be recognized by the faded appearance they take on during hot days; the leaves often turn purplish red, turn yellow and sometimes dry out.

◇ Wilted plants ⋯→ Cabbage Club Root: Underground part of the plant: root deformation or presence of galls on the roots. These galls are firm (full interior), whitish then turn brown and rot, leading to the death of the plant.

Roots or tubers
Deformation

◇ Roots abnormally increased or swellings ⋯→ Cabbage Club Root: Underground part of the plant: root deformation or presence of galls on the roots. These galls are firm (full interior), whitish then turn brown and rot, leading to the death of the plant.

Presence

◇ Presence of maggots in roots ⋯→ Cabbage Maggot, Cabbage Fly: The larvae of the cabbage fly penetrate into the fleshy parts and dig galleries. The root part is more or less destroyed. Attacked plants can be recognized by the faded appearance they take on during hot days; the leaves often turn purplish red, turn yellow and sometimes dry out.

Spots

◇ Small white mealy spots ⋯→ Potato Tuber Nematode. Potato Cyst Nematode: The nematode initially causes small white mealy spots just below the surface that are only visible if the skin is removed.

Stems
Dieback

◇ Damaged stems ⋯→ Dark Sword-grass Moth. Black cutworm. Greasy cutworm: Early larval stages feed on the leaves and create small holes with irregular contours. Later stages attack the stem, often during sowing, and consequently cut the seedlings at ground level.

Onion

Botanical name
Allium cepa

Class
Liliaceae

English name
Onion

Names in other languages
Oignon (FR), Ajuin. Ui (NL), Zwiebel (DE), Cipolla (IT), Cebola (PO), Cebolla (SP).

Related plants
Shallot, Scallion.

Description
Onion (*Allium cepa*) is an herbaceous biennial in the family Liliaceae grown for its edible bulb. The stem of the plant is a flattened disc at the base and the tubular leaves form a pseudostem where their sheaths overlap. The leaves are either erect or oblique and there are 3–8 per plant. The onion plant produces pink or white flowers clustered on stalks. The bulbs are formed just above the flattened stem of the plant by overlapping leaves. The bulb is made up of several layers, each corresponding to a leaf. They are are generally oval but shape can be variable and occur in clusters of 3–18 to a plant. The bulb is protected by a membrane which turns to a papery coat. Onion plants can reach a height of 50 cm (20 in) and are grown as annuals, harvested after one growing season.

Pests
American Serpentine Leaf Miner, Anthracnose Fruit Rot, Basal Rot, Beet Armyworm, Botrytis Rot, Neckrot, Click Beetle, Wireworms, Dark Sword-grass Moth, Black cutworm, Greasy cutworm, Downy Mildew of Alliums, Early Blight of Potato/Tomato, Garden Dart Moth, Leek Moth, Onion Moth, Onion and Leek Rust, Onion Fly, Onion Maggot, Onion Smut, Onion Thrips, Powdery Mildew, Stem Nematode, White Rot, Sclerotinia Wilt.

Symptoms on
Leaves
Damage

◇ Leaves with irregular holes ⋯→ Armyworms, Beet Armyworm: Older Spodoptera exigua caterpillars migrate to the apex of the plants where they feed mainly on the growing areas. They make large holes in the leaves and sometimes leave only the veins behind. The damage caused considerably affects the growth of the plants.

Decay

◇ Soft watery rot on lower leaves ⋯→ White Rot. White Mold. Sclerotinia Wilt: Pre and post-emergent damping off, crown rot, and blighting of foliage and petioles. Small, hard, irregular, black structures called sclerotia may be present on or in plant tissue (especially inside stem and petiole tissue).

Deformation

◇ Leaves distorted ⋯→ Stem Nematode. Bulb and Stem Nematode: Deformation and swelling of the stem, uncontrolled development and wilting of the leaves. The plant is stocky and is clearly less developed than a healthy plant.

Discoloring

◇ Leaves turn yellow and wilt ⋯→ Onion Fly: On young seedlings: the plant wilts and then dies. A larva can attack several seedlings in succession. If the plant is more developed, it wilts, especially in hot weather, and may die.

◇ Silvery marks on leaves ⋯→ Onion Thrips. Thrips: In a greenhouse, colonies can be very developed and direct damage is often significant. The larvae and adults of the tobacco and onion thrips puncture the contents of the subepidermal cells. The infested leaves are then dotted with numerous silver spots corresponding to groups of emptied cells. This symptom is typically associated with the presence of small piles of black feces.

Galleries

◇ Galleries in leaves ⋯⟶ Leek Moth, Onion Moth: The leaves are mined, perforated, partly consumed, the leaves end up having a lacerated appearance.

◇ Leaves with galleries ⋯⟶ Onion Maggot: In spring, damage occurs after the first flight. The first mines are very small, but leeks in cultivation are then small, and a few maggots are enough to kill a plant. In autumn, leeks are larger and survive even while hosting large populations of larvae. The mines do not rot; in some cases, they have a clean, whitish appearance. Sometimes the color is pinkish-brown, clearly visible on the white basal part of the leaves.

◇ Leaves with galleries ⋯⟶ American Serpentine Leaf Miner: The main damage is due to larvae which mine the leaves. This damage is particularly serious on small plants in nurseries or just transplanted, which can die.

Lesions

◇ Pale yellow or water-soaked regular or irregular lesions on leaves ⋯⟶ Anthracnose: Depending on the fungus responsible, these brown or black spots can be circular or irregular, they then appear either on the edge of the leaves or along the veins. The necrotic areas extend more or less concentrically, the limit with healthy tissue being very clear.

Presence

◇ White to gray powder coverage on leaves ⋯⟶ Powdery Mildew, Oidium: The heart leaves are covered with purplish-grey spores on the underside. They thicken, curl, and curl up. Older leaves turn yellow on the outside, then blacken and die. Only a few isolated plants or foci are damaged.

◇ Presence of maggots in leaves and bulbs ⋯⟶ Onion Maggot: In autumn, the leeks are larger and survive even while hosting large populations of larvae. The mines do not rot, in some cases they have a clean appearance of whitish hue. It also happens that the coloring is pinkish-brown, clearly visible on the white basal part of the leaves.

◇ Presence of cutworms ⋯⟶ Garden Dart Moth. Cutworm: The larvae feed on the roots of plants, cutting them at night.

◇ Presence of caterpillars ⋯⟶ Armyworms, Beet Armyworm: Older Spodoptera exigua caterpillars migrate to the apex of the plants where they feed mainly on the growing areas. They make large holes in the leaves and sometimes leave only the veins behind. The damage caused considerably affects the growth of the plants. In heavy infestations, the damage can extend to the stems and, in the worst cases, to the fruits, which the caterpillars consume entirely from the inside.

◇ Leaves with grey powder ⋯⟶ Downy Mildew of Alliums: At the beginning of vegetation: dwarf plants with chlorotic, deformed leaves, covered with a velvety gray mycelium. During vegetation: presence of elongated spots on leaves and stems of a yellowish appearance and covered with a gray felting.

Spots

◇ Leaves with yellow, brown, necrotic and concentric spots ⋯⟶ Early Blight of Potato/Tomato: Small yellow spots quickly turn brown-black, necrotic, circular and sharply outlined, measuring about 5 mm in diameter, which gradually spread concentrically.

◇ Bright-orange spots on leaves ⋯⟶ Onion and Leek Rust: Affected leek, garlic and onion leaves have small pustular lesions that are initially whitish to beige. These spread slightly and give rise to bright orange to brown pustules, with the leaves eventually drying out.

◇ Yellowish then brown spots on the upper surface of the leaf ⋯⟶ Powdery Mildew, Oidium: Yellowish then brown spots on the upper surface of the leaf, generally limited by the large veins, whitish felting on the lower surface.

Plantlets
Discoloring

◇ Black streaks and blisters on young plant parts ⋯⟶ Oignon Smut. Smut of Onion: Characterized by the presence of black streaks and blisters on leaves and bulbs; the streaks then split to release a cloud of black spores.

Plants whole
Spots

◇ Leaves with necrotic spots, turn yellow and die ⋯⟶ Basal Rot: Necrotic spots with dark brown, slightly sunken, irregular lesions on the leaves and stems, leading to wilting.

Stunted

◇ Plants stunted ⋯⟶ Leek Moth, Onion Moth: The plants age prematurely and the larvae move to the more turgid bulb where they dig galleries.

Roots or bulbs
Decay

◇ Rotted bulbs ⋯⟶ Basal Rot: In garlic and onion, rot typically initiates in the base of the bulb, then spreads into the bulb.

Dieback

◇ Roots and bulbs decay ⋯⟶ Onion Fly: Attacks by flies encourage the development of rot, visible only when pulled out, and which attract other saprophagous flies whose maggots are then found in the bulb.

Galleries

◇ Galleries in roots ⋯⟶ Click Beetle. Striped Elaterid Beetle. Wireworms: As larvae development takes up to four years, in an infected soil we can find larvae of different ages. They live at different depths, depending on the moment of the year, as they are highly sensitive to heat and dryness. They eat or pierce the underground organs of the plant: roots, crowns, bud leaves and turions.

Presence

◇ Rotten bulbs with white felting ⋯⟶ White Rot.

White Mold. Sclerotinia Wilt: The mycelium forms a white felt on the surface of the rotten parts, in which black sclerotia can b observed.

◇ Presence of white maggots ⋯→ Onion Fly: Maggots are found in the bulb.

◇ Decayed bulbs with gray mould ⋯→ Botrytis Rot. Neckrot: Botrytis bulb rot generally appears during storage, although infection originates in the field. Initial symptoms usually begin at the neck, where affected tissue softens, becomes water-soaked, and turns brown. In storage, a gray mold can be seen on the surface of the bulbs or between the scales. Black sclerotia cluster around the neck and between the scales.

Stems
Dieback

◇ Damaged stems ⋯→ Dark Sword-grass Moth. Black cutworm. Greasy cutworm: Early larval stages feed on the leaves and create small holes with irregular contours. Later stage attack the stem, often during sowing, and consequently cut the seedlings at ground level.

Presence

◇ White mold on the stem and collar ⋯→ White Rot. White Mold. Sclerotinia Wilt: Black or dark brown sclerotia form inside the stems. This uncommon disease can sometimes lead to the death of the plant.

◇ Stems with larvae ⋯→ Leek Moth, Onion Moth: The plants age prematurely and the larvae move to the more turgid bulb where they dig galleries.

Parsley

Botanical name
Petroselinum crispum

Class
Apiaceae

English name
Parsley

Names in other languages
Parsley, Garden parsley, Curly-leaf parsley, Flat-leaf parsley, Root parsley (EN), Persil, Persil cultivé, Persil odorant, Persin, Persil frisé, Persil plat, Persil de Naples, Persil tubéreux (FR), Peterselie, Krulpeterselie, Bladpeterselie, Wortelpeterselie (NL), Petersilie, Peterle, Peterli, Peterling, Petergrün, Wurzelpetersilie (DE), Prezzemolo, Petrosello (IT), Salsa, Salsinha, Perrexil (PO), Perejil (SP).

Description
Parsley is an herbaceous biennial or perennial plant grown for its leaves which are used as a herb. Parsley is an aromatic plant with an erect growth habit and possesses branched, hollow stems and dark green flat or curled leaves which are arranged alternately on the stems. The leaves form a rosette on younger plants. The plant produces small, yellow flowers on umbels. Parsley can reach 30–100 cm in height depending on the variety being grown and is commonly grown as an annual, harvested after one growing season.

Pests
Alternaria leaf blight, Armyworm, Black Scurf. Rhizoctonia Canker. Stem Canker. Crater spot, Carrot motley dwarf (CMD) virus, Carrot redeaf virus (CRLV), Carrot mottle virus (CMoV), Cercosporosa Leaf Spot, Cercosporia blight, Damping Off, Dark Sword-grass Moth. Black cutworm. Greasy cutworm, Onion and Leek Rust, Powdery Mildew, Oidium, Root knot nematode, Septoria leaf spot, Willow-Carrot Aphid.

Symptoms on:
Leaves
Damage

◇ Holes in leaves ⋯▸ Armyworm: Singular, or closely grouped circular to irregularly shaped holes in foliage; heavy feeding by young larvae leads to skeletonized leaves.

Lesions

◇ Brown black necrotic lesions ⋯▸ Alternaria leaf blight: Small brownish spots with a yellow halo on the edges of older leaves, developing into necrosis.

◇ Necrotic lesions with chlorotic halo ⋯▸ Cercosporosa Leaf Spot, Cercosporia blight: Small, necrotic flecks on leaves which develop a chlorotic halo and expand into tan brown necrotic spots; lesions coalesce and cause leaves to wither, curl and die

◇ Water-soaked lesions on leaves ⋯▸ Black Scurf. Rhizoctonia Canker. Stem Canker. Crater spot: Small, water-soaked lesions on crowns or petioles in contact with soil; collapse of petioles; petioles drying; lesions develop a sunken appearance and a dry, firm texture

Presence

◇ White to gray powder coverage on leaves ⋯▸ Powdery Mildew, Oidium: The heart leaves are covered with purplish-grey spores on the underside. They thicken, curl, and curl up. Older leaves turn yellow on the outside, then blacken and die. Only a few isolated plants or foci are damaged.

◇ Presence of honeydew and sooty moulds on leaves ⋯▸ Willow-Carrot Aphid: If aphid infestation is heavy it may cause leaves to yellow and/or distorted, necrotic spots on leaves and/or stunted shoots; aphids secrete a sticky, sugary substance called honeydew which encourages the growth of sooty mold on the plants.

Spots

◇ Bright-orange spots on leaves ⋯▸ Onion and

Leek Rust: Affected leek, garlic and onion leaves have small pustular lesions that are initially whitish to beige. These spread slightly and give rise to bright orange to brown pustules, with the leaves eventually **drying out.**

◇ Gray-brown angular spots ⋯⋅→ Septoria leaf spot: Small, angular, gray-brown spots with defined red-brown margins on leaves; black fungal fruiting bodies may be visible on surface of lesions; leaves becoming chlorotic and necrotic.

Plantlets
Wilting

◇ Wilted, collapsed and dead young seedlings ⋯⋅→ Damping Off: Seeds rot and fail to germinate, or even germinate, but seedlings fail to grow. A translucent area completely covers the stem near the soil surface. The affected tissues rot, leading to wilting and collapse of the seedlings.

Plants whole
Stunted

◇ Stunted plants ⋯⋅→ Carrot motley dwarf (CMD) virus, Carrot redeaf virus (CRLV), Carrot mottle virus (CMoV): Yellow and red leaves; stunted plant growth.

Roots or tubers
Deformation

◇ Galls on roots ⋯⋅→ Root knot nematode: Galls on roots which can be up to 3.3 cm (1 in) in diameter but are usually smaller; reduction in plant vigor; yellowing plants which wilt in hot weather.

Stems
Dieback

◇ Damaged stems ⋯⋅→ Dark Sword-grass Moth. Black cutworm. Greasy cutworm: Early larval stages feed on the leaves and create small holes with irregular contours. Later stages attack the stem, often during sowing, and consequently cut the seedlings at ground level.

Parsnip

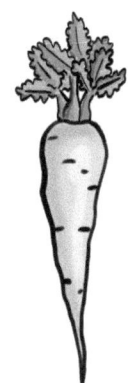

Botanical name
Pastinaca sativa

Class
Apiaceae

English name
Parsnip

Names in other languages
Panais (FR), Pastinaak (NL), Pastinake (DE), Pastinaca, (IT), Cherovia (PO), Chirivía (SP).

Description
Parsnip (*Pastinaca sativa)* is an herbaceous biennial plant in the family Apiaceae grown for its edible taproot resembling a pale carrot. The parsnip plant has an erect, branched stem with a rosette of leaves which are oblong or triangular in shape and 30–38 cm (12–15 in) in length. The leaves at the top of the plant are smaller and attached directly to the stem. The plant produces flowers on umbels which are yellow or orange in color with wide petals. The taproot of the plant is thick and fleshy and can grow between 10 and 23 cm (4–9 in) in length. The parsnip plant may grow to a height of 90–180 cm (35–70 in) in height and is usually grown as an annual for only one growing season.

Pests
Carrot Fly, Early Blight of Potato/Tomato, Itersonilia Canker. Parsnip Canker, Powdery Mildew, Rust, Violet Root Rot, White Rot, White Mold, Sclerotinia Wilt.

Symptoms on:
Leaves
Discoloring

◇ Leaves turn yellow ⋯⋙ Carrot Fly, Carrot Rust Fly: Yellowing or reddening of the foliage of affected plants is often observed.

Lesions

◇ Orange to brown lesions on leaves ⋯⋙ Itersonilia Canker. Parsnip Canker: On leaves, symptoms occur as small orange to brown lesions with a pale green halo. Infected inflorescences may be completely blighted.

Presence

◇ White to gray powder coverage on leaves ⋯⋙ Powdery Mildew, Oidium: The heart leaves are covered with purplish-grey spores on the underside. They thicken, curl, and curl up. Older leaves turn yellow on the outside, then blacken and die. Only a few isolated plants or foci are damaged.

Spots

◇ Leaves with yellow, brown, necrotic and concentric spots ⋯⋙ Early Blight of Potato/Tomato: Small yellow spots quickly turn brown-black, necrotic, circular and sharply outlined, measuring about 5 mm in diameter, which gradually spread concentrically.

◇ Reddish-orange spots on leaves ⋯⋙ Rust: On the upper side of the leaves, you will see tiny white, orange or even brown spots appear depending on the species. If you turn these leaves over, you will see that these spots correspond to tiny pustules of the same color. The lesions are generally yellow, brown or red, but can be dark brown or black at the end of the season.

Plants whole
Stunted

◇ Plants stunted ⋯⋙ Carrot Fly, Carrot Rust Fly: The roots have slowed growth and the plant can disappear in the event of an early attack.

Roots or tubers

Discoloring

◇ Purplish coloration of roots ⋯→ Violet Root Rot:
On roots, presence of superficial purple spots
in the form of felting of fine filaments,
developing from the base of the root and which
can develop over the entire root.

Galleries

◇ Galleries in roots ⋯→ Carrot Fly, Carrot Rust Fly:
The larvae dig galleries in the roots, especially
on the outer layer. Each root can host several
larvae (about ten). Attacked carrots have very
slow growth and take on a bitter taste.

Lesions

◇ Brown, black or purple black lesions on roots ⋯→
Itersonilia Canker. Parsnip Canker: On roots,
cankers form mainly on the crown and
shoulder, although lateral roots may be
affected. Lesions are superficial and brown,
black, or purple black. Secondary decay of
cankers can occur.

Presence

◇ Presence of yellow larvae in roots ⋯→ Carrot Fly,
Carrot Rust Fly: The larva is a very elongated
maggot (6 to 7 mm), shiny yellowish white. It is
the larvae that cause the damage by
penetrating the roots and digging winding
galleries.

Stems

Presence

◇ White mold on the stem and collar ⋯→ White Rot.
White Mold. Sclerotinia Wilt: Black or dark
brown sclerotia form inside the stems. This
uncommon disease can sometimes lead to the
death of the plant.

Peas

Botanical name
Pisum sativum

Class
Fabaceae

English name
Peas. Garden pea

Names in other languages
Pois (FR), Erwt (NL), Erbse (DE), Pisello (IT), Ervilha (PO), Guisante (SP).

Related plants
Sugar peas.

Description
Pea (*Pisum sativum*) is an annual herbaceous legume in the family Fabaceae grown for its edible seeds and seedpods. The pea plant can be bushy or climbing, with slender stems which attach to a substrate using tendrils. Each leaf has 1–3 pairs of oval leaflets and can reach 1–6 cm in length. The plant produces white, red or purple flowers and swollen or compressed green seedpods which can be straight or curved. The pods can range in size from 4 to 15 cm long and 1.5–2.5 cm wide. Each pod contains between 2 and 10 seeds, or peas. The pea plant is an annual plant, surviving only one growing season and can reach 30–150 cm in height.

Pests
American Serpentine Leaf Miner, Anthracnose Fruit Rot, Ascochyta Foot-rot, Pinodella Blight on Pea, Bacterial Blight, Bean Aphids, Bean Beetle, Pea beetle, Beet Armyworm, Celery Late Blight, Fusarium Root Rot, Fusarium Wilt, Gray Mold, Botrytis Blight, Thrips, Pea Aphid, Green Pea Louse, Pea Downy Mildew, Pea Midge, Pea Moth, Pea Root Nematode, Pea Seed-borne Mosaic Virus, Pea Weevil, Potato Aphid, Powdery Mildew, Slug and Snail, White Rot, White Mold, Sclerotinia Wilt.

Symptoms on:
Flowers
Deformation

◇ Flowers with swellings ⸱⸱⸱➜ Pea Midge: The larvae cause swelling of the floral organs, especially the sepals; the petals are strongly crimped; the attack on the terminal shoots leads to the reduction of the floral stems. The larvae also develop in the pods and feed on the internal surface of the latter or even on the seeds in formation.

Spots

◇ Blackish-brown spots, which may become covered with grayish mold ⸱⸱⸱➜ Gray Mold. Grey Mould. Botrytis Blight: Blackish-brown spots, extending from the base of the bracts, which may become covered with grayish mold (fruiting bodies). Sometimes, sclerotia are present. This disease develops secondarily following an injury or other disease.

Fruits
Dieback

◇ Fruit drop early ⸱⸱⸱➜ Pea Thrips: Its outbreaks cause the plant to weaken and flowers to abort, leading to crop losses. It is also a vector of different viruses.

Presence

◇ Presence of caterpillars in pods ⸱⸱⸱➜ Pea Moth: Each caterpillar damages up to 6 seeds but only 1 or 2 are heavily eaten. However, seed perforation, caterpillar presence and soiling result in loss.

Spots

◇ Fruits with spots ⸱⸱⸱➜ Bacterial Blight. Pea Bacterial Blight: Oily spots on all aerial organs (leaves, stipules, petioles, stem, pods) developing into light brown necrosis on leaves and brown on pods. The bacteria can also cause flower dripping.

Leaves
Damage

◇ Leaves with perforations ⤳ Slug and Snail. Garden Slug. Loach. Little Grey Slug. Vine Snail. White Garden Snail: The slug consumes the leaves of plants between the veins, which gives them a serrated appearance.

◇ Leaf edges eaten ⤳ Pea Weevil. Pea and Bean Weevil: Notches made by adults on the leaves can limit the density of young seedlings. In addition, attacks by larvae which feed on nodules and roots cause delays in vegetation.

◇ Leaves with irregular holes ⤳ Armyworms, Beet Armyworm: Older Spodoptera exigua caterpillars migrate to the apex of the plants where they feed mainly on the growing areas. They make large holes in the leaves and sometimes leave only the veins behind. The damage caused considerably affects the growth of the plants.

Deformation

◇ Curled leaves ⤳ Celery Late Blight: The disease first manifests itself by the appearance of small light brown spots on the foliage. In case of severe attacks, the petioles turn yellow, the leaves curl up and dry out.

◇ Leaves curled or shrivelled ⤳ Bean Aphids. Black Dolphin Aphids: Presence of black aphids on the leaves, on the flower stems and the flower heads. As soon as they appear, deformation of the attacked leaves and development of sooty mold.

◇ Leaves rolled ⤳ Pea Seed-borne Mosaic Virus: Symptoms on leaves: slight chlorosis, slight mosaic, rolling of leaflets on themselves, necrosis. On pods: deformation, small grains.

◇ Leaves shrivelled ⤳ Pea Thrips: Its outbreaks cause the plant to weaken and flowers to abort, leading to crop losses. It is also a vector of different viruses.

Discoloring

◇ Leaves turn yellow and wilt ⤳ Fusarium Wilt: An affected plant has a yellowing, stunted, wilted appearance, sometimes with gummosis on the stem. Discoloration and vascular browning of the collar progressing towards the stem and roots, and developing into cortical rot.

◇ Silvery marks on leaves ⤳ Onion Thrips. Thrips: In a greenhouse, colonies can be very developed and direct damage is often significant. The larvae and adults of the tobacco and onion thrips puncture the contents of the subepidermal cells. The infested leaves are then dotted with numerous silver spots corresponding to groups of emptied cells. This symptom is typically associated with the presence of small piles of black feces.

◇ Leaves turn yellow and die ⤳ Pea Root Nematode. Pea Cyst Nematode: The leaves turn yellow and fall prematurely, the plants twist at the base, growth is stopped and the plants remain dwarfed.

Galleries

◇ Leaves with galleries ⤳ American Serpentine Leaf Miner: The main damage is due to larvae which mine the leaves. This damage is particularly serious on small plants in nurseries or just transplanted, which can die.

Lesions

◇ Pale yellow or water-soaked regular or irregular lesions on leaves ⤳ Anthracnose: Depending on the fungus responsible, these brown or black spots can be circular or irregular, they then appear either on the edge of the leaves or along the veins. The necrotic areas extend more or less concentrically, the limit with healthy tissue being very clear.

Presence

◇ Coating of gray fungus spores on leaves ⤳ Grey Mold. Grey Mould. Botrytis Blight: Regardless of the organs affected, the dying tissues become covered with a very characteristic dense gray mold, consisting of the conidiophores and conidia of the fungus.

◇ White to gray powder coverage on leaves ⤳ Powdery Mildew, Oidium: The heart leaves are covered with purplish-grey spores on the underside. They thicken, curl, and curl up. Older leaves turn yellow on the outside, then blacken and die. Only a few isolated plants or foci are damaged.

◇ Presence of black aphids ⤳ Bean Aphids. Black Dolphin Aphids: Presence of black aphids on the leaves, on the flower stems and capitals. As soon as they appear, deformation of the attacked leaves and development of sooty mold.

◇ Presence of honey dew on leaves ⤳ Bean Aphids. Black Dolphin Aphids: Aphids suck large volumes of sap. The excess sugary fluid, honeydew, is secreted by the aphids. It adheres to plants, where it promotes growth of sooty molds.

◇ Presence of sooty mould on leaves ⤳ Bean Aphids. Black Dolphin Aphids: Aphids suck large volumes of sap. The excess sugary fluid, honeydew, is secreted by the aphids. It adheres to plants, where it promotes growth of sooty molds.

◇ Presence of aphids ⤳ Potato Aphid: The most classic symptoms are a curling of heavily infested leaves and a slowdown in the growth of the plants

◇ Slime trails ⤳ Slug and Snail. Garden Slug. Loach. Little Grey Slug. Vine Snail. White Garden Snail: Slime trail' that signals their presence.

◇ Presence of aphids ⤳ Pea Aphid. Green Pea Louse.: Aphid populations can literally explode and become damaging to crops if not controlled. In growing areas, leaves become deformed and turn yellow. This aphid is the main vector of several viruses.

◇ Presence of caterpillars ⤳ Armyworms, Beet Armyworm: Older Spodoptera exigua caterpillars migrate to the apex of the plants where they feed mainly on the growing areas.

They make large holes in the leaves and sometimes leave only the veins behind. The damage caused considerably affects the growth of the plants. In heavy infestations, the damage can extend to the stems and, in the worst cases, to the fruits, which the caterpillars consume entirely from the inside.

◇ Leaves with grey powder ⋯→ Pea Downy Mildew: Upper surface of leaves: discolored areas. Underside of leaves: gray-white mycelial felt. Drying of affected areas, as well as flowers that abort. Pods and seeds may also be affected.

Spots

◇ Pale brown spots on leaves ⋯→ Celery Late Blight: The disease first manifests itself by the appearance on the foliage of small light brown spots, often delimited by the fine veins of the leaves but sometimes with irregular contours, ranging in size from 1 to 4 mm. They gradually turn reddish-brown and have small black dots called pycnidia in their center on the upper surface.

◇ Yellowish then brown spots on the upper surface of the leaf ⋯→ Powdery Mildew, Oidium: Yellowish then brown spots on the upper surface of the leaf, generally limited by the large veins, whitish felting on the lower surface.

◇ Leaves with yellow-brown spots ⋯→ Bacterial Blight. Pea Bacterial Blight: Oily spots on all aerial organs (leaves, stipules, petioles, stem, pods) developing into light brown necrosis on leaves and brown on pods. The bacteria can also cause flower dripping.

◇ Brown spots on the leaves ⋯→ Ascochyta Foot-rot. Pinodella Blight on Pea : On leaves, flowers and pods, phoma causes symptoms very similar to those of ascochyta blight (Peyronellaea pinodes), however the spots do not become watery; they are round or oval in shape and concentric circles are visible.

◇ Leaves with yellow-brown spots ⋯→ Pea Downy Mildew: Upper surface of leaves: discolored areas. Underside of leaves: gray-white mycelial felt. Drying of affected areas, as well as flowers that abort. Pods and seeds may also be affected.

Plants whole
Stunted

◇ Plants stunted ⋯→ Fusarium Root Rot: Diseased plants wilt to a greater or lesser extent during the hottest times of the day; this wilting is sometimes reversible. In the most serious cases, the plants eventually dry out completely.

◇ Plants stunted ⋯→ Pea Seed-borne Mosaic Virus: Symptoms on plants: shortening of internodes giving a stunted appearance to the plant, abortion of flowers.

Roots or tubers
Decay

◇ Rotting of roots ⋯→ Fusarium Root Rot: The cause of these wilting is to be found at the level of the collar of the feet. At this location, a wet lesion has developed, a rot that has gradually spread to the lower part of the stem and the taproot, but also to the upper part of the root system. At the collar, the altered tissues are wet and show a dark to brownish tint. This lesion ends up girdling the stem for several centimetres. The roots located in the same layer of soil are also affected. Their cortex turns yellow, brown and decomposes.

Deformation

◇ Roots abnormally increased or swellings ⋯→ Pea Root Nematode. Pea Cyst Nematode: The roots are poorly developed and have only a limited number of bacterial nodules; the rootlets are abundant and bear clusters of cysts.

Dieback

◇ Roots damaged ⋯→ Pea Weevil. Pea and Bean Weevil: Notches made by adults on the leaves can limit the density of young seedlings. In addition, attacks by larvae which feed on nodules and roots cause delays in vegetation.

Seeds
Damage

◇ Beans with small holes ⋯→ Bean Beetle. Pea beetle: The presence of bruchids in beans, peas or beans makes them unfit for consumption, reduces the germination rate of seeds and presents risks of re-infestation of crops. A bean can accommodate 5 to 6 individuals.

Stems
Necrosis

◇ Necrotic stems ⋯→ Fusarium Wilt: An affected plant has a yellowing, stunted, wilted appearance, sometimes with gummosis on the stem. Discoloration and vascular browning of the collar progressing towards the stem and roots, and developing into cortical rot.

Presence

◇ Coating of gray fungus spores on stems ⋯→ Gray Mold. Grey Mould. Botrytis Blight: Lesions, even cankers, more or less extensive, are visible on the stems, mainly located at the level of pruning and disbudding wounds. Let us add that the lesions are generally covered with a very characteristic grayish to beige mold.

◇ White mold on the stem and collar ⋯→ White Rot. White Mold. Sclerotinia Wilt: Black or dark brown sclerotia form inside the stems. This uncommon disease can sometimes lead to the death of the plant.

◇ Presence of colonies of aphids ⋯→ Bean Aphids. Black Dolphin Aphids.

Pepper
Bell Pepper

Botanical name
Capsicum annuum

Class
Solanaceae

English name
Pepper. Bell Pepper

Names in other languages
Piment. Poivron (FR), Peper. Paprika (NL), Paprika (DE), Pimento. Peperone (IT), Pimento (PO), Pimentón, Pimiento (SP).

Related plants
Chili

Description
Peppers (*Capsicum annuum*) are a cultivar group of annual or perennial plants in the family Solanaceae grown for their edible fruits. Bell pepper plants are short bushes with woody stems that grow brightly colored fruits. The alternating leaves are elliptical, smooth edged, and come to a distinct point. The plant produces white or purple bell-shaped flowers which are 2.5 cm (1 in) in diameter. Red, yellow, purple, or brown fruit are produced each season about 3-6 weeks after flowering. Pepper plants can grow 1 m (3.3 ft) tall and are usually grown as annuals in temperate regions for only one growing season.

Pests
Anthracnose Fruit Rot, Bacterial Canker of Tomato, Beet Armyworm, Cercosporosa Leaf Spot, Cotton Aphid, Cotton Whitefly, Tobacco Whitefly, Cotton Worm, African Cotton Leafworm, Cucumber Mosaic Virus. CMV, Glasshouse Potato Foxglove Aphid, Gray Mold. Botrytis Blight, Green Peach Aphid, Mosaic Virus on Pepper, TMV. CMV, Potato Aphid, Red Spider Mite, Two-spotted Mite, Southern Green Stink bug, Tomato Leaf Miner, Tomato Russet Mite, Verticillium Wilt, White Rot, White Mold, Sclerotinia Wilt.

Symptoms on:
Flowers
Spots

◇ Blackish-brown spots, which may become covered with grayish mold ⋯➤ Gray Mold. Grey Mould. Botrytis Blight: Blackish-brown spots, extending from the base of the bracts, which may become covered with grayish mold (fruiting bodies). Sometimes, sclerotia are present. This disease develops secondarily following an injury or other disease.

Fruits
Deformation

◇ Fruits distortion ⋯➤ Mosaic Virus on Pepper. TMV. CMV: Infected plants may be stunted and have curled leaves and deformed fruit.

Spots

◇ Fruits with white spots ⋯➤ Southern Green Stink Bug: Young fruits have small, punctate spots, with the underlying tissues being lighter in color than the rest.

◇ Black spots on fruits ⋯➤ Bacterial Spot: Black spots on fruits about 1 cm in size, gradually widening.

Leaves
Damage

◇ Leaves with irregular holes ⋯➤ Armyworms, Beet Armyworm: Older Spodoptera exigua caterpillars migrate to the apex of the plants where they feed mainly on the growing areas. They make large holes in the leaves and sometimes leave only the veins behind.

◇ Leaf eaten (irregular holes) ⋯➤ Cotton Worm. African Cotton Leafworm: The damage caused by caterpillars, which vary in color from gray to reddish or yellowish, is recognizable by the large bites on the leaves.

Decay

◇ Soft watery rot on lower leaves ⋯➤ White Rot. White Mold. Sclerotinia Wilt: Pre and post-emergent damping off, crown rot, and blighting of foliage and petioles. Small, hard, irregular, black structures called sclerotia may be present on or in plant tissue (especially inside stem and petiole tissue).

Deformation

◇ Leaves curled or shrivelled ⋯▸ Green Peach Aphid: Myzus persicae is very polyphagous and, in summer, it has more than forty different families of host plants. The colonies secrete a honeydew that promotes the installation of sooty mold, a fungus that then slows down the photosynthesis of the covered parts. It is the most important aphid vector of viruses.

◇ Leaves curled or shrivelled ⋯▸ Cotton Aphid: Aphids, following their nutritional bites, are responsible for chlorotic spots and the deformation of young leaves which tend to roll up and more or less blister.

◇ Leaves curled and deformed ⋯▸ Glasshouse Potato Foxglove Aphid: Punctures by the aphids on lower leaves can cause deformations at the apex, with leaves becoming swollen and rolled. The immediate effects of these punctures are visible on lower leaves as yellow spots.

Discoloring

◇ Leaves discolouring bronzed or silvery ⋯▸ Red Spider Mite. Two-spotted Mite: They damage the plant by piercing its cells to feed on them. The leaves turn pale and become stained yellow. To protect themselves and improve their microclimate, they weave a web around the leaf. A strong attack of mites leads to the leaves rolling and drying out, then falling off.

◇ Leaves turn yellow ⋯▸ Cotton Whitefly. Tobacco Whitefly: The tobacco whitefly occupies the entire plant. Presence of numerous "white flies" and honeydew, slow growth of plants, development of sooty mold on aerial organs, yellowing and necrosis of the leaf blade.

Galleries

◇ Leaves with mines or galleries ⋯▸ Tomato Leaf Miner: Leafminer larvae dig mines and galleries on aerial organs. Leaves become mined with whitish spots that darken and become necrotic.

Lesions

◇ Pale yellow or water-soaked regular or irregular lesions on leaves ⋯▸ Anthracnose: Depending on the fungus responsible, these brown or black spots can be circular or irregular, they then appear either on the edge of the leaves or along the veins. The necrotic areas extend more or less concentrically, the limit with healthy tissue being very clear.

Mosaic pattern

◇ Yellow or whitish mosaic pattern on leaves ⋯▸ Mosaic Virus on Pepper. TMV. CMV: Typical symptoms of pepper plants infected with mosaic virus are a distinct yellow or whitish mosaic on leaves. Relative to uninfected plants, fruit may be stunted and misshapen.

Necrosis

◇ Shrivelling and necrosis of leaves ⋯▸ Tomato Russet Mite: The underside of the leaves or leaflets of the lower part of the plants takes on a greasy metallic tint. Subsequently, the leaves show a rather bronze coloration from which the name of this disease originates.

Presence

◇ Coating of gray fungus spores on leaves ⋯▸ Gray Mold. Grey Mould. Botrytis Blight: Regardless of the organs affected, the dying tissues become covered with a very characteristic dense gray mold, consisting of the conidiophores and conidia of the fungus. Presence of irregular, angular lesions ⋯▸ Bacterial Spot: On the underside, there are circular to angular spots, beige with a dark brown margin. They have a dry appearance and have a yellow halo.

◇ Presence of aphids ⋯▸ Potato Aphid: The most classic symptoms are a curling of heavily infested leaves and a slowdown in the growth of the plants

◇ Presence of honey dew on leaves ⋯▸ Cotton Aphid: In addition to aphid colonies, we often observe white molts and the presence of honeydew on the surface of the aerial organs of zucchini and other plants.

◇ Presence of sooty mould on leaves ⋯▸ Cotton Aphid: In addition to aphid colonies, we often observe white molts and the presence of honeydew on the surface of the aerial organs on which sooty mold develops. Remember that the latter can have several consequences, including a reduction in photosynthesis and leaf respiration and soiling of fruits thus rendered unmarketable.

◇ Leaves with fine silk webbing ⋯▸ Red Spider Mite. Two-spotted Mite: They damage the plant by piercing its cells to feed on them. The leaves turn pale and become stained yellow. To protect themselves and improve their microclimate, they weave a web around the leaf. A strong attack of mites leads to the leaves rolling and drying out, then falling off.

◇ Presence of red spider mites, cast skins and egg shells ⋯▸ Red Spider Mite. Two-spotted Mite: Spider mites always leave behind cast skins and egg shells.

◇ Presence of caterpillars ⋯▸ Silver-Y moth. Common Silver-Y moth. Cabbage Army Moth.: The caterpillar is active mainly at night, it devours the leaf blades and cuts the petioles. During the day, it remains attached to the underside of the leaves.

◇ Presence of honey dew on leaves ⋯▸ Cotton Whitefly. Tobacco Whitefly: The tobacco whitefly occupies the entire plant. Presence of numerous "white flies" and honeydew, slow growth of plants, development of sooty mold on aerial organs, yellowing and necrosis of the leaf blade.

◇ Presence of caterpillars ⋯▸ Cotton Worm. African Cotton Leafworm: The Mediterranean noctuid or cotton worm causes damage which is recognizable by the large portions eaten out of the leaves.

◇ Presence of caterpillars ⋯→ Armyworms, Beet Armyworm: Older Spodoptera exigua caterpillars migrate to the apex of the plants where they feed mainly on the growing areas. They make large holes in the leaves and sometimes leave only the veins behind. The damage caused considerably affects the growth of the plants.

Spots

◇ Yellow/brown spots ⋯→ Verticillium Wilt: Marginal drying, sometimes asymmetrical. In the stem, brown lesions at the level of the conductive tissue. Atrophied and deformed capitula.

◇ Leaf spots with brown-reddish margins ⋯→ Cercosporosa Leaf Spot, Cercosporia blight: Cercospora blight initially causes small, oval, gray to tan lesions with red borders. Severe infections may cause entire ferns to turn yellow or brown. Cercospora blight may cause reduced vigor and yield of spears the next spring.

Wilting

◇ Wilting of leaves ⋯→ Verticillium Wilt: Partial wilting of some lower leaves at the hottest times of the day, reversible during the night. Softening and progressive yellowing of sectors of the leaf blade, often interveinal and in the shape of a "V". The latter eventually turn brown and become necrotic.

Plants whole
Stunted

◇ Deformation and stunting of plants ⋯→ Cucumber Mosaic Virus. CMV: Artichoke latent virus (ALV, Potyvirus) is transmitted by aphids. Cucumber mosaic virus (CMV) induces deformation and stunting of plants.

Wilting

◇ Wilting of the entire plant ⋯→ Bacterial Canker of Tomato: Bacterial canker often manifests itself, at least at the beginning of its development, by the appearance on the leaflets of livid interveinal spots which quickly become necrotic. Very often, they are followed by leaf wilting, the leaflets tending in this case to curl downwards. Eventually, the seedlings, like adult plants, can wilt and dry out completely.

◇ Wilting of the entire plant ⋯→ Verticillium Wilt: The leaves soften and become duller. The leaves begin to yellow, then turn brown as they become necrotic. The characteristic feature is the asymmetry of the symptoms, with many leaves only affected on one half. The disease progresses from the bottom to the top of the plant. Verticillium wilt causes dark streaks under the bark.

Roots or tubers
Spots

◇ Small white mealy spots ⋯→ Potato Tuber Nematode. Potato Cyst Nematode: The nematode initially causes small white mealy spots just below the surface that are only visible if the skin is removed.

Stems
Presence

◇ Coating of gray fungus spores on stems ⋯→ Gray Mold. Grey Mould. Botrytis Blight: Lesions, even cankers, more or less extensive, are visible on the stems, mainly located at the level of pruning and disbudding wounds. Let us add that the lesions are generally covered with a very characteristic grayish to beige mold.

◇ White mold on the stem and collar ⋯→ White Rot. White Mold. Sclerotinia Wilt: Black or dark brown sclerotia form inside the stems. This uncommon disease can sometimes lead to the death of the plant.

Potato

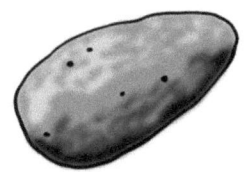

Botanical name
Solanum tuberosum

Class
Solanaceae

English name
Potato

Names in other languages
Pomme de terre (FR), Aardappel (NL), Kartoffel (DE), Patata (IT), Batata (PO), Patata (SP).

Description
Potato (*Solanum tuberosum*) is an herbaceous perennial plant in the family Solanaceae which is grown for its edible tubers. The potato plant has a branched stem and alternately arranged leaves consisting of leaflets which are both of unequal size and shape. The leaflets can be oval to oblong in shape and the leaves can reach 10–30 cm (4–12 in) in length and 5–15 cm (2–6 in) wide. The potato plant produces white or blue flowers and yellow-green berries. The potato tubers grow underground and generally located in the top 25 cm (10 in) of the soil. The tubers can range in color from yellow to red or purple depending on the variety. Potato plants can reach in excess of 1 m (3.3 ft) in height and are grown as annual plants, surviving only one growing season.

Pests
American Serpentine Leaf Miner, Anthracnose, Bacterial Spot, Bean Aphids, Beet Armyworm, Black Scurf, Rhizoctonia Canker, Cabbage Stem Flea Beetle, Cercosporosa Leaf Spot, Click Beetle, Wireworms, Colorado Potato Beetle, Common Swift Moth, Cotton Aphid, Whitefly, Cotton Worm, CMV, Black cutworm, Garden Dart Moth, Glasshouse Potato Foxglove Aphid, Botrytis Blight, Green Peach Aphid, June Beetles, Late Blight, Potato Aphid, PLRV, PVY, Potato Scab, Potato Tuber Nematode, Potato Tuberworm, PVA, PVX, Powdery Mildew, Verticillium Wilt, Sclerotinia Wilt.

Symptoms on:
Flowers
Spots

◇ Blackish-brown spots, which may become covered with grayish mold ⋯⋯ Gray Mold. Grey Mould. Botrytis Blight: Blackish-brown spots, extending from the base of the bracts, which may become covered with grayish mold (fruiting bodies). Sometimes, sclerotia are present. This disease develops secondarily following an injury or other disease.

Leaves
Damage

◇ Leaves with irregular holes ⋯⋯ Colorado Potato Beetle: They are very harmful because of their voracity and the fact that they can consume the entire foliage. The larvae begin to devour the leaves that carry them and then those neighboring up to the top of the plant. Their consumption is very important and rapid.

◇ Perforated leaves ⋯⋯ Cabbage Stem Flea Beetle: It is difficult to monitor the activity of the adult of the large rapeseed flea beetle: it occurs at night. Its damage, on the other hand, is easily recognizable because the insect bites the cotyledons and young leaves in a circular fashion. Perforations can also be observed.

◇ Leaves with irregular holes ⋯⋯ Armyworms, Beet Armyworm: Older Spodoptera exigua caterpillars migrate to the apex of the plants where they feed mainly on the growing areas. They make large holes in the leaves and sometimes leave only the veins behind. The damage caused considerably affects the growth of the plants.

◇ Leaf eaten (irregular holes) ⋯⋯ Cotton Worm. African Cotton Leafworm: The damage caused by caterpillars, which vary in color from gray to reddish or yellowish, is recognizable by the large bites on the leaves.

Deformation

◇ Leaves curled or shrivelled ⋯→ Bean Aphids. Black Dolphin Aphids: Presence of black aphids on the leaves, on the flower stems and the flower heads. As soon as they appear, deformation of the attacked leaves and development of sooty mold.

◇ Leaves curled or shrivelled ⋯→ Green Peach Aphid: Myzus persicae is very polyphagous and, in summer, it has more than forty different families of host plants. The colonies secrete a honeydew that promotes the installation of sooty mold, a fungus that then slows down the photosynthesis of the covered parts. It is the most important aphid vector of viruses.

◇ Leaves curled or shrivelled ⋯→ Cotton Aphid: Aphids, following their nutritional bites, are responsible for chlorotic spots and the deformation of young leaves which tend to roll up and more or less blister.

◇ Leaves shrivelled ⋯→ Potato Leaf-drop Streak. Potato Virus Y : Appearance of nerve necrosis or brown to black necrotic spots on the underside of the leaves. The leaves become brittle and dry out, remaining attached to the plant. Primary infection can also cause a deforming or curled mosaic, often localized on a stem or part of a plant.

◇ Leaves shrivelled ⋯→ Potato Leafroll Virus: The apical leaves are lighter in color and sometimes have an erect habit. The leaflets on the top of the plant are slightly curled inward at the base and show yellowing. We can sometimes note purple pigmentation at the edge of the leaflets.

◇ Leaves curled and deformed ⋯→ Glasshouse Potato Foxglove Aphid: Punctures by the aphids on lower leaves can cause deformations at the apex, with leaves becoming swollen and rolled. The immediate effects of these punctures are visible on lower leaves as yellow spots.

Discoloring

◇ Leaves turn yellow ⋯→ Cotton Whitefly. Tobacco Whitefly: The tobacco whitefly occupies the entire plant. Presence of numerous "white flies" and honeydew, slow growth of plants, development of sooty mold on aerial organs, yellowing and necrosis of the leaf blade.

Galleries

◇ Leaves with galleries ⋯→ South American Miner Fly. South American Leaf Miner: Feeding pits and mined leaves with galleries depreciate the harvest.

◇ Leaves with galleries ⋯→ American Serpentine Leaf Miner: The main damage is due to larvae which mine the leaves. This damage is particularly serious on small plants in nurseries or just transplanted, which can die.

◇ Leaves with galleries ⋯→ Potato Tuberworm. Potato Split-worm. Potato Tuber Moth: Damage to leaves, petioles and stems by perforations and mining which can weaken the plants. Grey felting on the surface.

Lesions

◇ Pale yellow or water-soaked regular or irregular lesions on leaves ⋯→ Anthracnose: Depending on the fungus responsible, these brown or black spots can be circular or irregular, they then appear either on the edge of the leaves or along the veins. The necrotic areas extend more or less concentrically, the limit with healthy tissue being very clear.

Mosaic pattern

◇ Leaves with mosaic pattern ⋯→ Potato Virus A: Infection may be associated with mild, fleeting mosaic symptoms that are visible especially on overcast days. These mosaics are discolorations of certain parts of the leaf, without deformation of the leaf blade and which are not limited by the veins.

◇ Leaves with mosaic pattern ⋯→ Potato Virus X: Contamination in the current year does not cause easily distinguishable symptoms. Only the infection of the previous year expresses them quite clearly with the appearance of mosaics limited by the veins.

Presence

◇ Coating of gray fungus spores on leaves ⋯→ Gray Mold. Grey Mould. Botrytis Blight: Regardless of the organs affected, the dying tissues become covered with a very characteristic dense gray mold, consisting of the conidiophores and conidia of the fungus.

◇ Presence of larvae and adult beetles ⋯→ Colorado Potato Beetle: Check plants every 3-4 days for presence of larvae and adults. It is considered to be the most important insect defoliator of potatoes. It may also cause considerable damage to tomato and aubergine crops with both adults and larvae feeding on the plant's foliage.

◇ White to gray powder coverage on leaves ⋯→ Powdery Mildew, Oidium: The heart leaves are covered with purplish-grey spores on the underside. They thicken, curl, and curl up. Older leaves turn yellow on the outside, then blacken and die. Only a few isolated plants or foci are damaged.

◇ Presence of black aphids ⋯→ Bean Aphids. Black Dolphin Aphids: Presence of black aphids on the leaves, on the flower stems and capitals. As soon as they appear, deformation of the attacked leaves and development of sooty mold.

◇ Presence of aphids ⋯→ Potato Aphid: The most classic symptoms are a curling of heavily infested leaves and a slowdown in the growth of the plants.

◇ Presence of honey dew on leaves ⋯→ Cotton Aphid: In addition to aphid colonies, we often observe white molts and the presence of honeydew on the surface of the aerial organs of zucchini and other plants.

◇ Presence of sooty mould on leaves ⋯→ Cotton Aphid:

◇ Leaves with white/grey felting ⋯→ Late Blight.

Potato and Tomato Late Blight: On the upper side of the leaves, small discolored spots are observed that turn brown and are surrounded by a light green to yellow halo. On the underside, in humid conditions, a characteristic white felting appears.

◊ Presence of aphids ⤳ Glasshouse Potato Foxglove Aphid: Bites on lower leaves can lead to deformations at the apex, with swollen and rolled leaves. Production of honeydew, and presence of colonies. Vector of viruses.

◊ Presence of honey dew on leaves ⤳ Cotton Whitefly. Tobacco Whitefly: The tobacco whitefly occupies the entire plant. Presence of numerous "white flies" and honeydew, slow growth of plants, development of sooty mold on aerial organs, yellowing and necrosis of the leaf blade.

◊ Presence of cutworms ⤳ Garden Dart Moth. Cutworm: The larvae feed on the roots of plants, cutting them at night.

◊ Presence of caterpillars ⤳ Bright-line Brown-eyes Moth: The damage caused by this moth on cabbage and beet leaves is generally not very significant.

◊ Presence of caterpillars ⤳ Cotton Worm. African Cotton Leafworm: The Mediterranean noctuid or cotton worm causes damage which is recognizable by the large portions eaten out of the leaves.

Spots

◊ Yellow/brown spots ⤳ Verticillium Wilt: Marginal drying, sometimes asymmetrical. In the stem, brown lesions at the level of the conductive tissue. Atrophied and deformed capitula.

◊ Yellowish then brown spots on the upper surface of the leaf ⤳ Powdery Mildew, Oidium: Yellowish then brown spots on the upper surface of the leaf, generally limited by the large veins, whitish felting on the lower surface.

◊ Leaf spots with brown-reddish margins ⤳ Cercosporosa Leaf Spot, Cercosporia blight: Cercospora blight initially causes small, oval, gray to tan lesions with red borders. Severe infections may cause entire ferns to turn yellow or brown.

◊ Brown spots surrounded by a halo ⤳ Late Blight. Potato and Tomato Late Blight: On the upper side of the leaves, small discolored spots are observed that turn brown and are surrounded by a light green to yellow halo. On the underside, in humid conditions, a characteristic white felting appears.

◊ Leaves with black spots ⤳ Potato Leaf-drop Streak. Potato Virus Y : Appearance of nerve necrosis or brown to black necrotic spots on the underside of the leaves. The leaves become brittle and dry out, remaining attached to the plant (leaf-drop). Primary infection can also cause a deforming or curled mosaic, often localized on a stem or part of a plant.

Plantlets
Dieback

◊ Damaged cotyledons ⤳ Dark Sword-grass Moth. Black cutworm. Greasy cutworm: Early larval stages feed on the leaves and create small holes with irregular contours. Later stages attack the stem, often during sowing, and consequently cut the seedlings at ground level.

Plants whole
Defoliation

◊ Plants defoliated ⤳ Colorado Potato Beetle: Larvae may defoliate potato plants resulting in yield losses up to 100% if the damage occurs prior to tuber formation. Larvae may consume 40 cm2 of potato leaves during the entire larval stage, but adults are capable of consuming 10 cm2 of foliage per day.

Stunted

◊ Deformation and stunting of plants ⤳ Cucumber Mosaic Virus. CMV: Artichoke latent virus (ALV, Potyvirus) is transmitted by aphids. Cucumber mosaic virus (CMV) induces deformation and stunting of plants.

◊ Stunted plants ⤳ Cabbage Stem Flea Beetle: It is difficult to monitor the activity of the adult of the large rapeseed flea beetle: it occurs at night. Its damage, on the other hand, is easily recognizable because the insect bites the cotyledons and young leaves in a circular fashion. Perforations can also be observed.

◊ Plants stunted ⤳ Potato Leafroll Virus: The size of the plants is reduced, the leaflets at the base are strongly curled and hardened, sometimes with a purple border.

Wilting

◊ Wilting of the entire plant ⤳ Verticillium Wilt: The leaves soften and become duller. The leaves begin to yellow, then turn brown as they become necrotic. The characteristic feature is the asymmetry of the symptoms, with many leaves only affected on one half. The disease progresses from the bottom to the top of the plant. Verticillium wilt causes dark streaks under the bark.

Roots or tubers
Galleries

◊ Galleries in roots ⤳ Click Beetle. Striped Elaterid Beetle. Wireworms: As larvae development takes up to four years, in an infected soil we can find larvae of different ages. They live at different depths, depending on the moment of the year, as they are highly sensitive to heat and dryness. They eat or pierce the underground organs of the plant: roots, crowns, bud leaves and turions.

◊ Tubers with galleries ⤳ Potato Tuberworm. Potato Split-worm. Potato Tuber Moth: Tubers with more or less superficial galleries often lined with silk threads and blackish excrement.

Lesions

◊ Brown lesions on tubers ⤳ Bacterial Spot: Reddish browning of the vascular ring, visible after cutting the tubers. A beige/brown rot then develops at the level of this vascular ring and the tuber ends up decomposing.

◇ Dark brown or black canker on tubers ⸱⸱⸱→ Black Scurf. Rhizoctonia Canker. Stem Canker. Crater spot: More or less extensive, rather moist, reddish-brown root lesions, becoming superficially corky.

Presence

◇ Grubs present in the soil ⸱⸱⸱→ June Beetles, May Beetles, Chafer beetles: The adults are phyllophagous and the larvae burrowd in the soil, called "white grubs", are root-eating. They deform the roots and cause the plant to wilt.

◇ Warty patches on tuber surface ⸱⸱⸱→ Potato Scab: Symptoms of common scab are formation of pustules and cork on the tubers surface.

Spots

◇ Small white mealy spots ⸱⸱⸱→ Potato Tuber Nematode. Potato Cyst Nematode: The nematode initially causes small white mealy spots just below the surface that are only visible if the skin is removed.

Wilting

◇ Wilted plants ⸱⸱⸱→ Tuber Rot: Dark depressed areas may be observed on tubers, characterised by blackish mark spots which are frequently found around the wounds, the eyes, the lenticels.

Stems
Dieback

◇ Damaged stems ⸱⸱⸱→ Dark Sword-grass Moth. Black cutworm. Greasy cutworm: Early larval stages feed on the leaves and create small holes with irregular contours. Later stages attack the stem, often during sowing, and consequently cut the seedlings at ground level.

Lesions

◇ Reddish and brown lesions ⸱⸱⸱→ Black Scurf. Rhizoctonia Canker. Stem Canker. Crater spot: Presence of reddish and brown lesion at the collar.

Presence

◇ Coating of gray fungus spores on stems ⸱⸱⸱→ Gray Mold. Grey Mould. Botrytis Blight: Lesions, even cankers, more or less extensive, are visible on the stems, mainly located at the level of pruning and disbudding wounds. Let us add that the lesions are generally covered with a very characteristic grayish to beige mold.

◇ White mold on the stem and collar ⸱⸱⸱→ White Rot. White Mold. Sclerotinia Wilt: Black or dark brown sclerotia form inside the stems. This uncommon disease can sometimes lead to the death of the plant.

◇ Presence of caterpillars ⸱⸱⸱→ Common Swift Moth. Garden Swift Moth: The roots and collars are eaten away, which leads to the gradual drying out of the plant.

Pumpkin

Botanical name
Cucurbita maxima, Cucurbita moschata

Class
Cucurbitaceae

English name
Pumpkin, Squash.

Names in other languages
Potiron (FR), Pompoen (NL), Risen-Kürbis (DE), Zucca (IT), Abóbora-menina (PO), Calabaza (SP).

Description
Pumpkin is the name given to a group of plant species in the genus Cucurbita, including *Cucurbita pepo*, *Cucurbita mixta*, *Cucurbita maxima*, and *Cucurbita moschata*. Pumpkin belongs to the family Cucurbitaceae and is grown primarily as a vegetable or ornamental plant. Pumpkin plants are short lived annual or perennial vines with branching tendrils and broad lobed leaves. The plant produces large yellow or orange flowers and a pepo fruit (berry with a thick rind) known as a pumpkin. The fruit can range greatly in size, from miniature pumpkins weighing a few ounces to giant pumpkins which can reach over 75 lbs (34 kg). The skin of the pumpkin is usually ribbed and is usually orange on color although some varieties are green, grey, yellow or red in color. Pumpkin plants are usually grown as annuals.

Pests
Anthracnose Fruit Rot, Celery Late Blight, Cotton Aphid, CMV, Damping Off, Early Blight of Potato/Tomato, Fusarium Root Rot, Fusarium Wilt, Gray Mold, Botrytis Blight, Thrips, Powdery Mildew, Red Spider Mite, Scab of Cucurbits, Verticillium Wilt, White Rot, White Mold, Sclerotinia Wilt.

Symptoms on:
Flowers
Spots

◇ Blackish-brown spots, which may become covered with grayish mold ⤳ Gray Mold. Grey Mould. Botrytis Blight: Blackish-brown spots, extending from the base of the bracts, which may become covered with grayish mold (fruiting bodies). Sometimes, sclerotia are present. This disease develops secondarily following an injury or other disease.

Fruits
Spots

◇ Hollow, brown spot with yellow halo ⤳ Scab of Cucurbits: Small moist lesions appear on the leaves, often the youngest. These lesions gradually expand to form more or less circular spots, turning brown and necrotic as they age. They can sometimes take on a grayish tint and be surrounded by a more or less large yellow halo.

Leaves
Deformation

◇ Curled leaves ⤳ Celery Late Blight: The disease first manifests itself by the appearance of small light brown spots on the foliage. In case of severe attacks, the petioles turn yellow, the leaves curl up and dry out.

◇ Leaves curled or shrivelled ⤳ Cotton Aphid: Aphids, following their nutritional bites, are responsible for chlorotic spots and the deformation of young leaves which tend to roll up and more or less blister.

Discoloring

◇ Leaves turn yellow and wilt ⤳ Fusarium Wilt: An affected plant has a yellowing, stunted, wilted appearance, sometimes with gummosis on the stem. Discoloration and vascular browning of the collar progressing towards the stem and roots, and developing into cortical rot.

◇ Silvery marks on leaves ⋯→ Onion Thrips. Thrips: In a greenhouse, colonies can be very developed and direct damage is often significant. The larvae and adults of the tobacco and onion thrips puncture the contents of the subepidermal cells. The infested leaves are then dotted with numerous silver spots corresponding to groups of emptied cells. This symptom is typically associated with the presence of small piles of black feces.

◇ Leaves discoulouring bronzed or silvery ⋯→ Red Spider Mite. Two-spotted Mite: They damage the plant by piercing its cells to feed on them. The leaves turn pale and become stained yellow. To protect themselves and improve their microclimate, they weave a web around the leaf. A strong attack of mites leads to the leaves rolling and drying out, then falling off.

Lesions

◇ Circular, brown, and necrotic lesions on leaves ⋯→ Early Blight of Potato/Tomato: Small yellow spots rapidly turning black-brown, necrotic, circular and sharply outlined, approximately 5 mm in diameter, which gradually expand concentrically.

◇ Pale yellow or water-soaked regular or irregular lesions on leaves ⋯→ Anthracnose: Depending on the fungus responsible, these brown or black spots can be circular or irregular, they then appear either on the edge of the leaves or along the veins. The necrotic areas extend more or less concentrically, the limit with healthy tissue being very clear.

Presence

◇ Coating of gray fungus spores on leaves ⋯→ Gray Mold. Grey Mould. Botrytis Blight: Regardless of the organs affected, the dying tissues become covered with a very characteristic dense gray mold, consisting of the conidiophores and conidia of the fungus.

◇ White to gray powder coverage on leaves ⋯→ Powdery Mildew, Oidium: The heart leaves are covered with purplish-grey spores on the underside. They thicken, curl, and curl up. Older leaves turn yellow on the outside, then blacken and die. Only a few isolated plants or foci are damaged.

◇ Presence of honey dew on leaves ⋯→ Cotton Aphid: In addition to aphid colonies, we often observe white molts and the presence of honeydew on the surface of the aerial organs of zucchini and other plants.

◇ Presence of sooty mould on leaves ⋯→ Cotton Aphid: In addition to aphid colonies, we often observe white molts and the presence of honeydew on the surface of the aerial organs on which sooty mold develops. Remember that the latter can have several consequences, including a reduction in photosynthesis and leaf respiration and soiling of fruits thus rendered unmarketable.

◇ Leaves with fine silk webbing ⋯→ Red Spider Mite. Two-spotted Mite: They damage the plant by piercing its cells to feed on them. The leaves turn pale and become stained yellow. To protect themselves and improve their microclimate, they weave a web around the leaf. A strong attack of mites leads to the leaves rolling and drying out, then falling off.

◇ Presence of red spider mites, cast skins and egg shells ⋯→ Red Spider Mite. Two-spotted Mite: Spider mites always leave behind cast skins and egg shells.

Spots

◇ Yellow/brown spots ⋯→ Verticillium Wilt: Marginal drying, sometimes asymmetrical. In the stem, brown lesions at the level of the conductive tissue. Atrophied and deformed capitula.

◇ Yellowish then brown spots on the upper surface of the leaf ⋯→ Powdery Mildew, Oidium: Yellowish then brown spots on the upper surface of the leaf, generally limited by the large veins, whitish felting on the lower surface.

◇ Leaves with angular spots ⋯→ Scab of Cucurbits: Small, necrotic brown spots appear on the leaves. They can also be grayish, brown on the periphery, sometimes angular, surrounded by a yellow halo. Brown nerve necroses also form.

Plantlets
Wilting

◇ Wilted, collapsed and dead young seedlings ⋯→ Damping Off: Seeds rot and fail to germinate, or even germinate, but seedlings fail to grow. A translucent area completely covers the stem near the soil surface. The affected tissues rot, leading to wilting and collapse of the seedlings.

Plants whole
Stunted

◇ Deformation and stunting of plants ⋯→ Cucumber Mosaic Virus. CMV: Artichoke latent virus (ALV, Potyvirus) is transmitted by aphids. Cucumber mosaic virus (CMV) induces deformation and stunting of plants.

◇ Plants stunted ⋯→ Fusarium Root Rot: Diseased plants wilt to a greater or lesser extent during the hottest times of the day; this wilting is sometimes reversible. In the most serious cases, the plants eventually dry out completely.

Wilting

◇ Wilting of the entire plant ⋯→ Verticillium Wilt: The leaves soften and become duller. The leaves begin to yellow, then turn brown as they become necrotic. The characteristic feature is the asymmetry of the symptoms, with many leaves only affected on one half. The disease progresses from the bottom to the top of the plant. Verticillium wilt causes dark streaks under the bark.

Roots or tubers
Decay

◇ Rotting of roots ⋯→ Fusarium Root Rot: The cause of these wilting is to be found at the level of the collar of the feet. At this location, a wet lesion has developed, a rot that has gradually spread to the lower part of the stem and the taproot, but also to the upper part of the root system. At the collar, the altered tissues are wet and show a dark to brownish tint. This lesion ends up girdling the stem for several centimetres. The roots located in the same layer of soil are also affected. Their cortex turns yellow, brown and decomposes.

Stems
Lesions

◇ Reddish and brown lesions ⋯→ Black Scurf. Rhizoctonia Canker. Stem Canker. Crater spot: Presence of reddish and brown lesion at the collar.

Necrosis

◇ Necrotic stems ⋯→ Fusarium Wilt: An affected plant has a yellowing, stunted, wilted appearance, sometimes with gummosis on the stem. Discoloration and vascular browning of the collar progressing towards the stem and roots, and developing into cortical rot.

Presence

◇ Coating of gray fungus spores on stems ⋯→ Gray Mold. Grey Mould. Botrytis Blight: Lesions, even cankers, more or less extensive, are visible on the stems, mainly located at the level of pruning and disbudding wounds. Let us add that the lesions are generally covered with a very characteristic grayish to beige mold.

◇ White mold on the stem and collar ⋯→ White Rot. White Mold. Sclerotinia Wilt: Black or dark brown sclerotia form inside the stems. This uncommon disease can sometimes lead to the death of the plant.

Radish

Botanical name
Raphanus sativus

Class
Brassicaceae

English name
Radish, Spring radish.

Names in other languages
Radis (FR), Radijs (NL), Rettich (DE), Rafano (IT), Rabanete (PO), Rábano (SP).

Related plants
Daikon (*Raphanus sativus var. longipinnatus*), Black radish (*Raphanus sativus var. niger*).

Description
Radish (*Raphanus sativus*) is an herbaceous annual or biennial plant in the family Brassicaceae, grown for its edible taproot. The radish plant has a short hairy stem and a rosette of oblong shaped leaves which measure 5–30 cm (2–12 in) in length. The taproot of the plant is cylindrical or tapering and commonly red or white in color. The radish plant produces multiple purple or pink flowers on racemes which produce 2–12 seeds. Radish is generally grown as an annual plant, surviving only one growing season and can reach 20–100 cm (8–39 in) in height depending on the variety.

Pests
Early Blight of Potato/Tomato, Damping Off, Dark Sword-grass Moth, Black cutworm, Greasy cutworm, Cabbage Maggot, Cabbage Stem Flea Beetle, Cabbage Aphid, Downy Mildew of Crucifers, Powdery Mildew, Turnip Gall Weevil, Cabbageworm, Turnip Maggot, Turnip Root Fly, Cabbage Fly, Cabbage Root Fly, Cabbage Bug, Crucifer Shield Bug, Brassica Bug.

Symptoms on:
Leaves
Damage

◇ Perforated leaves ⋯→ Cabbage Stem Flea Beetle: It is difficult to monitor the activity of the adult of the large rapeseed flea beetle: it occurs at night. Its damage, on the other hand, is easily recognizable because the insect bites the cotyledons and young leaves in a circular fashion. Perforations can also be observed.

◇ Leaves with holes ⋯→ Cabbageworm. Imported Cabbage Worms: Caterpillars devour the leaves of cruciferous plants, sometimes leaving only the large veins. In addition, their excrement, diluted by rain or dew, accumulates in the heart of the plant and makes it inedible.

Deformation

◇ Leaves curled or shrivelled ⋯→ Cabbage Aphid: In the event of an outbreak, the plant can be completely covered by aphids, their honeydew and their exuviae.

Discoloring

◇ Bleached leaves ⋯→ Cabbage Bug. Rape Bug. Crucifer Shield Bug. Brassica Bug: With their piercing-sucking apparatus, the larvae and adults feed by sucking the sap, which causes the leaves to turn white and slows down the growth of the cabbage. The very large number of punctures on the leaves of young plants can lead to the death of the host plant.

Lesions

◇ Purple or brown irregular shaped areas on leaves ⋯→ Downy Mildew of Crucifers: It first appears on older leaves, as white, yellow or brownish spots on the upper surfaces and downy grayish mold on the corresponding undersides.

◇ Brownish black lesions on leaves ⋯→ Early Blight of Potato/Tomato: Affected leaves and petioles turn yellow, then brown or black. Leaflets shrivel at the edges, and in severe infections the entire leaf wilts and dies.

Presence

◇ Presence of colonies of aphids ⸱⸱⸱→ Cabbage Aphid: In the event of an outbreak, the plant can be completely covered by aphids, their honeydew and their exuviae.

◇ White to gray, "downy" areas on under leaf surfaces. ⸱⸱⸱→ Downy Mildew of Crucifers: It first appears on older leaves, as white, yellow or brownish spots on the upper surfaces and downy grayish mold on the corresponding undersides.

◇ White to gray powder coverage on leaves ⸱⸱⸱→ Powdery Mildew, Oidium: The heart leaves are covered with purplish-grey spores on the underside. They thicken, curl, and curl up. Older leaves turn yellow on the outside, then blacken and die. Only a few isolated plants or foci are damaged.

◇ Presence of caterpillars ⸱⸱⸱→ Cabbageworm. Imported Cabbage Worms: Caterpillars devour the leaves of cruciferous plants, sometimes leaving only the large veins. In addition, their excrement, diluted by rain or dew, accumulates in the heart of the plant and makes it inedible.

◇ Presence of honeydew and sooty moulds on leaves ⸱⸱⸱→ Cabbage Aphid: In the event of an outbreak, the plant can be completely covered by aphids, their honeydew and their exuviae.

◇ Presence of bugs ⸱⸱⸱→ Cabbage Bug. Rape Bug. Crucifer Shield Bug. Brassica Bug: Presence of the adult insect and larva on leaves. Presence of eggs on the underside of the leaves. Observe the leaves to see the appearance of white spots. Be careful not to confuse these bugs with other red and black bugs such as Pyrrhocoris apterus, better known as the "firebug". These do not cause any damage to cabbage.

Spots

◇ Yellowish then brown spots on the upper surface of the leaf ⸱⸱⸱→ Powdery Mildew, Oidium: Yellowish then brown spots on the upper surface of the leaf, generally limited to the large veins, whitish felting on the lower surface.

Plantlets
Dieback

◇ Damaged cotyledons ⸱⸱⸱→ Dark Sword-grass Moth. Black cutworm. Greasy cutworm: Early larval stages feed on the leaves and create small holes with irregular contours. Later stages attack the stem, often during sowing, and consequently cut the seedlings at ground level.

Wilting

◇ Wilted, collapsed and dead young seedlings ⸱⸱⸱→ Damping Off: Seeds rot and fail to germinate, or even germinate, but seedlings fail to grow. A translucent area completely covers the stem near the soil surface. The affected tissues rot, leading to wilting and collapse of the seedlings.

Plants whole
Stunted

◇ Stunted plants ⸱⸱⸱→ Cabbage Stem Flea Beetle: It is difficult to monitor the activity of the adult of the large rapeseed flea beetle: it occurs at night. Its damage, on the other hand, is easily recognizable because the insect bites the cotyledons and young leaves in a circular fashion. Perforations can also be observed.

Roots or tubers
Deformation

◇ Swelling of roots ⸱⸱⸱→ Turnip Gall Weevil: The substances introduced at the time of egg laying and the larval secretions cause an enlargement of the collar or gall, which can reach 2 to 3 cm in diameter in cabbage.

Presence

◇ Presence of maggots in roots ⸱⸱⸱→ Cabbage Maggot, Cabbage Fly: The larvae of the cabbage fly penetrate into the fleshy parts and dig galleries. The root part is more or less destroyed. Attacked plants can be recognized by the faded appearance they take on during hot days; the leaves often turn purplish red, turn yellow and sometimes dry out.

◇ Roots with presence of maggots ⸱⸱⸱→ Turnip Maggot. Turnip Root Fly: On root vegetables, the larvae dig galleries that can go up to the petiole of the leaves and make the vegetable unfit for consumption. When the attack is massive, the plants stop growing, take on a leaden color and lack turgidity; little by little, they turn yellow and die.

Stems
Dieback

◇ Damaged stems ⸱⸱⸱→ Dark Sword-grass Moth. Black cutworm. Greasy cutworm: Early larval stages feed on the leaves and create small holes with irregular contours. Later stages attack the stem, often during sowing, and consequently cut the seedlings at ground level.

Romanesco Broccoli

Botanical name
Brassica oleracea var. botrytis

Class
Brassicaceae

English name
Romanesco, Romanesco broccoli, Roman cauliflower.

Names in other languages
Chou romanesco (FR), Romanesco (DE), Romanesco-broccoli (NL). Broccolo romanesco (IT), Brécol romanesco (SP).

Description
The Romanesco cauliflower (*Brassica oleracea var. botrytis*) belong to the family Brassicaceae. It superficially resembles a cauliflower, but it flowerhead is green in color, and its form is strikingly fractal, a pattern that endlessly repeats itself. The flavour is similar to that of cauliflower, but is milder, nuttier and has a crunchier texture.

Pests
Gray Mold, Grey Mould. Botrytis Blight, Early Blight of Potato/Tomato, Damping Off, Dark Sword-grass Moth, Black cutworm, Greasy cutworm, Cabbage Maggot, Cabbage Club Root, Cabbage Stem Flea Beetle, Cabbage Aphid, Downy Mildew of Crucifers, Turnip Gall Weevil, Cabbageworm, Imported Cabbage Worms.

Symptoms on:
Leaves
Damage

◇ Perforated leaves ⋯→ Cabbage Stem Flea Beetle: It is difficult to monitor the activity of the adult of the large rapeseed flea beetle: it occurs at night. Its damage, on the other hand, is easily recognizable because the insect bites the cotyledons and young leaves in a circular fashion. Perforations can also be observed.

◇ Leaves with holes ⋯→ Cabbageworm. Imported Cabbage Worms: Caterpillars devour the leaves of cruciferous plants, sometimes leaving only the large veins. In addition, their excrement, diluted by rain or dew, accumulates in the heart of the plant and makes it inedible.

Deformation

◇ Leaves curled or shrivelled ⋯→ Cabbage Aphid: In the event of an outbreak, the plant can be completely covered by aphids, their honeydew and their exuviae.

Discoloring

◇ Reddening, yellowing of the leaves ⋯→ Cabbage Club Root: Aerial part of the plant: reduced development, especially during early attacks, wilting or even reddening of the foliage.

Lesions

◇ Purple or brown irregular shaped areas on leaves ⋯→ Downy Mildew of Crucifers: It first appears on older leaves, as white, yellow or brownish spots on the upper surfaces and downy grayish mold on the corresponding undersides.

◇ Brownish black lesions on leaves ⋯→ Early Blight of Potato/Tomato: Affected leaves and petioles turn yellow, then brown or black. Leaflets shrivel at the edges, and in severe infections the entire leaf wilts and dies.

Presence

◇ Coating of gray fungus spores on leaves ⋯→ Gray Mold. Grey Mould. Botrytis Blight: Regardless of the organs affected, the dying tissues become covered with a very characteristic dense gray mold, consisting of the conidiophores and conidia of the fungus.

◇ Presence of colonies of aphids ⋯→ Cabbage Aphid: In the event of an outbreak, the plant can be completely covered by aphids, their honeydew and their exuviae.

◇ White to gray, "downy" areas on under leaf surfaces. ⋯→ Downy Mildew of Crucifers: It first appears on older leaves, as white, yellow or brownish spots on the upper surfaces and downy grayish mold on the corresponding undersides.

◇ Presence of caterpillars ⋯→ Cabbageworm. Imported Cabbage Worms: Caterpillars devour the leaves of cruciferous plants, sometimes leaving only the large veins. In addition, their excrement, diluted by rain or dew, accumulates in the heart of the plant and makes it inedible.

◇ Presence of honeydew and sooty moulds on leaves ⋯→ Cabbage Aphid: In the event of an outbreak, the plant can be completely covered by aphids, their honeydew and their exuviae.

Plantlets
Dieback

◇ Damaged cotyledons ⋯→ Dark Sword-grass Moth. Black cutworm. Greasy cutworm: Early larval stages feed on the leaves and create small holes with irregular contours. Later stages attack the stem, often during sowing, and consequently cut the seedlings at ground level.

Wilting

◇ Wilted, collapsed and dead young seedlings ⋯→ Damping Off: Seeds rot and fail to germinate, or even germinate, but seedlings fail to grow. A translucent area completely covers the stem near the soil surface. The affected tissues rot, leading to wilting and collapse of the seedlings.

Plants whole
Stunted

◇ Stunted plants ⋯→ Cabbage Stem Flea Beetle: It is difficult to monitor the activity of the adult of the large rapeseed flea beetle: it occurs at night. Its damage, on the other hand, is easily recognizable because the insect bites the cotyledons and young leaves in a circular fashion. Perforations can also be observed.

Wilting

◇ Wilted plants ⋯→ Cabbage Maggot, Cabbage Fly: Damage is observed in nurseries and at all stages of vegetation. On leafy vegetables, the root part is more or less destroyed. Attacked plants can be recognized by the faded appearance they take on during hot days; the leaves often turn purplish red, turn yellow and sometimes dry out.

◇ Wilted plants ⋯→ Cabbage Club Root: Underground part of the plant: root deformation or presence of galls on the roots. These galls are firm (full interior), whitish then turn brown and rot, leading to the death of the plant.

Roots or tubers
Deformation

◇ Roots abnormally increased or swellings ⋯→ Cabbage Club Root: Underground part of the plant: root deformation or presence of galls on the roots. These galls are firm (full interior), whitish then turn brown and rot, leading to the death of the plant.

◇ Swelling of roots ⋯→ Turnip Gall Weevil: The substances introduced at the time of egg laying and the larval secretions cause an enlargement of the collar or gall, which can reach 2 to 3 cm in diameter in cabbage.

Presence

◇ Presence of maggots in roots ⋯→ Cabbage Maggot, Cabbage Fly: The larvae of the cabbage fly penetrate into the fleshy parts and dig galleries. The root part is more or less destroyed. Attacked plants can be recognized by the faded appearance they take on during hot days; the leaves often turn purplish red, turn yellow and sometimes dry out.

Stems
Dieback

◇ Damaged stems ⋯→ Dark Sword-grass Moth. Black cutworm. Greasy cutworm: Early larval stages feed on the leaves and create small holes with irregular contours. Later stages attack the stem, often during sowing, and consequently cut the seedlings at ground level.

Rutabaga

Botanical name
Brassica napus subsp. *rapifera*

Class
Brassicaceae

English name
Rutabaga. Swede

Names in other languages
Chou-navet. Rutabaga (FR), Koolraap (NL), Kohlrübe (DE), Cavolo navone (IT), Nabo (PO), Colinabo (SP).

Description
Rutabaga (*Brassica napus*) is an herbaceous biennial in the family Brassicaceae grown primarily for its edible root. The leaves grow from a stout swollen stem (neck) close to the ground forming the crown. Rutabaga leaves are thick smooth and waxy. They are lobed and have a bluish hue. The plant produces light yellow flowers which are clustered at the top of a raceme. The taproot of the plant is is a bulbous tuber, almost perfectly round, which can be purple, white or yellow with yellow flesh. Rutabaga plants can reach in height of 30–46 cm (12–18 in) and although biennial, they are commonly grown as an annual, harvested after one growing season.

Pests
Gray Mold, Grey Mould, Botrytis Blight, Damping Off, Rust, Dark Sword-grass Moth, Black cutworm, Greasy cutworm, Cabbage Maggot, Cabbage Club Root, Cabbage Stem Flea Beetle, Cabbage Aphid, Downy Mildew of Crucifers, Slug and Snail, Garden Slug, Loach, Little Grey Slug, Vine Snail, White Garden Snail, Cabbageworm, Imported Cabbage Worms, Cabbage Bug, Rape Bug, Crucifer Shield Bug, Brassica Bug.

Symptoms on:
Leaves
Damage

◇ Perforated leaves ⋯⋅→ Cabbage Stem Flea Beetle: It is difficult to monitor the activity of the adult of the large rapeseed flea beetle: it occurs at night. Its damage, on the other hand, is easily recognizable because the insect bites the cotyledons and young leaves in a circular fashion. Perforations can also be observed.

◇ Leaves with perforations ⋯⋅→ Slug and Snail. Garden Slug. Loach. Little Grey Slug. Vine Snail. White Garden Snail: The slug consumes the leaves of plants between the veins, which gives them a serrated appearance. It digs small holes in the tubers. When the attack is serious, the stems are cut and consumed, the plants disappear.

◇ Leaves with holes ⋯⋅→ Cabbageworm. Imported Cabbage Worms: Caterpillars devour the leaves of cruciferous plants, sometimes leaving only the large veins. In addition, their excrement, diluted by rain or dew, accumulates in the heart of the plant and makes it inedible.

Deformation

◇ Leaves curled or shrivelled ⋯⋅→ Cabbage Aphid: In the event of an outbreak, the plant can be completely covered by aphids, their honeydew and their exuviae.

Discoloring

◇ Reddening, yellowing of the leaves ⋯⋅→ Cabbage Club Root: Aerial part of the plant: reduced development, especially during early attacks, wilting or even reddening of the foliage.

◇ Bleached leaves ⋯⋅→ Cabbage Bug. Rape Bug. Crucifer Shield Bug. Brassica Bug: With their piercing-sucking apparatus, the larvae and adults feed by sucking the sap, which causes the leaves to turn white and slows down the growth of the cabbage. The very large number of punctures on the leaves of young plants can lead to the death of the host plant.

Lesions

◇ Purple or brown irregular shaped areas on leaves ⋯▸ Downy Mildew of Crucifers: It first appears on older leaves, as white, yellow or brownish spots on the upper surfaces and downy grayish mold on the corresponding undersides.

Presence

◇ Coating of gray fungus spores on leaves ⋯▸ Gray Mold. Grey Mould. Botrytis Blight: Regardless of the organs affected, the dying tissues become covered with a very characteristic dense gray mold, consisting of the conidiophores and conidia of the fungus.

◇ Presence of colonies of aphids ⋯▸ Cabbage Aphid: In the event of an outbreak, the plant can be completely covered by aphids, their honeydew and their exuviae.

◇ White to gray, "downy" areas on under leaf surfaces. ⋯▸ Downy Mildew of Crucifers: It first appears on older leaves, as white, yellow or brownish spots on the upper surfaces and downy grayish mold on the corresponding undersides.

◇ Slime trails ⋯▸ Slug and Snail. Garden Slug. Loach. Little Grey Slug. Vine Snail. White Garden Snail: Slime trail' that signals their presence.

◇ Presence of caterpillars ⋯▸ Cabbageworm. Imported Cabbage Worms: Caterpillars devour the leaves of cruciferous plants, sometimes leaving only the large veins. In addition, their excrement, diluted by rain or dew, accumulates in the heart of the plant and makes it inedible.

◇ Presence of honeydew and sooty moulds on leaves ⋯▸ Cabbage Aphid: In the event of an outbreak, the plant can be completely covered by aphids, their honeydew and their exuviae.

◇ Presence of bugs ⋯▸ Cabbage Bug. Rape Bug. Crucifer Shield Bug. Brassica Bug: Presence of the adult insect and larva on leaves. Presence of eggs on the underside of the leaves. Observe the leaves to see the appearance of white spots. Be careful not to confuse these bugs with other red and black bugs such as Pyrrhocoris apterus, better known as the "firebug". These do not cause any damage to cabbage.

Spots

◇ Reddish-orange spots on leaves ⋯▸ Rust: On the upper side of the leaves, you will see tiny white, orange or even brown spots appear depending on the species. If you turn these leaves over, you will see that these spots correspond to tiny pustules of the same color. The lesions are generally yellow, brown or red, but can be dark brown or black at the end of the season.

Plantlets
Dieback

◇ Damaged cotyledons ⋯▸ Dark Sword-grass Moth. Black cutworm. Greasy cutworm: Early

larval stages feed on the leaves and create small holes with irregular contours. Later stages attack the stem, often during sowing, and consequently cut the seedlings at ground level.

Wilting

◇ Wilted, collapsed and dead young seedlings ⋯▸ Damping Off: Seeds rot and fail to germinate, or even germinate, but seedlings fail to grow. A translucent area completely covers the stem near the soil surface. The affected tissues rot, leading to wilting and collapse of the seedlings.

Plants whole
Stunted

◇ Stunted plants ⋯▸ Cabbage Stem Flea Beetle: It is difficult to monitor the activity of the adult of the large rapeseed flea beetle: it occurs at night. Its damage, on the other hand, is easily recognizable because the insect bites the cotyledons and young leaves in a circular fashion. Perforations can also be observed.

Wilting

◇ Wilted plants ⋯▸ Cabbage Maggot, Cabbage Fly: Damage is observed in nurseries and at all stages of vegetation. On leafy vegetables, the root part is more or less destroyed. Attacked plants can be recognized by the faded appearance they take on during hot days; the leaves often turn purplish red, turn yellow and sometimes dry out.

◇ Wilted plants ⋯▸ Cabbage Club Root: Underground part of the plant: root deformation or presence of galls on the roots. These galls are firm (full interior), whitish then turn brown and rot, leading to the death of the plant.

Roots or tubers
Deformation

◇ Roots abnormally increased or swellings ⋯▸ Cabbage Club Root: Underground part of the plant: root deformation or presence of galls on the roots. These galls are firm (full interior), whitish then turn brown and rot, leading to the death of the plant.

Presence

◇ Presence of maggots in roots ⋯▸ Cabbage Maggot, Cabbage Fly: The larvae of the cabbage fly penetrate into the fleshy parts and dig galleries. The root part is more or less destroyed. Attacked plants can be recognized by the faded appearance they take on during hot days; the leaves often turn purplish red, turn yellow and sometimes dry out.

Stems
Dieback

◇ Damaged stems ⋯▸ Dark Sword-grass Moth. Black cutworm. Greasy cutworm: Early larval stages feed on the leaves and create small holes with irregular contours. Later stages attack the stem, often during sowing, and consequently cut the seedlings at ground level.

Spinach

Botanical name
Spinacia oleracea

Class
Chenopodiaceae/Amaranthaceae

English name
Spinach

Names in other languages
Epinard (FR), Spinazie (NL), Spinat (DE), Spinacio (IT), Espinaca (PO), Espinaca (SP).

Description
Spinach (*Spinacia oleracea)* is a leafy herbaceous annual plant in the family Amaranthaceae (formerly in Chenopodiaceae) grown for its leaves which are used as a vegetable. The spinach plant has simple leaves which stem from the centre of the plant and measure about 2–30 cm (0.8–12.0 in) long and 1 to 15 cm (0.4–6.0 in) across. The leaves grow in a rosette and can appear crinkled or flat. The plant produces small yellow-green flowers which are 3–4 mm (0.1 in) in diameter. The flowers produce small fruit clusters which contain seeds. Spinach is an annual and survives only one growing season and can reach 30 cm (12 in) in height.

Pests
Damping Off, Seedcorn Maggot, Bean Seed Fly, Anthracnose Fruit Rot, Beet Fly, Mangold Fly, Dark Sword-grass Moth, Black cutworm, Greasy cutworm, June Beetles, May Beetles, Click Beetle, Wireworms, Powdery Mildew, Fusarium Wilt, Green Peach Aphid, Slug and Snail, Cladosporium Leaf Spot, CMV, BCTV, Silver-Y moth, Common Silver-Y moth, Cabbage Army Moth, Downy mildew, Bleu Mold.

Symptoms on:
Leaves
Damage

◇ Leaves with perforations ⋯→ Slug and Snail. Garden Slug. Loach. Little Grey Slug. Vine Snail. White Garden Snail: The slug consumes the leaves of plants between the veins, which gives them a serrated appearance. It digs small holes in the tubers. When the attack is serious, the stems are cut and consumed, the plants disappear.

◇ Leaves with perforations ⋯→ Silver-Y moth. Common Silver-Y moth. Cabbage Army Moth.: The caterpillar is active mainly at night, it devours the leaf blades and cuts the petioles. During the day, it remains attached to the underside of the leaves.

Deformation

◇ Leaves curled or shrivelled ⋯→ Green Peach Aphid: Myzus persicae is very polyphagous and, in summer, it has more than forty different families of host plants. The colonies secrete a honeydew that promotes the installation of sooty mold, a fungus that then slows down the photosynthesis of the covered parts. It is the most important aphid vector of viruses.

Discoloring

◇ Leaves discoulouring yellowish ⋯→ June Beetles, May Beetles, Chafer beetles: The adults are phyllophagous and the larvae, called "white grubs" are root-eating. They deform the roots and cause the plant to wilt.

◇ Leaves turn yellow and wilt ⋯→ Fusarium Wilt: An affected plant has a yellowing, stunted, wilted appearance, sometimes with gummosis on the stem. Discoloration and vascular browning of the collar progressing towards the stem and roots, and developing into cortical rot.

◇ Leaves turn yellow and wilt ⋯→ Beet Curly Top Virus. BCTV: Leaf curling and embossing, irregular and prominent veins are observed. Plants are sometimes stunted. Leaves are occasionally rough and eventually turn yellow.

Galleries
- ◇ Leaves with galleries ⋯▸ Beet Fly. Mangold Fly: The first generation beet fly larvae are the most harmful: they penetrate the leaves, between the two epidermis, and devour part of the tissue responsible for photosynthesis. They then dig galleries: whitish sinuosities can be observed. These galleries cause the leaves to dry out, turn brown, become pierced and lose their photosynthetic capacity.

Lesions
- ◇ Pale yellow or water-soaked regular or irregular lesions on leaves ⋯▸ Anthracnose: Depending on the fungus responsible, these brown or black spots can be circular or irregular, they then appear either on the edge of the leaves or along the veins. The necrotic areas extend more or less concentrically, the limit with healthy tissue being very clear.
- ◇ Brown lesions on leaves ⋯▸ Beet Fly. Mangold Fly: The first generation beet fly larvae are the most harmful: they penetrate the leaves, between the two epidermis, and devour part of the tissue responsible for photosynthesis. They then dig galleries: whitish sinuosities can be observed. These galleries cause the leaves to dry out, turn brown, become pierced and lose their photosynthetic capacity.

Presence
- ◇ White to gray powder coverage on leaves ⋯▸ Powdery Mildew, Oidium: The heart leaves are covered with purplish-grey spores on the underside. They thicken, curl, and curl up. Older leaves turn yellow on the outside, then blacken and die. Only a few isolated plants or foci are damaged.
- ◇ Presence of caterpillars ⋯▸ Silver-Y moth. Common Silver-Y moth. Cabbage Army Moth.: The caterpillar is active mainly at night, it devours the leaf blades and cuts the petioles. During the day, it remains attached to the underside of the leaves.

Spots
- ◇ Yellowish then brown spots on the upper surface of the leaf ⋯▸ Powdery Mildew, Oidium: Yellowish then brown spots on the upper surface of the leaf, generally limited by the large veins, whitish felting on the lower surface.
- ◇ Brown circular spots ⋯▸ Cladosporium Leaf Spot: Cladosporium leaf spot is characterized by round, tan leaf spots that rarely exceed 1 - 3 mm in diameter. Dark green spores and mycelium later develop in the centers of these spots.
- ◇ Leaves with yellow-brown spots ⋯▸ Downy mildew. Spinach Downy Mildew. Bleu Mold: Slightly yellow, irregular chlorotic lesions on leaves. Lesions can expand, become necrotic and/or desiccate. Heavily infected leaves can appear curled and distorted.

Plantlets
Dieback
- ◇ Damaged cotyledons ⋯▸ Seedcorn Maggot.

Bean Seed Fly: Fly larvae damage the sprouts of developing seeds and bulbs as well as transplanted plants. They often cause plant rot, leading to the total or partial destruction of seedlings and crops.
- ◇ Damaged cotyledons ⋯▸ Dark Sword-grass Moth. Black cutworm. Greasy cutworm: Early larval stages feed on the leaves and create small holes with irregular contours. Later stages attack the stem, often during sowing, and consequently cut the seedlings at ground level.

Wilting
- ◇ Wilted, collapsed and dead young seedlings ⋯▸ Damping Off: Seeds rot and fail to germinate, or even germinate, but seedlings fail to grow. A translucent area completely covers the stem near the soil surface. The affected tissues rot, leading to wilting and collapse of the seedlings.

Plants whole
Stunted
- ◇ Deformation and stunting of plants ⋯▸ Cucumber Mosaic Virus. CMV: Artichoke latent virus (ALV, Potyvirus) is transmitted by aphids. Cucumber mosaic virus (CMV) induces deformation and stunting of plants.

Roots or tubers
Galleries
- ◇ Galleries in roots ⋯▸ Click Beetle. Striped Elaterid Beetle. Wireworms: As larvae development takes up to four years, in an infected soil we can find larvae of different ages. They live at different depths, depending on the moment of the year, as they are highly sensitive to heat and dryness. They eat or pierce the underground organs of the plant: roots, crowns, bud leaves and turions.

Presence
- ◇ Grubs present in the soil ⋯▸ June Beetles, May Beetles, Chafer beetles: The adults are phyllophagous and the larvae burrowd in the soil, called "white grubs", are root-eating. They deform the roots and cause the plant to wilt.

Stems
Dieback
- ◇ Damaged stems ⋯▸ Dark Sword-grass Moth. Black cutworm. Greasy cutworm: Early larval stages feed on the leaves and create small holes with irregular contours. Later stages attack the stem, often during sowing, and consequently cut the seedlings at ground level.

Necrosis
- ◇ Necrotic stems ⋯▸ Fusarium Wilt: An affected plant has a yellowing, stunted, wilted appearance, sometimes with gummosis on the stem. Discoloration and vascular browning of the collar progressing towards the stem and roots, and developing into cortical rot.

Sweet Corn

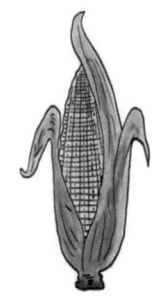

Botanical name
Zea mays convar. saccharata

Class
Poaceae

English name
Sweetcorn, Sugar corn.

Names in other languages
Maïs doux (FR), Suikermaïs (NL), Zuckermais (DE), Granoturco da zucchero (IT), Milho-doce (PO), Maïz dulce (SP).

Description
Sweet corn (*Zea mays convar. saccharata*) is a variety of maize belonging to the family of Poaceae. It is a maize with a high sugar content. Unlike field corn varieties, which are harvested when the kernels are dry and mature, sweet corn is picked when immature and prepared and eaten as a vegetable, rather than a grain.

Pests
Anthracnose Fruit Rot, Cercosporosa Leaf Spot, Click Beetle, Striped Elaterid Beetle, Wireworms, Common Swift Moth, Garden Swift Moth, European Chafer, White Grub, European Corn Borer, Maize Pyralid, Eyespot of maize, Grain Aphid, June Beetles, May Beetles, Leaf Blight of Maize, Maize Smut, Corn Smut, Seedcorn Maggot, Bean Seed Fly, Tomato Fruitworm, Old World Bollworm.

Symptoms on:
Cobs
Galleries

◇ Galleries in cobs ⋯➤ European Corn Borer. Maize Pyralid: Horizontal rows of holes in the young leaves, caused by larval feeding, provide an early indication of European corn borer attack. Later, frass and holes are easily visible on stems, or on the apical part of maize ears. Larval tunnelling weakens the stalks and causes them to break during windy weather.

Presence

◇ Cobs destroyed ⋯➤ Tomato Fruitworm. Old World Bollworm: First instar larvae feed on soft leaves, creating small holes. When they reach the second instar, they can penetrate fruit through a small hole, often bored near the stalk. During development, the caterpillars damage most fruits by mining.

Leaves
Damage

◇ Leaves with perforations ⋯➤ European Corn Borer. Maize Pyralid: Horizontal rows of holes in the young leaves, caused by larval feeding, provide an early indication of European corn borer attack. Later, frass and holes are easily visible on stems, or on the apical part of maize ears. Larval tunnelling weakens the stalks and causes them to break during windy weather.

Deformation

◇ Tumours on leaves ⋯➤ Maize Smut. Corn Smut: A prominent symptom of this disease is the formation of large tumors on the leaves, stems, tassels and ears. Initially galls are white to light green, turning dark when gall membranes rupture and a mass of dark spores emerge.

Discoloring

◇ Leaves discoulouring yellowish ⋯➤ June Beetles, May Beetles, Chafer beetles: The adults are phyllophagous and the larvae, called "white grubs" are root-eating. They deform the roots and cause the plant to wilt.

Lesions

◇ Pale yellow or water-soaked regular or irregular lesions on leaves ⋯→ Anthracnose: Depending on the fungus responsible, these brown or black spots can be circular or irregular, they then appear either on the edge of the leaves or along the veins. The necrotic areas extend more or less concentrically, the limit with healthy tissue being very clear.

Presence

◇ Trash deposit ⋯→ European Corn Borer. Maize Pyralid:Horizontal rows of holes in the young leaves, caused by larval feeding, provide an early indication of European corn borer attack. Later, frass and holes are easily visible on stems, or on the apical part of maize ears. Larval tunnelling weakens the stalks and causes them to break during windy weather.

◇ Presence of honeydew and sooty moulds on leaves ⋯→ Grain Aphid, English grain aphid: The aphids secrete honeydew, which gives the plants a bright, greasy look. Secondarily, black mould fungi can appear on the honeydew.

◇ Presence of caterpillars ⋯→ Tomato Fruitworm. Old World Bollworm: First instar larvae feed on soft leaves, creating small holes. When they reach the second instar, they can penetrate fruit through a small hole, often bored near the stalk. During development, the caterpillars damage most fruits by mining.

Spots

◇ Leaf spots with brown-reddish margins ⋯→ Cercosporosa Leaf Spot, Cercosporia blight: Cercospora blight initially causes small, oval, gray to tan lesions with red borders. Severe infections may cause entire ferns to turn yellow or brown. Cercospora blight may cause reduced vigor and yield of spears the next spring.

◇ Leaves with grey spots ⋯→ Eyespot of maize: The initial symptoms of eyespot are small, water-soaked or chlorotic circular spots. The tissue at the center of the spot later dies and turns tan-colored with a brown ring at the margin.

Plantlets
Dieback

◇ Damaged cotyledons ⋯→ Seedcorn Maggot. Bean Seed Fly: Fly larvae damage the sprouts of developing seeds and bulbs as well as transplanted plants. They often cause plant rot, leading to the total or partial destruction of seedlings and crops.

Plants whole
Stunted

◇ Stunted plants ⋯→ European Chafer. White Grub: The damage is done by the larvae (grubs). They feed on the fibrous roots of plants and cause them to become stunted and wilted.

Roots or tubers
◇ Roots damaged ⋯→ European Chafer. White

Grub: The damage is done by the larvae (grubs). They feed on the fibrous roots of plants and cause them to become stunted and wilted.

Galleries

◇ Galleries in roots ⋯→ Click Beetle. Striped Elaterid Beetle. Wireworms: As larvae development takes up to four years, in an infected soil we can find larvae of different ages. They live at different depths, depending on the moment of the year, as they are highly sensitive to heat and dryness. They eat or pierce the underground organs of the plant: roots, crowns, bud leaves and turions.

Presence

◇ Grubs present in the soil ⋯→ June Beetles, May Beetles, Chafer beetles: The adults are phyllophagous and the larvae burrowd in the soil, called "white grubs", are root-eating. They deform the roots and cause the plant to wilt.

Stems
Galleries

◇ Galleries in stems ⋯→ European Corn Borer. Maize Pyralid: Horizontal rows of holes in the young leaves, caused by larval feeding, provide an early indication of European corn borer attack. Later, frass and holes are easily visible on stems, or on the apical part of maize ears. Larval tunnelling weakens the stalks and causes them to break during windy weather.

Presence

◇ Trash deposit ⋯→ European Corn Borer. Maize Pyralid: Horizontal rows of holes in the young leaves, caused by larval feeding, provide an early indication of European corn borer attack. Later, frass and holes are easily visible on stems, or on the apical part of maize ears. Larval tunnelling weakens the stalks and causes them to break during windy weather.

◇ Presence of caterpillars ⋯→ Common Swift Moth. Garden Swift Moth: The roots and collars are eaten away, which leads to the gradual drying out of the plant.

Spots

◇ Long spots along the veins ⋯→ Leaf Blight of Maize:The most common leaf blight symptom is long elliptic tan lesions that appear on the lower leaves andspread upward. Small patches on leaves that are slightly oval and water-soaked are the first symptoms of infection. These develop into necrotic lesions that are elongated and spindle-shaped.

Tomato

Botanical name
Lycopersicum esculentum

Class
Solanaceae

English name
Tomato

Names in other languages
Tomate (FR), Tomaat (NL), Tomate (DE), Pomodoro (IT), Tomate (PO), Tomatera (SP).

Description
Tomato (*Lycopersicum esculentum*) is an herbaceous annual in the family Solanaceae grown for its edible fruit. The plant can be erect with short stems or vine-like with long, spreading stems. The stems are covered in coarse hairs and the leaves are arranged spirally. The tomato plant produces yellow flowers, which can develop into a cyme of 3–12, and usually a round fruit (berry) which is fleshy, smoothed skinned and can be red, pink, purple, brown, orange or yellow in color. The tomato plant can grow 0.7–2 m (2.3–6.6 ft) in height and as an annual, is harvested after only one growing season.

Pests
Anthracnose Fruit Rot, Bacterial Canker of Tomato, Bacterial Spot, Beet Armyworm, Cabbage Stem Flea Beetle, Celery Late Blight, Cercosporosa Leaf Spot, Chlorosis, Cotton Aphid, Cotton Whitefly, Cotton Worm, African Cotton Leafworm, CMV, Damping Off, Early Blight of Potato/Tomato, Fusarium Root Rot, Fusarium Wilt, Glasshouse Whitefly, Gray Mold, Botrytis Blight, Green Peach Aphid, Late Blight, Leaf Mould, Cladosporiosis of Tomato, Thrips, Phoma, Potato Aphid, Potato Tuberworm, Potato Tuber Moth, Powdery Mildew, Red Spider Mite, Seedcorn Maggot, South American Miner Fly, Southern Green Stink bug, ToCV, Tomato Corky Root, Tomato Fruitworm, Tomato Leaf Miner, Tomato Russet Mite, Verticillium Wilt, Sclerotinia Wilt.

Symptoms on:
Flowers
Decay

◇ Rotten inflorescences and flowers ⋯→ Gray Mold. Grey Mould. Botrytis Blight: Senescent petals are particularly vulnerable. They allow Botrytis to settle on the inflorescences and cause them to rot.

Spots

◇ Grayish colored soft, mushy spots on flowers ⋯→ Gray Mold. Grey Mould. Botrytis Blight: Regardless of the organs affected, the dying tissues become covered with a very characteristic dense gray mold, consisting of the conidiophores and conidia of the fungus.

◇ Blackish-brown spots, which may become covered with grayish mold ⋯→ Gray Mold. Grey Mould. Botrytis Blight: Blackish-brown spots, extending from the base of the bracts, which may become covered with grayish mold (fruiting bodies). Sometimes, sclerotia are present. This disease develops secondarily following an injury or other disease.

Fruits
Damage

◇ Black holes ⋯→ Tomato Fruitworm. Old World Bollworm: First instar larvae feed on soft leaves, creating small holes. When they reach the second instar, they can penetrate fruit through a small hole, often bored near the stalk. During development, the caterpillars damage most fruits by mining.

Discoloring

◇ Russeting of fruit ⋯→ Tomato Russet Mite: The affected fruits are more or less well colored; in the long term, they are often smaller and show more or less extensive corky areas, or even cracks.

Lesions

◇ Brownish black lesions on fruits ⋯→ Early Blight of Potato/Tomato: There are black spots measuring 1 to 2 cm, hollow, located at the base of the calyx.

Presence

◇ Fruits with brown marbling and white down ⋯→ Late Blight. Potato and Tomato Late Blight: Fruits affected at an early stage are often bumpy and have very characteristic brown marbling, which is rather slow to spread and has an irregular margin. A whitish down is occasionally visible on their surface.

◇ Fruits destroyed ⋯→ Tomato Fruitworm. Old World Bollworm: First instar larvae feed on soft leaves, creating small holes. When they reach the second instar, they can penetrate fruit through a small hole, often bored near the stalk. During development, the caterpillars damage most fruits by mining.

Spots

◇ Fruits with round, hollow spots ⋯→ Anthracnose: The first symptoms appear rather on ripe fruits in the form of small light brown lesions which develop into circular, slightly depressed and moist spots, distributed randomly. Several spots present on the fruits can merge and cause a large rot.

◇ Fruits with soft, pasty spots of a grayish tint ⋯→ Gray Mold. Grey Mould. Botrytis Blight: Soft, wet rots develop at the stalk scar of fruits, sometimes at the tips. Lesions are usually circular and elongated, pale brown to brown in color; the tissues often collapse.

◇ Fruits with white spots ⋯→ Southern Green Stink Bug: Young fruits have small, punctate spots, with the underlying tissues being lighter in color than the rest.

◇ Black spots on fruits ⋯→ Bacterial Spot: Black spots on fruits about 1 cm in size, gradually widening.

Leaves
Damage

◇ Perforated leaves ⋯→ Cabbage Stem Flea Beetle: It is difficult to monitor the activity of the adult of the large rapeseed flea beetle: it occurs at night. Its damage, on the other hand, is easily recognizable because the insect bites the cotyledons and young leaves in a circular fashion. Perforations can also be observed.

◇ Leaves with irregular holes ⋯→ Armyworms, Beet Armyworm: Older Spodoptera exigua caterpillars migrate to the apex of the plants where they feed mainly on the growing areas. They make large holes in the leaves and sometimes leave only the veins behind. The damage caused considerably affects the growth of the plants. In heavy infestations, the damage can extend to the stems and, in the worst cases, to the fruits, which the caterpillars consume entirely from the inside.

Decay

◇ Soft watery rot on lower leaves ⋯→ White Rot. White Mold. Sclerotinia Wilt: Pre and post-emergent damping off, crown rot, and blighting of foliage and petioles. Small, hard, irregular, black structures called sclerotia may be present on or in plant tissue (especially inside stem and petiole tissue).

Deformation

◇ Leaves shrivelled ⋯→ Southern Green Stink Bug: Presence of larvae and adults on affected organs. Wilting of apex leaves. Blisters on stems.

◇ Curled leaves ⋯→ Celery Late Blight: The disease first manifests itself by the appearance of small light brown spots on the foliage. In case of severe attacks, the petioles turn yellow, the leaves curl up and dry out.

◇ Leaves curled or shrivelled ⋯→ Green Peach Aphid: Myzus persicae is very polyphagous and, in summer, it has more than forty different families of host plants. The colonies secrete a honeydew that promotes the installation of sooty mold, a fungus that then slows down the photosynthesis of the covered parts. It is the most important aphid vector of viruses.

◇ Leaves curled or shrivelled ⋯→ Cotton Aphid: Aphids, following their nutritional bites, are responsible for chlorotic spots and the deformation of young leaves which tend to roll up and more or less blister.

Discoloring

◇ Russeting of leaves ⋯→ Tomato Russet Mite: The underside of the leaves of the lower part of the plants takes on a greasy to metallic tint. Later, the leaves show a rather bronze coloration.

◇ Yellow leaves on plants ⋯→ Chlorosis: Interveinal chlorosis of young leaflets starting at their base and gradually spreading to their tip. Iron deficiency.

◇ Leaves turn yellow and wilt ⋯→ Fusarium Wilt: An affected plant has a yellowing, stunted, wilted appearance, sometimes with gummosis on the stem. Discoloration and vascular browning of the collar progressing towards the stem and roots, and developing into cortical rot.

◇ Red stripes on roots, shoots and leaves ⋯→ Phoma: Known as a damping off agent, phoma also causes leaf necrosis. The first symptoms are often spots or Pink to wine-red streaks located on the leaves or taproot. These symptoms can progress to black necrosis with often diffuse borders located on leaves and cotyledons.

◇ Silvery marks on leaves ⋯→ Onion Thrips. Thrips: In a greenhouse, colonies can be very developed and direct damage is often significant. The larvae and adults of the tobacco and onion thrips puncture the contents of the subepidermal cells. The infested leaves are then dotted with numerous silver spots corresponding to groups of emptied cells. This symptom is typically associated with the presence of small piles of black faeces.

◇ Leaves discolouring bronzed or silvery ⋯→ Red Spider Mite. Two-spotted Mite: They damage the plant by piercing its cells to feed on them. The leaves turn pale and become stained yellow. To protect themselves and improve their microclimate, they weave a web around the leaf. A strong attack of mites leads to the leaves rolling and drying out, then falling off.

◇ Leaves turn yellow ⟶ Cotton Whitefly. Tobacco Whitefly: The tobacco whitefly occupies the entire plant. Presence of numerous "white flies" and honeydew, slow growth of plants, development of sooty mold on aerial organs, yellowing and necrosis of the leaf blade.

Galleries

◇ Leaves with mines or galleries ⟶ Tomato Leaf Miner: Leafminer larvae dig mines and galleries on aerial organs. Leaves become mined with whitish spots that darken and become necrotic.

◇ Leaves with galleries ⟶ South American Miner Fly. South American Leaf Miner: Feeding pits and mined leaves with galleries depreciate the harvest.

◇ Leaves with galleries ⟶ Potato Tuberworm. Potato Split-worm. Potato Tuber Moth: Damage to leaves, petioles and stems by perforations and mining which can weaken the plants.

Lesions

◇ Leaves with brownish-black lesions, with yellow halo ⟶ Bacterial Spot: Small, dark, brown to black spots suddenly appear on the leaflets, usually the youngest or on the edge of the blade.

◇ Circular, brown, and necrotic lesions on leaves ⟶ Early Blight of Potato/Tomato: Black, circular, necrotic spots, 4 to 7 mm in diameter, appear on the leaves and enlarge in the form of "concentric circles".

◇ Pale yellow or water-soaked regular or irregular lesions on leaves ⟶ Anthracnose: Depending on the fungus responsible, these brown or black spots can be circular or irregular, they then appear either on the edge of the leaves or along the veins. The necrotic areas extend more or less concentrically, the limit with healthy tissue being very clear.

◇ Black necrotic irregluar lesions on leaves ⟶ Anthracnose: The disease is recognizable by the brown or black spots it causes on the leaves. Depending on the fungus responsible, these spots can be circular or irregular, and appear either on the edge of the leaves or along the veins. The necrotic areas extend more or less concentrically, with the boundary with healthy tissues being very clear.

Mosaic pattern

◇ Leaves with mosaic pattern ⟶ Tomato Chlorosis Crinivirus. ToCV: Irregular chloritic mottling, interveinal yellowing in spots at first, then spreading to the entire blade of the lower leaves. The latter, the most affected, become hard and brittle.

Necrosis

◇ Shrivelling and necrosis of leaves ⟶ Tomato Russet Mite: The underside of the leaves or leaflets of the lower part of the plants takes on a greasy to metallic tint. Subsequently, the leaves show a rather bronze coloration from which the name of this disease originates.

Presence

◇ Presence of honey dew on leaves ⟶ Glasshouse Whitefly. Greenhouse Whitefly: We can observe the presence of numerous whiteflies and honeydew, plant growth is slowed, there is sooty mold on the aerial organs, as well as yellowing and necrosis of the leaf blade.

◇ Coating of gray fungus spores on leaves ⟶ Gray Mold. Grey Mould. Botrytis Blight: Regardless of the organs affected, the dying tissues become covered with a very characteristic dense gray mold, consisting of the conidiophores and conidia of the fungus.

◇ Presence of colonies of whiteflies ⟶ Glasshouse Whitefly. Greenhouse Whitefly:

◇ Presence of irregular, angular lesions ⟶ Bacterial Spot: On the underside, there are circular to angular spots, beige with a dark brown margin. They have a dry appearance and have a yellow halo.

◇ White to gray powder coverage on leaves ⟶ Powdery Mildew, Oidium: The heart leaves are covered with purplish-grey spores on the underside. They thicken, curl, and curl up. Older leaves turn yellow on the outside, then blacken and die. Only a few isolated plants or foci are damaged.

◇ Presence of aphids ⟶ Potato Aphid: The most classic symptoms are a curling of heavily infested leaves and a slowdown in the growth of the plants

◇ Presence of honey dew on leaves ⟶ Cotton Aphid: In addition to aphid colonies, we often observe white molts and the presence of honeydew on the surface of the aerial organs of zucchini and other plants.

◇ Presence of sooty mould on leaves ⟶ Cotton Aphid: In addition to aphid colonies, we often observe white molts and the presence of honeydew.

◇ Leaves with fine silk webbing ⟶ Red Spider Mite. Two-spotted Mite: They damage the plant by piercing its cells to feed on them. The leaves turn pale and become stained yellow. To protect themselves and improve their microclimate, they weave a web around the leaf. A strong attack of mites leads to the leaves rolling and drying out, then falling off.

◇ Presence of red spider mites, cast skins and egg shells ⟶ Red Spider Mite. Two-spotted Mite: Spider mites always leave behind cast skins and egg shells.

◇ Leaves with white/grey felting ⟶ Late Blight. Potato and Tomato Late Blight: On the upper side of the leaves, small discolored spots are observed that turn brown and are surrounded by a light green to yellow halo. On the underside, in humid conditions, a characteristic white felting appears.

◇ Presence of honey dew on leaves ⟶ Cotton Whitefly. Tobacco Whitefly: The tobacco whitefly occupies the entire plant. Presence of numerous "white flies" and honeydew, slow growth of plants, development of sooty mold on aerial organs, yellowing and necrosis of the leaf blade.

◇ Presence of caterpillars ⋯➤ Bright-line Brown-eyes Moth: The damage caused by this moth on cabbage and beet leaves is generally not very significant.

◇ Presence of caterpillars ⋯➤ Cotton Worm. African Cotton Leafworm: The Mediterranean noctuid or cotton worm causes damage which is recognizable by the large portions eaten out of the leaves.

◇ Leaves with grey powder ⋯➤ Leaf Mould. Cladosporiosis of Tomato: It causes light green to pale yellow spots with diffuse outlines, located mainly on the leaflets of the lower leaves. A downy growth, initially whitish then purplish to olive brown, gradually covers the spots on the underside of the leaf blade. Eventually, the tissues located in the center of the spots turn brown, necrotic and dry out while the leaves curl.

◇ Presence of caterpillars ⋯➤ Tomato Fruitworm. Old World Bollworm: First instar larvae feed on soft leaves, creating small holes. When they reach the second instar, they can penetrate fruit through a small hole, often bored near the stalk. During development, the caterpillars damage most fruits by mining.

Spots

◇ Leaves with gray spots ⋯➤ Gray Mold. Grey Mould. Botrytis Blight: Initially, the leaflets tend to have rather circular, wet spots. Their color varies from beigeish to light brown, they also have a parchment-like appearance and reveal concentric arabesques. These alterations can cause rot that then spreads and ends up damaging entire leaves, the tissues gradually collapsing and decomposing. Once the petioles have reached the stems, this rot can develop on the stems.

◇ Leaves with yellow, brown, necrotic and concentric spots ⋯➤ Early Blight of Potato/ Tomato: Small yellow spots quickly turn brown-black, necrotic, circular and sharply outlined, measuring about 5 mm in diameter, which gradually spread concentrically.

◇ Yellow/brown spots ⋯➤ Verticillium Wilt: Marginal drying, sometimes asymmetrical. In the stem, brown lesions at the level of the conductive tissue. Atrophied and deformed capitula.

◇ White spots on/in leaves ⋯➤ Tomato Leaf Miner: Leafminer larvae dig mines and galleries on aerial organs. Leaves have mines, irregular whitish spots that gradually become brown and necrotic.

◇ Pale brown spots on leaves ⋯➤ Celery Late Blight: The disease first manifests itself by the appearance on the foliage of small light brown spots, often delimited by the fine veins of the leaves but sometimes with irregular contours, ranging in size from 1 to 4 mm. They gradually

turn reddish-brown and have small black dots called pycnidia in their center on the upper surface.

◇ Yellowish then brown spots on the upper surface of the leaf ⋯➤ Powdery Mildew, Oidium: Yellowish then brown spots on the upper surface of the leaf, generally limited by the large veins, whitish felting on the lower surface.

◇ Leaf spots with brown-reddish margins ⋯➤ Cercosporosa Leaf Spot, Cercosporia blight: Cercospora blight initially causes small, oval, gray to tan lesions with red borders. Severe infections may cause entire ferns to turn yellow or brown. Cercospora blight may cause reduced vigor and yield of spears the next spring.

◇ Brown spots surrounded by a halo ⋯➤ Late Blight. Potato and Tomato Late Blight: On the upper side of the leaves, small discolored spots are observed that turn brown and are surrounded by a light green to yellow halo. On the underside, in humid conditions, a characteristic white felting appears.

◇ Leaves with yellow spots ⋯➤ Leaf Mould. Cladosporiosis of Tomato: It causes light green to pale yellow spots with diffuse outlines, located mainly on the leaflets of the lower leaves. A downy growth, initially whitish then purplish to olive brown, gradually covers the spots on the underside of the leaf blade. Eventually, the tissues located in the center of the spots turn brown, necrotic and dry out while the leaves curl.

Stunted

◇ Stunted leaves ⋯➤ Glasshouse Whitefly. Greenhouse Whitefly: The numerous bites and feeding suctions of whiteflies on the foliage, just like those of aphids, cause a slowdown in plant development.

Plantlets
Dieback

◇ Damaged cotyledons ⋯➤ Seedcorn Maggot. Bean Seed Fly: Fly larvae damage the sprouts of developing seeds and bulbs as well as transplanted plants. They often cause plant rot, leading to the total or partial destruction of seedlings and crops.

Wilting

◇ Wilted, collapsed and dead young seedlings ⋯➤ Damping Off: Seeds rot and fail to germinate, or even germinate, but seedlings fail to grow. A translucent area completely covers the stem near the soil surface. The affected tissues rot, leading to wilting and collapse of the seedlings.

Plants whole
Defoliation

◇ Plants defoliated ⋯➤ Colorado Potato Beetle: Larvae may defoliate potato plants resulting in yield losses up to 100% if the damage occurs prior to tuber formation. Larvae may consume 40 cm2 of potato leaves during the entire larval stage, but adults are capable of consuming 10 cm2 of foliage per day.

◇ Deformation and stunting of plants ⋯→ Cucumber Mosaic Virus. CMV: Artichoke latent virus (ALV, Potyvirus) is transmitted by aphids. Cucumber mosaic virus (CMV) induces deformation and stunting of plants.

◇ Stunted plants ⋯→ Cabbage Stem Flea Beetle: It is difficult to monitor the activity of the adult of the large rapeseed flea beetle: it occurs at night. Its damage, on the other hand, is easily recognizable because the insect bites the cotyledons and young leaves in a circular fashion. Perforations can also be observed.

◇ Plants stunted ⋯→ Fusarium Root Rot: Diseased plants wilt to a greater or lesser extent during the hottest times of the day; this wilting is sometimes reversible. In the most serious cases, the plants eventually dry out completely.

Wilting

◇ Wilting of the entire plant ⋯→ Bacterial Canker of Tomato: Bacterial canker often manifests itself, at least at the beginning of its development, by the appearance on the leaflets of livid interveinal spots which quickly become necrotic. Very often, they are followed by leaf wilting, the leaflets tending in this case to curl downwards. Eventually, the seedlings, like adult plants, can wilt and dry out completely.

◇ Wilting of the entire plant ⋯→ Verticillium Wilt: The leaves soften and become duller. The leaves begin to yellow, then turn brown as they become necrotic. The characteristic feature is the asymmetry of the symptoms, with many leaves only affected on one half. The disease progresses from the bottom to the top of the plant. Verticillium wilt causes dark streaks under the bark.

◇ Wilted plants ⋯→ Tomato Corky Root: Rotting and the disappearance of many rootlets. Brown changes are also visible on young roots. Larger roots have corky and rather dry lesions). The limitation of the root system, as well as the numerous lesions present, have the consequence of reducing the vigor of the plants.

Roots or tubers
Decay

◇ Rotting of roots ⋯→ Fusarium Root Rot: The cause of these wilting is to be found at the level of the collar of the feet. At this location, a wet lesion has developed, a rot that has gradually spread to the lower part of the stem and the taproot, but also to the upper part of the root system. At the collar, the altered tissues are wet and show a dark to brownish tint. This lesion ends up girdling the stem for several centimetres. The roots located in the same layer of soil are also affected. Their cortex turns yellow, brown and decomposes.

Deformation

◇ Roots abnormally increased or swellings ⋯→ Tomato Corky Root: Rotting and the disappearance of many rootlets. Brown changes are also visible on young roots. Larger roots have corky and rather dry lesions). The limitation of the root system, as

well as the numerous lesions present, have the consequence of reducing the vigor of the plants.

Spots

◇ Small white mealy spots ⋯→ Potato Tuber Nematode. Potato Cyst Nematode: The nematode initially causes small white mealy spots just below the surface that are only visible if the skin is removed.

Stems
Discoloring

◇ Russeting of stems ⋯→ Tomato Russet Mite: The underside of the leaves on the lower part of the plants takes on a greasy to metallic tint. Similar symptoms can be observed on the stem.

Lesions

◇ Brown lesions on stems ⋯→ Early Blight of Potato/Tomato: On the stems, the spots are brown or gray, also elliptical and concentric.

Necrosis

◇ Necrotic stems ⋯→ Fusarium Wilt: An affected plant has a yellowing, stunted, wilted appearance, sometimes with gummosis on the stem. Discoloration and vascular browning of the collar progressing towards the stem and roots, and developing into cortical rot.

Presence

◇ Coating of gray fungus spores on stems ⋯→ Gray Mold. Grey Mould. Botrytis Blight: Lesions, even cankers, more or less extensive, are visible on the stems, mainly located at the level of pruning and disbudding wounds. Let us add that the lesions are generally covered with a very characteristic grayish to beige mold.

◇ White mold on the stem and collar ⋯→ White Rot. White Mold. Sclerotinia Wilt: Black or dark brown sclerotia form inside the stems. This uncommon disease can sometimes lead to the death of the plant.

Spots

◇ Grayish colored soft, mushy spots on stems ⋯→ Gray Mold. Grey Mould. Botrytis Blight: The leaflets often have rather circular and initially damp spots. Beigeish to light brown in color, these also reveal a parchment-like appearance and reveal concentric arabesques. These alterations can give rise to rot which then spreads and ends up damaging entire leaves, the tissues collapsing and gradually becoming necrotic. Having reached the petioles, this rot can then settle on the stems.

Turnip

Botanical name
Brassica rapa subsp. *rapa*

Class
Brassicaceae

English name
Turnip

Names in other languages
Navet (FR), Raap (NL), Rübe (DE), Navone (IT), Nabo (PO), Nabo (SP).

Description
Turnip (*Brassica rapa*) is an herbaceous annual or biennial plant in the family Brassicaceae grown for its edible roots and leaves. The plant possesses erect stems and 8–12 leaves forming a crown. The leaves are light green in color, hairy and thin. The plant produces light yellow flowers which are clustered at the top of a raceme and are often extended above the terminal buds. The leaves can reach 30.5–35.5 cm (12–14 in) in length, while the branching flower stems can reach 30.5–91.5 cm (12–36 in). The taproot of the plant is is a bulbous tuber, almost perfectly round, which is usually a mixture of purple, white and yellow. Turnip is usually grown as an annual and harvested after one growing season.

Pests
Anthracnose Fruit Rot, Beet Armyworm, Boron Deficiency, Cabbage and Cauliflower Cyst Nematode, Cabbage Aphid, Cabbage Bug, Brassica Bug, Cabbage Club Root, Cabbage Fly, Cabbage Root Fly, Cabbage Maggot, Cabbage Stem Flea Beetle, Cabbageworm, Imported Cabbage Worms, Click Beetle, Wireworms, Damping Off, Dark Sword-grass Moth, Black cutworm, Downy Mildew of Crucifers, Gray Mold, Grey Mould, Botrytis Blight, Turnip Flea Beetle, Striped Turnip Flea Beetle, Turnip Gall Weevil, Turnip Maggot, Turnip Root Fly.

Symptoms on:
Leaves
Damage

◇ Perforated leaves ⋯→ Cabbage Stem Flea Beetle: It is difficult to monitor the activity of the adult of the large rapeseed flea beetle: it occurs at night. Its damage, on the other hand, is easily recognizable because the insect bites the cotyledons and young leaves in a circular fashion. Perforations can also be observed.

◇ Leaves with holes ⋯→ Cabbageworm. Imported Cabbage Worms: Caterpillars devour the leaves of cruciferous plants, sometimes leaving only the large veins. In addition, their excrement, diluted by rain or dew, accumulates in the heart of the plant and makes it inedible.

◇ Leaves with irregular holes ⋯→ Armyworms, Beet Armyworm: Older Spodoptera exigua caterpillars migrate to the apex of the plants where they feed mainly on the growing areas. They make large holes in the leaves and sometimes leave only the veins behind. The damage caused considerably affects the growth of the plants.

◇ Leaves with irregular holes ⋯→ Turnip Flea Beetle. Large Striped Flea Beetle, Striped Turnip Flea Beetle: When adults resume activity in the spring, they gather on wild and cultivated cruciferous plants and make small bites of 1 to 2 mm in diameter that do not penetrate the entire thickness of the leaf. If there are many flea beetles and the temperature is high, the damage can be significant, particularly on young seedlings that risk being destroyed.

Deformation

◇ Leaves curled or shrivelled ⋯→ Cabbage Aphid: In the event of an outbreak, the plant can be completely covered by aphids, their honeydew and their exuviae.

Discoloring

◇ Reddening, yellowing of the leaves ⋯→ Cabbage Club Root: Aerial part of the plant: reduced development, especially during early attacks, wilting or even reddening of the foliage.

◇ Yellow leaves on plants ⋯➔ Boron Deficiency: Symptoms appear on young leaves: wrinkled, fragile leaves, slowed growth. Then wilting of the leaves with the appearance of brown or black spots on the petioles. Young leaves wilt, turn black and dry out.

◇ Bleached leaves ⋯➔ Cabbage Bug. Rape Bug. Crucifer Shield Bug. Brassica Bug: With their piercing-sucking apparatus, the larvae and adults feed by sucking the sap, which causes the leaves to turn white and slows down the growth of the cabbage. The very large number of punctures on the leaves of young plants can lead to the death of the host plant.

Lesions

◇ Pale yellow or water-soaked regular or irregular lesions on leaves ⋯➔ Anthracnose: Depending on the fungus responsible, these brown or black spots can be circular or irregular, they then appear either on the edge of the leaves or along the veins. The necrotic areas extend more or less concentrically, the limit with healthy tissue being very clear.

◇ Purple or brown irregular shaped areas on leaves ⋯➔ Downy Mildew of Crucifers: It first appears on older leaves, as white, yellow or brownish spots on the upper surfaces and downy grayish mold on the corresponding undersides.

Presence

◇ Coating of gray fungus spores on leaves ⋯➔ Gray Mold. Grey Mould. Botrytis Blight: Regardless of the organs affected, the dying tissues become covered with a very characteristic dense gray mold, consisting of the conidiophores and conidia of the fungus.

◇ Presence of colonies of aphids ⋯➔ Cabbage Aphid: In the event of an outbreak, the plant can be completely covered by aphids, their honeydew and their exuviae.

◇ White to gray, "downy" areas on under leaf surfaces. ⋯➔ Downy Mildew of Crucifers: It first appears on older leaves, as white, yellow or brownish spots on the upper surfaces and downy grayish mold on the corresponding undersides.

◇ Presence of caterpillars ⋯➔ Cabbageworm. Imported Cabbage Worms: Caterpillars devour the leaves of cruciferous plants, sometimes leaving only the large veins. In addition, their excrement, diluted by rain or dew, accumulates in the heart of the plant and makes it inedible.

◇ Presence of honeydew and sooty moulds on leaves ⋯➔ Cabbage Aphid: In the event of an outbreak, the plant can be completely covered by aphids, their honeydew and their exuviae.

◇ Presence of bugs ⋯➔ Cabbage Bug. Rape Bug. Crucifer Shield Bug. Brassica Bug: Presence of the adult insect and larva on leaves. Presence of eggs on the underside of the leaves. Observe the leaves to see the appearance of white spots. Be careful not to confuse these bugs with other red and black bugs such as Pyrrhocoris apterus, better known as the "firebug". These do not cause any damage to cabbage.

Plantlets
Dieback

◇ Damaged cotyledons ⋯➔ Dark Sword-grass Moth. Black cutworm. Greasy cutworm: Early larval stages feed on the leaves and create small holes with irregular contours. Later stages attack the stem, often during sowing, and consequently cut the seedlings at ground level.

Wilting

◇ Wilted, collapsed and dead young seedlings ⋯➔ Damping Off: Seeds rot and fail to germinate, or even germinate, but seedlings fail to grow. A translucent area completely covers the stem near the soil surface. The affected tissues rot, leading to wilting and collapse of the seedlings.

Plants whole
Infested zone

◇ Infested plants form a circular area in the field ⋯➔ Cabbage and Cauliflower Cyst Nematode. Brassica Cyst Nematode: In the field, infested plants form a circular area and appear stunted.

Stunted

◇ Stunted plants ⋯➔ Cabbage Stem Flea Beetle: It is difficult to monitor the activity of the adult of the large rapeseed flea beetle: it occurs at night. Its damage, on the other hand, is easily recognizable because the insect bites the cotyledons and young leaves in a circular fashion. Perforations can also be observed.

◇ Plants stunted ⋯➔ Cabbage and Cauliflower Cyst Nematode. Brassica Cyst Nematode: In the field, infested plants form a circular area and appear stunted.

Wilting

◇ Wilted plants ⋯➔ Cabbage Maggot, Cabbage Fly: Damage is observed in nurseries and at all stages of vegetation. On leafy vegetables, the root part is more or less destroyed. Attacked plants can be recognized by the faded appearance they take on during hot days; the leaves often turn purplish red, turn yellow and sometimes dry out.

◇ Wilted plants ⋯➔ Cabbage Club Root: Underground part of the plant: root deformation or presence of galls on the roots. These galls are firm (full interior), whitish then turn brown and rot, leading to the death of the plant.

Roots or tubers
Decay

◇ Internal brown rot ⋯➔ Boron Deficiency: Boron deficiency causes inner tissue to be reddish brown, or brown or gray concentric rings develop inside the roots, it also causes brown heart rot.

Deformation

◇ Roots abnormally increased or swellings ⋯➔ Cabbage Club Root: Underground part of the plant: root deformation or presence of galls on the roots. These galls are firm (full interior), whitish then turn brown and rot, leading to the death of the plant.

◇ Swelling of roots ⋯→ Turnip Gall Weevil: The substances introduced at the time of egg laying and the larval secretions cause an enlargement of the collar or gall, which can reach 2 to 3 cm in diameter in cabbage.

Dieback

◇ Roots damaged ⋯→ Cabbage and Cauliflower Cyst Nematode. Brassica Cyst Nematode: On roots: formation of an abnormal abundance of fine browned rootlets bearing whitish pinhead-shaped cysts.

Galleries

◇ Galleries in roots ⋯→ Click Beetle. Striped Elaterid Beetle. Wireworms: As larvae development takes up to four years, in an infected soil we can find larvae of different ages. They live at different depths, depending on the moment of the year, as they are highly sensitive to heat and dryness. They eat or pierce the underground organs of the plant: roots, crowns, bud leaves and turions.

Presence

◇ Presence of maggots in roots ⋯→ Cabbage Maggot, Cabbage Fly: The larvae of the cabbage fly penetrate into the fleshy parts and dig galleries. The root part is more or less destroyed. Attacked plants can be recognized by the faded appearance they take on during hot days; the leaves often turn purplish red, turn yellow and sometimes dry out.

◇ Roots with presence of maggots ⋯→ Turnip Maggot. Turnip Root Fly: On root vegetables, the larvae dig galleries that can go up to the petiole of the leaves and make the vegetable unfit for consumption. When the attack is massive, the plants stop growing, take on a leaden color and lack turgidity; little by little, they turn yellow and die.

Stems
Dieback

◇ Damaged stems ⋯→ Dark Sword-grass Moth. Black cutworm. Greasy cutworm: Early larval stages feed on the leaves and create small holes with irregular contours. Later stages attack the stem, often during sowing, and consequently cut the seedlings at ground level.

Pests

American Serpentine Leaf Miner

Botanical name
Liriomyza trifolii (Burgess, 1880)

Class
Agromyzidae. Insect.

English name
American Serpentine Leaf Miner or Celery Leafminer.

Names in other languages
American Serpentine Leaf Miner (En). Mouche mineuse américaine, Mouche mineuse californienne (Fr). Floridaminierfliege (De). Floridamineervlieg (Nl).

Description
The American serpentine leaf miner fly are relatively small flies for their family. The adults measure less than 2 mm in length. They are mostly yellow in color, although parts of the abdomen and thorax are dark brown or grey. They typically have yellow legs. The American serpentine leaf miner (*Liriomyza trifolii*) larvae mines the leaves. The pattern of mining is irregular, tending to be blotch-like near the end of the mine. If the infestation is severe, photosynthetic capacity is reduced, thus causing a slowing in the development of flowers and fruits. On ornamental plants, damage may be due both to larvae and to adult females piercing the leaves to lay their eggs; many countries do not accept the importing of plants or cut flowers with a single blemish. In North America, this leaf miner is particularly harmful to chrysanthemums and celery; in France and the Netherlands it mostly attacks tomato, while in Italy, gerbera is most frequently damaged.

Symptoms
Leaves with galleries.

Vegetables
Celery, Leek, Melon, Onion, Peas, Potato.

American serpentine leaf miner adult and damage

Remedies: Immediate action
• Insecticide based on Azadirachta.

• Insecticide based on Pyrethrin.

Remedies: Proactive
• Chromatic trap (Yellow).

• Release Diglyphus isaea parasitic wasp in hot waether conditions (Summer).

• Release Dacnusa sibirica parasitic wasp in colder weather conditions (Spring & Automn).

• Remove plant debris and crop residues to eliminate overwintering sites.

• Use insect proof netting, with very small mesh.

• Install insects hotels, to promote ladybugs and lacewings who devore the eggs.

Anthracnose

Botanical name
Colletotrichum spp./ Gloeosporium spp.

Class
Phyllacoraceae, Fungus

Names in other languages
Anthracnose (En). Anthracnose (Fr). Anthraknose (De). Anthracnose (Nl).

Description
Anthracnose is a fungal disease caused by different species of *Colletotrichum*. Leaf symptoms begin as small, pale yellow or water-soaked lesions that rapidly enlarge and turn tan to dark brown or irregular and black. As lesions merge, large areas of the leaf may appear blighted or entire leaves may die. Although infections are not seen on green fruit, as soon as the tomato begins to ripen symptoms emerge as small, somewhat sunken, watersoaked circular spots. A semisoft decay occurs, resulting in large rotted areas over time.

Symptoms
Leaves with dark brown irregelar or pale yellow or water-soaked or black necrotic lesions. Fruits with depressed spots with concentric rings. Tubers with black dots.

Vegetables
Tomatoes, Potato, Courgette, Cucumber, Eggplant, Green bean, Common bean, Melon, Chinese cabbage, Onion, Peas, Pepper, Bell pepper, Pumpkin, Spinach, Sweet corn, Turnip.

Anthracnose on tomatoes

Remedies: Immediate action
- Bacillus subtilis

- Bicarbonate of potassium

- Bordeaux mixture

- Garlic decoction

- Horsetail decoction

- Liquid manure of comfrey

- Liquid manure of nettle

- Wettable sulphur

Remedies: Proactive
- Obtain certified seeds or plants

- Use resistant varieties

- Remove plant debris and crop residues

- Revieuw irrigation and watering

- Apply long rotation

Anthracnose of Cucurbits

Anthracnose of cucurbits on cucumbers

Botanical name
Colletotrichum lagenarium

Class
Phyllacoraceae, Fungus

Names in other languages
Anthracnose of Cucurbits (En). Anthracnose des Curcubitacées, ou nuile rouge (Fr). Anthraknose: Gurkengewächse, Brennfleckenkrankheit: Gurkengewächse (De). Brandvlekkenziekte (Nl).

Description
Anthracnose of Cucurbits is caused by a fungus (*Colletotrichum lagenarium*) Symptoms vary among the three principal cucurbits infected. On watermelon foliage the spots are irregular and turn dark brown or black. On cucumber and muskmelon the spots turn brown and can enlarge considerably. Stem lesions on muskmelon can girdle the stem and cause vines to wilt. Stem cankers are less obvious on cucumbers. On the fruit, where circular, black, sunken cankers appear.

Symptoms
Brown irregular spots on leaves and black circular lesions on fruits.

Vegetables
Cucumber, Melons.

Remedies: Immediate action
- Bacillus subtilis

- Bordeaux mixture

- Horsetail decoction

- Wettable sulphur

Remedies: Proactive
- Certified seeds or plants

- Long rotation. Crop rotation

- Use resistant varieties

- Remove plant debris and crop residues

Artichoke Moth

Botanical name
Gortyna xanthenes/Platyptilia carduidactyla

Class
Noctuidae, Insect

Names in other languages
Artichoke Moth (En). Noctuelle de l'artichaut (Fr). Artischockeneule, Artischockenmarkeule (De). Artisjokuil (Nl).

Artichoke plume moth adult and larvae (caterpillar)

Description
The artichoke moth (Gortyna xanthenes/*Platyptilia carduidactyla*) is a nocturnal moth, with 50 to 60 mm wingspan and greyish yellow for wings. The young caterpillar climbs along the plant and nibbles the upper epidermis of the leaves, it then penetrates the veins, perforating them to expel frass, it eats through the centre of the stem to reach the head, where it forms large galleries.

Symptoms
Galleries in stems and flowerheads

Vegetables
Artichoke

Remedies: Immediate action
*   Bacillus thuringiensis

*   Insecticide based on spinosad

Remedies: Proactive
*   Bait based on bran and pyrethrin

*   Elder decoction

*   Pheromone traps

*   Steinernema carpocapsae solution, soaking stumps before planting.

*   Tansy decoction

*   Wormwood decoction

*   Sanitation by cutting stalks. Remove infested plants parts.

Artichoke Pear-shaped Weevil

Botanical name
Apion carduorum

Class
Apionidae, Insect

Names in other languages
Artichoke pear-shaped weevil (En). Apion de l'artichaut (Fr). Artischockenspitzmäuschen (De). Artisjok snuitkever (Nl).

Description
The artichoke pear-shaped weevil (*Apion carduorum*) is a small shiny blackish bleu coleoptera. The larva are white and curved, they dig longitudinal galleries in the petioles and the large veins of the leaves of artichoke. The leaves develop pale spots, then yellow and decompose, the flowerhead develop badly.

Symptoms
Galleries in leaves. Leaves turn yellow and wilt.

Vegetables
Artichoke

Artichoke pear-shaped weevil adult

Remedies: Proactive
- Infusion of wormwood

- Tansy decoction

- Eliminate the infected plants

Artichoke Root Aphid

Botanical name
Protrama radicis

Class
Aphididae, Insect

Names in other languages
Artichoke Root Aphid (En). Puceron des racines de l'artichaut, Gros Puceron des racines de chicorée (Fr). Langfüßige Wurzellaus (De). Artisjok worteluis (Nl).

Description
The artichoke root aphid (*Protrama radicis*) is probably rather common, but is seldom seen because it lives underground feeding on the roots of plants. Sucking so much sap this causing leaves to turn yellow and plants stunted. Finding them is facilitated by the frequent presence of ants around the stem collar of an affected plant.

Symptoms
Stunted plants

Vegetables
Artichoke

Artichoke root aphid adulte

Remedies: Immediate action
- Black Soap

- Canola oil. Rapeseed oil

- Beauveria bassiana

- Insecticide based on azadirachta. Neem oil

- Insecticide based on spinosad

- Remove ants

- Steinernema nematodes

- Heterorhabditis nematodes

Remedies: Proactive
- Install insect hotels

- Remove plant debris and crop residues

Ascochyta Foot-rot

Botanical name
Phoma medicaginis and other species

Class
Phomaceae, Fungus

Names in other languages
Ascochyta Foot-rot, Collar rot of pea, Foot rot of pea (En). Anthracnose du pois, Ascochytose du pois, Pourridié ascochytique du pois (Fr). Brennfleckenkrankheit: Erbse, Fußkrankheit: Erbse (De). Voetziekte erwten (Nl).

Ascochyta foot-rot symptoms on peas

Description
Ascochyta blight attacks all parts of the plant. The infected leaves have small to large, round to irregular, dark brown to purple spots. Some of the spots may have ashy grey centres. The spots usually have purple margins and may have rings. Spots may join up to form brownish purple blotches. Severely diseased leaves shrivel and dry, starting at the base of the plant and progressing upwards. Spots on pods are sunken but have no rings. Stem symptoms consist of brownish to purple streaks. Infection from infected seeds can cause a brown to black stem and foot rot just above the soil line. Such plants may die and result in a poor stand in the field. Blossoms may be infected and drop off during extended wet weather. On the pods and the seeds, the spots are reddish-brown, have well defined margins and appear sunken on the skin of the pod. The infected seeds show dark lesions. Loss mainly affects the seedlings which die (damping-off).

Symptoms
Brown spots on leaves.

Vegetables
Peas

Remedies: Immediate action
• Bacillus subtilis

Remedies: Proactive
• Certified seed or plants

• Long Rotation. Crop Rotation

113

Ascochyta Rot

Botanical name
Ascochyta hortorum

Class
Phomaceae, Fungus

Names in other languages
Ascochyta Rot. Black Rot. Leaf Spot, Fruit spot of artichoke (En). Ascochytose de l'artichaut (Fr). Fleckenkrankheit (De). Ascochyta-ziekte van artisjok (Nl).

Ascochyta rot symptoms on artichoke

Description
Ascochyta rot or black rot is caused by a fungus (*Ascochyta hortorum*). It develops first on the tips of the outermost bracts of the flowerbuds. In wet conditions the bud may be affected by a dark rot. Brown lesions also occurs on stems and leaves.

Symptoms
Brown lesions on leaves. Brown lesions on fruits.

Vegetables
Artichoke

Remedies: Immediate action
- Bordeaux mixture

- Trichoderma

Remedies: Proactive
- Eliminate the infected plants

- Lithothamnion algae

- Long rotation

- Certified plants

Asparagus Aphid

Botanical name
Brachycorynella asparagi

Class
Aphididae, Insect

Names in other languages
Asparagus Aphid (En). Puceron de l'asperge (Fr).
Spargelblattlaus (De). Aspergebladluis (Nl).

Description
The asparagus aphid *(Brachycorynella asparagi)* damage is primarily from a toxin that the aphids inject into the plant when feeding. The toxin causes shortened internodes on subsequent growth, resulting in a tufted appearance. Heavy populations also produce massive amounts of honeydew that may lead to considerable ant activity. Asparagus aphid populations start very slowly and in widely dispersed patches, then seem to nearly explode. Populations often begin near field edges, so monitor the edges of fields regularly whenever leaves are present. It is best to collect plant samples and shake or beat them on a hard, light-colored surface to dislodge both the aphids and their natural enemies.

Symptoms
Presence of aphids on leaves. Presence of honey dew on leaves.

Vegetables
Asparagus

Asparagus aphid adulte

Remedies: Immediate action
- Insecticide based on pyrethrum

- Black Soap

- Beauveria bassiana

- Canola oil. Rapeseed oil. Plant oils

- Insecticide based on azadirachta. Neem oil

Remedies: Proactive
- Install insect hotels, bug hotels or insect houses

- Chromatic trap (Yellow)

- Use insect proof nett

Asparagus Beetles

Botanical name
Crioceris asparagi/Crioceris duodecimpunctata

Class
Chrysomelidae, Insect

Names in other languages
Asparagus Beetle (En). Criocère de l'asperge. (Fr). Gemeines Spargelhähnchen, Buntes Spargelhähnchen (De). Aspergehaantje, Aspergetorretje (Nl).

Asparagus beetles adults and larvae

Description
Two beetles feed on asparagus plants, Asparagus beetle (*Crioceris asparagi*) and the spotted asparagus beetle (*Crioceris duodecimpunctata*). Adults and larvae chew spears in spring. In summer they feed on the fronds, if present in high numbers they may defoliate the plants.

Symptoms
Plants defoliated and presence of larvae and beetles.

Vegetables
Asparagus.

Remedies: Immediate action
- Insecticide based on pyrethrum

- Insecticide based on azadirachta

- Black soap

- Steinernema carpocapsae. S. feltae nematodes

- Remove manually pests

Remedies: Proactive
- Nematode Heterorhabditis bacteriophora

- Install insect hotels, bug hotels or insect houses

- Remove plant debris and crop residues

- Trap cropping. Leave a few asparagus shoots growing on one plant, while you harvest the other plants, to attract the first beetles to manage them.

Asparagus Fly

Botanical name
Platyparea poeciloptera / Plioreocepta poecilioptera

Class
Tephritidae, Insect

Names in other languages
Asparagus Fly, Asparagus maggot (En). Mouche de l'asperge (Fr). Spargelfliege (De). Aspergevlieg (Nl).

Description
The asparagus fly (*Platyparea poeciloptera*) larvae make tunnels/galeries in the asparagus turions. The galleries prevent the sap from circulating, resulting in deficient nutrition and a gradual weakening of the crown.

Symptoms
Deformed turions or stems.

Vegetables
Asparagus

Asparagus fly adult

Remedies: Immediate action
- Tansy infusion

- Rue maceration

- Liquid manure or maceration of tomato

- Eliminate the infected plants

- Nematode Heterorhabditis bacteriophora

Remedies: Proactive
- Chromatic trap.

- Remove plant debris and crop residues

Asparagus Moth

Botanical name
Parahypopta caestrum. Hypopta caestrum

Class
Cossidae, Insects.

Names in other languages
Asparagus Moth (En). Chenille à fourreau de l'asperge, Teigne de l'asperge (Fr). Spargelmotte (De). Aspergemot (Nl).

Description
The asparagus moth, Parahypopta caestrum is among the most damaging pests of Asparagus spp.. Adults lay eggs in the soil near the shoots and larvae bore the roots causing the destruction of asparagus plantations in a few years. Due to the cryptic nature of immature stages, control of this pest is very difficult. The asparagus moth larvae feeds on the buds and hollows out the roots. This leads to the disappearance of plants which dry up in the course of the summer.

Symptoms
Plant slowly desiccates.

Vegetables
Asparagus

Asparagus moth adult and larvae

Remedies: Immediate action
- Remove infested plants parts:

- Heterorhabditis bacteriophora Nematode

- Steinernema carpocapsae

Remedies: Proactive
- Pheromone traps

Bacterial Blight of Garlic

Botanical name
Pseudomonas salomonii

Class
Pseudomonadaceae, Bacterium.

Names in other languages
Bacterial Blight of Garlic, Café au lait disease of garlic (En). Maladie du café au lait, Café au lait de l'ail (Fr). Café-au-lait-Krankheit (De). Gele randen (Nl).

Bacterial blight of garlic

Description
Bacterial blight of garlic is caused by a bacterium (*Pseudomonas salomonii*) provoke white lesions in the leaf sheaths and striated lesions on the leaf that sometimes leads to soft rot and plant death.

Symptoms
White and striated lesions on leaves.

Vegetables
Garlic.

Remedies: Immediate action
• Reynoutria sachalinensis extract. Giant Knotweed

Remedies: Proactive
• Certified seed

• Long Rotation. Crop Rotation

• Review irrigation. Watering

Bacterial Blight of Pea

Botanical name
Pseudomonas syringae

Class
Pseudomonadaceae, Bacterium.

Names in other languages
Bacterial Blight of pea. Pea Bacterial Blight (EN), Graisse du Pois (FR), Bakterienbrand (DE), Bacterieverwelkingsziekte (NL).

Description
Bacterial blight (*Pseudomonas syringae*) first appears as small, dark green, water-soaked spots on leaves and stipules, often near the leaf base. The spots enlarge and merge but are often limited by the veins. The leaf spots turn yellowish and later brown and papery. Spots on pods are sunken and olive brown.

Symptoms
Leaves wit yellow-brown spots. Pods with olive brown sunken spots.

Vegetables
Peas.

Bacterial blight of pea

Remedies: Immediate action
• Reynoutria sachalinensis extract. Giant Knotweed

• Review irrigation. Watering

• Remove infested plants

Remedies: Proactive
• Long Rotation. Crop Rotation

• Certified seed or plants

• Remove plant debris and crop residues

Bacterial Brown Spot

Bacterial brown spot of beans

Botanical name
Pseudomonas syringae

Class
Pseudomonadaceae, Bacterium.

Names in other languages
Bacterial Brown Spot, Bacterial blight of bean, Grease spot of bean, Halo blight of bean (En). Graisse du haricot, Taches aréolées du haricot, Tison du haricot (Fr). Eckige Fleckigkeit: Bohne, Fettfleckenkrankheit: Bohne (De). Bruinrot (Nl).

Description
Bacterial brown spot is caused by a bacterium (*Pseudomonas syringae*) on bean foliage and pods. The lesions are generally circular, brown, and necrotic and are often surrounded by a blight yellow zone. Lesions occasionally fall out, giving the leaves a shot-hole appearance. Lesions on pods are circular and initially water-soaked. They become brown and necrotic. Infected pods may be twisted or bent where lesions develop.

Symptoms
Circular, brown, and necrotic lesions on leaves. Translucent lesions on leaves.

Vegetables
Green bean, Common bean

Remedies: Immediate action
- Eliminate the infected plants

- Reynoutria sachalinensis extract. Giant Knotweed

- Bordeaux mixture

- Review irrigation. Watering

- Remove infested plants

- Streptomyces avermitilis

Remedies: Proactive
- Long rotation

- Certified seed

- Use resistant varieties/cultivars

- Remove plant debris and crop residues

Bacterial Canker of Tomato

Botanical name
Clavibacter michiganensis

Class
Microbacteriaceae, Bacterium

Names in other languages
Bacterial Canker of Tomato, Bird's eye of tomato fruits, Vascular wilt of tomato (En). Chancre bactérien de la tomate (Fr). Bakterienkrebs, Bakterienwelke (De). Bakterie kanker (Nl).

Description
Bacterial canker is a tomato disease caused by a bacterium (*Clavibacter michiganensis*). Unilateral wilting or withering of leaflets on one side of the leaf, and bird's eye-spot lesions (raised white spot developing a necrotic centre) on the fruit surface are the outstanding features diagnostic of tomato bacterial canker. In the field, the first symptom is desiccation of the edge of the leaflets. The plant slowly desiccates, with or without exhibiting wilting. Plants infected as young seedlings become stunted and wither rapidly. Numerous small whitish or tan pustules may appear on leaf veins, petioles and peduncles.

Symptoms
Desiccation of the edge of the leaflets. Whole plant slowly desiccates

Vegetables
Eggplant, Pepper, Bell pepper, Tomatoes.

Bacterial canker of tomato

Remedies: Immediate action
- Bordeaux mixture

- Horsetail decoction

- Eliminate the infected plants

- Reynoutria sachalinensis extract. Giant Knotweed

Remedies: Proactive
- Use certified seeds or plants

- Long crop rotation

- Sanitation. If bacterial canker was a problem the previous year, sanitize implements, tools, and cages prior to use.

Bacterial Spot

Bacterial spot on tomato

Botanical name
Pseudomonas and *Xanthomonas*

Class
Pseudomonaceae, Bacterium

Names in other languages
Bacterial Spot (EN), Tache bactérienne (FR), Bakteriell Fleck (DE), Bacteriele vlekziekte (NL).

Description
Bacterial spot is caused by a bacterium (*Xanthomonas campestris*). Leaf spots appear as small, 2 to 3 mm in diameter, water-soaked, translucent lesions that later turn brownish black and may have a yellow halo. The lesions are somewhat irregular and appear greasy on the upper leaf surface, with a translucent centre and a black margin. The centres of the lesions dry out and frequently tear. Only a few spots may cause a leaflet to turn yellow, wither, and drop prematurely.

Symptoms
Circular, irregular, brownish-black, necrotic lesions on leaflets. Dried up leaves. Black spots on fruits. and in potato brown lesions on tubers.

Vegetables
Tomato, Potato.

Remedies: Immediate action
*   Bordeaux mixture

*   Horsetail decoction

*   Bacillus subtilis

*   Reynoutria sachalinensis extract. Giant Knotweed

*   Streptomyces avermitilis

Remedies : Proactive
*   Long rotation

*   Certified seed

*   Use resistant varieties/cultivars

*   Hot water treatment of seeds

*   Remove plant debris and crop residues

Basal Rot

Basal rot on garlic

Botanical name:
Fusarium oxysporum, Fusarium proliferatum, Fusarium solani

Class
Tuberculariaceae, Fungus

Names in other languages
Basal Rot, Foot rot, Root rot (En). Fusariose du collet, Pourriture du collet, Pourridié fusarien (Fr). Basalfäule, Fußfäule, Stengelgrundfäule, Zwiebelfäule (De). Fusariumrot (Nl).

Description
Fusarium basal rot is a fungal disease affecting onion and garlic, as well as other Allium crops such as leek. In field situations, Fusarium basal rot can cause damping-off of young plants, as well as foliar chlorosis, stunting, death of mature plants, and bulb rot. In garlic and onion, rot typically initiates in the basal plate (base of the bulb), then spreads into the bulb. In some cases, rot can start on the side of the bulb, potentially via wounds, or on the neck, necrotizing the bulb from the top down. When cut vertically, an infected bulb will show brown discoloration of the stem plate tissue. Later, the stem plate tissue becomes pitted and shows a dry rot.

Symptoms
Leaves or plant turn yellow and die. Rotted bulbs or cloves.

Vegetables
Garlic, Onion.

Remedies: Immediate
• Trichoderma

• Streptomyces lydicus

• Remove fallen leaves and dead material

• Review irrigation. Watering

Remedies: Proactive
• Long rotation:

• Soil solarization

• Certified seed or plants

• Remove plant debris and crop residues

Bean Aphids

Black Dolphin Aphids

Botanical name
Aphis fabae

Class
Aphididae, Insects

Names in other languages
Bean Aphids, Black bean aphid (En). Puceron noir de la fève, Puceron du haricot (Fr). Schwarze Bohnenblattlaus, Schwarze Rübenblattlaus (De). Zwarte bonenluis (Nl).

Bean aphids adults

Description
The black aphids (*Aphis fabae*) can seriously damage the broad kidney or runner bean crop, if unattended, in a few days. It cover the plants with numerous black aphids, produce a film of honeydew who is on its turn infested by black fungus fumagine.

Symptoms
Leaves curled or shrivelled, Presence of aphids, colonies of aphids, honey dew, sooty mould on leaves or stems.

Vegetables
Artichoke, Beetroot, Broad bean, Carrot. Chard, Green bean, Peas, Potato.

Remedies: Immediate action
- Black soap:

- Insecticide based on pyrethrum

- Liquid manure of fern

- Elder decoction

- Common Rue Maceration

- Liquid manure of wormwood

- Liquid manure or maceration of tomato

- Aphidius matricariae

- Beauveria bassiana

- Lithothamnium algae. Calcified Seaweed. Maerl

Remedies: Proactive
- Early seeding

- Install insect hotels, bug hotels or insect houses. Natural enemies include parasitic wasps, ladybirds, hoverflies, lacewings, and insect-pathogenic fungi.

Bean Beetle

Pea beetle

Botanical name
Bruchus rufimanus. Bruchus pisorum

Class
Chrysomelidae, Insects

Names in other languages
Bean Beetle, Broad-bean weevil (En). Bruche de la fève, Bruche de la gourgane (Fr). Ackerbohnenkäfer, Bohnenkäfer, Pferdebohnenkäfer (De). Tuinbonenkever (Nl).

Bean beetle adult

Description
The Bean beetle (Bruchus rufimanus and other Bruchus spp.) are small coleoptera who attacks broad bean but also pea and bean. The main signs of pea beetle feeding are ragged, scalloped cuts around the edges of the leaves, along with damage to flowers. They causes small holes in the seeds. This are the distinctive exit holes left by emerging adults after the insect's pupation stage.The presence of beetles in the seeds renders them unsuitable for consumption and reduce the germination rate.

Symptoms
Beans with small holes.

Vegetables
Broad bean, Green bean, Peas.

Remedies: Immediate action
*   Remove manually pests

*   Beauveria bassiana

*   Pyrethrum insecticide

*   Liquid manure of wormwood

Remedies: Proactive
*   Pheromone traps

*   Freeze seeds

*   Insect-proof net. Insect net. Mesh Crop Cover

*   Remove plant debris and crop residues

*   Install insect hotels, bug hotels or insect houses

Bean Yellow Mosaic Virus

Bean yellow mosaic virus symptoms

Botanical name
Potyvirus phaseoluteum, BYMV

Class
Potyviridae, Virus.

Names in other languages
Bean Yellow Mosaic Virus, Bean top necrosis (En).
Mosaïque jaune des haricots (Fr).
Bohnengelbmosaik-Virus (De).
Bonenscherpmozaïekvirus (Nl).

Description
The diagnostic symptom of bean yellow mosaic is the bright yellow to green mosaic or mottle appearance of infected leaves, which becomes most apparent on leaves as they age. Infected leaves also show varying degrees of leaf distortion, downward cupping, and wrinkling. Plants infected at a young age may show stunted growth. The striking yellow mosaic symptoms differentiate bean yellow mosaic infections from those of bean common mosaic, which causes light and dark green mosaic patterns of infected leaves. The virus is transmitted by over 20 species of aphids (e.g., the pea, green peach, and bean aphids). Transmission of the virus to the bean plant occurs within seconds once virus-carrying aphids begin feeding on the crop. Aphids can effectively spread the virus within a field, resulting in high rates of infection.

Symptoms
Leaves with mosaic pattern.

Vegetables
Green bean, Common bean

Remedies: Immediate action
· Remove aphids

· Eliminate the infected plants

Remedies: Proactive
· Long rotation

· Use resistant varieties/cultivars

· Certified seed or plants

Beet Armyworm

Botanical name
Spodoptera exigua

Class
Noctuidae, Insects

Names in other languages
Beet Armyworm (EN), Noctuelle de la betterave (FR), Florida-uil (NL)

Description
The beet army worm (Spodoptera exigua) adult are small, mottled gray- or dusky-winged moths. Females deposit pale greenish or pinkish striated eggs on leaves in small or large masses covered with white cottony material. Eggs hatch in a few days and tiny caterpillars begin feeding on the plant. When caterpillars are full grown in about 2 to 3 weeks, they are about 3 cm long. The color down the middle of the back may be olive green to almost black with a yellow stripe on each side of the body. There is a dark spot on each side of the thorax just above the middle leg. Beet armyworms can kill seedlings, consume large portions of leaves, and stunt growth by feeding on buds. Young larvae or caterpillars feed gregariously and skeletonize foliage. As they mature, larvae become solitary and eat large irregular holes in foliage.

Symptoms
Leaves with irregular holes and presence of caterpillars.

Vegetables
Asparagus, Beetroot, Broccoli, Cabbage, Cauliflower, Celery, Eggplant, Onion, Peas, Pepper, Potato, Tomato, Turnip.

Beet Armyworm adult and larvae

Remedies: Immediate action
*   Auxiliary Beauveria brongniartii

*   Steinernema carpocapsae. S. feltae nematodes

*   Insecticide based on pyrethrum

*   Bacillus thuringiensis. Bt

*   Insecticide based on azadirachta. Neem oil

*   Remove manually pests

*   Spinosad

Remedies: Proactive
*   Pheromone traps

*   Install insect hotels, bug hotels or insect houses. Many natural enemies attack beet armyworms. Common parasites include the wasps Chelonus insularis and Hyposoter exiguae, and the tachinid fly Lespesia archippivora. .

*   Remove plant debris and crop residues

Beet Curly Top Virus

Beet curly top virus symptoms

Botanical name
Curtovirus betae, BCTV

Class
Geminiviridae, Virus.

Names in other languages
Beet Curly Top Virus. BCTV, Curly top of beet (En).
Virus de l'enroulement apical de la betterave (Fr).
Kräuselschopfkrankheit: Rübe (De). Krulvirus van biet (Nl).

Description
Beet curly top virus (BCTV) is caused by a virus. The leaves are dwarfed and crinkled and curl upwards. Leaves turn yellow, wilt and die. The only known vector of BCTV is the beet leafhopper, Circulifer tenellus. The beet leafhopper is a small insect that can accumulate BCTV while feeding on annual and perennial weeds. Once the BLH have accumulated the virus, they can then transmit BCTV as they feed on agricultural commodities in search of new host plants, potentially causing severe damage and crop losses.

Symptoms
Leaves turn yellow and wilt.

Vegetables
Beetroot, Chard, Spinach.

Remedies: Immediate action
• Eliminate the infected plants

Remedies: Proactive
• Install insect hotels, bug hotels or insect houses. There are many natural enemies of beet leafhopper, including spiders, green lacewings, assassin bugs, bigeyed bugs, and certain species of parasitic flies and wasps. When possible, these natural enemies should be promoted.

• Insect-proof net. Insect net. Mesh Crop Cover

Beet Fly

Botanical name
Pegomyia betae/Pegomya hyoscyami

Class
Anthomyidae, Insects

Names in other languages
Beet Fly, Beet leaf miner, Mangold fly, Spinach leaf miner (En). Mouche de la betterave, Mineuse de l'épinard (Fr). Spinatfliege, Bilsenkrautfliege (De). Bietenvlieg, bilzenkruidvlieg (Nl).

Beet Fly adult and symptoms

Description
The beet leafminer (Pegomyia betae Curtis) and the spinach leafminer (Pegomya hyoscyami (Panzer)) are very similar in appearance and life cycle. Both primarily attack members of the family Chenopodiaceae including spinach, beet, swiss chard, and lambsquarter. The adult leafminer is a small fly (5-7mm), which lays elongated white eggs that measure around 1mm x 0.3mm. Once the eggs hatch, in 3-6 days, the larvae burrow immediately into the leaf. The larvae feed between the upper and lower leaf epidermis, forming transparent "mines" that eventually become large blotches. The larvae live for 7-12 days (depending on temperature), and then pupate, usually dropping into the soil first. New adult flies hatch after 10-20 days, except in late fall, when they enter diapause. The damage to the crop may be insignificant, or it may be very severe if attacked when leaves are at or near marketable stage.

Symptoms
Brown lesions and galleries in leaves.

Vegetables
Beetroot, Chard, Spinach.

Remedies: Immediate action
- Insect-proof net

- Eliminate the infected plants

- Steinernema carpocapsae. S. feltae nematodes

Remedies: Proactive
- Long Rotation. Crop Rotation

- Install insect hotels, bug hotels or insect houses

Beet Moth, Beet Worm

Botanical name
Scrobipalpa ocellatella. Phthorimaea ocellatella

Class
Gelechiidae, Insect

Names in other languages
Beet Moth, Beet worm (En). Teigne de la betterave (Fr). RuebenmotteRunkelruebenmotte (De). Bietzandvleugeltje (Nl).

Description
The beet moth (Scrobipalpa ocellatella) mines can be detected in the leaves and leaf stems. The caterpillars skeletonize leaves, braiding them with silk threads. In spring and in the beginning of summer, they mine leaves, usually along main veins, also piercing holes in petioles. The damaged leaves roll and blacken. A black clump of rotten leaves fastened with silk threads is formed instead of the central rosette. In hot and dry years, such damage frequently causes the whole plant to die since the outer leaves die off quickly and new ones are not formed because of the central rosette loss. Caterpillars of the following generations penetrate into roots.

Symptoms
Leaves with galleries. Stems stunted.

Vegetables
Beetroot, Beet.

Beet Moth adult and larvae

Remedies: Immediate action
- Remove manually pests

- Beauveria bassiana

- Insecticide based on spinosad

- Azadirachta. Neem oil insecticide

- Heterorhabditis bacteriophora Nematode

- Steinernema carpocapsae. S. feltae nematodes

Remedies: Proactive
- Pheromone traps

- Insect-proof net. Insect net. Mesh Crop Cover

- Install insect hotels, bug hotels or insect houses

- Remove plant debris and crop residues

Black Leg

Botanical name
Leptosphaeria maculans. Phoma lingum

Class
Pleosporaceae, Fungus.

Names in other languages
Black leg of cabbage, Crucifer Collar Rot, Canker of crucifers, Dry rot of crucifers, Leaf spot of crucifers (En). Pied noir, Phoma ou nécrose du collet des crucifères, Chancre du chou, Jambe noire du chou, Nécrose du collet (Fr). Fußfäule: Kohl, Halsnekrose: Raps, Stengelfäule: Raps, Trockenfäule: Kohl, Umfallkrankheit: Kohl (De). Zwarte voet, Phoma of kroonnecrose van kruisbloemige (Nl).

Description
Black leg or collar rot (Leptosphaeria maculans) can develop pale, irregular spots on leaves, which later become ashy gray with scattered black dots on the surface. Stem lesions are elongated with purple borders near the ground level and extend below the soil surface, causing a black rot of lower stem and roots. Severely affected plants remain stunted and finally wilt. As plants mature, they fall sideways from lack of root anchorage.

Symptoms
Leaves with yellow spots, Rotting of collar.

Vegetables
Cabbage

Black leg or collar rot symptoms

Remedies: Immediate action
• Remove infested plants or plant parts

Remedies: Proactive
• Certified seed or plants

• Long Rotation. Crop Rotation

• Remove plant debris and crop residues

• Hot water treatment of seeds ((25 to 30 minutes in 50°C water)

Black Rot of Cabbage

Black rot of cabbage symptoms

Botanical name
Xanthomonas campestris pv. campestris

Class
Xanthomonadaceae, Bacterium

Names in other languages
Black Rot of Cabbage (En). Nervation noire des Crucifères (Fr). Adernschwärze: Kohl, Gefässbakteriose Kohl (De). Zwartnervigheid (Nl).

Description
Black rot, caused by the bacterium *Xanthomonas campestris pv. campestris (Xcc)*, is a significant disease of cabbage and other crucifer crops worldwide. Symptoms of black rot generally begin with yellowing at the leaf margin, which expands into the characteristic "V"-shaped lesion. The bacterial infection becomes systemic, meaning that the bacterium can enter the veins of the plant and spread into the cabbage head, which can lead to serious losses in storage. Blackening of the vascular tissue is typical in severe infections.

Symptoms
Leaves turn yellow. Leaves with V-shaped lesions.

Vegetables
Cabbage

Remedies: Immediate action
• Review irrigation. Watering

• Bordeaux mixture

• Remove infested plants or plant parts

Remedies: Proactive
• Certified seed or plants

• Long Rotation. Crop Rotation

• Use resistant varieties/cultivars

• Remove plant debris and crop residues

Black Scurf

Botanical name
Rhizoctonia solani

Class
Ceratobasidiaceae, Fungus

Names in other languages
Black Scurf. Rhizoctonia Canker. Stem Canker (En). Rhizoctone brun, Chancre du pied de la pomme de terre, Pied noir, Rhizoctone brun (Fr). Pockenkrankheit: Kartoffel, Wurzeltöterkrankheit: Kartoffel (De). Zwartpoten (Nl).

Description
Black scurf or rhizoctonia canker is caused by a fungus (Rhizoctonia solani). Symptoms are reddish and brown lesions found on stolons and roots. Black Scurf forms a hard, dark brown or black mass on the surface of the underground tuber, which can range in size from small and flat, to large, raised lumps. Rhizoctonia diseases are initiated by seed-borne or soil-borne inoculum. The pathogen overwinters as sclerotia and mycelium on infected tubers, in plant residue or in infested soils.

Symptoms
Reddish-brown lesions on stolons, roots. Dark brown or black canker on tubers.

Vegetables
Potato

Black scurf on potato

Remedies: Immediate action
- Trichoderma

- Streptomyces lydicus

Remedies: Proactive
- Certified seed

- Long rotation

- Biofumigation

Boron Deficiency

Boron deficiency symptoms

Botanical name
B

Class
Nutrient deficiency

Names in other languages
Boron Deficiency (En). Carence en bore (Fr). Bormangel (De). Boriumgebrek (Nl).

Description
Boron deficiency occurs when plants do not receive sufficient amounts of boron, leading to impaired growth and development. This deficiency is more likely to occur in sandy or acidic soils, as boron can easily leach away or become unavailable to plants in such conditions. Additionally, high rainfall and excessive irrigation can exacerbate the leaching of boron from the soil. Symptoms vary between crop species, but generally occur in the growing points or flower and fruiting parts of the plant. Young leaves will often show a general chlorosis. The upper leaves may show a reddish color. Crops with high boron requirements: Broccoli, cabbage, cauliflower, rutabaga, turnips, beets, and spinach. Crops with medium boron requirements: Asparagus, carrots, cucurbits, eggplants, leeks, okra, onions, parsnips, radishes, strawberries, sweet corn, tomatoes, potatoes. Crops with low boron requirements: Peppers, sweet potatoes. Crops with very low boron requirements: Beans, peas

Symptoms
Yellow leaves.

Vegetables
Beetroot, Celeriac, Celery, Garlic, Turnip.

Remedies: Immediate action
- Lithothamnion algae

- Liquid manure of nettle

- Liquid manure of comfrey

Remedies: Immediate action
- Soil pH (Keep pH in between 6 - 6.5)

- Review irrigation. Watering

Botrytis Rot

Botrytis neck rot symptoms

Botanical name
Botrytis

Class
Sclerotiniaceae, Fungus

Names in other languages
Neckrot. Botrytis Rot (EN), Botrytis (FR), Koprot (NL)

Description
Botrytis neck rot is caused by Botrytis acclada and B. allii. The fungi are specific to members in the Alliaceae (onion and garlic) and can be found in all onion producing regions around the world. They occur in the soil and can be seedborne. Botrytis can grow and produce spores on dry onion leaf tissue in the field and spores are blown around by wind and can infect wounded bulbs. However, the single most important point of infections is through soft, green neck tissue of the onion bulb. Botrytis aclada and B. allii become a problem in storage when onions are harvested immature and can result in more than 30% yield loss. The symptoms include water-soaked stems and gray fuzzy fungal growth. The disease may develop on stored bulbs.

Symptoms
Decayed bulbs with gray mould

Vegetables
Garlic, Onion

Remedies: Immediate action
- Eliminate the infected plants

- Horsetail decoction

- Liquid manure of horsetail

- Bacillus subtilis

- Bicarbonate of potassium or sodium

- Streptomyces lydicus

Remedies: Proactive
- Long rotation

- Certified seed or plants

- Use resistant varieties/cultivars

- Remove plant debris and crop residues

Brachyserus of Garlic

Brachycerus beetle of garlic

Botanical name
Brachycerus undatus

Class
Brachyceridae, Insects

Names in other languages
Brachyserus of Garlic (En). Charançon d'ail (Fr). Knoblauchkäfer (De). Knoflook kever (Nl).

Description
The brachycerus beetles of garlic (Brachycerus undatus) larvae feeds on the bulbs of garlic and other Liliaceae. Attacked bulbs are internally hollowed. Damage to garlic can involve one or more cloves. Around the hollowed parts, the external membrane is sunken and soft to the touch and there is often a dark plug present, composed of larval faecal droppings mixed with other debris.

Symptoms
Damaged bulbs.

Vegetables
Garlic

Remedies: Immediate action
*   Remove manually pests

*   Steinernema carpocapsae. S. feltae nematodes

Remedies: Proactive
*   Insect-proof net

*   Certified seed or plants

*   Chromatic trap

Bright-line Brown-eyes Moth

Botanical name
Mamestra oleracea. Polia oleracea. Melanchra oleracea. Lacanobia oleracera

Class
Noctuidae, Insects

Names in other languages
Bright-line Brown-eyes Moth, Glasshouse tomato moth, Tomato moth (En). Noctuelle potagère (Fr). Gemüseeule, Salateule (De). Groenteuil. Kooluil (Nl).

Bright-line brown-eyes moth adult and larvae

Description
The bright-line brown-eyes moth (*Mamestra oleracea*) caterpillar feeds at night, rarely during the day: it moves along and eats across the leaves. If disturbed, it drops at the end of a silk thread and remains still. During the day, it hides.

Symptoms
Presence of caterpillars.

Vegetables
Asparagus, Beetroot, Cabbage, Cucumber, Green bean, Potato, Tomato.

Remedies: Immediate action
- Insecticide based on spinosad
- Remove infested plants parts
- Azadirachta. Neem oil insecticide
- Bacillus thuringiensis. Bt
- Garlic macerate oil
- Remove manually pests
- Pheromone traps
- Insect-proof net. Insect net. Mesh Crop Cover
- Apply mulch or straw

Remedies: Proactive
- Pheromone traps
- Install insect hotels, bug hotels or insect houses.
- Long Rotation. Crop Rotation
- Remove plant debris and crop residues

Cabbage Cyst Nematode

Botanical name
Heterodora cruciferae

Class
Heteroderidae, Nematodes

Names in other languages
Cabbage and Cauliflower Cyst Nematode. Brassica Cyst Nematode (En). Nématode des crucifères (Fr). Kohlzystenälchen (De). Koolcystenaaltje (Nl).

Cabbage cyst nematode symptoms

Description
The cabbage and cauliflower nematode (*Heterodora cruciferae*) first field symptom is the appearance of small, conspicuous areas where plants are stunted. In severely infested fields, areas of decline usually can be identified by excessive leaf wilting during hot weather. Infected plants are much smaller than normal ones. Frequently, they have a dense system of secondary roots, called a hairy-root condition. Examination with a hand lens usually shows numerous small, white, bead-like structures on roots of infected plants.

Symptoms
Plants turn yellow. Plants stunted. Roots damaged.

Vegetables
Cabbage, Cauliflower, Turnip.

Remedies: Immediate action
- French marigolds infusion

Remedies: Proactive
- Long Rotation. Crop Rotation (3 to 5 years)

- Soil solarization. The soil should be moist but not wet. Cover the soil with a clear plastic tarp and bury the edges of the plastic. Leave the plastic on the soil for at least 4 to 6 weeks. Do not remove the plastic until you are ready to plant.

- Repellent plants. Companion plants. Marigolds. Tomato, Pepper, Peas.

- Certified seed or plants

Cabbage Aphid

Botanical name
Brevicoryne brassicae

Class
Aphididae, Insects

Names in other languages
Cabbage Aphid, Grey cabbage aphid, Mealy cabbage aphid (En). Puceron cendré du chou. Puceron blanc du chou (Fr). Mehlige Kohlblattlaus (De). Melige koolluis (Nl).

Cabbage aphid adult

Description
The cabbage aphid (*Brevicoryne brassicae*) is globe-shaped and green in colour. They are entirely coated with a characteristic grey-white powder. The feeding of aphids causes imperfect growth and wither of cabbage and rape. The plants may be covered entirely by aphids, honeydew and moult.

Symptoms
Leaves curled or shrivelled. Presence of colonies of aphids. Presence of honey dew and sooty mould.

Vegetables
Broccoli, Brussels sprout, Cabbage, Cauliflower, Kohlrabi, Chinese cabbage, Radish, Romanesco, Rutabaga, Turnip.

Remedies: Immediate action
- Black soap

- Liquid manure of nettle

- Tansy infusion

- Liquid manure of fern

- Garlic decoction

- Insecticide based on pyrethrum

- Elder decoction

- Canola oil. Rapeseed oil. Plant oils

- Insecticide based on azadirachta. Neem oil:

- Beauveria bassiana

- Common Rue Maceration

- Liquid manure of wormwood

- Liquid manure or maceration of tomato

- Lithothamnium algae. Calcified Seaweed. Maerl

Remedies: Proactive
- Predator Macrolophus caliginosus/M. pygmaeus. Predatory bug

- Remove plant debris and crop residues

Cabbage Bug.
Rape Bug. Crucifer Shield Bug. Brassica Bug

Botanical name
Eurydema oleraceum, Strachia oleracea

Class
Pentatomidae, Insects

Names in other languages
Cabbage Bug, Brassica bug (En). Punaise verte du chou, Punaise potagère (Fr). Gemüsewanze, Kohlwanze (De). Koolwants, Koolschildwants (Nl).

Description
The adults and nymphs of the Cabbage bug (*Eurydema oleraceum*) sucking sap from leaves causes damaged areas to become yellowish. Severe attacks can cause all leaves and flowers to turn yellow and may lead to the death of young plants. Among cultivated crops the bugs damage cabbage, radish, turnip, rutabaga, horseradish and rape.

Symptoms
Leaves turn yellow. Presence of bugs.

Vegetables
Cabbage, Kohlrabi, Radish, Rutabaga, Turnip.

Cabbage bug adult

Remedies: Immediate action
* Remove manually pests

* Garlic Decoction

* Garlic macerate oil

* Bacillus thuringiensis. Bt

* Diatomaceous Earth

* Insect-proof net. Insect net. Mesh Crop Cover

Remedies: Proactive
* Association with another crop or culture. Companion culture. (Onion, Tomato).

* Install insect hotels, bug hotels or insect houses. Diaeretiella rapae parasitic wasp, fungal pathogens, lady beetles, and syrphid fly larvae are important natural enemies.

Cabbage Club Root

Cabbage club root symptoms

Botanical name
Plasmodiophora brassicae

Class
Plasmodiophoradae, Fungus

Names in other languages
Cabbage Club Root, Club root of crucifers (En).
Hernie des Crucifères. Hernie du chou (Fr).
Kohlhernie, Knotensucht: Kohl (De). Knolvoet (Nl).

Description
Cabbage Club Root is caused by a fungus (*Plasmodiophora brassicae*). The disease rarely kills plants but induces them to wilt when under slight water stress. Initial foliar wilting is followed by reddening of the leaves which become chlorotic and eventually necrotic. Plants may become stunted. The roots become abnormally increased and swell up at different regions.

Symptoms
Reddening, yellowing of the leaves. Wilted plants, Roots abnormally increase

Vegetables
Broccoli, Brussels sprout, Cabbage, Cauliflower, Kohlrabi, Chinese cabbage, Romanesco, Rutabaga, Turnip.

Remedies: Immediate action
* Eliminate the infected plants

Remedies: Proactive
* Long rotation:

* Use resistant varieties/cultivars:

* Raise your soil pH

* Lithothamnium algae. Calcified Seaweed. Maerl

Cabbage Fly

Botanical name
Anthomye brassicae. Delia radicum

Class
Antomylidae, Insects

Names in other languages
Cabbage Maggot, Cabbage root fly, Radish fly (En). Mouche du chou (Fr). Kkleine Kohlfliege, Kohlmade, Schnauzenwurzelfliege (De). Koolvlieg (Nl).

Description
Cabbage maggot are the larvae of a fly (*Delia radicum*) it provoke tunnels into the roots and stems, causing plants to wilt in the sun and eventually stunting growth. Larvae are white maggots who can be observed in the collar or the surrounding soil.

Symptoms
Presence of maggots in roots, Wilted plants.

Vegetables
Broccoli, Brussels sprout, Cabbage, Cauliflower, Kohlrabi, Chinese cabbage, Radish, Romanesco, Rutabaga, Turnip.

Cabbage fly adult and maggots

Remedies: Immediate action
*   Cardboard. Cabbage Collars

*   Insect-proof net. Insect net. Mesh Crop Cover

*   Diatomaceous Earth

*   Insecticide based on pyrethrum

*   Steinernema carpocapsae. S. feltae nematodes

*   Liquid manure of tansy

*   Liquid manure of wormwood

*   Remove infested plants parts

Remedies: Proactive
*   Pheromone traps

*   Long Rotation. Crop Rotation

*   Remove plant debris and crop residues

Cabbage Stem Flea Beetle

Botanical name
Psylliodes chrysocephala

Class
Chrysomelidaceae, Insects

Names in other languages
Cabbage Stem Flea Beetle, Rape flea beetle (En).
Grosse altise du colza, Altise d'hiver du colza,
Altise du navet, Altise à tête dorée (Fr).
Rapserdfloh (De). Koolzaadaardvlo (Nl).

Cabbage stem flea beetle adult

Description
The Cabbage stem flea beetle (*Psylliodes chrysocephala*) are small coleoptera with a metallic sheen. The young adults nibbles the leaves of cultivated brassicas.The larvae penetrates the plant, it gnaws within the pith, passes into the stem and may reach the terminal bud. This plants becomes bushy and stunted.

Symptoms
Leaves perforated. Stunted plants.

Vegetables
Beetroot, Broccoli, Brussels sprout, Cabbage, Cauliflower, Chard, Kohlrabi, Chinese cabbage, Potato, Radish, Romanesco, Rutabaga, Tomato, Turnip.

Remedies: Immediate action
• Elder decoction

• Garlic decoction

• Tansy decoction

• Liquid manure of nettle

• Insecticide based on pyrethrum

• Wood ash

• Liquid manure or maceration of tomato

• Heterorhabditis bacteriophora nematode

• Black Soap

• Azadirachta. Neem oil insecticide

• Beauveria bassiana

Remedies: Proactive
• Insect-proof net

• Install insect hotels, bug hotels or insect houses. Flower strips provide nectar resources for parasitic wasps and beetle banks provide habitats for ground beetles. Minimising cultivations may also help by reducing mortality of soil dwelling natural enemies (e.g. ground beetles and pupae of parasitic wasps).

Cabbageworm
Imported Cabbage Worms

Botanical name
Pieris brassicae/Pieris rapae

Class
Pieridae, Insects

Names in other languages
Cabbageworm. Imported Cabbage Worms, Cabbage caterpillar, Cabbage white (En). Piéride du chou, Grand papillon blanc du chou (Fr). Großer Kohlweißling (De). Groot koolwitje. Klein koolwitje. Koolrupsen (Nl).

Description
The cabbageworm is the larvae of a common white butterfly (*Pieris brassicae/Pieris rapae*) with two or three small black spots. The caterpillars chew large holes in leaves. They produce dark green excrement.

Symptoms
Leaves with holes. Presence of caterpillars.

Vegetables
Broccoli, Brussels sprout, Cabbage, Cauliflower, Kohlrabi, Chinese cabbage, Radish, Romanesco, Rutabaga, Turnip.

Pieris adult and caterpillars

Remedies: Immediate action
- Remove manually pests

- Insecticide based on pyrethrum

- Bacillus thuringiensis

- Liquid manure or maceration of tomato

- Tansy infusion

- Liquid manure of wormwood

- Infusion of wormwood

- Steinernema carpocapsae nematodes.

- Azadirachta. Neem oil insecticide

Remedies: Proactive
- Association with another crop or culture, Repellent plants. Companion plants. Thym, Oregano, Dill, Onions, Garlic, Marigolds.

- Trap cropping. Cabbageworms are attracted to mustard plants.

Carrot Fly Carrot Rust Fly

Botanical name
Psilla rosae

Class
Psilidae, Insects

Names in other languages
Carrot Fly, Carrot rust fly (En). Mouche de la carotte (Fr). Eisenmade, Möhrenfliege (De). Wortelvlieg (Nl).

Description
The carrot fly (*Psila rosae*) is a small black fly with yellow legs. They attack carrots, celery and more rarely parsley and parsnip. The larvae penetrates into the roots, forms twisting galleries, the carrots are stunted and rot.

Symptoms
Galleries in roots, Presence of yellow larvae (maggots) in roots. Plants stunted.

Vegetables
Carrot, Celeriac, Fennel, Parsnip.

Carrot fly adult and maggot

Remedies: Immediate action
- Lavender decoction or infusion

- Elder decoction

- Liquid manure of pyrethrum

- Tansy decoction

- Liquid manure of lavender

Remedies: Proactive
- Insect-proof net

- Chromatic trap (Yellow)

- Association with another crop or culture

- Install insect hotels, bug hotels or insect houses. Preserve predators such as ground beetles and rove beetles, which feed on the eggs and larvae of carrot rust flies.

- Long Rotation. Crop Rotation

Carrot Root Nematode
Carrot Cyst Nematode

Botanical name
Heterodera carotae

Class
Heteroderidae, Insects

Names in other languages
Carrot Root Nematode. Carrot Cyst Nematode (En). Nématode à kystes de la carotte (Fr). Möhrenzystenälchen (De). Peencystenaaltje (Nl).

Description
The carrot root nematode (*Heterodera carotae*) symptoms appear as signs of nutrient deficiency. The symptoms include patches of the crop with reduced and stunted growth and yellowish foliage. Compared to healthy carrots, the diseased carrots are small with numerous beard-like rootlets, small distorted roots, a tangled overgrowth of rootlets and the characteristic cysts.

Symptoms
Stunted plants, Roots damaged.

Vegetables
Carrot.

Carrot root nematode symptoms

Remedies: Immediate action
- French marigolds infusion

Remedies: Proactive
- Long Rotation. Crop Rotation with brassicas, sorghum.

- Use resistant varieties/cultivars

- Soil solarization. It requires a 4- to 6-week (up to 60°C) treatment during the hottest time of the year.

- Repellent plants. Companion plants

Celery Fly

Botanical name
Philophylla heraclei. Euleia heraclei

Class
Tephritidae, Insects

Names in other languages
Celery Fly (En). Mouche du céléri (Fr).
Selleriblattfliege, Selleriefliege, Selleriminierfliege
(De). Selderijvlieg (Nl).

Celery fly adult and maggot

Description
The celery fly (Euleia heraclei) is blackish in colour
with yellow legs and measures 4 to 5 mm in
length. The maggots are elongated, more than 5
mm in length and yellowish-white in colour. The
larvae dig galleries causing the leaves to turn
yellow and dry out.

Symptoms
Galleries in leaves, Presence of white larvae,
Leaves turn yellow and wilt.

Vegetables
Celeriac, Celery.

Remedies: Immediate action
- Liquid manure of lavender

- Eliminate the infected plants

- Liquid manure of tansy

- Liquid manure of wormwood

- Beauveria bassiana

Remedies: Proactive
- Association with another crop or culture

- Insect-proof net

- Chromatic trap (Yellow)

Celery Late Blight

Botanical name
Septoria apiicola

Class
Phomaceae, Fungus

Names in other languages
Celery Late Blight, Fire blight of celery, Leaf spot of celery, Leaf spot of parsley (En). Septoriose du céleri, Brûlure tardive du céleri (Fr). Blattfleckenkrankheit: Sellerie (De). Bladvlekkenziekte (Nl).

Description
Celery late blight is caused by a fungus (*Septora apiicola*).Pale brown well defined spots occur on the leaves. They carry black specks (pycnidia) and they rapidly increase in number. The leaf blade turns yellow, the curled leaves dry out. The disease is most troublesome during mild, damp weather, especially warm, humid nights. Once late blight on celery is established, it is very difficult to control.

Symptoms
Pale brown spots on leaves, Curled leaves, Dry out leaves.

Vegetables
Carrot, Celeriac, Celery, Courgette, Cucumber, Lettuce, Peas, Pumpkin, Tomato.

Celery late blight symptoms

Remedies: Immediate action
- Horsetail decoction

- Eliminate the infected plants

- Dandelion infusion

- Bordeaux mixture

Remedies: Proactive
- Long rotation. If possible, avoid planting other vulnerable plants in the affected soil, including dill, cilantro, parsley, or fennel for three growing seasons before planting celery.

- Certified seed or plants

- Use resistant varieties/cultivars

Celery Miner Fly

Botanical name
Liriomyza bryoniae

Class
Agromyzidae, Insect

Names in other languages
Celery Miner Fly, Potato leaf miner, Tomato leafminer (En). Mouche de la bryone, Mouche mineuse du céleri (Fr). Kartoffelminierfliege, Tomatenminierfliege (De). Mineervlieg (Nl).

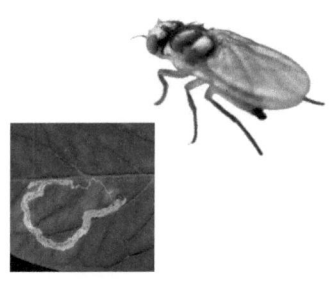

Celery miner fly adult and leaf with galleries

Description
The celery miner fly (*Liriomyza bryoniae*) adults are small black to gray flies with yellow markings. Females puncture leaves to feed on plant sap and lay eggs within the leaf tissues. After 2 to 4 days eggs hatch and larvae feed between the upper and lower surface of the leaves, making distinctive winding, whitish tunnels or mines that are often the first clue that leafminers are present. It reduce the plant's photosynthetic capacity.

Symptoms
Leaves with galleries

Vegetables
Celery

Remedies: Immediate action
*   Diglyphus isaea. Parasitic wasp

*   Insecticide based on azadirachta. Neem oil

*   Insecticide based on pyrethrum

*   Insecticide based on spinosad

*   Remove infested plants or plant parts

Remedies: Proactive
*   Chromatic trap (Yellow or blue)

*   nsect-proof net. Insect net. Mesh Crop Cover

*   Long Rotation. Crop Rotation

*   Remove plant debris and crop residues

Celery Root Rot
Phoma crown and root rot

Celery root rot symptoms

Botanical name
Phoma apiicola

Class
Phomaceae, Fungus

Names in other languages
Celery Root Rot, Root rot of celeriac, Scab of celeriac (En). Gale rugueuse du céleri, Pourriture du collet du céleri (Fr). Schorf: Sellerie (De). Schurft (Nl).

Description
Celery root rot (*Phoma apiicola*) causes brown spots on the root surface in the proximity of the collar. In this area cortical crusts with a scaly aspect occur. The affected foot is soft and the leaves wilt. The lesions caused by this fungus can develop rot.

Symptoms
Brown lesions on tubers

Vegetables
Celeriac.

Remedies: Immediate action
*   Streptomyces lydicus

*   Trichoderma

*   Bordeaux mixture

*   Remove infested plants or plant parts

Remedies: Proactive
*   Certified seed or plants

*   Hot water treatment of seeds. (48 °C for 30 minutes)

Cercosporosa Leaf Spot
Cercosporia blight

Botanical name
Cercospora et *Mycosphaerella*

Class
Dothideaceae, Fungus

Names in other languages
Cercosporosa Leaf Spot (En). Cercosporiose (Fr). Blattfleckenkrankheit (De). Bladvlekkenziekte (Nl).

Description
Cercospora leaf spot (Cercospora and Mycosphaerella) symptoms begin as small, circular to angular, brown to dark green spots with a reddish brown margin form on older leaves. The pathogen is favored by high humidity. The spores from the lesions are spread by rain and wind. Remove and burn the infected plant material and crop residue. Avoid over head application of water.

Symptoms
Leaf spots with brown-reddish margins.

Vegetables
Asparagus, Beetroot, Carrot, Celeriac, Celery, Chard, Green bean, Leek, Lettuce, Melon, Pepper, Potato, Sweet corn, Tomato.

Cercosporosa leaf spot symptoms

Remedies: Immediate action
- Eliminate the infected plants

- Micronized sulphur for pulverization

- Reynoutria sachalinensis extract. Giant Knotweed

- Bordeaux mixture

- Wettable sulphur

Remedies: Proactive
- Certified seed

- Long rotation

- Review irrigation. Watering

- Remove plant debris and crop residues

- Apply mulch or straw. To prevent spores from splashing up to lower leaves.

Chlorosis

Class
Nutrient deficiency

Names in other languages
Chlorosis (En). Chlorose (Fr). Chlorose (De). Chlorose (Nl).

Description
Chlorosis or yellowing of plant foliage due to a lack of chlorophyll development. Often the leaf veins remain green. At first the plant may appear lighter green than usual. Usually, the youngest leaves show the most yellowing. In some cases only part of the plant may be affected. Many different situations can cause chlorosis. These include soil compaction, poor drainage, nutrient deficiencies, high pH soils, root injury, flooding, and drought.

Symptoms
Yellow leaves on plants.

Vegetables
Tomato

Chlorosis symptoms

Remedies: Immediate action
- Liquid manure of nettle

- Liquid manure of comfrey

Cladosporium Leaf Spot

Botanical name
Cladosporium variabile

Class
Cladosporiaceae, Fungus

Names in other languages
Cladosporium Leaf Spot, Leaf spot of spinach (En). Cladosporiose sur épinard (Fr). Blattfleckenkrankheit: Spinat (De). Bladvlekkenziekte van spinazie (Nl).

Description
Cladosporium leaf spot is caused by the fungus Cladosporium variabile. This disease is frequently observed on spinach and has been reported from USA, Europe (including the UK) and Asia. In the UK, it is reported to be more severe in cool, wet autumn conditions. Leaf lesions are initially white, circular and up to 0.5 cm diameter. Older lesions are usually round, white/yellow with a dark margin and up to 1 cm in diameter, becoming irregular in shape when they merge with other lesions. Dark green fungal growth (spore clusters) may be visible in lesion centres, and this helps to distinguish cladosporium leaf spot from symptoms of anthracnose and stemphylium leaf spot.

Symptoms
Brown circular spots on leaves.

Vegetables
Spinach

Cladosporium leaf spot symptoms

Remedies: Immediate action
*   Liquid manure of nettle

*   Reynoutria sachalinensis extract. Giant Knotweed

*   Bacillus amyloliquefaciens

Remedies: Proactive
*   Certified seed

*   Long Rotation. Crop Rotation

*   Review irrigation. Watering

*   Remove plant debris and crop residues

Click Beetle
Striped Elaterid Beetle
Wireworms

Botanical name
Agriotes lineatus

Class
Elateridae, Insect

Names in other languages
Lined click beetle. Wireworms, Striped elaterid beetle (En). Taupin des moissons, Taupin rayé (Fr). Feldhumus-Schnellkäfer, Saatschnellkäfer (De). Gestreepte kniptor, Ritnaalden (Nl).

Description
The click beetle (*Agriotes lineatus*) larvae are called "wireworm". They are extremely polyphagous and feeds on roots of numerous plant species. Beet seedlings are destroyed. Potato tubers are attacked at maturity, revealing narrow, shallow galleries. The underground parts of carrot, tomato, onion, leek, chicory, lettuce, broad been can be seriously attacked.

Symptoms
Galleries in roots.

Vegetables
Asparagus, Beetroot, Carrot, Lettuce, Onion, Potato, Spinach, Sweet corn, Turnip.

Click beetle adult and larvae (wireworm)

Remedies: Immediate action
- Liquid manure of fern

- Click beetle traps

- Steinernema carpocapsae. S. feltae nematodes

- Heterorhabditis bacteriophora Nematode

Remedies: Proactive
- Pheromone traps

- Long rotation

- Trap cropping. Wheat and a mixture of wheat, bean, lupine, white mustard, buckwheat, and ryegrass in between the main crop.

- Install insect hotels, bug hotels or insect houses. Besides general vertebrate predators such as birds, moles and amphibians, arthropods including carabid beetles, rove beetles and the stiletto fly Thereva nobilitata larvae have been reported to prey upon wireworms.

Colorado Potato Beetle

Botanical name
Leptinotarsa decemlineata

Class
Chrysomelidae, Insect

Names in other languages
Colorado Potato Beetle (En). Doryphore, Doryphore de la pomme de terre (Fr). Kolorado-Käfer (De). Coloradokever (Nl).

Description
The Colorado potato beetle (*Leptinotarsa decemlineata*) are yellowish orange beetles with 10 black stripes on their wing covers and dark spots just behind the head. Larvae are dark, orange grubs with black legs and two rows of black spots on each side. They feed on leaves and shoots and if present in high numbers they may defoliate the plants.

Symptoms
Leaves with irregular holes, Presence of larvae and adult beetles, Plants defoliated.

Vegetables
Eggplant. Potato.

Colorado potato beetle adulte and larvae

Remedies: Immediate action
*   Bacillus thuringiensis

*   Remove manually pests

*   Insecticide based on pyrethrum

*   Steinernema carpocapsae. S. feltae nematodes

*   Heterorhabditis bacteriophora Nematode

*   Insecticide based on spinosad

*   Steinernema carpocapsae. S. feltae nematodes

*   Remove manually pests

Remedies: Proactive
*   Install insect hotels, bug hotels or insect houses.

*   Long Rotation. Crop Rotation

*   Apply mulch or straw

*   Insect-proof net. Insect net. Mesh Crop Cover

Common Swift Moth
Garden Swift Moth

Botanical name
Korscheltellus lupulinus. Hepialus lupulinus

Class
Hepialidae, Insect

Names in other languages
Common Swift Moth. Garden Swift Moth (En). Petite Hépiale du houblon (Fr). Kleiner Hopfen-Wurzelbohrer, Wurzelspinner. (De). Slawortelboorder (Nl).

Common swift moth adult and larvae (caterpillar)

Description
Swift moths include the ghost moth (also known as the ghost swift moth) and the common swift or garden swift moth. They are minor and localised pests of carrots, cereals and lettuce. The larvae cut off plants just below ground level or tunnel into roots or stems. The Swift moth (Hepialus lupulinus) caterpillars are dirty-white with brown heads. They live in the soil and feed on plant roots and at the base of plant stems causing gradual drying-out of the plant.

Symptoms
Presence of caterpillars

Vegetables
Lettuce, Potato, Carrots, Sweet corn.

Remedies: Immediate action
* Insecticide based on spinosad

* Remove manually pests

* Steinernema carpocapsae. S. feltae nematodes

Remedies: Proactive
* Install insect hotels, bug hotels or insect houses.Several polyphagous predators attack these pests, including birds and moles. The larvae may also be parasitised by certain species of wasp that eventually kill the larvae.

Cotton Aphid

Botanical name
Aphis gossypii

Class
Aphididae, Insect

Names in other languages
Cotton Aphid, Melon and cotton aphid, Melon aphid (En). Puceron du cotonnier, Puceron du melon (Fr). Grüne Baumwollblattlaus, Grüne Gurkenblattlaus (De). Katoenluis (Nl).

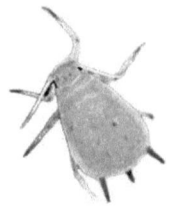

Cotton aphid adult

Description
The cotton aphid (*Aphis gossypii*) can affect a big number of vegetables. The first symptoms of attack is a yellowing of the leaves. As aphids become more numerous, leaves become puckered, and curled. Plants also become stunted and the stems become twisted. Development of black sooty mould which grows on the honeydew excreted by the aphid. This aphid transmit several virus.

Symptoms
Leaves curled or shrivelled, Presence of honeydew and presence of sooty mould on leaves.

Vegetables
Courgette, Cucumber, Eggplant, Melon, Pepper, Potato, Pumpkin, Tomato.

Remedies: Immediate action
- Garlic macerate oil
- Black soap
- Insecticide based on pyrethrum
- Horsetail decoction
- Comfrey infusion
- Nettle infusion
- Liquid manure of fern
- Canola oil. Rapeseed oil. Plant oils
- Insecticide based on azadirachta. Neem oil
- Beauveria bassiana

Remedies: Proactive
- Ladybird Predatory beetle
- Predator Macrolophus caliginosus/M. pygmaeus
- Install insect hotels, bug hotels or insect houses. The parasitic wasp *Lysiphlebus testaceipes* and a group of aphid predators including the lady beetles and the predatory larvae of syrphid flies are important natural enemies.

Cotton Whitefly
Tobacco Whitefly

Botanical name
Bemisia tabaci

Class
Aleyrodidae, Insect

Names in other languages
Cotton Whitefly. Tobacco Whitefly, Silverleaf whitefly (En). Aleurode du tabac (Fr). Baumwollmottenschildlaus, Tabakmottenschildlaus (De). Tabakswittevlieg (Nl).

Description
The cotton whitefly (*Bemisia tabaci*) damage is caused by the suction of plant fluids, an abundant production of honeydew and, above all, the transmission of viruses. Infected plants could exhibit any one or a combination of the following symptoms: vein yellowing, inter-vein yellowing, leaf yellowing, yellow blotching of leaves, yellow mosaic of leaves, leaf curling, leaf crumpling, leaf vein thickening, leaf cupping, stem twisting, plant stunting.

Symptoms
Leaves turn yellow, Presence of honeydew on leaves.

Vegetables
Eggplant, Pepper, Potato, Tomato.

Cotton whitefly adult

Remedies: Immediate action
- Insecticide based on spinosad

- Canola oil. Rapeseed oil. Plant oils

- Black Soap

- Beauveria bassiana

- Encarsia formosa

- Insecticide based on azadirachta. Neem oil

- Insecticide based on pyrethrum:

- Amblydromalus limonicus Predatory mites

- Steinernema carpocapsae. S. feltae nematodes

- Orius insidiosus pirate bug

Remedies: Proactive
- Ladybird Predatory beetle

Cotton Worm
African Cotton Leafworm

Botanical name
Spodoptera littoralis. Spodoptera litura. Prodenia litura

Class
Noctuidae, Insect

Names in other languages
Cotton Worm, Cotton leafworm, Mediterranean climbing cutworm (En). Ver du cotonnier, Noctuelle méditerranéenne (Fr). Afrikanischer Baumwollwurm, ägyptische Baumwollraupe (De). Katoenuil (Nl).

Description
The cotton leafworm (Spodoptera littoralis) is a highly polyphagous species feeding on plants of 40 families, containing 87 species of economic importance. It originates in Egypt, and is currently found in Africa, the Canary Islands, the Middle East and parts of Mediterranean Europe including the Balearic Islands, Madeira and the Azores. Most of the damage is caused by the older caterpillars which are voracious leaf feeders. Extensive feeding by the larvae may lead to complete stripping and skeletisation of the leaves, whereby all that remains are the bigger veins.

Symptoms
Presence of caterpillars, Leaves skeletonized.

Vegetables
Artichoke, Cabbage, Pepper, Potato, Tomato.

Cotton worm adult and larvae (caterpillar)

Remedies: Immediate action
- Bacillus thuringiensis. Bt

- Insecticide based on pyrethrum

- Insecticide based on azadirachta. Neem oil

- Steinernema carpocapsae. S. feltae nematodes

Remedies: Proactive
- Pheromone traps

- Install insect hotels, bug hotels or insect houses

- Ladybird Predatory beetle

Cucumber Mosaic Virus

Botanical name
Cucumovirus, CMV

Class
Bromoviridae, Virus

Names in other languages
Cucumber Mosaic Virus. CMV (En). Virus de la mosaïque du concombre, CMV (Fr). Gurkenmosaikvirus (De). Komkommermozaïekvirus (NI).

Description
Cucumber mosaic, caused by the cucumber mosaic virus (abbreviated as CMV) is a worldwide, highly infectious viral disease that affects a wide range of hosts. The number one vector for spreading this disease is aphids. Cucumber mosaic virus causes white or yellow mottled areas on leaves. Leaf margins roll downward. Plants are stunted, with shortened stems between leaves.

Symptoms
Leaves turn yellow, Plants stunted.

Vegetables
Artichoke, Celeriac, Celery, Courgette, Cucumber, Eggplant, Green bean, Melon, Pepper, Potato, Pumpkin, Spinach, Tomato.

Cucumber mosaic virus symptoms

Remedies: Immediate action
• Eliminate the infected plants

Remedies: Proactive
• Use resistant varieties/cultivars

• Remove aphids

• Install insect hotels, bug hotels or insect houses.Attract aphid predators, such as ladybugs.

Damping Off

Botanical name
Rhizoctonia. Fusarium. Phytophthora

Class:

Names in other languages:
Damping Off (En). Fonte des semis (Fr). Wurzelfäule (De). Omvalziekte (Nl).

Description
Damping off is a soil-borne disease caused by severel fungi (Rhizoctonia, Fusarium, Phytophthora) it provokes the rotting of stem and root tissues at and below the soil surface. Infected plants will germinate and come up, but within a few days they become water-soaked and mushy, fall over at the base and die. Damping off is most active in cool, moist conditions, especially in spring when these conditions are common. Too wet soil and poor ventilation in greenhouses contribute to its spread. Damping off is highly contagious and can spread quickly, affecting most seedlings in a tray if left unchecked.

Damping off

Symptoms
Collapse and dying o young seedlings

Vegetables
Broccoli, Brussels sprout, Cabbage, Cauliflower, Celeriac, Celery, Courgette, Cucumber, Eggplant, Green bean, Kohlrabi, Lamb's Lettuce, Lettuce, Chinese cabbage, Pumpkin, Radish, Romanesco, Rutabaga, Spinach, Tomato, Turnip.

Remedies: Immediate action
*   Horsetail decoction

*   Garlic decoction

*   Lithothamnion algae

*   Liquid manure of nettle

*   Liquid manure of horsetail

*   Trichoderma seed treatment

*   Wettable sulphur

*   Streptomyces lydicus

*   Bacillus subtilis

Remedies: Proactive
*   Charcoal dust

*   Review irrigation. Watering

Dark Sword-grass Moth
Black cutworm
Greasy cutworm

Botanical name
Agrotis ipsilon

Class
Noctuidae, Insect

Names in other languages
Dark Sword-grass Moth, Black cutworm (En). Noctuelle ipsilon, Ver gris noir (Fr). Ypsiloneulen (De). Grote worteluil (Nl).

Description
The Dark sword-grass moth (*Agrotis ipsilon*) has brown forewings with a clearer area on the apical quarter. The caterpillars can attack a very wide range of cultivated plants. The caterpillar feeds at night, it nibbles the leaves, the petioles and the plant collar, during the day it hides.

Symptoms
Leaves with perforations, Damaged cotyledons, Damaged stems.

Vegetables
Beetroot, Broccoli, Brussels sprout, Cabbage, Cauliflower, Kohlrabi, Lettuce, Chinese cabbage, Radish, Romanesco, Rutabaga, Spinach, Turnip.

Dark Sword-grass Moth adult and larvae (caterpillars)

Remedies: Immediate action
- Elder decoction

- Tansy decoction

- Steinernema carpocapsae. S. feltae nematodes

- Insecticide based on spinosad

- Bacillus thuringiensis. Bt

- Beauveria bassiana

- Heterorhabditis bacteriophora Nematode

Remedies: Proactive
- Trichogramme wasps predators

- Bait based on bran and pyrethrum

- Pheromone traps

- Trap cropping. Plant sunflowers along the edge of your garden. Sunflowers are a favorite target of cutworms. The plants will attract the larvae giving you a chance to pick them from the ground

- Diatomaceous Earth. Spreading a line of diatomaceous earth around the base of plants sets up a barrier to larvae.

Diamond-back Moth

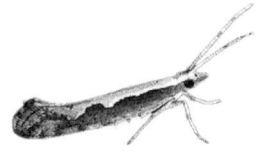

Botanical name
Plutella xylostella. Plutella maculipennis

Class
Plutellidae, Insect

Names in other languages
Diamond-back Moth, Cabbage moth (En). Teigne des crucifères, Teigne du chou (Fr). Gemüsemotte, Kohlschabe, Schleiermotte (De). Koolmot (Nl).

Diamond-back moth adult and larvae (caterpillars)

Description
The adult is a small moth about 10 -12 mm long. The male moth is dark brown with 3 grey-brown uneven diamond-shaped patterns on its back. The female moth is tan coloured and its diamond patterns are less distinct than those of the male. DBM larvae (caterpillars) are pale yellowish-green and tapered at both ends. They undergo 4 growth stages growing to approximately 12 mm in length. The diamond-back moth (Plutella xylostella) damage is important on almost all cruciferae. The caterpillars first gnaw the outer leaves and then progressively move towards the young central leaves. They unite them with silken threads and soil them with their frass.

Symptoms
Leaves with holes. Presence of caterpillars.

Vegetables
Broccoli, Brussels sprout, Cabbage, Cauliflower, Chinese cabbage.

Remedies: Immediate action
- Insecticide based on spinosad

- Bacillus thuringiensis. Bt

- Insect-proof net. Insect net. Mesh Crop Cover

- Trichogramme wasps predators

Remedies: Proactive
- Pheromone traps

- Association with another crop or culture. Companion culture

- Long Rotation. Crop Rotation. Crop rotation with cucurbits, beans, peas, tomato and melon

- Remove infested plants parts

- Trap cropping. Grow mustard as trap crop at 2:1 ratio (cabbage: mustard) to attract Diamond-Back Moth for oviposition at least 10 days ahead of planting of main crop.

Downy Mildew of Alliums

Botanical name
Peronospora destructor

Class
Peronosporaceae, Fungus

Names in other languages
Downy Mildew of Alliums, Downy mildew of onion (En). Mildiou de l'Oignon, Mildiou des alliacées (Fr). Knoblauchsorten falscher Mehltau, Falscher Mehltau: Zwiebel (De). Valse meeldauw (Nl).

Description
Downy mildew of garlic, leeks or onios is caused by a fungus-like mircoorganism (Peronospora destructor). It causes slightly pale spots first on leaves or seed stalks, later taking on a light brown or purplish shade. As spots enlarge, often girdling the leaves, a grayish violet furry mold develops on the spot's surface. Plants may be dwarfed, distorted, and pale green if they are systemically infected. Plants often are not killed, but bulb quality is poor and often spongy. This disease is favored by cool (less than 20°C) and humid weather. Spores (conidia) can be wind-blown long distances and are produced at 6° to 26°C (optimum is 11° to 13°C); no spores are produced when conditions are dry with temperature above 13°C.

Symptoms
Translucid spots on leaves, Leaves with grey powder.

Vegetables
Garlic, Leek.

Downy mildew of alliums symptoms

Remedies: Immediate action
• Horsetail decoction

• Bordeaux mixture

• Diluted milk

• Garlic decoction

• Liquid manure of horsetail

• Elder infusion

• Bicarbonate of potassium or sodium

• Trichoderma

• Streptomyces lydicus

• Reynoutria sachalinensis extract. Giant Knotweed

Remedies: Proactive
• Certified seed or plants

• Use resistant varieties/cultivars

• Remove plant debris and crop residues

• Long Rotation. Crop Rotation

• Review irrigation. Watering

Downy Mildew of Crucifers

Downy mildew of crucifers symptoms

Botanical name
Peronospora parasitica

Class
Peronosporaceae, Fungus

Names in other languages
Downy Mildew of Crucifers (En). Mildiou (Fr). Falschen Mehltau (De). Valse meeldauw (Nl).

Description
Downy mildew of crucifers (Hyaloperonospora parasitica/Peronospora parasitica) manifests as yellow, purple or brown irregular shaped areas on upper leaf surfaces, which correspond to white to gray, "downy" masses on under leaf surfaces.The disease cycle begins when young seedlings are infected by overwintering spores that germinate and penetrate young plants. The fungus colonizes the above-ground plant parts and produces spores on the lower surface of leaves. The spores may be rain-splashed or windblown to other plants and fields. Spread of the pathogen occurs during temperatures of 10-20° C. Survival of the downy mildew fungus occurs via thick-walled spores which remain in the soil after the crop decays.

Symptoms
Purple or brown irregular shaped areas. White to gray downy areas under leaves.

Vegetables
Broccoli, Brussels sprout, Cabbage, Cauliflower, Kohlrabi, Chinese cabbage, Radish, Romanesco, Rutabaga, Turnip.

Remedies: Immediate action
*   Horsetail decoction:

*   Bicarbonate of potassium or sodium:

*   Bordeaux mixture

*   Wettable sulphur

*   Diluted milk

*   Garlic decoction

*   Liquid manure of horsetail

*   Elder infusion

*   Reynoutria sachalinensis extract. Giant Knotweed

*   Bacillus subtilis

*   Streptomyces lydicus

Remedies: Proactive
*   Long Rotation. Crop Rotation

*   Watering only at the root

*   Lithothamnium algae. Calcified Seaweed. Maerl

Downy mildew of Cucurbits

Downy mildew of cucurbits symtoms

Botanical name
Pseudoperonospora cubensis

Class
Peronosporaceae, Fungus

Names in other languages
Downy mildew of Cucurbits (En). Mildiou des Cucurbitacées, Mildiou du concombre (Fr). Falschen Mehltau (De). Valse meeldauw (Nl).

Description
Downy mildew (Pseudoperonospora cubensis) appear first asa pale green areas on the upper leaf surfaces. These changes to yellow angular spots. A fine white-to grayish downy growth soon appears an the lower leaf surface. Infected leaves generally die but my remain erect while the edges of the leaf blade curl inward. The entire plant may eventually be killed. Downy mildew can infect plants in a wide range of temperatures (5-30° C) but is most severe from 15-20° C. The pathogen needs moisture on the leaf surface in order to germinate and start a new infection. Under humid conditions, downy mildew rapidly reproduces and spreads, resulting in severe crop damage. The pathogen can move on air currents, splashing water and on the tools and hands of growers.

Symptoms
Leaves with mosaic pattern. Leaves with yellow spots. Leaves with grey powder.

Vegetables
Cucumber, Melon.

Remedies: Immediate action
- Bicarbonate of potassium or sodium

- Reynoutria sachalinensis extract

- Bacillus subtilis

- Bordeaux mixture

- Remove infested plants or plant parts

Remedies: Proactive
- Use resistant varieties/cultivars

- Review irrigation. Watering

Downy mildew of Spinach

Downy mildew of spinach symptoms

Botanical name
Peronospora farinosa. Peronospora spinaciae

Class
Peronosporaceae, Fungus

Names in other languages
Downy mildew of spinach. Spinach Downy Mildew. Bleu Mold (EN), Mildiou de l'Epinard (FR), Spinat falscher Mehltau)DE), Spinazie valse meeldauw (NL).

Description
Spinach downy mildew (Peronospora spp) often begins as irregular yellow patches on upper leaf surfaces. Purplish-gray sporulation will be observed on the undersides of leaves. Occasionally, sporulation may be seen on upper leaf surfaces as well. Lesions may eventually dry out and turn brown. Cool temperatures with long periods of leaf wetness or high humidity is favorable for disease development. Wet foliage is especially favorable.

Symptoms
Leaves with yellow-brown spots. Leaves with purple gray spots.

Vegetables
Spinach.

Remedies: Immediate action
• Bicarbonate of potassium or sodium

• Reynoutria sachalinensis extract. Giant Knotweed

• Remove infested plants or plant parts

Remedies: Proactive
• Long Rotation. Crop Rotation

• Use resistant varieties/cultivars

• Review irrigation. Watering

Early Blight of Potato/Tomato

Early blight of tomato

Botanical name
Alternaria dauci. Alternaria solani. Alternaria alternata

Class
Peronosporaceae, Fungus

Names in other languages
Early Blight of Potato/Tomato (En). Alternariose (Fr). Blattbrand (De). Loofverbruining, Purpervlekkenziekte (Nl).

Description
Early blight of potato and tomato (Alternaria spp) have circular, dark brown spots with a pattern of concentric rings. the leaves turns yellow and may drop. Brown lesions may develop on the stems. On tomatoes brown patches may appear on green fruit, while more mature fruits will decay rapidly.Mild temperatures and humidity (rain, morning dew, condensation in a greenhouse or tunnel) are factors that favor this disease, whose spores and mycelium survive from one year to the next in the soil and plant debris. Do not crowd your plants. Always water at the base and not on the foliage. Apply plant rotation (the fungus persists in the soil). Destroy (burn) the affected plants. Mild temperatures and humidity (rain, morning dew, condensation in a greenhouse or tunnel) are factors that favor this disease, whose spores and mycelium survive from one year to the next in the soil and plant debris. Please note that seeds from an affected plant are contaminated. Do not collect tomato seeds from a plant carrying Alternaria.

Symptoms
Circular, brown, necrotic lesions on leaves of cucurbits. Brownish black lesions on leaves of crucifers. Brownish black lesions on fruits.

Vegetables
Courgette, Cucumber, Melon, Pumpkin, Tomato. Broccoli, Brussel Sprout, Cabbage, Carrot, Cauliflower, Kohlrabi, Radish, Romanesco.

Remedies: Immediate action
• Bicarbonate of potassium or sodium:

• Garlic decoction

• Horsetail decoction

• Bordeaux mixture

• Streptomyces lydicus

• Bacillus subtilis

Remedies: Proactive
• Certified seed

• Review irrigation. Watering

• Use resistant varieties/cultivars

• Certified seed or plants

• Remove plant debris and crop residues

European Corn Borer Maize Pyralid

Botanical name
Ostrinia nubilalis

Class
Crambodae, Insect

Names in other languages
European Corn Borer, European maize borer, Maize pyralid, Stalk borer (En). Pyrale du maïs (Fr). Hirsezünsler, Hopfenzünsler, Maiszünsler (De). Europese maisboorder (Nl).

European Corn Borer adult and larvae

Description
The maize pyralid (*Ostrinia nubilalis*) is a small Lepidoptera. The larva is yellowish grey, they penetrate the maize leaf sheath and feed at its base causing the presence of characteristic perforations. They also dig galleries in the peduncle of the ear and in the ear itself.

Symptoms
Leaves with perforations, Galleries in stems, fruits, Trash deposit.

Vegetables
Sweet corn

Remedies: Immediate action
• Trichogramme wasps predators

• Bacillus thuringiensis

• Steinernema carpocapsae. S. feltae nematodes

• Beauveria bassiana

Remedies: Proactive
• Pheromone traps

• Install insect hotels, bug hotels or insect houses. European corn borer eggs and larvae are attacked by predators (lady beetles, lacewings, spiders, insidious flower bugs, and predatory mites), parasitoids (wasps and flies), and pathogens (Beauvaria bassiana, a fungus).

Eyespot of Maize

Botanical name
Kabatiella zeae

Class
Tuberculariaceae, Fungus

Names in other languages
Eyespot of maize (En). Kabatiellose du Maïs, Brunissure du maïs, Taches oculaires du maïs (Fr). Augenfleckenkrankheit: Mais (De). Oogvlekkenziekte van mais (Nl).

Description
Eyespot of maize (*Kabatiella zeae*) presents as many circular to oval spots on the leaf which may coalesce to form large areas of dead tissue. Initially spots appear water-soaked eventually forming tan to cream colored centers surrounded by brownish purple margins with a narrow yellow halo. The haloed spots give the appearance of an "eyespot." The disease can cause severe shrivelling of the ears.

Symptoms
Leaves with grey spots.

Vegetables
Sweet corn.

Eyespot of maize

Remedies: Immediate action
• Remove aphids

Remedies: Proactive
• Long Rotation. Crop Rotation

• Use resistant varieties/cultivars

• Certified seed or plants

• Remove plant debris and crop residues

Frosted Orange Moth
Artichoke Moth

Botanical name
Gortyna flavago. Xanthoecia flavago. Gortyna xanthenes

Class
Noctuidae, Insect

Names in other languages
Frosted Orange Moth (En). Noctuelle jaune de l'artichaut, Teigne de l'artichaut, Drap d'or (Fr). Kartoffeltriebbohrer, Markeule (De). Goudgele boorder (Nl).

Description
The larvae of the frosted orange moth (*Gortyna flavago)* and the artichoke moth (*Gortyna xanthenes*) are a pest on artichokes. Early instars feed on the upper epidermis of the leaves. Later, they penetrate the veins and finally eat through the center of the stem and reach the head where they form large galleries.

Symptoms
Sawdust at the base of stems, Galleries in flowerhead.

Vegetables
Artichoke

Frosted Orange Moth adult and larvae

Remedies: Immediate action
- Insecticide based on spinosad

Remedies: Proactive
- Pheromone traps

- Install insect hotels, bug hotels or insect houses.

Fusarium Root Rot

Fusarium root rot

Botanical name
Fusarium solani et Fusarium oxysporum

Class
Tuberculariaceae, Fungus

Names in other languages
Fusarium Root Rot, Dry rot of potato, Foot rot, Stem canker (En). Maladie de la pourriture des racines, Flétrissement fusarien du concombre, Fusariose du pied, Pourriture fusarienne du planton de la pomme de terre, Pourriture rose de l'oignon (Fr). Fußfäule, Wurzelfäule (De). Voetziekte (Nl).

Description
Specialized forms of Fusarium solani and Fusarium oxysporum parasitize the roots and crowns of legumes and cucurbits. Fusarium crown rot (Fusarium solani and Fusarium oxysporum) causes roots to rot, turning black or brown. Root rot can cause foliar symptoms such as yellowing, stunting, and defoliation.

Symptoms
Rotting of roots, Plants stunted.

Vegetables
Asparagus, Broad bean, Celeriac, Celery, Courgette, Cucumber, Eggplant, Green bean, Melon, Peas, Pumpkin, Tomato.

Remedies: Immediate action
• Eliminate the infected plants

• Streptomyces lydicus

Remedies: Proactive
• Soil solarization

• Use resistant varieties/cultivars

• Long rotation

• Soil pH. Maintain a soil pH of 6 to 7, as the fungus thrives in low pH soil.

• Remove plant debris and crop residues

Fusarium Wilt

Fusarium wilt

Botanical name
Fusarium oxysporum. Fusarium roseum

Class
Tuberculariaceae, Fungus

Names in other languages
Fusarium Wilt, Basal rot, Foot rot, Seedling wilt (En). Fusariose, Flétrissement fusarien, (Fr). Basalfäule, Fußfäule, Stengelgrundfäule, Zwiebelfäule (De). Fusarium (Nl).

Description
Fusarium wilt is a soil-borne pathogen the fungi (Fusarium oxysporum) enter through the roots and interfere with the water conducting vessels of the plant. As the infection spreads up into the stems and leaves it restricts water flow causing the foliage to wilt and turn yellow. Plant only disease free seed. Minimize stress to plants by following good fertilization and watering practices. Plant tolerant varieties. The disease is most active during cool, moist seasons, especially in poorly drained soils. These conditions provide an ideal environment for Fusarium spp., allowing them to multiply rapidly. The disease is highly contagious, as spores are easily spread by water splash, contaminated soil, tools and wind.

Symptoms
Leaves turns yellow and wilt, Necrotic stems.

Vegetables
Beetroot, Celery, Courgette, Cucumber, Green bean, Melon, Peas, Pumpkin, Spinach, Tomato.

Remedies: Immediate action
- Eliminate the infected plants

- Remove fallen leaves and dead material

- Trichoderma

- Streptomyces lydicus

Remedies: Proactive
- Use resistant varieties/cultivars

- Certified seed or plants

- Soil solarization

- Review irrigation. Watering

- Long rotation

- Remove plant debris and crop residues

Garden Dart Moth Cutworm

Garden dart moth adult and larvae (cutworm)

Botanical name
Euxoa nigricans

Class
Noctuidae, Insect.

Names in other languages
Garden Dart Moth, Cutworm (En). Noctuelle noirâtre, Vers gris (Fr). Violettschwarze Erdeule (De). Rookkleurige worteluil (Nl).

Description
The larvae of the Garden dart moth (*Euxoa nigricans*) is called a cutworm and cause serious losses around end of April beginning of May when they feed on the stems or roots of seedling crops and young shoots.

Symptoms
Presence of caterpillars.

Vegetables
Beetroot, Cabbage, Green bean, Onion, Potato.

Remedies: Immediate action
- Insecticide based on pyrethrum

- Remove manually pests

- Steinernema carpocapsae. S. feltae nematodes

- Bacillus thuringiensis. Bt

Remedies: Proactive
- Install insect hotels, bug hotels or insect houses. Frogs and toads, birds, rodents, other arthropods such as ants and wasps are natural predators.

Glasshouse Potato Foxglove Aphid

Botanical name
Aulacorthum solani. Dysaulacorthum vincae

Class
Aphidae, Insect.

Names in other languages
Glasshouse Potato Foxglove Aphid, Green potato aphid (En). Puceron à taches vertes de la pomme de terre, Puceron de la pomme de terre (Fr). Gefleckte Kartoffelblattlaus, Grünfleckige Kartoffelblattlaus (De). Boterbloemluis (Nl).

Glasshouse potato foxglove aphid

Description
Foxglove aphids are also known as the glasshouse potato aphid. The pale green, shiny foxglove aphids have large dark green spots at the base of their cornicles. They also have black markings on their leg joints and antennae. Foxglove aphids also have an indentation between their antennae. The glasshouse potato aphid (Aulacorthum solani) is a native European species of aphids, seriously affecting crops of sweet pepper in particular. These aphids further affect ornamental crops, such as begonia, as well as potato, lettuce, beans, aubergine and sometimes tomato. This species is an active vector of potato leaf roll virus (PLRV) and, being polyphagous, also transmits cucumber mosaic virus (CMV) to various cultivated plants and beet yellows virus (BYV) to beet. The glasshouse potato aphid can cause curly tops in capsicums and potatoes by injecting a toxic substance into the plant while feeding.

Symptoms
Leaves curled or shrivelled. Presence of aphids.

Vegetables
Pepper, Potato.

Remedies: Immediate action
*   Insecticide based on pyrethrum

*   Black Soap

*   Canola oil. Rapeseed oil. Plant oils

*   Insecticide based on azadirachta. Neem oil

*   Aphelinus Predatory wasp

*   Aphidius colemani. Predatory Wasp

*   Beauveria bassiana

Remedies: Proactive
*   Ladybird Predatory beetle

*   Lacewings Predators

*   Predatory gall midges

Glasshouse Whitefly
Greenhouse Whitefly

Botanical name
Trialeurodes vaporariorum

Class
Aleyrodidae

Names in other languages
Glasshouse Whitefly (En). Aleurode des serres, Mouche blanche des serres (Fr). Weiße Fliege (De). Witte vlieg. Kaswittevlieg (Nl).

Description
The greenhouse white fly (*Trialeurodes vaporariorum*) are minuscule insects coated with pure white waxy bloom. They are very polyphagous and are living in huge colonies on the under surface of the leaves. By sucking the sap, production of honey dew and the formation of sooty mould they provoke very severe damage. The may transmit viruses.

Symptoms
Stunted leaves, Presence of colonies of whitefly, Presence of honeydew and sooty mould on leaves.

Vegetables
Asparagus, Eggplant, Tomato.

Glasshouse whitefly

Remedies: Immediate action
*   Black soap

*   Liquid manure of nettle

*   Elder infusion

*   Comfrey infusion

*   Liquid manure of pyrethrum

*   French marigolds infusion

*   Remove manually pests

*   Garlic macerate oil

*   Auxiliary Encarsia formosa

*   Auxiliary Macrolophus caliginosus

*   Auxiliary Beauveria brongniartii

*   Predator Macrolophus caliginosus/M. pygmaeus. Predatory bug

*   Transeius montdorensis. Predatory mite

*   Insecticide based on pyrethrum

*   Canola oil. Rapeseed oil. Plant oils

*   Lecanicillium muscarium beneficial fungi

Remedies: Proactive
*   Whitefly traps (Yellow)

Grain Aphid, English grain aphid

Botanical name
Sitobion avenae, Metopolophium dirhodum, Rhopalosiphum padi,

Class
Aphidadae, Insect.

Names in other languages
Grain Aphid (En). Puceron vert des céréales, Puceron du blé (Fr). Große Getreideblattlaus (De). Bladluis, Grote graanluis (Nl).

Description
The grain aphid (*Sitobion avenae*, and others) are a major pest of cereals and maize in spring. By sucking juice, by carrying infectious plant virus diseases and by encouraging developing of sooty moulds on the honeydew they secrete.

Symptoms
Distorted leaves. presence of aphids, honeydew and sooty mould.

Vegetables
Sweet corn.

Grain aphid

Remedies: Immediate action
- Insecticide based on pyrethrum

- Liquid manure of fern

- Predator Macrolophus caliginosus/M. pygmaeus. Predatory bug

- Trichogramme wasps predators

- Black Soap

- Canola oil. Rapeseed oil. Plant oils

- Insecticide based on azadirachta. Neem oil

- Beauveria bassiana

- Liquid manure of wormwood

- Liquid manure or maceration of tomato

- Lithothamnium algae. Calcified Seaweed. Maerl

Remedies: proactive
- Lacewings Predators

- Ladybird Predatory beetle

- Install insect hotels, bug hotels or insect houses. Natural enemies, such as lady beetles, lacewing larvae and hoverfly larvae.

Gray Mold
Grey Mould
Botrytis Blight

Botanical name
Botrytis cinerea

Class
Sclerotiniaceae, Fungus.

Names in other languages
Gray Mold. Grey Mould. Botrytis Blight (EN), Pourriture grise (FR), Grauschimmel (DE), Grauwe schimmel (NL).

Description
Gray mold (Botrytis cinerea) is a fungal disease found on a wide range of plants. Symptoms appear as grayish colored soft, mushy spots on leaves, stems, flowers and on produce. Spots may become covered with a coating of gray fungus spores, especially if humidity is high. Plant in light, well-draining, fertile soils; avoid overcrowding plants and planting seeds too deeply; do not wet foliage when watering, water plants at base; remove crop debris from soil after harvest.

Symptoms
Grayish colored spots on leaves and fruits. Coating of gray fungus spores on leaves and fruits.

Vegetables
Broccoli, Brussels sprout, Cabbage, Cauliflower, Courgette, Cucumber, Eggplant, Green bean, Kohlrabi, Lamb's lettuce, Lettuce, Melon, Chinese cabbage, Peas, Pepper, Potato, Pumpkin, Romanesco, Rutabaga, Tomato, Turnip.

Gray mold on tomato

Remedies: Immediate action
• Bordeaux mixture

• Review irrigation. Watering. Irrigate crops in the morning using a drip system rather than a sprinkler one to avoid moisture pooling on foliage.

• Eliminate the infected plants

• Horsetail decoction

• Garlic decoction

• Liquid manure of horsetail

• Bacillus subtilis

• Streptomyces lydicus

• Remove infested plants or plant parts

Remedies: Proactive
• Remove plant debris and crop residues

• Pseudomonas chlororaphis

Green Artichoke Aphid

Botanical name
Capitophorus horni. Capitophorus elaeagni

Class
Aphidadae, Insect.

Names in other languages
Green Artichoke Aphid, Thistle aphid (En). Puceron vert de l'artichaut (Fr). Artischockenblattlaus (De). Groene artisjok bladluis (Nl).

Green artichoke aphid

Description
Artichoke aphids are pale greenish-white to yellowish-green, almost translucent aphids with pale appendages. Large numbers of these aphids cause artichoke leaves to curl and turn yellow and the plants to show retarded growth, resulting in the formation of undersized or deformed artichoke buds. In addition, bud stalks weaken and can no longer support the weight of developing buds, causing them to droop. Also, buds that are close to harvest get contaminated with aphid bodies. Besides this direct-feeding damage, artichoke aphid characteristically secretes copious amount of honeydew, which is deposited onto leaves and developing artichoke buds in the lower canopy, giving them a wet and shiny appearance. Honeydew deposits on the foliage result in the growth of sooty mold, which covers the leaf surface and interferes with photosynthesis.

Symptoms
Presence of aphids. Leaves curled.

Vegetables
Artichoke

Remedies: Immediate action
*   Insecticide based on pyrethrum

*   Black Soap

*   Canola oil. Rapeseed oil. Plant oils

*   Insecticide based on azadirachta. Neem oil

*   Beauveria bassiana

*   Strong spray of water

Remedies: Proactive
*   Install insect hotels, bug hotels or insect houses. General predators including lady beetles, syrphid fly, and lacewings.

*   Ladybird Predatory beetle

*   Lacewings

*   Remove plant debris and crop residues

Green Leaf Beetle
Green Tortoise Beetle

Botanical name
Cassida deflorata

Class
Chrysomelidae

Names in other languages
Green Tortoise Beetle, Green Leaf Beetle, Tortoise beetle (En). Casside de l'artichaut (Fr). Artischockenschildkäfer (De). Groene schildpadtor (Nl).

Green tortoise beetle

Description
The Green tortoise beetle is one of a group of several closely related beetles. When disturbed, the adults behave just like tortoises, retracting their antennae and feet, and pulling their 'shell' tight down around them as they grip tightly on to the leaf they are on. The green leaf beetles (Cassida deflorata) are found on artichoke and cardoon. The adults and larvae eat the leaf surface leaving a pale or brown translucent membrane.

Symptoms
Leaf surface eaten. Presence of bugs.

Vegetables
Artichoke.

Remedies: Immediate action
- Insecticide based on pyrethrum

- Azadirachta. Neem oil insecticide

- Kaolin clay spray

- Remove manually pests

Remedies: Proactive
- Install insect hotels, bug hotels or insect houses. Wasps, Parasitic flies such as Tachinid fly, Lady beetle larvae, Damsel bugs, Shield bugs, Assassin bugs are natural predators.

- Remove plant debris and crop residues

Hawthorn Aphids

Botanical name
Dysaphis apiifolia

Class
Aphidadae

Names in other languages
Hawthorn aphids, Parsley aphid, Rusty banded aphid (En). Puceron cendré (Fr). Braunbindige Sellerieblattlaus (De). Bruinbandselderijbladluis (Nl).

Description
Hawthorn-parsley aphid, Rusty banded aphid (*Dysaphis apiifolia*), Hawthorn-carrot (*Dysaphis crataegi*), Hawthorn-fennel (*Dysaphis feoniculum*). Hawthorn aphids can damage crops by stunting growth, by transmitting virus and by contaminating the crop with honeydew and debris. The hawthorn aphids lives in dense colonies and ants can transport them from one plant to another.

Symptoms
Presence of colonies of aphids.

Vegetables
Carrot, Celeriac, Celery, Fennel.

Remedies: Immediate action
- Remove ants

- Insecticide based on pyrethrum

- Liquid manure of fern

- Predator Macrolophus caliginosus/M. pygmaeus. Predatory bug

- Black Soap

- Canola oil. Rapeseed oil. Plant oils

- Insecticide based on azadirachta. Neem oil

- Beauveria bassiana

- Strong spray of water

Remedies: Proactive
- Install insect hotels, bug hotels or insect houses. Encourage natural enemies including ladybird beetles, lacewings, syrphid (hover) fly larvae, and parasitic wasps.

- Insect-proof net. Insect net. Mesh Crop Cover

Itersonilia Canker
Parsnip Canker

Itersonilia canker.

Botanical name
Itersonilia perpexans

Class
Cystofiliobasidiaceae, Fungus

Names in other languages
Itersonilia canker, Canker parsnip, Petal blight of chrysanthemum (En). Chancre à Itersonilia, Brunissure des bractées de l'artichaut (Fr). Blattspitzendürre, Blütenfäule: Chrysantheme (De). Itersonilia bacteriekanker (Nl).

Description
The fungus, *Itersonilia perplexans*, is a common saprophyte on umbelliferous crops as well as some weeds and other cultivated plants including brassicas. It overwinters as chlamydospores in soil or plant debris, on living parsnip roots, and can also infest seed. Parsnip canker or Itersonilia causes small brown necrotic lesions on leaves with pale green halos. The lesions may coalesce to form large necrotic patches and gray to black lesions on bases of petioles. The roots shown red-brown cankers mostly on the crown and shoulder with a rough texture.

Symptoms
Brown, black or purple black lesion on roots. Orange to brown lesions on leaves.

Vegetables
Carrot, Parsnip.

Remedies: Immediate action
• Remove infested plants parts

• The disease can be reduced by keeping the shoulder of parsnip roots covered with soil throughout the growing season

Remedies: Proactive
• Long rotation. Keep burdock, Chinese aster, and chrysanthemum away from susceptible crops, as they may carry the disease.

• Certified seed or plants

• Use resistant varieties/cultivars

• Insect-proof net. Insect net. Mesh Crop Cover. Manage carrot rust flies whose larvae predispose plants to infection.

June Beetles
May Beetles
Chafer beetles

Botanical name
Phyllophaga anxia. Melolontha melolontha

Class
Melolonthidae, Insect

Names in other languages
June Beetles, Common European cockchafer, May bug, White grub (En). Hanneton commun, Ver blanc (Fr). Feldmaikäfer, Gemeiner Maikäfer, Engerling (De). Gewone meikever, Engerlingen (Nl).

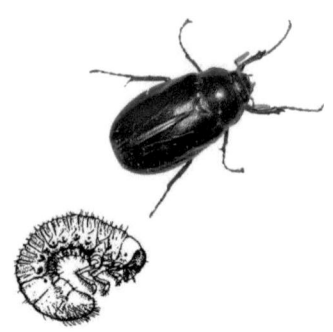

June Beetles adult and larvae (white grub)

Description
June beetles also called May beetles or Chafer are oval, stout, and12 to 25 mm long, reddish brown without patterns such as spots or stripes, and rather hairy beneath. June beetle larvae, called white grubs with cream-colored bodies and brown head capsules are C-shaped, and about 25 mm long. They have three pairs of legs, one on each of the first three segments behind the head, and live in the soil. Adults of june beetles feed on leaves. Larvae (grubs) are most dangerous they feed on roots. If damage is importent leaves are discolouring yellowish and plants die off.

Symptoms
Presence of grubs in the soil. Leaves discolouring yellow.

Vegetables
Beetroot, Lettuce, Potato, Spinach, Sweet corn.

Remedies: Immediate action
- Remove manually pests

- Remove infested plants parts

- Beauveria brongniartii

- Heterorhabditis bacteriophora Nematode

- Steinernema carpocapsae. S. feltae nematodes

- Bacillus thuringiensis. Bt

- Milky spore

- Azadirachta. Neem oil insecticide

Remedies: Proactive
- Light trap

- Insect-proof net. Insect net. Mesh Crop Cover

Late Blight
Potato and Tomato
Late Blight

Late blight of potato

Botanical name
Phytophthora infestans

Class
Pythiaceae, Fungus

Names in other languages
Late Blight. Potato and Tomato Late Blight, Downy mildew of potato (En). Mildiou de la pomme de terre. Mildiou de la tomate (Fr). Kartoffelfäule, Braunfäule: Kartoffel, Braunfäule: Tomate (De). Aardappelziekte (Nl).

Description
Late blight is caused by a fungus (Phytophthora infestans). It appears on the lower, older leaves as water-soaked, gray-green spots. These spots darken and a white fungal growth forms on the undersides. Eventually the entire plant will become infected. Crops can be severely damaged. Warm, humid conditions with poor air circulation promote the spread of these pathogens. The disease can be easily spread to other nearby plants through airborne spores, water splashes, or contaminated tools.

Symptoms
Leaves shrivelled, Leaves dark brown and papery. Fruits brown rotting.

Vegetables
Potato, Tomato.

Remedies: Immediate action
- Bordeaux mixture

- Trichoderma

- Streptomyces lydicus

- Reynoutria sachalinensis extract. Giant Knotweed

- Remove infested plants parts

- Compost tea

- Bacillus subtilis

- Liquid manure of fern

Remedies: Proactive
- Use resistant varieties/cultivars

- Review irrigation. Watering

- Certified seed or plants

- Remove plant debris and crop residues

Leaf Blight of Maize

Leaf blight of maize

Botanical name
Setosphaeria turcica. Trichometasphaeria turcica

Class
Pleosporaceae, Fungus

Names in other languages
Leaf Blight of Maize, Northern corn leaf blight (En). Helminthosporiose du maïs, Brûlure du maïs, Suie du maïs (Fr). Blattdürre: Mais, Streifenkrankheit: Mais (De). Bladvlekkenziekte (Nl).

Description
Leaf blight of maize (*Setosphaeria turcica*) first symptoms on maize plants appear on the lower leaves. At the beginning of the infestation small, longish, watery stains arise which can grow into elongated bands of grey-green to light brown lesions. The patches converge and can reach a size of up to 20 cm long and 5 cm wide. Thus big parts of the leaf blade can die back but rarely the whole leaf does.

Symptoms
Long spots along the veins.

Vegetables
Sweet corn.

Remedies: Immediate action
*   Remove infested plants parts

*   Wettable sulphur

*   Bacillus subtilis

*   Trichoderma fungus

*   Bordeaux mixture

Remedies: Proactive
*   Use resistant varieties/cultivars

*   Long Rotation. Crop Rotation

*   Remove plant debris and crop residues

Leaf Mould
Cladosporiosis of Tomato

Leaf mould of tomato

Botanical name
Fulvia fulva. Cladosporium fulvum. Passalora fulva.

Class
Mycosphaereliaceae, Fungus

Names in other languages
Cladosporiosis of Tomato, Leaf mould of tomato (En). Cladosporiose de la tomate, Moisissure olive de la tomate (Fr). Braunfleckigkeit: Tomate, Samtfleckenkrankheit: Tomate (De). Bladvlekkenziekte van tomaten (Nl).

Description
Leaf mould (*Passalora fulva*) is a fungal disease that affects the foliage of tomatoes, particularly those grown in greenhouses. Symptoms are: Lower leaves are generally attacked first. Yellow blotches develop on the upper leaf surface. A pale, greyish-brown mould growth is found on the corresponding lower surface. Where the disease is severe the mould growth may also be found on the upper surface. Heavily infected leaves turn brown and shrivel, but do not fall.

Symptoms
Leaves with yellow spots, Leaves with grey powder.

Vegetables
Tomato.

Remedies: Immediate action
- Review irrigation. Watering

- Remove infested plants parts

- Hansfordia pulvinata

- Bordeaux mixture

Remedies: Proactive
- Use resistant varieties/cultivars

- Remove plant debris and crop residues

Leek Moth
Onion Moth

Botanical name
Acrolepiopsis assectella. Acrolepa assectella

Class
Glyphipteridae, Insect

Names in other languages
Leek Moth (En). Teigne du poireau (Fr). Lauchmotte, Zwiebelmotte (De). Preimot (Nl).

Description
Leek or onion moth (Acrolepia assectella/ Acrolepiopsis assectella) feed on top of and inside the leaf material. They bore through folded leaves towards the centre of the plant, causing a series of pinholes on the inner leaves. Larval mines in the central leaves become longitudinal grooves in the mature plant. On leek, larvae prefer to feed on the youngest leaves but can consume leaves more than 2 months old. Leek moth larvae enter hollow leaves, such as those of onions and chives, to feed internally, creating translucent "windows" on the plant surface. Occasionally, larvae attack reproductive parts of the host plant but usually avoid the flowers, which contain saponins that inhibit insect growth. Affected plants may appear distorted and are more susceptible to plant pathogens. In general, damage is more prevalent near field perimeters.

Symptoms
Galleries in leaves, Plants stunted.

Vegetables
Garlic, Leek, Onion.

Leek moth adult and larvae

Remedies: Immediate action
• Liquid manure of horsetail

• Tansy decoction

• Bacillus thuringiensis

• Insecticide based on pyrethrum

• Liquid manure or maceration of tomato

• Trichogramme predatory wasps

• Lithothamnium algae. Calcified Seaweed. Maerl

Remedies: Proactive
• Insect-proof net

• Pheromone traps

• Chromatic trap

• Repellent plants. Companion plants. Grow carrot in between leek rows to keep moths away. In reverse, leek also keeps the carrot fly away. You can also grow plants that emit strong smells around your plots of leek. They confuse the moth, which can no longer find the leeks. Examples are fennel, celery, lavender, wild thyme.

• Remove plant debris and crop residues

Lettuce Bacterial Rot

Lettuce bacterial rot

Botanical name
Pseudomonas cichorii, Pseudomonas marginalis, and Pseudomonas viridiflava.

Class
Pseudomonadaceae, Bacterium

Names in other languages
Lettuce bacterial rot, Bacterial blight of celery, Bacterial blight of endive, Varnish spot of lettuce (En). Bactériose à Pseudomonas sur Laitue, Pourriture bactérienne de la laitue (Fr). Bakterienfäule von Salat (De). Bacteriële rotting van sla (Nl).

Description
In lettuce the symptoms are observed close to the harvest time. The tissue, mostly around inside the head of head lettuce softens and becomes mushy or watery. Slimy masses of bacteria and cellular debris frequently ooze out from cracks in the tissues. Decaying tissue, which may be opaque, white, cream-colored, gray, brown, or black frequently gives off a characteristically putrid odor. The bacteria overwinter in infected fleshy tissues in storage, in the field, garden or greenhouse, in the soil, and on contaminated tools, equipment, containers, and in certain insects. The bacteria enter primarily through wounds made during planting, cultivating, harvesting, grading, and packing and through freezing injuries, insect and hail wounds, growth cracks, and sunscald. They may also follow other disease-producing organisms. Uninjured tissues may become infected when the humidity approaches 100 percent or when free moisture is present. Rains, poorly drained or waterlogged soils, and warm temperatures favor infection in the field.

Symptoms
Leaves with brown spots.

Vegetables
Lettuce

Remedies: Immediate action
• Remove infested plants parts

• Review irrigation. Watering. Maintain well aerated field, avoid close planting and overhead irrigation.

• Reynoutria sachalinensis extract. Giant Knotweed

Remedies: Proactive
• Long Rotation. Crop Rotation

• Certified seed or plants

189

Lettuce Drop

Lettuce drop

Botanical name
Sclerotinia minor, Sclerotinia sclerotiorum

Class
Sclerotiniaceae, Fungus

Names in other languages
Lettuce drop, Sclerotinia disease of lettuce (En). Sclérotiniose de la laitue, Sclérotiniose des cultures maraîchères (Fr). Halsfäule: Salat (De). Sclerotiniarot in sla (Nl).

Description
Two species of *Sclerotinia* infect lettuce and cause the lettuce drop disease: *Sclerotinia minor* is the primary species, while *S. sclerotiorum* is more prevalent. *Sclerotinia minor* only infects the stems and leaves in contact with the soil. Once infection takes place, the fungus will cause a brown, soft decay that eventually destroys the plant crown tissue. Older leaves then wilt and later the entire plant will wilt and collapse, making it unharvestable. Plant collapse usually occurs when lettuce is near maturity. Profuse amounts of white mycelia and small, black, hard, resting bodies (sclerotia) form on the outside of the decayed crown. *Sclerotinia sclerotiorum* can also infect lower leaves and stems, causing symptoms similar to those of S. minor. In addition, *S. sclerotiorum* has an aerial spore that can infect any of the upper leaves. Spores usually infect damaged or senescent tissue when the weather is cool and moist. Infection results in a watery, soft rot that is accompanied by white mycelial growth and formation of sclerotia. *Sclerotinia sclerotiorum* forms sclerotia that are larger than those of S. minor.

Symptoms
Leaves wilted, Collar rot.

Vegetables
Lettuce

Remedies: Immediate action
• Remove infested plants parts

• Coniothyrium minitans

• Trichoderma

• Streptomyces lydicus

• Reynoutria sachalinensis extract

Remedies: Proactive
• Long Rotation. Crop Rotation. Avoid known crop hosts including beans, cauliflower, celery, corn salad, endive, escarole, fennel, pepper, radicchio, and tomato. Cover crop hosts to avoid include Austrian winter pea, mustards, phacelia, and vetch.

• Review irrigation. Watering. Avoid overly wet soils and keep the bed surface as dry as possible with careful irrigation.

Lettuce Mosaic Virus

Lettuce mosaic virus

Botanical name
Potyvirus lactucae, LMV

Class
Potyviridae, Virus

Names in other languages
Lettuce mosaic virus (En). Mosaïque de la Laitue, LMV (Fr). Mosaikvirus: Salat (De). Slamozaïekvirus (Nl).

Description
Lettuce mosaic virus (LMV) characteristic symptoms on susceptible cultivars are dwarfism, mosaic, distortion and yellowing of the leaves with sometimes a very reduced lettuce heart.

Symptoms
Leaves with mosaic pattern.

Vegetables
Lettuce

Remedies: Immediate action
* Remove infested plants parts

* Remove aphids

Remedies: Proactive
* Certified seed or plants

* Use resistant varieties/cultivars

Lettuce Root Aphid

Botanical name
Pemphigus bursarius

Class
Aphidadae. Insect

Names in other languages
Lettuce Root Aphid, Poplar gall aphid (En).
Puceron lanigère des racines de laitue, Puceron
du peuplier (Fr). Salatwurzellaus,
Pappelblattstielgallenlaus (De). Wollige
slawortelluis (Nl).

Lettuce root aphid

Description
The aphids (all females) that hatch from the
overwintering eggs are greyish green and lightly
covered with wax. These aphids suck sap from
leaf stalks of poplar leaves, which results in the
formation of hollow galls that enclose the aphid.
The female aphids produce 100-250 offspring
inside the gall, which are winged. The winged
aphids leave the galls and migrate to lettuce and
other Compositae. They infest the foliage and
produce wingless daughters which are yellowish
white with waxy patches on hind part of the body,
and which colonise the roots. In late summer, the
wingless aphids produce winged, sexual females
and males, which fly back to poplar, where they
mate. The females lay the overwintering eggs in
crevices in the bark. Some, however, do not get
wings and these ar able to overwinter in the soil.
Roots of lettuce and chicory become covered in a
white, waxy secretion. Because of the aphids
feeding from the roots, lettuces have difficulty
forming heads. Leaves may turn yellow and plants
may wilt and die.

Symptoms
Presence of colonies of gray aphids on roots,
Roots covered with sooty mould. Wilted plants.

Vegetables
Artichoke, Carrot, Green bean, Lettuce.

Remedies: Immediate action
* Tansy decoction

* Remove ants

* Liquid manure of fern

* Black Soap

* Beauveria bassiana

* Canola oil. Rapeseed oil. Plant oils

* Remove infested plants parts

Remedies: Proactive
* Insect-proof net. Insect net. Mesh Crop Cover

* Install insect hotels, bug hotels or insect
  houses. Natural enemies, including ladybirds
  and hoverflies, attack the aphids in galls on
  poplar and on lettuce roots. For ground
  beetles, leave a heap of dead leaves in a
  corner to provide them with shelter, or place
  overturned flower pots nearby with uneven
  rims in which they can shelter.

Maize Smut
Corn Smut

Maize smut

Botanical name
Ustilago maydis. Ustilago zeae

Class
Ustilaginaceae, Fungus

Names in other languages
Maize Smut, Corn Smut (EN), Charbon à Ustilago (FR), Maisbeulenbrand (DE), Builenbrand (NL).

Description
Frequently found in gardens, corn smut is caused by the fungus *Ustilago zeae* and can appear in the stalks, leaves, tassels or ears. Symptoms are most commonly noticed when the ears produce mushroom-like tumors or galls. These "swellings" begin as small, whitish-gray irregularities which expand and turn black as they fill with spores. Ear galls can grow to 10 cm in diameter and release thousands of spores as they rupture. These fungal spores are blown by the wind for considerable distances to infect new plants. Galls on leaves remain small and eventually become hard and dry. Corn smut overwinters on garden debris and in the soil. It is carried by wind, rain and irrigation and does best in hot, dry weather. Spores may remain viable for 5- to 7-years. Wounds from various injuries, including cultivation and abrasion from blowing soil, provide points for the fungus to enter the plant.

Symptoms
Tumours on leaves, stems, flowers and cobs.

Vegetables
Sweet corn.

Remedies: Immediate action
- Eliminate the infected plants. Bag or burn infected plant parts — do NOT compost.

Remedies: Proactive
- Certified seed

- Use resistant varieties/cultivars

- Long Rotation. Crop Rotation

- Remove plant debris and crop residues

March Crane Fly Leatherjackets

Botanical name
Tipula spp.

Class
Tipulidae, Insect

Names in other languages
March Crane Fly, Common crane fly, Leather jacket (En). Tipule potagère, Tipule des prairies (Fr). Sumpfschnake, Wiesenschnake (De). Weidelangpootmug, Emelten (Nl).

March crane fly adult and larvae (leatherjackets)

Description
Two species of crane fly are considered pests, the invasive European crane fly and another species commonly referred to as the common or marsh crane fly. Crane fly eggs and larvae require high moisture for survival, and most species reproduce in aquatic or semi-aquatic habitats. The March crane fly (Tipula paludosa) is often called "daddy longlegs" it resembles a big mosquito. The larva known commonly as leatherjackets, dig underground galleries and devours roots and some aerial parts of young plants. They damage the underground part of the stem, the plants yellow and die.

Symptoms
Wilted plants. Roots damaged.

Vegetables
Lettuce.

Remedies: Immediate action
* Liquid manure of fern

* Steinernema carpocapsae. S. feltae nematodes

* Beauveria bassiana

Remedies: Proactive
* Bait based on bran and pyrethrum

Molybdenum Deficiency

Molybdenum deficiency on cauliflower

Botanical name
Mo

Class
Nutrient deficiency

Names in other languages
Molybdenum Deficiency. Whiptail (En). Carence en molybdene (Fr). Molybdänmangel (De). Molybdeentekort (Nl).

Description
Whiptail disorder is caused due to deficiency of molybdenum. In young plants the deficiency symptoms are chlorosis of leaf margins and the whole leaves may turn white. The leaf blades do not develop properly. When the deficiency is severe, only the midribs develop.

Symptoms
Leaves turn white, Only midrib develops.

Vegetables
Melon, Cauliflower

Remedies: Immediate action
• Liquid manure of comfrey

Remedies: Proactive
• Lithothamnion algae

Mosaic Virus on Pepper

Mosaic virus on pepper

Botanical name
TMV. CMV

Class
Geminiviridae, Virus

Names in other languages
Mosaic Virus on Pepper. Pepper mosaic, TMV. CMV (En). Virus mosaïque du poivron, TMV, CMV, Mosaïque du tabac (Fr). Paprikamosaik, Tabakmosaikvirus (De). Pepermozaïekvirus, Tabakmozaïekvirus (Nl).

Description
The main signs of pepper plants with mosaic virus are stunted, pale green or leathery leaves, specks or ring spots, and a tell-tale mosaic appearance consisting of dark and light spots or streaks on the foliage – and sometimes the peppers. Other signs of mosaic virus in peppers include curled or wrinkled leaves and stunted plant growth. Peppers with the disease may display blistered or warty areas. Mosaic is a viral disease that affects quality and reduces yield in a wide variety of plants, including sweet and hot peppers. Once infection occurs, there are no cures for mosaic virus on pepper plants, which is spread by pests.

Symptoms
Fruit and stem decay.

Vegetables
Pepper, Bell pepper.

Remedies: Immediate action
*   Remove aphids

*   Remove infested plants or plant parts

Remedies: Proactive
*   Use resistant varieties/cultivars

*   Insect-proof net. Insect net. Mesh Crop Cover

Oignon Smut
Smut of Onion

Oignon smut

Botanical name
Urocytis cepulae

Class
Tilletiaceae, Fungus

Names in other languages
Oignon Smut, Smut of leek (En). Charbon de l'Oignon, Charbon des feuilles de l'oignon (Fr). Brand: Zwiebel (De). Lookbrand (Nl).

Description
Onion smut is caused by the soil-borne fungus *Urocytis cepulae*. Onion smut has distinctive narrow, dark streaks, usually on the cotyledon (embryonic leaf) or the first true leaf. These streaks thicken, which is the most visible symptom on the plant. The infection inside the leaf later bursts through the surface and releases masses of dark-brown powdery spores. Plants that survive onion smut become stunted, distorted, develop blisters on the green leaf tissue, and the leaves may curve downward due to large lesions.

Symptoms
Black streaks and blisters on young plants

Vegetables
Onion

Remedies: Immediate action
• Remove infested plants

Remedies: Proactive
• Long rotation:

• Certified seed

• Remove plant debris and crop residues

197

Onion and Leek Rust

Botanical name
Puccinia allii

Class
Pucciniaceae, Fungus

Names in other languages
Onion and Leek Rust, Rust of garlic (En). Rouille de l'Ail (Fr). Rost: Lauch, Rost: Zwiebel (De). Prei en uiroest, Lookroest (Nl).

Description
Rust (Puccinia alli) is primarily a disease of garlic, although onion, leeks, shallots, and wild species of Allium are also hosts. Symptoms begin as small flecks, which expand into slightly larger, oval- to square shaped reddish- to dull-orange pustules that develop on leaf blades. Lesions typically form first on older leaves, and then spread to younger leaves. Reddish airborne spores are produced copiously within the lesions. Later in the growing season, the lesions may appear dark because black survival spores develop within the pustules. Older leaves are usually attacked first. Severely affected leaves can be completely covered with pustules, turn yellow and then dry out and die.

Symptoms
Bright-orange spots on leaves.

Vegetables
Garlic, Leek, Onion

Onion and leek rust

Remedies: Immediate action
- Horsetail decoction

- Bordeaux mixture

- Liquid manure of horsetail

- Camomile infusion

- Dandelion infusion

- Wettable sulphur

- Garlic decoction

- Liquid manure of comfrey

- Liquid manure of wormwood

- Elder infusion

Remedies: Proactive
- Remove plant debris and crop residues

- Use resistant varieties/cultivars

- Review irrigation. Watering. Don't grow plants too closely together, always use the recommended spacings, as close spacing raises humidity and increases the likelihood of infection.

Onion Fly
Onion Maggot

Botanical name
Delia antiqua

Class
Anthomylidae, Insect

Names in other languages
Onion Fly, Onion maggot (En). Mouche de l'oignon (Fr). Zwiebelfliege (De). Uienvlieg, Preivlieg (Nl).

Description
The onion fly (*Delia antiqua*) adults looks like a large domestic fly. It attacks onion, shallot and leek. The larvae penetrates the tissue between the leaf shoots or at the base of the roots. It occurs on seedlings on thinned out provoking yellowing and wilting of the plants which rot.

Symptoms
Leaves turn yellow and wilt, Presence of white maggots, Roots and bulbs decay.

Vegetables
Garlic, Leek, Onion.

Onion fly adult and larvae (maggot)

Remedies: Immediate action
*   Eliminate the infected plants

*   Lavender decoction or infusion

*   Steinernema carpocapsae. S. feltae nematodes

*   Liquid manure of fern

*   Insecticide based on spinosad

*   Insecticide based on pyrethrum

*   Azadirachta. Neem oil insecticide

*   Steinernema carpocapsae. S. feltae nematodes

Remedies: Proactive
*   Insect-proof net

*   Chromatic trap (Yellow)

*   Long Rotation. Crop Rotation

*   Install insect hotels, bug hotels or insect houses. (Rove beetles)

*   Remove plant debris and crop residues

*   Use resistant varieties/cultivars. Red onios are less prone to attacks by onion fly.

Onion Thrips

Botanical name
Thrips tabaci

Class
Thripidae, Insect

Names in other languages
Onion Thrips. Thrips, Common cotton thrips, Potato thrips (En). Thrips de l'oignon, Thrips du tabac (Fr). Tabakthrips, Tabakblasenfuß, Zwiebelblasenfuß (De). Trips. Tabakstrips (Nl).

Description
Onion thrips (Thrips tabaci) are small insectes, very polyphagous, its attacks onion, leek, tomato, potato, tobaco, peach, cabbage, lucerne and red beet. In the glasshouse, infested foliage is disfigured by many silvery marks, with the presence of specks of black frass. This thrips is a vector of spotted-wilt virus on tomato. Thrips prefare hot dry weather. Thrips can spread quickly and widely due to their small size, high reproductive rate, and ability to fly or be carried by the wind.

Symptoms
Silvery marks on leaves, Speckled damage on leaves.

Vegetables
Courgette, Cucumber, Eggplant, Green bean, Leek, Onion, Peas, Pumpkin, Tomato.

Onion thrips adult

Remedies: Immediate action
- Amblyseius/Neoseiulus californicus. Californicus Spider Mite

- Garlic macerate oil

- Black soap

- Insecticide based on pyrethrum

- Auxiliary Beauveria brongniartii

- Predator Macrolophus caliginosus/M. pygmaeus. Predatory bug

- Orius insiduous pirate bug

- Kaolin clay spray

- Canola oil. Rapeseed oil. Plant oils

- Beauveria bassiana

- Transeius montdorensis. Predatory mite

- Steinernema carpocapsae. S. feltae nematodes

- Heterorhabditis bacteriophora Nematode

Remedies: Proactive
- Chromatic trap (Blue and Yellow)

- Install insect hotels, bug hotels or insect houses. A variety of natural enemies, including predatory mites, predatory bugs, predatory thrips, lacewings, ladybirds and parasitoid wasps, can all contribute to the control of thrips.

Pea Aphid
Green Pea Louse

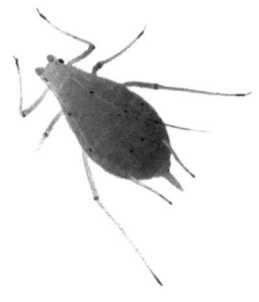

Pea aphid

Botanical name
Acyrthosiphon pisum

Class
Aphididae

Names in other languages
Pea Aphid, Destructive pea louse, Green pea louse (En). Puceron vert ou rose du pois, Puceron du pois (Fr). Grüne Besenginsterblattlaus, grüne Erbsenblattlaus (De). Erwtenbladluis (Nl).

Description
The pea aphid (*Acyrthosiphon pisum*) damage the plant because they feed on the sap, and the vegetal tissue is altered and the aphid's saliva is toxic for the plants. Usually, along with the attack, there is also a sugared secretion called "honey dew", on which, later on, sooty mould can appear. This aphid is a major vector of several plant virus diseases.

Symptoms
Presence of aphids, Presence of honeydew on leaves.

Vegetables
Green bean, Common bean, Peas.

Remedies: Immediate action
* Insecticide based on pyrethrum

* Black Soap

* Canola oil. Rapeseed oil. Plant oils

* Insecticide based on azadirachta. Neem oil

* Beauveria bassiana

* Remove infested plants or plant parts

Remedies: Proactive
* Long Rotation. Crop Rotation

* Beauveria bassiana

* Install insect hotels, insect houses, or insect houses. Encourage predators such as ladybugs, hoverfly and lacewing larvae, and Aphidius ervi parasitoids, which help control pea aphid populations.

Pea Downy Mildew

Pea downy mildew

Botanical name
Peronospora viciae

Class
Peronosporaceae, Fungus

Names in other languages
Pea Downy Mildew (En). Mildiou du Pois (Fr). Erbse falschen Mehltau (De). Erwten valse meeldauw (Nl).

Description
Downy mildew (*Peronospora viciae*) symptoms include a fuzzy, soft looking growth that can be white, grey, brown or purple. This growth is most commonly seen on the lower leaves of the plant. Other common symptoms for downy mildew include mottling or spots on the leaves. The spotting will be yellow, light green, brown, black or purple. In some cases, the mottling may look like chlorosis. Plants that are affected by downy mildew, may be stunted or have leaf loss.

Symptoms
Leaves with yellow-brown spots, Leaves with grey powder.

Vegetables
Peas.

Remedies: Immediate action
*   Bicarbonate of potassium or sodium

*   Reynoutria sachalinensis extract. Giant Knotweed

*   Review irrigation. Watering

*   Remove fallen leaves and dead material

Remedies: Proactive
*   Certified seed or plants

*   Use resistant varieties/cultivars

*   Long Rotation. Crop Rotation

Pea Midge

Botanical name
Contarinia pisi

Class
Cecidomyidae, Insect

Names in other languages
Pea Midge (En). Cécidomyie du pois (Fr). Erbsengallmücke (De). Erwtengalmug (Nl).

Description
The pea midge (*Contarinia pisi*) is a small fly black-yellowish in color. The larvae feeding causes swelling of the floral parts which leads to desiccation and abortion of the flowers. The larvae also develop in the pods and feed on the inner pod and the seeds.

Symptoms
Flowers with swellings.

Vegetables
Peas.

Pea midge adult

Remedies: Immediate action
*   Insecticide based on pyrethrum

Remedies: Proactive
*   Insect-proof net

*   Pheromone traps

Pea Moth

Botanical name
Laspeyresia nigricana, Cydia nigricana

Class
Geometridae, Insect

Names in other languages
Pea Moth (En). Tordeuse du pois (Fr). Rehfarbener Erbsenwickler (De). Erwtenpeulboorder (Nl).

Description
The pea moth (*Cydia nigricana*) is a small butterfly. Pea Moths are dull grey-brown with white and black markings on the leading edge of each forewing. They are approximately 6 mm long, with a 15 mm wingspan. Eggs are small and flattened. Caterpillars are pale yellow with a black head and legs. When mature, they are around 10 mm long. They have a brown ring on the prothorax, with eight brown dots on the following segments. Its penetrates the pods and damage up to 6 seeds (peas).

Symptoms
Presence of caterpillars in pods.

Vegetables
Peas.

Pea Moth adult and larvae (caterpillars)

Remedies: Immediate action
*   Insecticide based on pyrethrum

*   Insecticide based on spinosad

*   Liquid manure or maceration of tomato

*   Azadirachta. Neem oil insecticide

*   Bacillus thuringiensis. Bt

*   Kaolin clay spray

Remedies: Proactive
*   Early seeding. Timing pea planting to avoid the peak egg-laying period of the pea moth.

*   Insect-proof net

*   Pheromone traps

*   Chromatic trap

*   Long Rotation. Crop Rotation

*   Long Rotation. Crop Rotation

Pea Root Nematode
Pea Cyst Nematode

Botanical name
Heterodera goettingiana

Class
Heteroderidae, Insect

Names in other languages
Pea Root Nematode. Pea Cyst Nematode (En).
Nématode du pois, Anguillule à kyste du pois (Fr).
Erbsenzystenälchen,   Erbsenälchen   (De).
Erwtecystenaaltje (Nl).

Description
Pea root nematode (*Heterodera goettingiana*)
infected peas are stunted with yellowing leaves,
and leaves tend to point up. At bloom, yellowing
spreads rapidly from the bottom of the plant to the
top. Sometimes the color is a very bright yellow.
Invaded plants lack fibrous roots and nitrogen-
fixing nodules. Tiny (less than 0.5 mm) cream-
color, lemon-shaped cysts can be found
embedded in root tissue, but once cysts mature
and turn dark brown, they detach easily from root
systems and are difficult to detect.

Symptoms
Leaves turn yellow and die, Roots abnormally
increased.

Vegetables
Broad bean, Green bean, Peas.

Pea root nematode symptoms

Remedies: Immediate action
- French marigolds infusion

Remedies: Proactive
- Long Rotation. Crop Rotation. Non-host
  plants include cowpea, soybean, oats, wheat
  and woolly pod vetch. A rotation of 2 years or
  more between susceptible crops is needed to
  control a serious outbreak. Vegetable crops
  resistant to nematodes include broccoli, corn,
  brussels sprouts, chives and leeks.

- Repellent plants. Companion plants. Plants
  that contain high levels of bio-fumigant
  compounds include: rapeseed (canola)
  Brassica napus, marigolds and Indian
  mustard.

- Use resistant varieties/cultivars

- Certified seed or plants

- Soil solarization. The aim is to raise the
  temperature to between 45°C and 50°C in the
  top 10 cm of soil. This is high enough to kill
  disease pathogens but most beneficial soil
  organisms will survive. Leave the plastic in
  place for 4 to 6 weeks and then plant as usual.

Pea Seed-borne Mosaic Virus

Botanical name
Potyvirus pisumsemenportati, PSbMV

Class
Potyviridae, Virus

Names in other languages
Pea Seed-borne Mosaic Virus (En). Mosaïque du Pois, PSbMV (Fr). Erbsenrollenmosaikvirus (De). Erwtenrolmozaïekvirus (Nl).

Description
Pea seed-borne mosaic virus symptoms of the disease include leaf chlorosis, whole plant stunting, shortening and downward rolling of the leaflets, vein clearing and swelling, apical malformation (rosetting), mosaic, distorted flowers or seed pods and failure to set pods.

Symptoms
Leaves rolled, Plants stunted.

Vegetables
Peas

Pea seed-borne mosaic virus symptoms

Remedies: Immediate action

- Remove aphids

Remedies: Proactive

- Certified seed or plants

- Use resistant varieties/cultivars

Pea Thrips

Pea thrips

Botanical name
Frankliniella robusta

Class
Thripidae, Insect

Names in other languages
Pea Thrips, Bean thrips, Blackfly (En). Thrips du pois, Thrips de la fève et du pois (Fr). Erbsenthrips, Erbsenblasenfuß (De). Erwtentrhips, Donderbeestjes (Nl).

Description
The pea thrips (Frankliniella robusta) feeds on young parts of peas, field beans, broad beans, and beans, by sucking the nymphs weaken the shoots and the flowers shrivel or remain sterile. The pods stay small and may dry up and drop off. Late sowings and late varieties of peas are particularly vulnerable. Thrips can damage plants in multiple ways. First, egg laying within plant tissues can leave scarring. This can be particularly problematic in bean and pea pods. The feeding of thrips can leave brown or silvery scarring and stippling on shoots, stems and leaves, and can also damage flowers. Feeding of thrips usually only causes cosmetic damage, though heavier infestations can cause leaf curling, stunted growth and death of the plant. Furthermore, hot and dry conditions can favor outbreaks of thrips while plants are already stressed, leading to more severe damage. Lastly, thrips act as a carrier and transmitter of important plant viruses, which can spread through plant populations and cause much more severe damage and widespread plant death.

Symptoms
Leaves shrivelled, Fruit drop early.

Vegetables
Broad bean, Green bean, Peas.

Remedies: Immediate action
- Kaolin clay spray

- Canola oil. Rapeseed oil. Plant oils

- Insecticide based on azadirachta. Neem oil

- Insecticide based on pyrethrum

- Insecticide based on spinosad

- Beauveria bassiana

- Lecanicillium muscarium beneficial fungi

- Transeius montdorensis. Predatory mite

- Orius insidiosus pirate bug

Remedies: Proactive
- Install insect hotels, bug hotels or insect houses. To promote lacewings, minute pirate bugs, ladybugs and predatory thrips.

- Use resistant varieties/cultivars

- Insect-proof net. Insect net. Mesh Crop Cover

Pea Weevil
Pea and Bean Weevil

Botanical name
Sitona lineatus

Class
Curculionidae, Insect

Names in other languages
Pea Weevil, Pea and bean weevil, Striped bean weevil (En). Sitone du pois, Charançon rayé du pois, Sitone linéaire (Fr). Gestreifter Blattrandkäfer (De). Bladrandkever (Nl).

Pea weevil adult. Pea leaf edges eaten

Description
The pea weevil (Sitona lineatus) belong to the coleoptera, is a small, grey-brown weevil. The Adults are 4–5 mm long and light brown, with faint creamy yellow stripes along the length of the wing cases. They have a short 'snout' with the 'elbowed' antennae typical of weevils. The adults provoke notches on the leaves of many bean and pea species. The larvae feed on root nodules and roots.

Symptoms
Leaf edges eaten. Roots damaged.

Vegetables
Broad bean, Common bean, Peas.

Remedies: Immediate action
* Nematode Heterorhabditis bacteriophora

* Beauveria bassiana

Remedies: Proactive
* Certified seed

* Pheromone traps

* Install insect hotels, bug hotels or insect houses.

* Trap cropping. Early spring-planted faba beans or winter peas planted around the perimeter of later-planted spring field peas (main crop) can reduce adult and larval damage in the main crop.

Penicillium Decay
Seed Clove Decay
Bleu Mold

Botanical name
Penicillium spp.

Class
Trichocornaceae, Fungus

Names in other languages
Bleu Mold, Clove rot of garlic, Decay of garlic (En). Pourriture bleue. Pourriture verte de l'ail (Fr). Zwiebelfäule (De). Blauwe of groene schimmel (Nl).

Description
Penicillium decay of garlic (Penicillium hirsutum) is responsible for poor plant stand in the field and storage decay. Symptoms in the field include clove decay after planting and wilted, yellowed, or stunted seedlings. Infected plants are weak and stands are poor. In storage symptoms of the disease start as pale blemishes, yellow lesions, and soft spots. A blue-green mold develops on lesions. When bulbs are cut open, one or more of the fleshy scales may be discolored and water-soaked. In advanced stages, bulbs may deteriorate into complete decay. The fungus does not survive long in soil and is transmitted generally on seed cloves. Infection occurs on wounds sustained when cloves are separated from the parent bulb.

Symptoms
Plants stunted, Bluish-green area on cloves.

Vegetables
Garlic

Penicillium decay of garlic

Remedies: Immediate action
- Eliminate the infected plants. Dispose of infected bulbs off-farm: do not compost them.

Remedies: Proactive
- Certified seed or plants.

- Long Rotation. Crop Rotation

Phoma

Botanical name
Phoma valerianellae

Class
Phomaceae, Fungus

Names in other languages
Phoma (En). Nécrose de phoma, Phoma de la mâche (Fr). Phoma, Fäule: Feldsalat (De). Phoma. Schurft (Nl).

Description
Phoma is a seed-borne disease caused by a fungus *(Phoma valerianellae)*. Some seedlings will die shortly after germination, red stripes develop on roots, shoots and leaves, followed by the appearance of brown or black spots on the leaves.

Symptoms
Red stripes on roots, shoots and leaves.

Vegetables
Asparagus, Celery, Lamb's lettuce, Tomato

Phoma on asparagus

Remedies: Proactive
- Certified seed

- Use resistant varieties/cultivars

- Hot water treatment of seeds. Seed-borne pathogens could be reduced without significant losses of germination by hot water treatments at 50 °C for 20 to 30 min up to 53 °C for 10 to 30 min.

- Long rotation

- Remove plant debris and crop residues

Potato Aphid

Botanical name
Macrosiphum euphorbiae

Class
Aphidae, Insect

Names in other languages
Potato Aphid, Tomato aphid (En). Puceron vert et rose de la pomme de terre, Puceron de la pomme de terre (Fr). Gestreifte Kartoffelblattlaus, Grünstreifige Kartoffelblattlaus (De). Toprol. Aardappeltopluis (Nl).

Description
The potato aphid (*Macrosiphum euphorbiae*) is rather large sized for an aphid, from greyish-green to pink. It is very polyphagous and it infest potato, beet, cabbage. lettuce, pepper, aubergine and many others. It transmit phytopathogenic viruses as the potato virus and the beet yellow virus.

Symptoms
Presence of aphids

Vegetables
Beetroot, Cabbage, Cucumber, Eggplant, Lettuce, Peas, Pepper, Potato, Tomato.

Potato aphid

Remedies: Immediate action
- Garlic macerate oil

- Black soap

- Insecticide based on pyrethrum

- Horsetail decoction

- Comfrey infusion

- Nettle infusion:

- Liquid manure of fern

- Elder decoction

- Predator Macrolophus caliginosus/M. pygmaeus. Predatory bug

- Canola oil. Rapeseed oil. Plant oils

- Insecticide based on azadirachta. Neem oil

- Beauveria bassiana

- Aphelinus Predatory Wasps

- Aphidius Predatory Wasps

Remedies: Proactive
- Ladybird Predatory beetle. Among the more common predators are lady beetles and their larvae, lacewing larvae, and syrphid fly larvae.

- Weed control

- Insect-proof net. Insect net. Mesh Crop Cover

Potato Leaf Roll Virus

Potato leaf roll virus

Botanical name
Potyvirus yituberosi, PVY

Class
Luteoviridae, Virus

Names in other languages
Potato Leaf-drop Streak. Potato Virus Y (En). Mosaïque de la Pomme de terre, PVY (Fr). Kartoffelvirus Y (De). Aardappelvirus Y (Nl).

Description
Potato leaf roll virus (PRLV) primary symptoms develop in plants infected with the virus during the current season and are usually restricted to chlorosis or purpling of the tops of the plants and slight leafrolling of the leaflets. Typical secondary symptoms are stunting of the plants and severe upward rolling of the basal leaves which progresses during season to the upper leaves.

Symptoms
Leaves shrivelled, Plants stunted.

Vegetables
Potato.

Remedies: Immediate action
*   Remove aphids

*   Remove infested plants parts

Remedies: Proactive
*   Certified seed or plants

*   Use resistant varieties/cultivars

Potato Scab

Botanical name
Streptomyces scabies

Class
Streptomycetaceae, Fungus

Names in other languages
Potato Scab, Common scab of potato (En). Gale commune de la pomme de terre, Gale commune de la carotte, Gale commune du navet (Fr). Kartoffelschorf, Gewöhnlicher Schorf: Kartoffel (De). Aardappelschurft (Nl).

Potato scab

Description
Potato scab is caused by a bacterium-like organism (*Streptomyces scabies*). Symptoms include dark brown, pithy patches that may be raised and "warty." These lesions can affect just a small portion of the tuber surface, or may completely cover it.

Symptoms
Warty patches on tuber.

Vegetables
Potato

Remedies: Proactive
*   Certified seed

*   Use resistant varieties/cultivar

*   Long rotation. Rotation with small grains, corn, or alfalfa appears to reduce disease in subsequent potato crops

*   Green manure. Growing a green manure crop like mustard or oilseed radish can help suppress the bacteria that cause potato scabs. These plants can be turned into the soil about two weeks before planting potatoes.

Potato Tuber Nematode
Potato Cyst Nematode

Botanical name
Ditylenchus destructor. Globodera rostochiensis

Class
Anguinidae, Insect

Names in other languages
Potato Tuber Nematode. Potato Cyst Nematode, Potato root nematode, Potato rot nematode (En). Nématode de la pomme de terre, Nématode à galle et à kyste, Maladie vermiculaire de la pomme de terre (Fr). Kartoffelkrätzeälchen, Krätzeälchen (De). Destructoraaltje (Nl).

Description
Potato tuber nematode (*Ditylenchus destructor* and *Globodera species*). Infested plants are stunted and may wilt, leaves may yellow or display a dull colour. Plants have a reduced root system which is abnormally branched and brownish in colour. At flowering or later, minute-white, yellow or brown spheres or cysts, about the size of a pin head (0.5 mm), can be seen on the outside of roots.

Symptoms
Wilted plants, Roots abnormally increased.

Vegetables
Potato

Potato tuber nematode

Remedies: Immediate action
*   French marigolds infusion

Remedies: Proactive
*   Long rotation

*   Association with another crop or culture like Tagetes, Cereals and Alfalfa.

*   Certified seed or plants

*   Use resistant varieties/cultivars

*   Soil solarization. In summer the soil is irrigated very well to increase its heat conductivity. The plastic should be left in place for about 4 to 6 weeks.

Potato Tuberworm
Potato Split-worm
Potato Tuber Moth

Botanical name
Phthorimaea operculella. Gnorimoschema operculella

Class
Gelechiidae, Insect

Names in other languages
Potato Tuberworm, Potato moth, Potato tuber moth (En). Teigne de la pomme de terre (Fr). Kartoffelmotte (De). Aardappelmot (Nl).

Description
The potato tuberworm (*Phthorimaea operculella*) or potato tuber moth. The larvae (caterpillar) feed on potato leaves, stems, petioles, and more importantly potato tubers in the field and in storage. The newly hatched larvae create mines on leaves by feeding on leaf tissue while leaving the upper and lower epidermis of the leaf intact. They prefer feeding on young foliage. Typical damage results from larvae boring tunnels in tubers. As a result also fungi and mites develop inside the galleries, causing the decomposition of the tuber.

Symptoms
Leaves with galleries, Tubers with galleries.

Vegetables
Potato

Potato tuberworm adult and larvae

Remedies: Immediate action
- Insecticide based on spinosad

- Bacillus thuringiensis. Bt

- Heterorhabditis bacteriophora Nematode

- Steinernema carpocapsae. S. feltae nematodes

Remedies: Proactive
- Pheromone traps

- Certified seed or plants

- Use resistant varieties/cultivars

- Long Rotation. Crop Rotation

- Remove plant debris and crop residues

- Install insect hotels, bug hotels or insect houses

Potato Virus A

Botanical name
Potyvirus atuberosi, PVA

Class
Potyviridae, Virus

Names in other languages
Potato Virus A, Common mosaic of potato, Mild mosaic of potato, Veinal mosaic of potato (En). Mosaïque commune de la Pomme de terre, Virus A de la pomme de terre. PVA (Fr). Kartoffelvirus A (De). Aardappelvirus A (Nl).

Potato virus A

Description
Potato virus A leaves of infected potatoes may show a mild mosaic, roughness of the surface, waviness of the leaf margin, or no symptoms at all depending on the variety and on the weather. Some hypersensitive varieties develop top necrosis. Potatoes infected with potato virus A in combination with potato virus X or potato virus Y show crinkle symptoms.

Symptoms
Leaves with mosaic pattern.

Vegetables
Potato.

Remedies: Immediate action
• Remove infested plants or plant parts

Remedies: Proactive
• Certified seed or plants

• Use resistant varieties/cultivars: The cheapest, easiest and most efficient way for gardeners to reduce losses from diseases is to plant resistance varieties. Many seed companies, offer seeds that are resistant to certain common pathogens

Potato Virus X

Potato virus X

Botanical name
Potexvirus ecspotati, PVX

Class
Alphaflexiviridae, Virus

Names in other languages
Potato Virus X, Potato mottle, Potato mild mosaic (En). Mosaïque de la Pomme de terre, PVX (Fr). Kartoffelvirus X (De). Aardappelvirus X (Nl).

Description
Potato Virus X is found mainly in potatoes and is only transmitted mechanically. There are no insect or fungal vectors for this virus. This virus causes mild or no symptoms in most potato varieties, but when Potato Virus Y is present, synergy between these two viruses causes severe symptoms in potatoes. It causes mild mosaic symptoms.

Symptoms
Leaves with mosaic pattern.

Vegetables
Potato

Remedies: Immediate action
• Remove infested plants or plant parts

Remedies: Proactive
• Certified seed or plants

• Use resistant varieties/cultivars

Potato Virus Y

Potato Leaf Roll Virus

Potato virus Y

Botanical name
Potyvirus yituberosi, PVY

Class
Potyviridae, Virus

Names in other languages
Potato Leaf-drop Streak. Potato Virus Y (En). Mosaïque de la Pomme de terre, PVY (Fr). Kartoffelvirus Y (De). Aardappelvirus Y (Nl).

Description
Potato Virus Y causes a severe disease called mosaic or rugose mosaic. Symptoms are variable depending on viral strain, host cultivar, climatic conditions, and whether it is a primary infection (inoculation by aphid vectors) or secondary infection (when mother tuber is infected) Symptoms in the aerial parts of the plants consist of a mild to severe mottle, often associated with distortion (crinkling) of the leaves. Yellowing and necrosis (vein necrosis and necrotic spots) frequently occur in the lower leaves. Symptoms also include collapse and dropping of intermediate leaves (leaf drop), which remain clinging to the stem. Secondarily infected plants are dwarfed and brittle, with crinkled and puckered leaves. Necrosis in tubers may occur in numerous cultivars.

Symptoms
Leaves shrivelled, Leaves with black spots.

Vegetables
Potato

Remedies: Immediate action
•   Remove aphids

Remedies: Proactive
•   Certified seed or plants

•   Use resistant varieties/cultivars

•   Long Rotation. Crop Rotation

Powdery Mildew

Powdery mildew

Botanical name
Peronospora, Bremia, Pseudoperonospora, Phytophthora. Sphaerotheca fuliginea

Class
Peronosporaceae, Fungus

Names in other languages
Powdery Mildew (EN), Mildou. Oidium (FR), Mehltau (DE), Echte meeldauw (NL).

Description
Powdery mildew is caused by a variety of closely related fungal species (*Peronospora, Bremia, Pseudoperonospora, Phytophthora*). Low soil moisture combined with high humidity levels at the plant surface favors this disease. Powdery mildew starts on young leaves as raised blister-like areas that cause leaves to curl, exposing the lower leaf surface. Infected leaves become covered with a white to gray powdery growth, usually on the upper surface. Leaves of severely infected plants turn brown and drop.

Symptoms
Raised blister-like areas on leaves. White to grey powder coverage on leaves.

Vegetables
Artichoke, Beetroot, Broad bean, Carrot, Celeriac, Celery, Courgette, Cucumber, Eggplant, Fennel, Green bean, Lamb's lettuce, Leek, Lettuce, Onion, Peas, Potato, Pumpkin, Radish, Spinach, Tomato.

Remedies: Immediate action
• Review irrigation. Watering

• Eliminate the infected plants

• Lithothamnion algae

• Horsetail decoction

• Bordeaux mixture

• Liquid manure of nettle

• Diluted milk

• Garlic decoction

• Liquid manure of horsetail

• Elder infusion

• Wettable sulphur

• Liquid manure of fern

• Bacillus subtilis

Remedies: Proactive
• Watering only at the root

• Long rotation

Ramularia Leaf and Bract Spot

Botanical name
Ramularia cynarae

Class
Mycosphaerelliaceae

Names in other languages
Ramularia Leaf and Bract Spot (En). Ramulariose (Fr). Blattfleckenkrankheit (De). Ramularia (Nl).

Description
Ramularia leaf and bract spot (*Ramularia cynarae*) leaf symptoms consist of small in pale green to yellow-green circular spots that develops on the older foliage. Most of the leaf can turn brown and dry up.

Symptoms
Pale green to yellow-green circular spots on leaves, Leaves turn brown and dry up.

Vegetables
Artichoke.

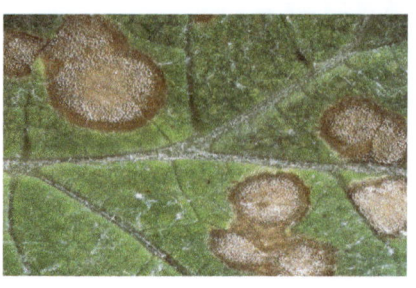

Ramularia leaf and bract spot

Remedies: Immediate action
• Bordeaux mixture

• Eliminate the infected plants

Ring Spot on Lettuce

Botanical name
Marssonina panattoniana

Class
Tuberculariaceae, Fungus

Names in other languages
Ring Spot of Lettuce, Anthracnose of lettuce, Shot-hole (En). Anthracnose de la laitue (Fr). Blattfleckenkrankheit: Endivie, Blattfleckenkrankheit: Salat (De). Vuur (Nl).

Description
Ring spot on lettuce also known as shot hole or Anthracnose (Marssonina panattoniana) development is particularly severe on the underside of the lower leaves. Spots enlarge, turn yellow, and are usually irregular and angular in shape. If the disease is severe, the lesions will coalesce and cause significant dieback of the leaf and in some cases result in stunting of the plant. As spots age, the affected tissue will dry up and become papery in texture. Eventually the centers of these spots will fall out, resulting in the shot hole symptom. This disease requires cool, wet conditions for infection and symptom development. Anthracnose is always associated with rainy springs. Splashing water moves microsclerotia onto lettuce leaves, resulting in infection.

Symptoms
Leaves with yellow spots.

Vegetables
Lettuce

Ring spot on lettuce

Remedies: Immediate action
*   Remove infested plants parts

*   Bacillus subtilis

*   Wettable sulphur

Remedies: Proactive
*   Long Rotation. Crop Rotation

*   Certified seed or plants:

*   Use resistant varieties/cultivars

*   Review irrigation. Watering

*   Remove plant debris and crop residues

*   Hot water treatment of seeds. Treat the seeds with hot water at 50°C for 30 minutes. Treat a small amount of each batch of seeds, and test for germination before treating each seed.

Rust

Rust

Botanical name
Puccinia asparagi. Phragmidium

Class
Pucciniacaea, Fungus

Names in other languages
Rust, Rust of asparagus (En). Rouille, Rouille de l'asperge (Fr). Rost: Spargel (De). Roestziekte, Aspergeroest (Nl).

Description: Rust is a term used for a group of fungal species which attack a broad range of plants. The disease is usually seen on the underside of leaves where small rusty brown spores develop. Spores can be other colours, including orange and yellow, and can also occur on other parts of a plant. Infected leaves usually show yellow discolouration on the upper side of the leaf corresponding to where the rust spore is located on the underside. Badly infected leaves will drop and younger plants can be severely stunted or die. Manage irrigation and ensure plants are not under or over-watered. Pick off and destroy infected leaves and frequently rake under plants to remove all fallen debris. Burn or bag infected plants after the growing season. Do NOT compost.

Symptoms
Reddish-orange spots on leaves.

Vegetables
Asparagus, Broad bean, Carrot, Celeriac, Celery, Chard, Green bean, Parsnip, Rutabaga.

Remedies: Immediate action
*   Bordeaux mixture

*   Eliminate the infected plants

*   Horsetail decoction

*   Liquid manure of fern

*   Liquid manure of tansy

*   Wettable sulphur

*   Garlic decoction

*   Liquid manure of horsetail

*   Liquid manure of wormwood

*   Elder infusion

*   Bacillus subtilis

*   Remove infested plants or plant parts

Remedies: Proactive
*   Watering only at the root

*   Use resistant varieties/cultivars

*   Remove plant debris and crop residues

Scab of Cucurbits

Botanical name
Cladosporium cucumerinum

Class
Cladosporiaceae, Fungus

Names in other languages
Scab of Cucurbits, Gummosis of cucumber (En). Cladosporiose du concombre, Nuile grise du melon, Gale du concombre (Fr). Gummifluß: Gurke, Gurkenkrätze (De). Schurft van komkommer (Nl).

Description
Scab of cucurbits is provoked by a fungus (Cladosporium cucumerinum). On leaves, symptoms are gray to brown angular lesions with a yellow halo. On fruit, appear small brown pockmarks, resembling insect damage. Later, the spots enlarge and finally become distinct sunken cavities. This pathogen overwinters on infected crop debris for up to 3 years. It may also spread through seeds. Spores develop under moist conditions when temperatures are between 15° and 25°C. Spores are spread by insects, farm equipment, and people brushing against infected plants.

Symptoms
Leaves with angular spots, Brown pockmarks on fruits.

Vegetables
Courgette, Melon, Pumpkin.

Scab of cucurbits

Remedies: Immediate action
· Horsetail decoction

· Bordeaux mixture

· Liquid manure of nettle

· Certified seed or plants

· Reynoutria sachalinensis extract. Giant Knotweed

Remedies: Proactive
· Use resistant varieties/cultivars

· Long rotation

· Revieuw irrigation system

· Remove plant debris and crop residues

Seedcorn Maggot
Bean Seed Fly

Botanical name
Delia platura

Class
Anthomyiidae, Insect

Names in other languages
Seedcorn Maggot. Bean Seed Fly, Onion maggot (En). Mouche des semis, Mouche grise des semis, Mouche de la graine du haricot, Mouche de l'oignon (Fr). Bohnenfliege, Graue Wurzelfliege, Kammschienenwurzelfliege, Saatenfliege, Schalottenfliege (De). Bonenvlieg (Nl).

Description
The bean seed fly (*Delia platura*) is extremely polyphagous, more than 40 hosts are recorded. The female deposits several hundred eggs in the ground the preference in humid soils rich in organic matter. The larvae feed on germinating seeds and young plants, forming galleries in the cotyledons, the small stems and the young shoots. They often cause the plants to rot.

Symptoms
Damaged cotyledons.

Vegetables
Green bean, Lamb's lettuce, Spinach, Sweet corn, Tomato.

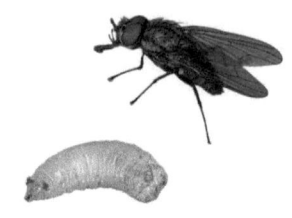

Bean seed fly adult, larvae (seedcorn maggot)

Remedies: Immediate action
- Infusion of wormwood

- Steinernema carpocapsae. S. feltae nematodes

Remedies: Proactive
- Insect-proof net

- Chromatic trap

- No-till. Fields that have been recently tilled (less than 2 to 3 weeks prior to planting) and were in sod, cover crops, or were recently manured are at the highest risk for egg laying. The adult flies are looking for decaying vegetation or high organic matter fields that have been recently tilled.

Silver-Y moth
Common Silver-Y moth
Cabbage Army Moth

Botanical name
Autographa gamma/Mamestra brassicae

Class
Noctuidae, Insect

Names in other languages
Silver-Y moth. Common Silver-Y moth. Cabbage Army Moth. (En). Noctuelle gamma, Noctuelle défoliatrice, Noctuelle grise des jardins (Fr). Gammaeule (De). Gamma-uil (Nl).

Silver-Y moth adult and larvae (caterpillar)

Description
The silver-Y moth (*Autographa gamma*) fore wings are brownish-yellow with at their centre a white spot resembling the shape of the Greek letter gamma. The caterpillars light green with longitudinal white lines are particularly voracious. The silver-Y moth is a migrant moth that appears in northern parts of Europe until November, migrating back to southern Europe for the winter months. The moths can fly 2,000 to 2,500 km. In temperate climates, the species produces one to two overlapping generations, and it is the second generation that inflicts much damage to agricultural crops, particularly brassicas, from August onward. The silver-Y moth feeds on plants of 14 families and is sometimes also encountered in greenhouse crops such as sweet pepper, lettuce, beans,

Symptoms
Leaves with perforations, Presence of caterpillars

Vegetables
Cabbage, Eggplant, Spinach, Lettuce, Pepper.

Remedies: Immediate action
- Bacillus thuringiensis

- Wormwood decoction

- Tansy decoction

- Bait based on bran and pyrethrum

- Elder decoction

- Insecticide based on spinosad

- Steinernema carpocapsae. S. feltae nematodes

Remedies: Proactive
- Pheromone traps

Skin Blotch of Garlic

Skin blotch of garlic

Botanical name
Embellisia allii. Helminthosporium allii

Class
Pleosporaceae, Fungus

Names in other languages
Skin Blotch of Garlic, Canker of garlic, Dry rot of garlic (En). Suie des bulbes d 'ail (Fr). Ruß von Knoblauchknollen (De). Embellisia schimmelvlekken (Nl).

Description
Skin blotch of garlic is caused by the fungal pathogen (*Embellisia allii/Helminthosporium allii*). Symptoms start as small water-soaked lesions on the bulbs and develop into brown to black lesions. The disease may progress into cankers on the cloves.

Symptoms
Brown or black lesions on bulbs.

Vegetables
Garlic.

Remedies: Immediate action
*   Bordeaux mixture

*   Eliminate the infected plants

Remedies: Proactive
*   Certified seed or plants

Slug and Snail
Garden Slug. Loach. Little Grey Slug. Vine Snail. White Garden Snail

Botanical name
Arion hortensis. Deroceras reticulatum. Agriolimax reticulatum. Euparypha pisana. Helix pisana

Class
Insect

Names in other languages
Common garden slug, Field slug (En). Lmace des jardins, ILmace des champs, Cagouille (Fr). Gartenschnecke (De). Tuinslak, Akkerslak (Nl).

Description
Slug and snail are most active at night, they feed on a variety of living plants as well as on decaying plant material. It chew large holes in foliage and may cause extensive damage to seedlings, tender, low-growing, leafy vegetables and ripening fruit, depositing trash.

Symptoms
Leaves with perforations, Traces of trash.

Vegetables
Beetroot, Chard, Cucumber, Lettuce, Peas, Rutabaga, Spinach

Slug and snail

Remedies: Immediate action
- Nematode Phasmarhabditis hermaphrodita

- Fern decoction

- Granule on the basis of iron phospahate

- Liquid manure of fern

- Infusion of wormwood

- Rue maceration

Remedies: Proactive
- Beer traps

- Physical barriers

- Diatomaceous earth

- Reppelent and trap plants Garlic, Lawn Chamomile, chives. Some plants repel most slugs and snails and these may have a deterrent effect when planted alongside or used to make an extract.

- Install insect hotels, bug hotels or insect houses. Frogs, lizards, chooks, ducks and other birds find snails and slugs irresistible.

Soft rot
White Rot on Carrot
Cottony rot

Botanical name
Sclerotinia sclerotiorum. Sclerotinia libertiana

Class
Sclerotiniaceae, Fungus

Names in other languages
White Rot on Carrot, Cottony rot, Storage rot, White mould (En). Pourriture blanche sur carotte, Maladie à sclérotes, Pourriture du collet, Sclérotiniose (Fr). Pelzfäule, Rapskrebs, Stengelfäule, Weißfäule (De). Rattenkeutelziekte (Nl).

Description
The cottony rot disease is caused by the fungal pathogen, *Sclerotinia sclerotiorum*. In the field the early signs of the disease would be a water soaked lesion at the base of the foliage, and if humidity is high, the infection could be accompanied with cottony white mycelial growth on the carrots and crop residue. In the storage, the white mycelium of the pathogen grows rapidly and infects carrots over large areas.

Symptoms
Wilting of leaves, Leaves with water soaked lesions.

Vegetables
Carrot

Soft rot on carrot

Remedies: Immediate action
*   Coniothyrium minitans

*   Trichoderma

*   Streptomyces lydicus

*   Reynoutria sachalinensis extract. Giant Knotweed

*   Bacillus subtilis

Remedies: Proactive
*   Long Rotation. Crop Rotation

*   Manage soil conditions

South American Miner Fly
South American Leaf Miner

South American leaf miner adult and larvae (maggots)

Botanical name
Liriomyza huidobrensis

Class
Agromyzidae, Insect

Names in other languages
South American Miner Fly. South American Leaf Miner (EN), Mouche mineuse sud-américaine (FR), Südamerikanische Minierfliege (DE), Nerfmineervlieg (NL).

Description
The South American leaf miner (*Liriomyza huidobrensis*) is highly polyphagous. The larva is primarily a leaf miner. Mines are usually white with dampened black and dried brown areas, and are usually associated with the midrib and lateral leaf veins. Mines are typically serpentine, of irregular shape, increasing in width as larvae mature.

Symptoms
Leaves with galleries.

Vegetables
Cabbage, Celery, Cucumber, Lettuce, Potato, Tomato.

Remedies: Immediate action
* Diglyphus isaea. Parasitic wasp

* Bacillus thuringiensis. Bt

* Insecticide based on azadirachta. Neem oil

Remedies: Proactive
* Chromatic trap

Southern Green Stink Bug

Botanical name
Nezara viridula

Class
Pentatomidae, Insect

Names in other languages
Southern Green Stink bug, Green plant bug, Green shield bug, Tomato and bean bug (En). Punaise verte à front jaune, Punaise verte, Punaise verte du sud, Punaise verte ponctuée, Punaise verte puante (Fr). Grüne Reiswanze (De). Zuidelijke groene schildwants (Nl).

Description
Stink bugs are large triangular bugs in the Pentatomidae family of insects. They usually appear in green or brown colors. Their common name is derived from disagreeable odors produced by their scent glands to deter predators. They give an awful odor when crushed. The insects possess piercing-sucking mouthpart and use it to suck sap from plants. Several species of stink bugs have been reported on a large number of crops and they cause significant damage as they feed on these crops. However, they cause most damage to tomato, pepper, bean, okra and fruit crops. The Southern green stink bug (*Nezara viridula*) has piercing sucking mouthparts. All plant parts are likely to be fed on but growing shoots and developing floral buds are preferred. In case of many piercings young buds withers and drops.

Symptoms
Leaves shrivelled. White spots on fruits.

Vegetables
Cucumber, Eggplant, Freen bean, Pepper, Tomato.

Southern green stink bug adult

Remedies: Immediate action
• Remove manually pests

• Kaolin clay spray

• Black Soap

• Insecticide based on azadirachta. Neem oil

• Diatomaceous Earth

• Garlic macerate oil

• Trissolcus basalis Parasitic wasp

• Pyrethrum insecticide

Remedies: Proactive
• Insect-proof net

• Chromatic trap (Yellow)

• Trap cropping (Sorghum, millet, sunflower, buckwheat, okra, field peas also work)

• Install insect hotels, bug hotels or insect houses

Stem Nematode
Bulb and Stem Nematode

Botanical name
Ditylenchus dipsaci

Class
Anguinidae, Nematode

Names in other languages
Stem Nematode. Bulb and Stem Nematode (En). Anguillule, Nématode des tiges, Nématode des bulbes, Anguillule commune des tiges (Fr). Rübenkopfälchen, Stengelälchen, Stockälchen (De). Stengelaaltje (Nl).

Stem nematode symptoms

Description
Stem nematode (Ditylenchus dipsaci) affects apart from the Liliaceae (onion, leeks, garlic) many aother vegetables belonging to Solanaceae (potato), Cruciferae (Cabbage, ...), Leguminosae (Peas, ...). The base of young onion, leek, garlic and shallot plants becomes swollen and leaves distorted. Bulbs later become blistered and cracked. Stem nematodes are known to reproduce sexually. All juvenile and adult stages of the nematode can infect a host plant, although the fourth juvenile stage is the main infective stage. The life cycle is temperature dependent and takes approximately 20 days to complete at 15°C. Every female may lay 200–500 eggs. As a result an infestation starting with lower initial population densities can quickly increase to large numbers.

Symptoms
Leaves with red spots and distorted.

Vegetables
Garlic, Onion

Remedies: Immediate action
- Eliminate the infected plants

- French marigolds infusion

Remedies: Proactive
- Repellent crops (French marigolds)

- Long rotation

- Certified seed or plants

- Soil solarization. The soil is irrigated with 15–20 mm water, then covered with virtually impermeable film and left for at least 6 weeks at a soil temperature of at least 16°C.

Thistle Aphid
Plum - thistle aphid

Thistle aphid

Botanical name
Brachycaudus cardui

Class
Aphididae

Names in other languages
Thistle Aphid (En). Puceron de l'artichaut, puceron du chardon (Fr). Große Pflaumenblattlaus (De). Distelkortstaartluis (Nl).

Description
The thistle aphid (Brachycaudus cardui) is brownish-yellow, pale green or brwon with a large black spot situated dorsally on the abdomen. Leaves of artichoke undergo severe curling and dense colonies occur at the base of the flower heads and on the leaves. Colonies of Thistle-aphids are usually attended by ants which feed on the honeydew the aphids produce and drive away predators. The primary host of B. cardui is plum, cherry, apricot, peach or damson, but during the summer months it moves to a secondary host. This is often a thistle in the genera Carduus or Cirsium where it is commonly seen on the stems and flowerheads. Alternatively, other plants in the aster family or plants in the borage family (Boraginaceae) may be used as secondary hosts. Winged individuals fly back to the primary hosts in the autumn.

Symptoms
Leaves curled or shrivelled, Presence of colonies of aphids.

Vegetables
Artichoke

Remedies: Immediate action
* Horsetail decoction

* Insecticide based on pyrethrum

* Black soap

* Garlic macerate oil

* Comfrey infusion

* Nettle infusion

* Liquid manure of fern

* Elder decoction

* Predator Macrolophus caliginosus/M. pygmaeus. Predatory bug

* Canola oil. Rapeseed oil. Plant oils

* Insecticide based on azadirachta. Neem oil

* Beauveria bassiana

Remedies: Proactive
* Ladybird Predatory beetle

Tobacco Mosaic Virus

Tobacco mosaic virus on eggplant

Botanical name
Tobamovirus tabaci, TMV

Class
Virgaviridae, Virus

Names in other languages
Tobacco Mosaic Virus (En). Virus de la mosaïque du tabac (Fr). Tabakmosaikvirus (De). Tabaksmozaïekvirus (Nl).

Description
Mosaics are caused by a virus. Symptoms include yellow and green mottling, upward curling, necrotic leaf spots, leaf distortion, and overall stunting. TMV is not transmitted by insects, but is transmitted mechanically in sap, by contact with contaminated equipment, by vegetative propagation, and it can be carried in seed.

Symptoms
Leaves with mosaic pattern.

Vegetables
Eggplant.

Remedies: Immediate action
• Remove infested plants parts

Remedies: Proactive
• Certified seed or plants

• Use resistant varieties/cultivars

Tomato Chlorosis Crinivirus

Tomato chlorosis crinivirus

Botanical name
Crinivirus tomatichlorosis, ToCV

Class
Closteroviridae, Virus

Names in other languages
Tomato Chlorosis Crinivirus. ToCV (En). Virus de la chlorose de la tomate, ToCV (Fr). Tomatenchlorosevirus (De). Tomaten Chlorose Virus (Nl).

Description
Tomato plants infected with Tomato Chlorosis Crinivirus show an irregular chlorotic mottle that develops first on lower leaves and gradually advances toward the growing point. In between the veins yellow areas develop on leaves with red and brown necrotic flecks. The tomato chlorosic virus (ToCV) is transmitted by the adults of the white fly Trialeurodes vaporariorum and Bemisia tabaci (Tobacco white fly).

Symptoms
Leases with mosaic pattern, Leaves turn yellow.

Vegetables
Tomato

Remedies: Immediate action
*   Remove aphids

*   Remove infested plants parts

*   Remove white fly

*   Macrolophus caliginosus/M. pygmaeus. Predatory bug

*   Lecanicillium muscarium

Remedies: Proactive
*   Insect-proof net. Insect net. Mesh Crop Cover

*   Chromatic trap (Yellow)

*   Remove plant debris and crop residues

234

Tomato Corky Root

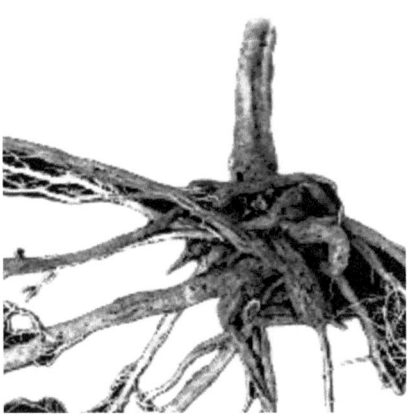

Tomato corky root symptoms

Botanical name
Pyrenochaeta lycopersici

Class
Phomaceae, Fungus

Names in other languages
Tomato Corky Root, Brown root rot of tomato (En).
Maladie des racines liégeuses (Fr).
Korkwurzelkrankheit: Tomate (De). Kurkwortel (Nl).

Description
Corky root (*Pyrenochaeta lycopersici*) attacks the
root system of the tomato plant, causing rotting of
smaller feeder roots, brown lesions on small roots
and typical corky lesions on larger roots. Wilting of
the affected plants, brown corky swelling of the
roots which show a corrugated surface.

Symptoms
Wilted plants, Roots abnormally increased.

Vegetables
Tomato

Remedies: Immediate action
- Remove infested plants parts

- Compost tea

- Bacillus subtilis

- Streptomyces lydicus

Remedies: Proactive
- Use resistant varieties/cultivars

Tomato Fruitworm
Old World Bollworm

Tomato fruitworm adult and larvae

Botanical name
Helicoverpa armigera. Heliothis armigera. Heliothis zea. Heliothis obsoleta

Class
Noctuidae, Insect

Names in other languages
Tomato Fruitworm, African cotton bollworm, Corn earworm, Tomato grub (En). Noctuelle de la tomate, Chenille des épis du maïs, Ver de la capsule (Fr). Altweltlicher Baumwollkapselwurm (De). Katoendaguil (Nl).

Description
The Old World bollworm (Helicoverpa armigera) larvae (caterpillars) feed externally and internally on all above-ground parts but prefer flowers, buds, seeds, and fruit. Internal feeding is revealed by boreholes or cutting open fruit and buds. Feeding damage often is accompanied by fungal and bacterial infection. Tomato fruitworm adult is a moth that lays single creamy white eggs at night during mid-May to early June on lower side of leaves or leaflets close to flowers or fruits. Newly hatched larvae/caterpillars are creamy white, brown headed with distinctive black tubercles and hairs. Larvae usually measure about 3 to 5 cm (1.5 to 2 inches) in size, fully grown large caterpillars vary in color from greenish-yellow to brown, pink, yellow or even black with densely covered microscopic hairs and paler white stripes running along the body. Signs of fruitworm damage can be identified by a visible black hole at the base of stems of infested plants.

Symptoms
Flower buds destroyed, Presence of caterpillars. Black holes.

Vegetables
Sweet corn, Tomato.

Remedies: Immediate action
- Insecticide based on spinosad

- Bacillus thuringiensis. Bt

- Azadirachta. Neem oil insecticide

- Black Soap. Marseille soap

- Remove manually pests, hand picking and destruction of the larvae

Remedies: Proactive
- Pheromone traps

- Insectary plants. Planting crops (coriander, fennel, mint) that attract natural predators like minute pirate bugs, lacewings, big-eyed bugs and damsel bugs that feed on fruitworm eggs and young larvae should be encouraged.

Tomato Leaf Miner

Botanical name
Tuta absoluta

Class
Gelechidae, Insect

Names in other languages
Tomato Leaf Miner, Tomato borer, South American tomato moth (En). Mineuse de la tomate (Fr). Tomatenminiermotte (De). Tomatenmineermot (Nl).

Description
The tomato leaf miner (*Tuta absoluta*) larvae feed on leaves and fruits. It provoke tunnels or galleries in the leaves and stems appearing as white spots.

Symptoms
Tunnels or galleries in leaves, White spots on leaves.

Vegetables
Eggplant, Pepper, Tomato.

Tomato leaf miner adult and larvae

Remedies: Immediate action
- Eliminate the infected plants

- Liquid manure of rhubarb

- Auxiliary Macrolophus caliginosus

- Auxiliary Nesidiocoris tenuis

- Diglyphus isaea. Parasitic wasp

Remedies: Proactive
- Insect-proof net

- Pheromone traps

Tomato Russet Mite

Botanical name
Aculops lycopersici

Class
Eriophydae, Spider mite

Names in other languages
Tomato Russet Mite, Tomato mite (En). Acariose bronzée de la tomate, Acarien de la tomate (Fr). Tomatenmilbe, Bronzenfleckenmilbe der Tomate (De). Tomatengalmijt (NI).

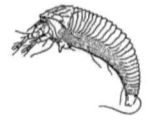

Tomato russet mite

Description
The tomato russet mite (Aculops lycopersici) is a species of mite. It is an important pest in tomato plants. Feeding on the foliage, inflorescence and young fruit of tomato plants causes shrivelling and necrosis of leaves, dropping of flowers, russeting of fruit and, if uncontrolled, death of the plants. Russet mites grow to a length of 1/5 mm and cannot be seen without a microscope or powerful hand lens. Due to their size, this pest is often only detected after substantial crop damage has occurred. They have slender, cone-shaped bodies that are cream, tan, or yellow in color, with only two pairs of legs located at the front. Russet mites do not produce webbing as spider mites do. Avoid treatments on the entire crop and instead carry out targeted applications on hot spots to avoid reducing the activity of auxiliaries and pollinators.

Symptoms
Shrivelling and necrosis of leaves, stems and fruits, Russeting of leaves, stems and fruits.

Vegetables
Eggplant, Pepper, Tomato.

Remedies: Immediate action
- Feltiella acarisuga. Predatory midge

- Wettable sulphur

- Liquid manure of fern

- Garlic macerate oil

- Nettle infusion

- Amblyseius/Neoseiulus californicus. Californicus Spider Mite

- Liquid manure of pyrethrum

- Black Soap

- Canola oil. Rapeseed oil. Plant oils

- Bacillus thuringiensis. Bt

- Transeius montdorensis. Predatory mite

Remedies: Proactive
- Lacewings Predators

Tuber Rot

Botanical name
Boeremia exigua var. exigua

Class
Didymellaceae, Fungi.

Names in other languages
Tuber Rot, Dry rot of potato (En). Gangrène, Pourriture sèche de la pomme de terre (Fr). Knollenfäule, Pustelfäule: Kartoffel, Trockenfäule: Kartoffel (De). Knolrot (Nl).

Potato tuber rot

Description
During the vegetative cycle, dark small marks (pycnidia) occur at the base of the stems and become visible after the wilting.When the tubers are lifted slightly depressed lesions can be noticed on the skin usually located at wounds, eyes or lenticels. During storage brown rot can be observed on a contaminated section ; its extension is rapid in the medullar area and slower in the cortical zone, it causes cavities in which mycelium develops.

Symptoms
Wilted plants

Vegetables
Potato.

Remedies: Immediate action
• Remove infested plants parts

Remedies: Proactive
• Long Rotation. Crop Rotation

• Use resistant varieties/cultivars

• Certified seed or plants

• Remove plant debris and crop residues

Turnip Flea Beetle
Large Striped Flea Beetle
Striped Turnip Flea Beetle

Botanical name
Phyllotreta atra. Phyllotreta nemorum

Class
Chrysomelidae, Insect

Names in other languages
Turnip Flea Beetle, Cabbage flea beetle (En). Altise des crucifères, Altise du chou (Fr). Schwarzer Erdfloh (De). Zwarte koolaardvlo (Nl).

Turnip flea beetle

Description
The turnip flea beetle (Phyllotreta atra) adults are active leaf-feeders that can, in large numbers, rapidly defoliate and kill plants. Symptoms of flea beetle feeding are small, rounded, irregular holes. Heavy feeding makes leaves look as if they had been peppered with fine shot. Flea beetles are so small that identifying them is tricky, though you can certainly catch a few with a yellow or white sticky trap and look at them with a magnifying glass. These crucifer flea beetles are among the first garden pests to appear in spring, with young seedlings of arugula, bok choy, Chinese cabbage, mustard, radishes and turnips at high risk for damage. Crucifer flea beetles prefer hairy or glossy leaves from plants in the mustard family, though they also can damage young broccoli or cabbage plants. A few flea beetles on fast-growing plants can be ignored, but unprotected seedlings can be so heavily damaged that the leaves appear to have been scorched. Flea beetles overwinter as adults, which emerge in early spring and lay eggs at the base of host plants, including wild mustard. By early May, garden plants are being threatened by overwintered flea beetles and a new generation, too.

Remedies: Immediate action
*   Insecticide based on pyrethrum

*   Black Soap

*   Long Rotation. Crop Rotation

*   Canola oil. Rapeseed oil. Plant oils

*   Kaolin clay spray

*   Spinosad

*   Beauveria bassiana

Remedies: Proactive
*   Chromatic trap (Yellow, White)

*   Insect-proof net. Insect net. Mesh Crop Cover

Symptoms
Leaves with irregular holes.

Vegetables
Cabbage, Cauliflower, Turnip.

Turnip Gall Weevil

Botanical name
Ceuthorynchus pleurostigma

Class
Curculionidae, Insect

Names in other languages
Turnip Gall Weevil, Cabbage gall weevil (En). Charançon gallicole du chou, Ceutorrhynque du chou (Fr). Kohlgallenrüssler (De). Galboorsnuitkever (Nl).

Description
The turnip gall weevil (*Ceuthorynchus pleurostigma*) is a small blackish-grey coleoptera. The weevil lay eggs in the brassicas, the eggs and larvae, due to substances introduced, cause hyperthophisation (a gall) of the collar. Do not confuse with cabbage hernia, which never contain a larval cell. Rove beetles prey on eggs and young maggots. Rove larvae parasitize the pupa stage of the maggot. The parasitic wasp *Trybliographa rapae* lays its eggs in the maggot larvae if the larvae are close enough to the soil surface.

Symptoms
Swelling of roots.

Vegetables
Brussels sprout, Cabbage, Cauliflower, Kohlrabi, Radish, Romanesco, Turnip.

Turnip gall weevil

Remedies: Immediate action
*   Tansy infusion

*   Heterorhabditis bacteriophora Nematode

*   Azadirachta. Neem oil insecticide

*   Pyrethrum insecticide

Remedies: Proactive
*   Insect-proof net. Insect net. Mesh Crop Cover

*   Install insect hotels, bug hotels or insect houses.

Turnip Maggot
Turnip Root Fly

Botanical name
Delia floralis

Class
Anthomyidae, Insect

Names in other languages
Turnip Maggot, Summer cabbage fly, Turnip root fly (En). Mouche du navet, Mineuse du radis, Mouche de la racine de la rave, Mouche du radis (Fr). Große Kohlfliege, Rettichfliege (De). Grote koolvlieg, Raapvlieg (Nl).

Description
The turnip root fly (Delia floralis) maggots are feeding on the roots and young plants die. However, older plants can often tolerate maggot activity, making early detection difficult because damage is not visible until after harvest. Some signs of maggots might include wilting, lighter green foliage than normal, and overall poor growth.

Symptoms
Presence of maggots.

Vegetables
Cabbage, Cauliflower, Radish, Turnip.

Turnip root fly adult and larvae (maggots)

Remedies: Immediate action
- Insecticide based on azadirachta. Neem oil

- Insecticide based on pyrethrum

Remedies: Proactive
- Insect-proof net. Insect net. Mesh Crop Cover

- Chromatic trap

- Install insect hotels, bug hotels or insect houses

Verticillium Wilt

Botanical name
Verticillium spp.

Class
Moniliaceae, Fungus

Names in other languages
Verticillium Wilt (En). Verticilliose (Fr). Verticillium-Welke (De). Verwelkingsziekte (Nl).

Description
Verticillium wilt is caused by fungus (*Verticillium species*). Plants may be infected for a while before symptoms become visible. Initial symptoms include wilting either the entire plant may wilt or only parts of the plant may wilt. The leaves soon begin to yellow then turn brown and die.

Symptoms
Leaves wilt, turn yellow than brown. Wilting of the entire plant.

Vegetables
Artichoke, Brussel sprout, Courgette, Cucumber, Eggplant, Pepper, Potato, Pumpkin, Tomato.

Verticillium wilt

Remedies: Immediate action
*   Bordeaux mixture

*   Eliminate the infected plants

*   Horsetail decoction

*   Liquid manure of nettle

*   Streptomyces lydicus

Remedies: Proactive
*   Soil solarization

*   Use resistant varieties/cultivars

*   Review irrigation. Watering

*   Long Rotation. Crop Rotation

Violet Root Rot

Botanical name
Helicobasidium brebissonii. Rhizoctonia violacea

Class
Auriculariaceae, Fungus

Names in other languages
Violet Root Rot, Root rot of asparagus, (En). Rhizoctone violet de la carotte, Rhizoctone violet du céleri (Fr). Violetterwurzeltöter (De). Violet wortelrot (Nl).

Violet root rot

Description
The violet root rot (Helicobasidium brebissonii. Rhizoctonia violaceae. R. crocorum) causes a thick mycelial weft and spores cover the root and appear as a purplish coloration and usually decay.

Symptoms
Purple to light brown stems.

Vegetables
Asparagus

Remedies: Immediate action
• Eliminate the infected plants

• Trichoderma

• Wettable sulphur

• Streptomyces lydicus

Remedies: Proactive
• Long rotation

White Rot
White Mold
Sclerotinia Wilt

Botanical name
Sclerotinia sclerotiorum

Class
Sclerotiniaceae, Fungus

Names in other languages
White mould, Watery soft rot, Storage rot, Stem rot, Stalk break, Seedling blight, Root rot, Cottony rot (En). Pourriture blanche,Pourriture du collet, Pourriture à sclérotes, sclérotiniose (Fr). Pelzfäule, Rapskrebs, Stengelfäule, Weißfäule (De). Witrot, Sclerotienrot (Nl).

Description
White rot is a fungus (Sclerotinia sclerotiorum) it provoke wilting of the leaves. Rot on the collar who can extend into the roots. A thick white mycelium covers the surface of the affected parts and large black sclerotia can be seen in the decaying tissues. Promoted by cool, damp weather, especially during dense canopy growth that maintains high humidity. Spores can easily spread to nearby plants under suitable conditions.

Symptoms
Wilting of leaves, Soft watery rot on lower leaves, Thick white mycelium.

Vegetables
Artichoke, Beetroot, Carrot, Celeriac, Celery, Courgette, Cucumber, Garlic, Green bean, Leek, Onion, Parsnip, Pepper, Peas, Pepper, Potato, Pumpkin, Tomato.

White rot

Remedies: Immediate action
- Review irrigation. Watering

- Eliminate the infected plants

- Horsetail decoction

- Bordeaux mixture

- Coniothyrium minitans

- Trichoderma

- Streptomyces lydicus

- Reynoutria sachalinensis extract

- Bacillus amyloliquefaciens bacterium

Remedies: Proactive
- Long rotation

Xanthomonas Disease of Artichoke

Botanical name
Xanthomonas cynarae

Class
Xanthomonadaceae, Bacterium

Names in other languages
Bacterial bract spot of artichoke, Xanthomonas Disease of Artichoke (En). Graisse de l'Artichaut (Fr). Bloemhoofdjesziekte (Nl).

Description
The Xanthomonas disease is provoked by a bacterium (*Xanthomonas cynarae*) it invades the bract within a few days entering through a wound. The symptoms occur in spring, on the flower head, which shows little water-soaked lesions exudating a yellowish mucus. The lesions on the flower bracts become dark brown. This bacteria only affects globular type artichokes (Camus and Castel). Xanthomonas are mainly disseminated by infected seeds or cuttings and can be further dispersed by wind and rain, or mechanically transferred during planting and cultivation.

Symptoms
Water-soaked lesions on leaves and flowers.

Vegetables
Artichoke.

Xanthomonas disease of artichoke

Remedies: Immediate action
- Bordeaux mixture

- Eliminate the infected plants

Remedies: Proactive
- Certified seed or plants

- Use resistant varieties/cultivars

Remedies

Amblydromalus limonicus Predatory mites

Botanical name
Amblydromalus limonicus

Class
Predators

English name
Amblydromalus limonicus Predatory mites

Names in other languages
Amblydromalus limonicus Predatory mites (En).
Amblydromalus limonicus acarien prédateur (Fr).
Amblydromalus limonicus Raubmilben (De).
Amblydromalus limonicus roofmijt (Nl).

Description
Amblydromalus limonicus is a highly effective predatory mite that plays a vital role in bolstering the biological control of common greenhouse pests such as whiteflies and thrips. Measuring less than 0.5mm in length, these minute predators feature a distinctive beige-pink hue and possess a droplet-shaped body with eight short legs.One of Amblydromalus limonicus' standout attributes is its rapid lifecycle, spanning just 7 to 10 days. This characteristic allows them to manage substantial pest populations swiftly and effectively. Female mites exhibit impressive reproductive capabilities, laying 2 to 4 oblong, transparent white eggs per day. These eggs develop into larvae within a mere 1 to 2 days, rapidly progressing to a stage where they can engage with and counter pest infestations.

Amblydromalus limonicus

Use on Vegetables
Courgette, Cucumber, Eggplant, Melon, Onion, Peas, Pepper, Tomatoes

Use for
Amblydromalus limonicus exhibits a diverse diet, targeting various pests such as thrips, whiteflies, spider mites, and even pollen. Notably, this predatory mite demonstrates a particular penchant for consuming the larvae of different thrips species during their first and second larval stages. Additionally, it efficiently preys on the eggs and larvae of glasshouse and cotton whiteflies.

How to use
Start introduction as soon as the first pests are detected in the crop. Introduction rates typically range from 50-250 per m2/release. Releases should be repeated once or twice, or until control is achieved. Amblydromalus limonicus is most effective at temperatures between 13 and 25°C (55 and 77°F). It is not effective above 30°C (86°F). *A. limonicus* is sensitive to relative humidity below 70%. Can be combined with Orius spp. and whitefly parasitoids. Do not combine with other generalist predatory mites (*Amblyseius swirskii, Neoseiulus cucumeris, Transeius montdorensis, Amblyseius andersoni*).

Warning
Amblydromalus limonicus has a very short life expectancy and therefore need to be introduced into the crop as soon as possible after receipt. Storing them for a period can have a negative impact on their quality.

Amblyseius californicus Spider Mite

Botanical name
Amblyseius californicus/Neoseiulus californicus

Class
Predators

English name
Californicus Spider Mite, Amblyseius californicus/ Neoseiulus californicus.

Names in other languages
Amblyseius/Neoseiulus Spider mite (En).
Amblyseius/Neoseiulus Tétranyque (Fr).
Amblyseius/Neoseiulus Rote Spinne (De).
Amblyseius/Neoseiulus Spint (Nl).

Description
Neoseiulus californicus is a predatory mite that feeds on Tetranychid mites. This species was first described on lemons from California under the name *Typhlodromus californicus* in 1954. The mite 0.04 mm long is pinkish red to pale white in colour with six legs. Males are smaller than females. The larvae are translucent. Females lay 2-4 eggs a day. Eggs take 1.5–4 days to hatch depending on temperatures. This species is found in California, Texas, Florida, Chile, Argentina, Japan, South Africa, parts of southern Europe, and all along the border of the Mediterranean Sea inhabiting fruiting and vegetable crops. This mites are known for their ability to actively hunt in conditions where prey is few and far between.

Amblyseius californicus

Use on Vegetables
Artichoke, Carrot, Courgette, Cucumber, Eggplant, Green Bean, Common Bean, Leek, Melon, Onion, Peas, Pepper, Pumpkin, Tomatoes

Use for
The Californicus spider mite is used for the prevention, control, and management of various spider mites: Tomato Russet Mite, Red Spider Mite, Two-spotted Mite, European Red Mite.

How to use
The Californicus Spider Mite (Neoseiulus californicus) can be bought online and introduced in greenhouses, preventive and curative. They are active in high temperature and under dry conditions. In case you made any treatments, it is often necessary to wait a few days or weeks to release auxiliary organisms.

Warning
Natural predators are living organisms and needs to be introduced in the garden or glasshouse as soon as possible after receiving them.

Aphelinus Predatory Wasp

Botanical name
Aphelinus abdominalis

Class
Predators

English name
Aphelinus Predatory Wasp

Names in other languages:
Aphelinus predatory wasp (En). Aphelinus guêpes parasites (Fr). Aphelinus parasitische Wespe (De). Aphelinus sluipwesp (Nl).

Description
Aphelinus abdominalis (Aphelinus) is a parasitoid wasp which attacks over 200 species of aphids. Aphelinus wasps are about 3mm long and black with a yellowish-brown abdomen. The legs and antennae are relatively short. Although winged, they are not strong fliers. Males are slightly smaller and darker. The female lays eggs singly into mid age nymphal stages of target aphids. The egg hatches after 2-3 days and the larva feeds on the aphid without immediately killing it. At 20 °C, it pupates after 7 days and transforms the aphid into a distinctive black 'mummy'. Mummies first appear 2-3 weeks after introduction. The adult wasp chews a rough exit hole in the back to emerge 8 days later. Oviposition starts after 3-4 days. Direct killing through predatory feeding on non-parasitised younger nymphs, is also significant. Aphelinus has a relatively long life and oviposition period of several weeks and can lay 5-10 eggs/day.

Aphelinus abdominalis

Used on Vegetables
Aphelinus can be used on all crops where aphids are present. It is primarily used in greenhouse production, but can also be used in field crops. Cucumber, Eggplant, Pepper, Bell Pepper, Potato, Tomatoes.

How to use
Aphelinus works best when used preventatively, or when aphids are first noticed in the crop. It is not a good disperser so needs to be placed near aphid colonies for maximum efficacy. If aphid numbers are already high it is advisable to use a repellent to lower the aphid population prior to release.

Warning
Natural predators are living organisms and needs to be introduced in the garden or glasshouse as soon as possible after receiving them.

Aphidius colemani Predatory Wasp

Botanical name
Aphidius colemani

Class
Predators

English name
Aphidius colemani Predatory Wasp

Names in other languages:
Aphidius colemani predatory wasp (En). Aphidius colemani guêpes parasites (Fr). Aphidius colemani parasitische Wespe (De). Aphidius colemani sluipwesp (Nl).

Description
Aphidius colemani predatory wasps are about 2-3 mm long and black with brown legs. They look very similar to a small black ant with wings, but the antennae are long and slender. The parasite deposits an egg into the aphid in a matter of seconds. The aphid continues to move and feed for 3 days after the egg has been deposited. When the egg hatches, the Aphidius larva begins feeding on the aphid, eventually killing it. The parasitoid develops within the aphid body which at this stage is called a "mummy". The mummy looks like an over inflated bronze aphid. The Aphidius chews a hole through the back of the mummy and emerges as an adult wasp ready to deposit eggs in live aphids. Complete development time is temperature dependent, but is about 12 days at 25°C. This is longer than the development time of aphids, but each Aphidius female can parasitise over 300 aphids in her lifetime which can last 2-3 weeks when food and water are available.

Aphidius colemani

Use on Vegetables
Carrot, Lettuce, Melon, Pepper, Bell Pepper, Potato, Spinach, Tomatoes.

Use for
Aphidius will parasitise many aphid species including the green peach aphid (*Myzus persicae*) and the cotton or melon aphid (*Aphis gossypii*)

How to use
Aphidius colemani are all natural aphid parasites and very useful and effective for the prevention and low-infestation management of various aphid species. The Aphidius-wasps are best used for preventing the establishment of more than 40 species of aphids. They can also tackle light to medium infestations. And, if established, they can adequately protect a crop throughout the season.

Warning
Natural predators are living organisms and needs to be introduced in the garden or glasshouse as soon as possible after receiving them.

Yellow sticky traps used for monitoring pests will also trap Aphidius. If yellow traps are necessary for monitoring whitefly, do not release Aphidius near the yellow traps, and use no more than 1 yellow card per 100 plants. Aphidius are not attracted to blue sticky traps (which can be used for monitoring thrips where Aphidius is being released).

Aphidius matricariae Predatory Wasp

Botanical name
Aphidius matricariae

Class
Predators

English name
Aphidius matricariae predatory wasp

Names in other languages
Aphidius matricariae predatory wasp (En). Aphidius matricariae guêpe parasite (Fr). Aphidius matricariae parasitische Wespe (De). Aphidius matricariae sluipwesp (Nl).

Description
The adult Aphidius matricariae is black with brown legs. This parasitoid wasp has long antennae and is approximately 2-3 mm long. After mating, the female lays her eggs inside juvenil or adult aphids. Aphidius matricariae larvae develops and feeds on the internal organs of the aphid. After 7 days, the aphid becomes immobile, swells and turn beige and become a "mummy". A new adult emerges from the parasitised aphid after a few days.

Aphidius matricariae

Used on Vegetables
Artichoke, Beetroot, Beet. Broad Bean, Carrot, Chard, Citrus Green Bean, Common Bean, Peas, Potato

Used for
The predatory wasp Aphidius matricariae suppresses effectively aphids even faster than the more common parasitic wasps. It targets in particular the tobacco aphid (Myzus persicae nicotianae) and peach potato aphid (Myzus persicae persicae). Bean Aphids. Black Dolphin Aphids, Black Citrus Aphid

How to use
Purchase from biocontrol companies and follow instructions for release. It is advised to use Aphidius matricariae in prevention. Aphidius wasps can be used together with the Aphid predatory midge *Aphidoletes aphidimyza.*

Warning
Yellow sticky traps used for monitoring pests will also trap Aphidius. If yellow traps are necessary for monitoring whitefly, do not release Aphidius near the yellow traps, and use no more than 1 yellow card per 100 plants. Aphidius are not attracted to blue sticky traps (which can be used for monitoring thrips where Aphidius is being released).

Apply Mulch or Straw

Class
Cultural control practices

English name
Apply mulch or straw

Names in other languages
Apply mulch or straw (En). Appliquer du paillis ou de la paille (Fr). Mulch oder Stroh auftragen (De). Breng mulch of stro aan (Nl).

Description
Mulches can play a surprising role in pest control and soil health. Organic mulch, such as wood chips, cover crop residues, or straw, can reduce thrips and leaf miner numbers significantly. Additionally, organic mulch (e.g. wood mulch) can reduce foliar fungal pathogens by mitigating soil splashing and, therefore, preventing spores from reaching the leaves. Organic mulches also help to conserve soil moisture and increase beneficial soil organisms that play a role in nutrient cycling and biocontrol, which results in a significantly greater yield.

Used on Vegetables
Artichoke, Asparagus, Beetroot, Beet, Broad Bean, Broccoli, Brussels Sprout, Cabbage, Carrot, Cauliflower, Celeriac, Celery, Chard, Courgette, Cucumber, Eggplant, Fennel, Green Bean, Common Bean, Kohlrabi, Leek, Lettuce, Melon, Napa/Chinese Cabbage, Onion, Peas, Pepper, Bell Pepper, Potato, Pumpkin, Radish, Romanesco Broccoli, Rutabaga, Spinach, Sweet Corn , Tomatoes, Turnip.

Used for
Colorado Potato Beatle, Cercosporosa Leaf Spot, Bright-line Brown-eyes Moth and many other pests and diseases..

How to use
There are many different types of mulches that you can use in your vegetable garden. The best mulch for your vegetable garden is the type that is readily available to you and works with your garden management practices. Straw is widely used for mulching vegetable gardens. Its loose structure usually allows for plenty of airflow while reducing light infiltration to the soil. It is also readily available and inexpensive. To effectively prevent "weeds" from growing, mulch layers need to be 5 – 10 cm thick. This provides an adequate reduction of light to prevent many seeds from germinating and creates a layer thick enough so that many seedlings will expend all available stored energy trying to grow through the layer up toward the light. Ensure that the mulch is not in direct contact with any of the stems of your plants. Leave an air gap to keep your plants growing healthy and strong.

Association with another Crop or Culture

Class
Cultural control practices

English name
Association with another crop or culture.
Companion culture

Names in other languages
Association with another crop (En). Culture
associée (Fr). Assoziation mit einer kultur (De).
Tussengewas (Nl).

Description
Companion planting is based on the principle that
certain plants can attract or repel insects or
provide beneficial support to other plants. It can
also work the other way around where one plant
can be detrimental to another's growth. Rotation
and use of companion plants are part of biological
pest control strategies.

Used on Vegetables
Broccoli, Brussels Sprout, Cabbage, Carrot,
Cauliflower, Celeriac, Celery, Fennel, Kohlrabi,
Lettuce, Napa/Chinese Cabbage, Parsnip, Potato,
Radish, Romanesco Broccoli, Rutabaga, Turnip

Used for
Carrot Fly, Celery Fly, Potato Tuber Nematode,
Potato Cyst Nematode, Cabbageworm, Imported
Cabbage Worms, Bean Bruchid, Cabbage Bug,
Rape Bug, Crucifer Shield Bug, Brassica Bug,
Lettuce Aphid. Current-lettuce Aphid, Diamond-
back Moth.

How to use
Beneficial and antagonist vegetables associations
tables can be find in books and on the internet.

Azadirachta Insecticide

Botanical name
Azadirachta indica

Class
Insecticide

English name
Insecticide based on azadirachta. Neem oil

Names in other languages
Insecticide based on azadirachta. Neem oil (En).
Insecticide à base d'azadirachta. L'huile de neem.
Neem insecticide (Fr). Neembaums Extrakt
Insektizid (De). Neemboomolie spuitmiddel (Nl).

Description
Neem products are derived from the Neem tree
(*Azadirachta indica*). Neem pesticide products are
usually made by crushing neem tree seeds, and
then using water or a solvent, such as alcohol, to
extract the pesticidal constituents. Neem extracts
have been shown to affect over 200 insect
species, including some species of white flies,
thrips, leafminers, caterpillars, aphids, scales,
beetles, true bugs, and mealybugs.

Azadirachta indica

Used on Vegetables
Artichoke, Asparagus, Beetroot, Beet, Broad
Bean, Broccoli, Brussels Sprout, Cabbage,
Carrot, Cauliflower, Celeriac, Celery, Chard,
Courgette, Cucumber, Eggplant, Fennel, Green
Bean, Common Bean, Kohlrabi, Leek, Lettuce,
Melon, Napa/Chinese Cabbage, Onion, Peas,
Pepper, Bell Pepper, Potato, Pumpkin, Radish,
Romanesco Broccoli, Rutabaga, Spinach, Sweet
Corn , Tomatoes, Turnip.

Used for
Southern Green Stink bug, Thistle Aphid,
Cabbage Aphid, Potato Aphid, Cotton Aphid,
Grain Aphid, Hawthorn Aphids, Beet Armyworm,
Bean Bruchid, Pea Aphid, Green Pea Louse,
Asparagus Aphid, Green Artichoke Aphid, Turnip
Maggot, Turnip Root Fly, Pea Thrips, Celery Miner
Fly, Lettuce Aphid, Current-lettuce Aphid,
Artichoke Root Aphid, Daisy-root Aphid.

How to use
Follow product label. Neem oil is practically non-
toxic to birds, mammals, bees and plants. Neem
oil is slightly toxic to fish and other aquatic
organisms. Azadirachtin, a component of neem
oil, is moderately toxic to fish and other aquatic
animals. It is important to remember that insects
must eat the treated plant to be killed. Therefore,
bees and other pollinators are not likely to be
harmed.

Bacillus amyloliquefaciens

Botanical name
Bacillus amyloliquefaciens

Class
Biopesticide

English name
Bacillus amyloliquefaciens bacterium

Names in other languages
Bacillus amyloliquefaciens bacterium (En). Bactérie Bacillus amyloliquefaciens (Fr). Bacillus amyloliquefaciens Bakterium (De). Bacillus amyloliquefaciens bacterie (Nl).

Description
Bacillus amyloliquefaciens bacterium is a broad-spectrum preventive biofungicide and bactericide. It utilizes the power of a naturally occurring beneficial bacterium, to control and suppress fungal and bacterial diseases in plants. This bacterium triggers the plant's immune response to fight off pathogens. It will also colonise plant roots, which prevents fungi and bacteria from establishing there. *Bacillus amyloliquefaciens* biofungicide is used to fight root pathogens such as *Ralstonia solanacearum*, *Pythium*, *Rhizoctonia solani*, *Alternaria tenuissima* and *Fusarium* as well it improve root tolerance to salt stress.

Used on Vegetables
Artichoke, Beetroot, Beet, Carrot, Celeriac, Celery, Courgette, Cucumber, Garlic, Green Bean, Common Bean, Leek, Onion, Parsnip, Peas, Pepper, Bell Pepper, Potato, Pumpkin, Spinach, Tomatoes,

Used for
Cladosporium Leaf Spot. White rot, White mold, Soft rot.

How to use
Bacillus amyloliquefaciens bacterium can be used as a foliar spray and as a soil drench. For top to bottom disease control, use it both ways. You can apply indoors or outdoors, but should only use it as a soil treatment on indoor plants.

Bacillus subtilis

Botanical name
Bacillus subtilis

Class
Biopesticide

English name
Bacillus subtilis preparation

Names in other languages
Bacillus subtilis preparation (En). Préparation de Bacillus subtilis (Fr). Zubereitung aus Bacillus subtilis (De). Preparaat Bacillus subtilis (Nl).

Description
Bacillus subtilis inhibits plant pathogen spore germination, disrupts germ tube growth, and interferes with the attachment of the pathogen to the plant. It is also reported to induce systemic acquired resistance (SAR) against bacterial pathogens.

Used on Vegetables
Artichoke, Asparagus, Beetroot, Beet, Broad Bean, Broccoli, Brussels Sprout, Cabbage, Carrot, Cauliflower, Celeriac, Celery, Chard, Courgette, Cucumber, Eggplant, Fennel, Garlic, Green Bean, Common Bean, Kohlrabi, Lamb's Lettuce, Leek, Lettuce, Napa/Chinese Cabbage, Onion, Parsnip, Pepper, Bell Pepper, Potato, Pumpkin, Radish, Romanesco Broccoli, Rutabaga, Spinach, Sweet Corn, Tomatoes, Turnip.

Used for
Gray Mold. Grey Mould. Botrytis Blight, Early Blight of Potato/Tomato, Anthracnose Fruit Rot, Bacterial Spot, Rust, Downy Mildew of Crucifers, Powdery Mildew, Anthracnose of Cucurbits, Botrytis Rot, Neckrot, Soft rot. White Rot on Carrot, Cottony rot, Tomato Corky Root, Downy mildew of Cucurbits, Ascochyta Foot-rot, Pinodella Blight on Pea, Ring Spot on Lettuce, Anthracnose.

How to use
Bacillus subtilis preparation can be used as a foliar spray and soil drench on ornamentals, trees, shrubs, flowering plants and greenhouse crops and vegetables grown under cover.

Bacillus thuringiensis

Bt

Botanical name
Bacillus thuringiensis

Class
Biopesticide

English name
Bacillus thuringiensis. Bt

Names in other languages
Bacillus thuringiensis (En). Idem (Fr). Idem (De). Idem (Nl).

Description
Bacillus thuringiensis (or Bt) is a Gram-positive, soil-dwelling bacterium, commonly used as a biological pesticide. *Bacillus thuringiensis* (Bt) proteins are allowed in organic farming as a insecticide because Bt is a natural, non-pathogenic bacterium that is found naturally in the soil. Bt has also been found to be safe to all higher animals tested.

Used on Vegetables
Artichoke, Asparagus, Beetroot, Beet, Broccoli, Brussels Sprout, Cabbage, Cauliflower, Celery, Cucumber, Eggplant, Garlic, Kohlrabi, Leek, Lettuce, Napa/Chinese Cabbage, Onion, Pepper, Bell Pepper, Potato, Radish, Romanesco Broccoli, Rutabaga, Spinach, Sweet Corn, Tomatoes, Turnip.

Used for
Tomato Russet Mite, Artichoke Moth. Artichoke Plume Moth, Leek Moth. Onion Moth, Colorado Potato Beetle, Dark Sword-grass Moth. Black cutworm. Greasy cutworm, June Beetles, May Beetles, European Corn Borer. Maize Pyralid,Cabbageworm. Imported Cabbage Worms, Silver-Y moth. Common Silver-Y moth, Cabbage Army Moth, Beet Armyworm, Tent Caterpillars, Cabbage Bug. Rape Bug. Crucifer Shield Bug. Brassica Bug, Tomato Fruitworm, Old World Bollworm, South American Miner Fly, South American Leaf Miner, Potato Tuberworm, Potato Split-worm, Potato Tuber Moth, Diamond-back Moth, Cotton Worm, African Cotton Leafworm.

How to use
Bt products are commonly sprays, dusts, granules, and pellets. Apply Bt products that are approved for use in organic agriculture. Always follow label instructions and take steps to avoid exposure.

Bait based on Bran and Pyrethrum

Botanical name
Tanacetum cinerariifolium

Class
Cultural control practices

English name
Bait based on bran and pyrethrum

Names in other languages
Bait based on bran and pyrethrum (En). Appât au son de blé et pyrèthre (Fr). Lockmittel Kleie und Pyrethrum (De). Lokmiddel gebaseerd op zemelen en pyrethrum (Nl).

Description
Baits are traps prepared with molasses, bran, water and pyrethrum powder. Traditionally, dried ground flowers from pyrethrum *(Tanacetum cinerariifolium)* have been used to make dusts and sprays.

Used on Vegetables
Artichoke, Beetroot, Beet, Broccoli, Brussels Sprout, Cabbage, Cauliflower, Eggplant, Kohlrabi, Leek, Lettuce, Napa/Chinese Cabbage, Onion, Potato, Radish, Romanesco Broccoli, Rutabaga, Spinach, Turnip.

Used for
Artichoke Moth, Artichoke Plume Moth, Dark Sword-grass Moth, Black cutworm, Greasy cutworm. March Crane Fly, Silver-Y moth, Common Silver-Y moth, Cabbage Army Moth.

How to use
Example given a bait for cutworms. Mix 100 grams (g) of bran, 10 g of sugar, 200 g of water, 5 g of pyrethrum powder. Spread around the base of the plants protected from the rain in jars or bottles.

Warning
When handling or making or using pyrethrum based products always wear gloves, goggles and a mask over the nose and mouth.

Beauveria bassiana

Botanical name
Beauveria bassiana

Class
Biopesticide

English name
Beauveria fungus

Names in other languages
Beauveria fungus (En). Beauveria champignon entomopathogène (Fr). Insektenparasitischen Pilz Beauveria (De). Beauveria schimmel (Nl).

Description
Beauveria bassiana, a beneficial fungus, it can control a wide variety of soft-bodied insects in greenhouse, field and nursery crops such as Whiteflies, Thrips, Aphids, Psyllids, Mealybugs, scarab beetles and Weevils. The insect disease caused by the fungus is a muscardine which has been called white muscardine disease. When the microscopic spores of the fungus come into contact with the body of an insect host, they germinate, penetrate the cuticle, and grow inside, killing the insect within a matter of days. Afterwards, a white mold emerges from the cadaver and produces new spores.

Used on Vegetables
Artichoke, Asparagus, Beetroot, Beet, Broad Bean, Broccoli, Brussels Sprout, Cabbage, Carrot , Cauliflower, Celeriac, Celery, Chard, Courgette, Cucumber, Eggplant, Fennel, Garlic, Green Bean, Common Bean, Kohlrabi, Leek, Lettuce, Melon, Napa/Chinese Cabbage, Onion, Pepper, Bell Pepper, Potato, Pumpkin, Radish, Romanesco Broccoli, Rutabaga, Spinach, Sweet Corn, Tomatoes, Turnip.

Used for
Thistle Aphid, Dark Sword-grass Moth, Black cutworm, Greasy cutworm, Cabbage Aphid, Bean Aphids, Black Dolphin Aphids, Potato Aphid, Cotton Aphid, Grain Aphid, Onion Thrips, Thrips, Bean Beetle, Pea beetle, Pea Weevil. Pea and Bean Weevil, Bean Bruchid, Pea Aphid, Green Pea Louse, Asparagus Aphid, Green Artichoke Aphid, Pea Thrips, Lettuce Aphid, Current-lettuce Aphid, Artichoke Root Aphid, Daisy-root Aphid, Beet Moth.

How to use
Beauveria bassiana should be used as prevention rather than a cure. Due to the infection incubation period, it takes several days to kill pests. The best practice is to start foliar applications at the beginning of the season, when you receive the plants, or on cuttings before pests first appear. You can even do soakings. *Beauveria bassiana* spores are very sensitive to UV rays. For this reason, apply this product in the late afternoon or evening. You can also do foliar application on cloudy or rainy days.

Beauveria brongniartii

Botanical name
Beauveria brongniartii

Class
Biopesticide

English name
Beauveria brongniartii fungus

Names in other languages
Beauveria brongniartii fungus (En). Fungi Beauveria brongniartii (Fr). Beauveria brongniartii Pilz (De). Beauveria brongniartii schimmel (Nl).

Description
The fungus Beauveria brongniartii is a pathogen which occurs naturally in soils. It is commonly isolated from larvae and adults of Otiorhynchus spp.

Used on Vegetables
Asparagus, Beetroot, Beet, Broccoli, Cabbage, Cauliflower, Celery, Courgette, Cucumber, Eggplant, Green Bean, Common Bean, Leek, Lettuce, Onion, Pepper, Bell Pepper, Potato, Pumpkin, Spinach, Sweet Corn, Tomatoes, Turnip.

Used for
The fungus *Beauveria brongniartii* can be used specifically against white grubs. Glasshouse Whitefly, Greenhouse Whitefly, June Beetles, May Beetles, Onion Thrips, Thrips, Beet Armyworm.

How to use
Incorporated in to the soil. or pot ground.

Beer Traps

Class
Cultural control practices

English name
Beer traps

Names in other languages
Beer traps (En). Pièges à bière (Fr). Bierfallen (De).
Biervallen (Nl).

Description
Slugs and snails are attracted to the yeasty, fermented odor of beer and even prefer it to the fresh smell of your growing plants. Beer traps – fill saucers or jars with beer and place around the garden at soil level. Snails and slugs will be attracted to the beer and end up drowning in it. To be effective you need to keep the traps fresh by cleaning out the dead bodies regularly and replacing the beer.

Beer traps

Used on Vegetables
Beetroot, Celeriac, Celery, Chard, Cucumber, Lettuce, Peas, Spinach.

Used for
Slugs and snails.

How to use
Place these traps about every square meter in the areas where you're seeing slug activity. If you don't have access to cheap beer or would simply rather concoct your own substitute, here's a formula that works just as well. Mix these ingredients and pour the liquid into your traps. You can add a touch of honey, and these measurements don't need to be exact: 1 tablespoon (15 ml.) yeast, 1 tablespoon (15 ml.) flour, 1 tablespoon (15 ml.) sugar, 1 cup (237 ml.) water

Bicarbonate of Potassium or Sodium

Class
Fungicide

English name
Bicarbonate of potassium or sodium. Potassium bicarbonate

Names in other languages
Bicarbonate of potasium or sodium (En). Bicarbonate de sodium (Fr). Natriumbicarbonat (De). Natriumbicarbonaat (Nl).

Description
Potassium bicarbonate can be used as a contact fungicide against powdery mildew disease in a variety of crops, e.g. grapevine, pome and stone fruit, berries and soft fruit, vegetables and cereals.

Bicarbonate of potassium

Used on Vegetables
Broccoli, Brussels Sprout, Cabbage, Carrot, Cauliflower, Courgette, Cucumber, Eggplant, Garlic, Green Bean, Common Bean, Kohlrabi, Leek, Melon, Napa/Chinese Cabbage, Onion, Parsnip, Peas, Pepper, Bell Pepper, Potato, Pumpkin, Radish, Romanesco Broccoli, Rutabaga, Spinach, Sweet Corn, Tomatoes, Turnip.

Used for
Early Blight of Potato/Tomato, Anthracnose Fruit Rot, Downy Mildew of Alliums, Downy Mildew of Crucifers, Botrytis Rot. Neckrot, Powdery Mildew, Downy mildew of Cucurbits, Downy mildew. Spinach Downy Mildew. Bleu Mold, Pea Downy Mildew, Powdery mildew.

How to use
Potassium bicarbonate is effective at 10 g/L when used as preventive sprays at 10 days interval. Several studies have shown much better efficacy against powdery mildew when oils are added to bicarbonate products, typically at the rate of 0.5-1.0%

Biofumigation

Mustard

Class
Cultural control practices

English name
Biofumigation

Names in other languages
Biofumigation (En). Biofumigation (Fr).
Biofumigation (De). Biofumigatie (Nl).

Description
Biofumigation involves incorporating cultivated plants (especially mustard) into the soil to combat certain organisms: most commonly nematodes, various soil-borne diseases, and weed seeds. The decomposition of biofumigant plants produces gaseous compounds toxic to these organisms. Biofumigant compounds are emitted within the first few minutes of shredding mustard or other cruciferous plants. It is therefore crucial that the soil be incorporated immediately after this step. The penetration of volatile compounds is improved if the soil is sealed with plastic mulch or compacted with a roller. Furthermore, the soil must be moist to promote biofumigation. It is therefore important not to carry out the incorporation in dry weather or to plan for irrigation.

Used on Vegetables
Celery, Courgette, Cucumber, Eggplant, Parsley, Potato. Pumpkin.

Used for
Nematodes, Black scurf, Rhictonia camker

How to use
Biostimulant bacteria (such as Trichoderma harzanium and Coniothyrium minitans) are favored by biofumigation, demonstrating that the beneficial effects of biofumigation go beyond the direct consequence by influencing several aspects of integrated management. Biofumigant plants also constitute a form of green manure.

Plants used for incorporation are mostly Brassicas like mustard and radish, also sorghum and sorghum-sudan grass can be used.

Black Soap

Black soap

Class
Insecticide

English name
Black Soap. Marseille soap

Names in other languages
Black Olive Soap. Marseille soap (EN), Savon noir à l'huile d'olive. Savon de Marseille (FR), Zwarte zeep op basis van olijfolie. Marseille zeep (NL).

Description
Black soap made from olive oil is a effective spray to protect your plants from greenfly, mealybugs, red spider mite. It can be added to other plant sprays to increase efficiency and to clean plants from honeydew and sooty mould.

Used on Vegetables
Asparagus, Beetroot, Beet, Broad Bean, Broccoli, Brussels Sprout, Cabbage, Carrot, Cauliflower, Celeriac, Celery, Chard, Courgette, Cucumber, Eggplant, Fennel, Green Bean, Common Bean, Kohlrabi, Leek, Lettuce, Melon, Napa/Chinese Cabbage, Onion, Peas, Pepper, Bell Pepper, Potato, Pumpkin, Radish, Romanesco Broccoli, Rutabaga, Spinach, Sweet Corn, Tomatoes, Turnip.

Used for
Glasshouse Whitefly. Greenhouse Whitefly, Southern Green Stink bug, Tomato Russet Mite, Thistle Aphid, Asparagus Beetle. Twelve-spotted Asparagus Beetle, Cabbage Stem Flea Beetle, Cabbage Aphid, Lettuce Root Aphid, Bean Aphids. Black Dolphin Aphids, Potato Aphid, Cotton Aphid, Grain Aphid, Onion Thrips, Thrips, Red Spider Mite, Two-spotted Mite, Rust Mite, Pea Aphid, Green Pea Louse.

How to use
Dilute 5 tablespoons of liquid olive oil black soap in 1l of lukewarm water. Leave to cool. Spray all over the infested plants making sure you cover the upper and underside of the leaves. Spray in the morning well before the hottest time of day, or in the evening. Repeat several times, if necessary.

Bordeaux Mixture

Class
Fungicide

English name
Bordeaux Mixture

Names in other languages
Bordeaux mixture (En). Bouillie bordelaise (Fr).
Bordeauxbrühe (De). Bordeauxse pap (Nl).

Description
Bordeaux mixture is a blue-colored fungicide
prepared from copper and lime. This powder or
spray acts as a fungicide with insecticidal and
insect repellant properties and can offer control of
anthracnose, bacterial wilt, rust, powdery mildew,
and fire blight. It should only be used as last resort
solution.

Bordeaux mixture

Used on Vegetables
Artichoke, Asparagus, Beetroot, Beet, Broad
Bean, Broccoli, Brussels Sprout, Cabbage,
Carrot, Cauliflower, Celeriac, Celery, Chard,
Courgette, Cucumber, Eggplant, Fennel, Garlic,
Green Bean, Common Bean, Kohlrabi, Lamb's
Lettuce, Leek, Lettuce, Melon, Napa/Chinese
Cabbage, Onion, Parsnip, Peas, Pepper, Bell
Pepper, Potato, Pumpkin, Radish, Romanesco
Broccoli, Rutabaga, Spinach, Sweet Corn,
Tomatoes, Turnip.

Used for
Gray Mold. Grey Mould. Botrytis Blight, Early
Blight of Potato/Tomato, Anthracnose Fruit Rot,
Bacterial Spot, Ramularia Leaf and Bract Spot,
Ascochyta Rot, Black Rot, Leaf Spot, Bacterial
Canker of Tomato, Xanthomonas Disease of
Artichoke, Onion and Leek Rust, White Rot. White
Mold. Sclerotinia Wilt, Skin Blotch of Garlic,
Downy Mildew of Alliums, Rust, Verticillium Wilt,
Downy Mildew of Crucifers, Celery Late Blight ,
Powdery Mildew, Anthracnose of Cucurbits, Scab
of Cucurbits, Cercosporosa Leaf Spot, Bacterial
Brown Spot, Late Blight. Potato and Tomato Late
Blight, Black Rot of Cabbage

How to use:
Refer to product label for detailed instructions.

Canola Oil

Class
Insecticide

English name
Canola oil. Rapeseed oil. Plant oils

Names in other languages
Canola oil. Rapeseed oil (En). Huile de Colza, Canola, Huiles végétales (Fr). Rapsöl (De). Koolzaadolie (Nl).

Rapeseed

Description
Canola, like other vegetable oils, is safe for most plants and won't harm humans or pets. The effects of canola oil differ, depending on the pest. Insecticidal oils kill insects on contact by disrupting respiration, cell membrane function or structure. They also kill them by disrupting their feeding on oil-covered surfaces. Their toxic action is more physical than chemical and is short-lived. They are most commonly used against mites, aphids, whiteflies, thrips, mealybugs and scale insects.

Used on Vegetables
Artichoke, Asparagus, Beetroot, Beet, Broad Bean, Broccoli, Brussels Sprout, Cabbage, Carrot, Cauliflower, Celeriac, Celery, Courgette, Cucumber, Eggplant, Fennel, Green Bean, Common Bean, Kohlrabi, Leek, Lettuce, Melon, Napa/Chinese Cabbage, Onion, Peas, Pepper, Bell Pepper, Potato, Pumpkin, Radish, Romanesco Broccoli, Rutabaga, Spinach, Sweet Corn, Tomatoes, Turnip.

Used for
Glasshouse Whitefly, Greenhouse Whitefly, Tomato Russet Mite, Thistle Aphid, Cabbage Aphid, Lettuce Root Aphid, Green Peach Aphid, Potato Aphid, Cotton Aphid, Grain Aphid, Onion Thrips, Thrips, Asparagus Aphid, Green Artichoke Aphid, Pea Thrips

How to use
Combine 1 cup of canola oil and 1 tablespoon of mild liquid dish soap. Fill a spray bottle with 1 cup of water. Add 1 or 2 teaspoons of the oil-soap mixture to the water. Put the lid on the bottle and shake well to evenly distribute the ingredients. Spray plants with oil on a dry day.

Cabbage Collars

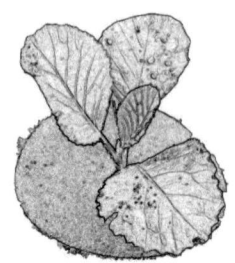

Class
Cultural control practices

English name
Cardboard. Cabbage Collars

Names in other languages
Cabbage Collars (En). Collerettes carrés de carton (Fr). Wellpappenhülsen (De). Koolkragen (Nl).

Description
To keep cabbage root maggots from decimating your cabbages, make simple collars to prevent adult flies from laying eggs. They can be bought from garden centres but are easy to make yourself.

Cabbage collars

Used on Vegetables
Broccoli, Brussels Sprout, Cabbage, Cauliflower, Kohlrabi, Napa/Chinese Cabbage, Radish, Romanesco Broccoli, Rutabaga, Turnip.

Used for
Cabbage Maggot.

How to use
You can easily make your own collars by cutting a square or circle of thick cardboard and then cutting a cross in the middle where the stem will go. As the stem grows it can expand because of the cross in the middle. Place each collar around the stem immediately after planting the cabbages.

Certified Seed or Plants

Class
Cultural control practices

English name
Certified seed or plants

Names in other languages
Certified seed or plants (En). Semences ou plantes certifiées (Fr). Zertifiziertes Saat- und Pflanzgut (De). Gecertificeerd zaad en plantgoed (Nl).

Description
Seed and plant certification is to supply high quality seed or plants, which are true to identity, high in purity and germination capacity and free from certain pests and diseases. If you have the choice prefer certified organic planting or seeding material.

Used on Vegetables
Artichoke, Asparagus, Beetroot, Beet, Broad Bean, Broccoli, Brussels Sprout, Cabbage, Carrot , Cauliflower, Celeriac, Celery, Chard, Courgette, Cucumber, Eggplant, Garlic, Green Bean, Common Bean, Kohlrabi, Leek, Lamb's Lettuce, Leek, Lettuce, Melon, Napa/Chinese Cabbage, Onion, Parsnip, Peas, Pepper, Bell Pepper, Potato, Pumpkin, Radish, Romanesco Broccoli, Spinach, Sweet Corn, Tomatoes, Turnip.

Used for
Early Blight of Potato/Tomato, Anthracnose Fruit Rot, Bacterial Spot, Xanthomonas Disease of Artichoke, Penicillium Decay. Seed Clove Decay. Bleu Mold, Bacterial Blight of Garlic, Skin Blotch of Garlic, Downy Mildew of Alliums, Stem Nematode. Bulb and Stem Nematode, Brachyserus of Garlic, Tobacco Mosaic Virus. TMV, Celery Late Blight , Anthracnose of Cucurbits, Scab of Cucurbits, Maize Smut. Corn Smut, Cercosporosa Leaf Spot, Phoma, Cladosporium Leaf Spot, Bacterial Brown Spot , Onion Smut. Smut of Onion, Pea Weevil. Pea and Bean Weevil, Black Scurf. Rhizoctonia Canker. Stem Canker, Potato Tuber Nematode. Potato Cyst Nematode, Potato Scab, Bean Bruchid, Potato Tuberworm. Potato Split-worm. Potato Tuber Moth, Black Rot of Cabbage, Xanthomonas Disease of Strawberry Strawberry Bacterial Angular Leaf Spot Disease, Bacterial Blight. Pea Bacterial Blight, Potato Leaf-drop Streak. Potato Virus Y , Potato Leaf Roll Virus, Potato Virus X, Celery Root Rot, Ascochyta Foot-rot. Pinodella Blight on Pea, Pea Downy Mildew, Pea Seed-borne Mosaic Virus, Ring Spot on Lettuce. Anthracnose, Lettuce mosaic virus, Black Leg. Crucifer Collar Rot.

How to use
Ask your provider for organic certified seeds and plants free from pests and diseases.

Chamomile

Matricaria chamomilla

Botanical name
Chamaemelum nobile/Matricaria chamomilla

Class
Repellent

English name
Chamomile

Names in other languages
Chamomile infusion (En). Infusion de camomille (Fr). Kamille infusion (De). Kamille infusie (Nl).

Description
Chamomile s the common name for several daisy-like plants of the family Asteraceae. *Chamaemelum nobile* or Roman chamomile, has daisy-like white flowers and procumbent stems; the leaves are alternate, bipinnate, finely dissected, and downy to glabrous. The solitary, terminal flowerheads, rising 20–30 cm (8–12 in) above the ground, consist of prominent yellow disk flowers and silver-white ray flowers. *Matricaria chamomilla* or the German chamomile has a branched, erect and smooth stem, which grows to a height of 15–60 cm (6–23.5 in). The long and narrow leaves are bipinnate or tripinnate. The flowers are borne in paniculate flower heads (capitula). The white ray florets are furnished with a ligule, while the disc florets are yellow. The hollow receptacle is swollen and lacks scales. Infusion can be used preventive or curative. It can be made out of German chamomile (*Matricaria chamomilla),* Roman chamomile (*Chamaemelum nobile*)

Treatment name
Chamomile infusion

Names in other languages
Chamomile infusion (EN), Infusion de camomille (FR), Kamille infusie (NL), Kamille infusion (D).

Used on Vegetables
Garlic, Leek, Onion.

Preparation
Collect flowers. For 1 litre of water. Use non-chlorinated water like rainwater use 500 grammes fresh chamomile flowers or 50 grammes dried chamomile flowers. Bring to a boil and cut the heat. Let cool down and infuse for 24 hours. Filter the liquid through a sieve. Preparation time: Two days.

Use
Use as a spray on plants. Diluted prior to utilisation at 5%. Repeat, if necessary, every 3 to 4 days. Infusion has to be used before it starts to ferment.

Charcoal Dust

Class
Cultural control practices

English name
Charcoal dust

Names in other languages
Charcoal dust (En). Poudre de charbon (Fr). Holzkohle puder (De). Houtskool poeder (Nl).

Description
Dusting with powdered charcoal on the soil surface will help prevent damping-off.

Used on Vegetables
Broccoli, Brussels Sprout, Cabbage, Cauliflower, Celeriac, Celery, Courgette, Cucumber, Eggplant, Green Bean, Common Bean, Kohlrabi, Lamb's Lettuce, Lettuce, Napa/Chinese Cabbage, Pumpkin, Radish, Romanesco Broccoli, Rutabaga, Spinach, Tomatoes, Turnip.

Used for
Damping Off

How to use
To make your own charcoal dust. Grab any black coals from your barbecue or wood stove or other source, put them in a heavy cloth/burlap bag on a flat piece of cement and hammer it, then empty your crude black gravel and dust into a blender to produce charcoal powder, or just sieve it and throw the gravel on your compost heap. A one-time light dusting of powdered charcoal on the soil surface should assist your seedlings against damping off.

Chromatic Trap

Chromatic insect trap

Class
Cultural control practices

English name
Chromatic insect trap

Names in other languages
Chromatic insect trap (En). Piège chromatique à insectes (Fr). Chromatische Insektenfallen (De). Chromatische insectenvangers (Nl).

Description
Chromatic traps are small squares of yellow (or other colour) cardboard with sticky glue on them. Insects are attracted by the colour and attach to the trap and can't fly away. You can purchase them from garden centres, online or make them yourself. Different colours target different insects.

Used on Vegetables
Cabbage, Carrot, Cauliflower, Celeriac, Celery, Courgette, Cucumber, Eggplant, Fennel, Garlic, Green Bean, Common Bean, Lamb's Lettuce, Leek, Lettuce, Melon, Onion, Parsnip, Peas, Pepper, Bell Pepper, Potato, Pumpkin, Radish, Spinach, Sweet Corn, Tomatoes, Turnip.

Used for
Seedcorn Maggot, Bean Seed Fly, Southern Green Stink bug, Onion Fly, Carrot Fly, Celery Fly. Onion Thrips, Thrips, Onion Maggot, Pea Moth, Turnip Maggot, Turnip Root Fly, Celery Miner Fly, South American Miner Fly. South American Leaf Miner, American Serpentine Leaf Miner.

How to use
Blue traps for thrips, yellow traps for aphids, whitefly, fly and other insects. Black for South American tomato pinworm *Tuta absoluta*.

Click Beetle Wireworms Traps

Botanical name:

Class
Cultural control practices

English name
Click beetle traps

Names in other languages
Click beetle traps (En). Pièges à taupin (Fr). Drahtwurm Fallen (De). Ritnaalden vallen (Nl).

Description
Click beetle larvae, called wireworms, are usually saprophagous, living on dead organisms, this habit can be used to bait trap them. Burrowing cut pieces of potatoes, on specific spots in your garden, and check the bait and remove the attracted wireworms every two days. To attract adult beetles solar powered spotlight traps are used and can be homemade.

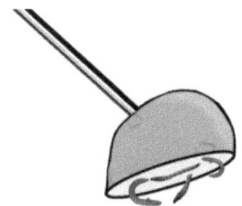

Click beetle traps

Used on Vegetables
Asparagus, Beetroot, Beet, Carrot, Lettuce, Onion, Potato, Spinach, Sweet Corn, Turnip.

Used for
Click Beetle, Striped Elaterid Beetle, Wireworms.

How to use
Cut a raw potato into pieces of at least 1 x 2 inches (3 cm x 5 cm) in size and insert a skewer into each one (this is so you can find them readily later). Now bury the pieces in the garden about 2 to 6 inches (5 to 15 cm) deep and about 3 feet (1 m) apart, leaving the skewer visible above the ground. After 24 to 48 hours, dig up the potato chunk using the skewer as a guide (this is best done in the evening when wireworms are most active). Remove the wormy potato segment with its wireworms and replace it with a fresh piece. Repeat as long as you keep finding wireworms (they're active from mid-spring through fall).

Comfrey

Botanical name
Symphytum officinale, Symphytum asperum, Symphytum × uplandicum

Class
Repellent

English name
Comfrey

Names in other languages
Comfrey infusion (En). Infusion de consoude (Fr). Beinwell infusion (De). Smeerwortel infusie (Nl).

Description
Comfrey is a perennial plant in the borage family, Boraginaceae. The hardy plant can grow to a height of 1–3 ft (0.3–0.9 m). It is a herb with a black, turnip-like root and large, hairy broad leaves that bears small bell-shaped flowers of various colours, typically cream or purplish, which may be striped. A common hybrid is formed between *Symphytum officinale* and *S. asperum*, *Symphytum × uplandicum*, known as Russian comfrey, and which interbreeds with S. officinale. Compared to S. officinale, S. ×uplandicum is generally more bristly and has flowers which tend to be more blue or violet. The most commonly used species is Russian comfrey.

Cultivation
By seeds or dividing plants. Russian comfrey is not seeding (sterile).

Symphytum officinale

Treatment name
Comfrey infusion

Names in other languages
Comfrey infusion (EN), Infusion de consoude (FR), Smeerwortel infusie (NL), Beinwell infusion (DE)

Used on Vegetables
Artichoke, Asparagus, Beetroot. Beet, Cabbage, Carrot, Courgette, Cucumber, Eggplant, Lettuce, Melon, Peas, Pepper. Bell Pepper, Potato, Pumpkin, Spinach, Tomatoes

Used for
The comfrey infusion is a repellent for whiteflies and aphids.

Preparation
Use the leaves. For 1 litre of water. Use non-chlorinated water like rainwater. Use 100 grams of fresh comfrey or 10 grams dried leaves. Bring to a boil and cut the heat. Let cool down and infuse for 12 hours. Filter the liquid through a sieve. Preparation time: One day. Infusion has to be used before it starts to ferment.

How to use
As a spray on plants. Not diluted. Repeat every 6 to 7 days, if necessary.

Treatment name
Liquid manure of comfrey

Names in other languages
Liquid manure of comfrey (EN), Purin de consoude
(FR), Smeerwortelgier (NL), Beinwelljauche (DE)

Used on Vegetables
Beetroot. Beet, Cauliflower, Celeriac, Celery,
Courgette, Cucumber, Eggplant, Garlic, Green
Bean. Common Bean, Melon, Napa/Chinese
Cabbage, Onion, Peas, Pepper. Bell Pepper,
Potato, Pumpkin, Spinach, Sweet Corn,
Tomatoes, Turnip

Used for
Liquid manure of comfrey is used for Chlorosis,
Anthracnose or Fruit Rot, Boron Deficiency,
Molybdenum Deficiency, Whiptail.

Preparation
Collect the whole plant, without the roots, broken
or chopped into small pieces. For 1 litre of water.
Use non-chlorinated water like rainwater use 100
grams of fresh comfrey or 10 grams of dried
plants. Macerate for one to two weeks. Stir or
shake the mixture regularly. Strain after
fermentation is complete or no air bubbles form.
The undiluted manure can be stored for a few
weeks, in a cool and dark place, preferable in
glass or plastic containers. Preparation time: Two
weeks.

How to use
As a spray on plants and soil. Diluted prior to
utilisation at 20%. Repeat every 6 to 7 days, if
necessary.

Common Rue

Ruta graveolens

Botanical name
Ruta graveolens

Class
Repellent

English name
Common rue

Names in other languages
Common rue maceration (En). Macération rue des jardins ou rue fétide (Fr). Weinraute Mazeration (De). Wijnruit maceratie (Nl).

Description
Ruta graveolens, commonly known as rue, common rue or herb-of-grace belongs to the Rutaceae family. It is a glabrous, glaucous, woody-based, shrubby perennial with aromatic, fern-like, compound leaves. It typically grows in a mound to one metre tall. Leaves are pinnately divided, blue green with oblong/spatulate segments. Small, 4- to 5-petaled, dull yellow flowers in clusters (flattened corymbs) bloom above the foliage in early summer. Fruit is a brown seed capsule. A maceration made with common rue (*Ruta graveolens*) can repel snail and slugs and some animals likes cats, field mice and meadow voles. Most cats dislike the smell of it, and it can, therefore, be used as a deterrent to them.

Propagation
By seeds and cuttings.

Treatment name
Common rue maceration

Names in other languages
Common rue maceration (EN), Macération rue des jardins ou rue fétide (FR), Wijnruit maceratie (NL), Weinraute Mazeration (DE).

Used on Vegetables
Asparagus, Beetroot. Beet, Celeriac, Celery, Chard, Cucumber, Lettuce, Peas, Rutabaga, Spinach

Used for
Common rue maceration is repellent for Asparagus Fly, Asparagus Maggot. Slug and Snail. Garden Slug. Loach. Little Grey Slug. Vine Snail. White Garden Snail.

Preparation
Use the leaves. For 1 litre of water. Use non-chlorinated water like rainwater use 100 grams of fresh common rue or 10 grams of dried common rue. Macerate in full sun. Macerate for 10 to 12 days. Stir or shake the mixture regularly. Filter the liquid through a sieve. Preparation time: Two weeks.

How to use
Spray on plants and soil. Diluted prior to utilisation at 20%.

Warning
Exposure to common rue, or herbal preparations derived from it, can cause severe burn-like blisters on the skin.

Compost Tea

Class
Repellent

English name
Compost tea

Names in other languages
Compost tea (En). Thé de compost (Fr). Kompost-Extraktes (De). Compost thee (Nl).

Description
The simplest method to produce compost watery extract is by suspending a burlap sack containing compost in a barrel of water for 7 to 14 days. By mixing one volume of compost with 4–10 volumes of water in an open container. Initially, the mixture is stirred, then allowed to stand undisturbed at 15–20C for at least 3 days with no or minimal stirring. Strain and use. Other more sophisticated methods are described which you can check on the internet.

Compost tea

Used on Vegetables
Tomatoes

Used for
Tomato Corky Root

How to use
Non diluted as a drench, diluted 1 to 3 as a spray.

Coniothyrium minitans Fungus

Botanical name
Coniothyrium minitans

Class
Biopesticide

English name
Coniothyrium minitans fungus

Names in other languages
Coniothyrium minitans fungus (En). Coniothyrium minitans fungi (Fr). Coniothyrium minitans Pilz (De). Coniothyrium minitans schimmel (Nl).

Description
Coniothyrium minitans is a fungus that can be utilized as a biological control against the fungal pathogens Sclerotinia sclerotiorum and Sclerotinia minor (causal agents of white mold on many plant species).

Used on Vegetables
Artichoke, Beetroot, Beet, Carrot, Celeriac, Celery, Courgette, Cucumber, Garlic, Green Bean, Common Bean, Leek, Lettuce, Onion, Parsnip, Peas, Pepper Bell Pepper, Potato, Pumpkin, Tomatoes.

Used for
Coniothyrium minitans is a fungus that can be utilized as a biological control against the fungal pathogens Sclerotinia sclerotiorum and Sclerotinia minor (causal agents of white mold on many plant species). White Rot, White Mold, Sclerotinia Wilt, Soft rot, White Rot on Carrot, Cottony rot, Lettuce drop.

How to use
Coniothyrium biocontrol fungus is sold as conidia (spores), which are dried and mixed with glucose. The product is then mixed with water and sprayed onto the soil.

Copper Tape or Wire

Class
Cultural control practices

English name
Copper tape/wire

Names in other languages
Copper tape/ wire (En). Ruban/fil de cuivre (Fr). Kupferband/-draht (De). Kopertape/draad (Nl).

Description
Copper tape – thin adhesive copper tape is available from stores to act as a barrier. Snails and slugs simply won't cross over the tape. Wrap a continuous line around pots or planter boxes for protection.

Copper tape/wire

Used on Vegetables
All in containers, raised beds.

Used for
Slug and snail.

How to use
Trials have shown that to have the best possible effect a wide strip of copper tape is best. If you find that a single band isn't an effective deterrent, use a double band to increase the width. Cut back any overhanging foliage or branches that may act as a 'bridge' between the outside of the taped area and the plants you want to protect.

Dacnusa sibirica Parasitic Wasp

Botanical name
Dacnusa sibirica

Class
Predators

English name
Dacnusa sibirica. Parasitic wasp

Names in other languages
Dacnusa sibirica Parasitic wasp (En). Dacnusa sibirica Guêpe parasite (Fr). Dacnusa sibirica Parasitäre Wespe (De). Dacnusa sibirica Parasitaire wesp (Nl).

Description
Dacnusa sibirica is a small parasitic wasp belonging to the family Braconidae. This insect is known for its role as a biological control agent, particularly in the control of leaf miners of the genus Liriomyza. The species is native to Europe and can appear spontaneously in greenhouses in all seasons. Adults are dark brown to black in colour and 2 to 3 mm in size. The parasitic wasp has long antennae and its wings are longer than its abdomen. The larval stages develop inside the host.

Dacnusa sibirica

Used on Vegetables
Celery, Cucumber, Eggplant, Leek, Lettuce, Melon, Onion, Peas, Pepper, Potato, Tomato.

Used for
Celery Miner Fly, South American Miner Fly, American Serpentine Leaf Miner, Tomato Leaf Miner.

How to use
The performance of D. sibirica is better in crops raised in autumn, winter and spring. Dosage can vary depending on the crop and the level of the pest. 0.25-0.5 individuals/m2, in two consecutive releases. When the temperature is high, it is advisable to use *Diglyphus isaea* instead of *D. sibirica*.

Dandelion

Botanical name
Taraxacum officinale

Class
Repellent

English name
Dandelion

Names in other languages
Dandelion (En). Pissenlit (Fr). Löwenzahn (De). Paardenbloem (Nl).

Description
Taraxacum officinale belongs to the Asteraceae family. It grows from generally unbranched taproots and produces one to more than ten stems that are typically 5–40 cm (2.0–15.7 in) tall. The stems are upright or lax, and produce flower heads that are held as tall or taller than the foliage. The foliage may be upright-growing or horizontally spreading; the leaves have petioles that are either unwinged or narrowly winged. The stems can be glabrous or sparsely covered with short hairs. Plants have milky latex and the leaves are all basal; each flowering stem lacks bracts and has one single flower head. The yellow flower heads lack receptacle bracts and all the flowers, which are called florets, are ligulate and bisexual.

Treatment name
Dandelion infusion

Names in other languages
Dandelion infusion (En). Infusion de pissenlit (Fr). Löwenzahn infusion (De). Paardenbloem infusie (Nl).

Used on Vegetables
Carrot, Celeriac, Celery, Courgette, Cucumber, Garlic, Leek, Lettuce, Onion, Peas, Pumpkin, Tomatoes.

Used for
Dandelion is used as infusion to repel fungi like Onion and Leek Rust, Celery Late Blight.

Preparation
Collect the whole plant, without the roots. Chop the plant in very small pieces. For 1 litre of water. Use non-chlorinated water like rainwater. Use 200 grammes fresh dandelion or 20 grammes dried dandelion. Bring to a boil and cut the heat. Let cool down covered. Filter the liquid through a sieve. Infusion has to be used before it starts to ferment. Preparation time: One hour.

How to use
Spray on plants. Not diluted. Repeat every 6 to 7 days, if necessary.

Diatomaceous Earth

Class
Cultural control practices

English name
Diatomaceous Earth

Names in other languages
Diatomaceous Earth (En). Terre diatomée (Fr). Kieselgur (De). Diatomeeënaarde (Nl).

Description
Diatomaceous earth is a powder made from prehistoric crustaceans called diatoms. The sharp edges of diatomaceous earth cut into insects' bodies, causing them to die of dehydration. Diatomaceous earth is most useful in dry situations.

Used on Vegetables
Broccoli, Brussels Sprout, Cabbage, Cauliflower, Cucumber, Eggplant, Green Bean, Common Bean, Kohlrabi, Napa/Chinese Cabbage, Pepper, Bell Pepper, Radish, Romanesco Broccoli, Rutabaga, Tomatoes, Turnip.

Used for
Southern Green Stink bug, Cabbage Maggot.

How to use
Apply a light dusting to the plants. Diatomaceous earth must be reapplied after every rain or heavy dew to be effective.

Diglyphus
Parasitic Wasp

Botanical name
Diglyphus isaea

Class
Predators

English name
Diglyphus isaea parasitic wasp

Names in other languages
Diglyphus isaea parasitic wasp (En). Diglyphus isaea guêpe parasite (Fr). Diglyphus isaea parasitische Wespe (De). Diglyphus isaea sluipwesp (Nl).

Diglyphus isaea

Description
Diglyphus isaea is an Eulophid wasp that can be found anywhere in the Mediterranean Basin associated with *Liriomyza spp*. The Diglyphus adult is 1.5-2 mm long with a black elongated body and short antennae. Establishment within a crop is very rapid and is remarkable the ability to survive in difficult circumstances. Before laying eggs beside the larval host body, the female stings it inducing paralysis. The adult will emerge through a round hole cut in the leaf tissues. Egg to adult development is sharply influenced by temperature and could be very quick (10 days at 25ºC). Longevity is very high comparing to other parasitoids. A female can lay 60 to 100 eggs depending on different conditions. Not only parasitisation but also host feeding causes significant mortality in leaf miner population. This combined with a high searching capability makes also very early ('preventive') introductions successful. Even if high population of the parasitoid could rapidly overcome heavy pest outbreaks,

Used on Vegetables
Among the natural enemies commercially available, this tiny wasp is regarded as one of the most efficient and easy to apply in several crops. Cabbage, Celery, Cherries, Cucumber, Eggplant, Leek, Lettuce, Melon, Onion, Peas, Pepper. Bell Pepper, Potato, Tomatoes

Used for
Tomato Leaf Miner, Celery Miner Fly, South American Miner Fly. South American Leaf Miner, American Serpentine Leaf Miner

How to use
The parasitic wasp can be purchased from garden centres or online or biocontrol companies. Starting early with multiple releases and small quantities (up to a total rate of 0.5 to 2/m2) is generally the best method of application in any crop.

Diluted Milk

Class
Repellent

English name
Diluted milk

Names in other languages
Diluted milk (En). Lait dilué (Fr). Verdünnt Milch (De). Verdunde melk (Nl).

Description
A spray of diluted milk is also effective against mildew. To use milk as an antifungal spray. Mix 1 part skimmed milk to 5 to 9 parts water in a spray bottle. Spray the solution onto the leaves of plants, preferably unaffected plants, when the plant is in bright sun. Soak both sides of the leaves until the solution is dripping. Repeat the spray application every 6 to 7 days. Milk works best preventive.

Diluted milk

Used on Vegetables
Artichoke, Beetroot. Beet, Broad Bean Broccoli, Brussels Sprout, Cabbage, Carrot, Cauliflower, Celeriac, Celery, Chard Courgette, Cucumber, Eggplant, Fennel, Garlic, Green Bean, Common Bean, Kohlrabi, Lamb's Lettuce, Leek, Lettuce, Melon, Napa/Chinese, Onion, Parsnip, Peas, Potato, Pumpkin, Radish, Romanesco Broccoli, Rutabaga, Spinach, Tomatoes, Turnip.

Used for
Downy Mildew of Alliums, Downy Mildew of Crucifers, Powdery Mildew.

How to use
Use a mixture 1 to 1 ratio of milk to water. Reapply the milk treatment every 10 to 14 days.

Early Seeding

Class
Cultural control practices

English name
Early seeding

Names in other languages
Early seeding (En). Ensemencement précoce (Fr).
Frühsaaten (De). Vroeg zaaien (Nl).

Description
The timing of crop development can have a great effect on it's susceptibility to insect pests. For many pest and crop systems, planting date will dictate whether or not a pest will be present in sufficient numbers to become a problem. The method of planting direct-seeded versus transplants can also affect a crop's ability to resist pests. Direct-seeded crops require optimal growing conditions to emerge quickly and grow fast. The use of transplants, when possible, can speed crop development and make them more tolerant of pest attack.

Early seeding

Used on Vegetables
Artichoke, Beetroot, Beet, Broad Bean, Carrot, Chard, Green Bean, Common Bean, Peas, Potato.

Used for
Bean Aphids. Black Dolphin Aphids, Pea Moth.

How to use
Early sowing of fast maturing peas varieties will have a good chance of cropping before the pea moth lays her eggs.

Elder

Sambucus nigra

Botanical name
Sambucus nigra

Class
Repellent

English name
Elder

Names in other languages
Elder (En). Sureau (Fr). Holunder (De). Vlier (Nl).

Description
The elder (*Sambucus nigra*) belong in the family Adoxaceae. It common names are elderberry, black elder, European elder, European elderberry and European black elderberry. Elderberry is a deciduous shrub or small tree growing to 6 m (20 ft) tall and wide,] rarely reaching 10 m (33 ft) tall). The bark, light grey when young, changes to a coarse grey outer bark with lengthwise furrowing, lenticels prominent. The leaves are arranged in opposite pairs, 10–30 cm long, pinnate with five to seven (rarely nine) leaflets, the leaflets are 5–12 cm long and 3–5 cm broad, with a serrated margin. The young stems are hollow. The hermaphroditic flowers have five stamens, which are borne in large, flat corymbs 10–25 cm diameter in late spring to mid-summer, the individual flowers are ivory white, 5–6 mm diameter, with five petals; they are pollinated by flies. The fruit is a glossy, dark purple to black berry, 3–5 mm diameter, produced in drooping clusters in late autumn.

Propagation
Elders grow very well from cuttings or find young trees near parent plants.

Warning
Except for the flowers and ripe berries, all parts of the plant are poisonous to mammals.

Treatment name
Elder decoction

Names in other languages
Elder decoction (En). Décoction de sureau (Fr). Holunder Pflanzenabsuds (De). Vlier aftreksel (Nl).

Used on Vegetables
Artichoke, Beetroot, Beet, Broad Bean, Broccoli, Brussels Sprout, Cabbage, Carrot, Cauliflower, Celeriac, Chard, Cucumber, Eggplant, Fennel, Green Bean. Common Bean, Kohlrabi, Leek, Lettuce, Melon, Napa/Chinese Cabbage, Onion, Parsnip, Peas, Pepper, Bell Pepper, Potato, Radish, Romanesco Broccoli, Rutabaga, Spinach, Tomatoes, Turnip

Used for
Artichoke Moth, Artichoke Plume Moth, Thistle Aphid, Dark Sword-grass Moth. Black cutworm, Greasy cutworm, Cabbage Stem Flea Beetle, Cabbage Aphid, Carrot Fly, Bean Aphids. Black Dolphin Aphids, Green Peach Aphid, Potato Aphid, Silver-Y moth. Common Silver-Y moth, Cabbage Army Moth.

Preparation
Use the leaves. Chop in very small pieces. For 1 litre of water. Use non-chlorinated water like rainwater. Use 100 grams of fresh elder or 10 grams of dried plants. Bring to a boil, cover and let simmer for 30 minutes. Let cool down covered and let Macerate for 12 to 24 hours. Filter the liquid through a sieve. Preparation time: Two days.

How to use
As a spray on plants. Not diluted. Repeat every 2 to 3 days, if necessary.

Treatment name
Elder infusion

Names in other languages
Elder infusion (En). Infusion de surreau (Fr). Holunder infusion (De). Vlier infusie (Nl).

Used on vegetables
Artichoke, Asparagus, Beetroot. BeetBroad, Bean, Broccoli, Brussels Sprout, Cabbage, Carrot, Cauliflower, Celeriac, Celery, Chard, Courgette, Cucumber, Eggplant, Fennel, Garlic, Green Bean, Common Bean, Kohlrabi, Lamb's Lettuce, Leek, Lettuce, Melon, Napa/Chinese Cabbage, Onion, Parsnip, Peas, Potato, Pumpkin, Radish, Romanesco, Broccoli, Rutabaga, Spinach, Tomatoes, Turnip.

Used for
The infusion made from elder is repellent to fungi and white fly. Glasshouse Whitefly, Greenhouse Whitefly, Onion and Leek Rust, Downy Mildew of Alliums, Rust, Downy Mildew of Crucifers, Powdery Mildew.

Preparation
Use leaves, For 1 litre of water. Use non-chlorinated water like rainwater. Use 100 grams of fresh elder or 10 grams dried plants. Bring to a boil and cut the heat. Let cool down and infuse for 12 hours. Filter the liquid through a sieve. Preparation time: One day. Infusion has to be used before it starts to ferment.

Use
As a spray on plants. Not diluted. Repeat every 2 to 3 days, if necessary.

Eliminate the Infected Plants

Class
Cultural control practices

English name
Eliminate the infected plants

Names in other languages
Eliminate the infected plants (En). Eliminer les plantes infectées (Fr). Eliminieren infizierte Pflanz (De). Elimineer besmette planten (Nl).

Description
Remove infected plants, and dispose of plant debris. Avoid composting them, some pathogens survive through the composting process and you risk reinfecting your garden by using this compost.

Used on Vegetables
Artichoke, Asparagus, Beetroot, Beet, Broad Bean, Broccoli, Brussels Sprout, Cabbage, Carrot, Cauliflower, Celeriac, Chard, Courgette, Cucumber, Eggplant, Fennel, Garlic, Green Bean, Common Bean, Kohlrabi, Lamb's Lettuce, Leek, Lettuce, Melon, Napa/Chinese Cabbage, Onion, Parsnip, Peas, Pepper, Bell Pepper, Potato, Pumpkin , Radish, Romanesco Broccoli, Rutabaga, Spinach, Sweet Corn, Tomatoes, Turnip.

Used for
Gray Mold, Grey Mould. Botrytis Blight, Tomato Leaf Miner, Ramularia Leaf and Bract Spot, Ascochyta Rot, Black Rot, Leaf Spot, Bacterial Canker of Tomato, Xanthomonas Disease of Artichoke, Artichoke Pear-shaped Weevil, Onion Fly, White Rot, White Mold. Sclerotinia Wilt, Penicillium Decay, Seed Clove Decay, Bleu Mold, Skin Blotch of Garlic, Violet Root-rot of Asparagus, Rust, Asparagus Fly, Asparagus Maggot, Stem Nematode, Bulb and Stem Nematode, Beet Fly, Mangold Fly, Verticillium Wilt, Cabbage Club Root, Violet Root Rot, Celery Late Blight , Powdery Mildew, Celery Fly, Fusarium Wilt, Maize Smut, Corn Smut, Cercosporosa Leaf Spot, Onion Maggot, Cucumber Mosaic Virus. CMV, Beet Curly Top Virus. BCTV, Bean Yellow Mosaic Virus. BYMV, Bacterial Brown Spot, Botrytis Rot, Neckrot, Fusarium Root Rot.

How to use
Remove infected foliage, stems or plants as soon as you see them.

Encarsia Parasitic Wasp

Botanical name
Encarsia formosa

Class
Predators

English name
Encarsia formosa parasitic wasp

Names in other languages
Encarsia formosa parasitic wasp (En). Encarsia formosa guêpes parasites (Fr). Encarsia formosa parasitische Wespe (De). Encarsia formosa sluipwesp (Nl).

Description
Encarsia formosa, a parasitoid of greenhouse whiteflies, is one of the first natural enemies being used. The Encarsia adult female is a tiny wasp, 0.6 mm long, with a black and yellow body. Once found a whitefly an egg is inserted within the host body. The host "pupa" changes its colour and turns black or brown. After the end of larval development the adult cut a rounded hole to emerge from the host. Encarsia is one of the most reliable natural enemies when conditions are suitable having a very high searching capability. Also the host feeding is very important for the pest control as many host pupae are killed to obtain a food source.

Encarsia formosa

Used on Vegetables
Asparagus, Eggplant, Pepper, Bell Pepper, Potato, Tomatoes.

Used for
It is mainly released to control whitefly in greenhouses. Glasshouse Whitefly, Greenhouse Whitefly, Cotton Whitefly, Tobacco Whitefly.

How to use
Introduction rates vary from 2 to 6 individuals/m2 per week, starting very early in the season as the first whiteflies is detected. Expose the predator away from direct sunlight.

Episyrphus balteatus Hoverflies

Botanical name
Episyrphus balteatus

Class
Predators

English name
Episyrphus balteatus Hoverflies. The Marmalade hoverfly.

Names in other languages
Marmalade hoverfly (En). Syrphe ceinturé (Fr). Hainschwebfliege (De). Snorzweefvlieg (Nl).

Description
The Marmalade hoverfly is around 9–12mm (0.35–0.45in) long with distinctive orange and black banding. The third and fourth dorsal tergites have a secondary thinner black band that is notched in the center giving it the appearance of a "moustache", and the thorax has three feint grey longitudinal stripes. Hoverfly eggs are oval, whitish-grey in colour and up to 1mm long, so not easy to spot. The larvae are up to 11mm long, a transparent beige type colour with no legs. The larvae develop into beige brown coloured pupae. The pupae hatch into adult Hoverfly that are 10-13mm long with a dark yellow face and a golden abdomen with black stripes.

Episyrphus balteatus

Used on Vegetables
Hoverflies can be used in both greenhouse and outdoor crops, whenever aphids are present.

Used for
All species or stages of aphids.

How to use
The introduction of hoverfly depends on climate, crop and aphid density and should always be adjusted to the particular situation. Start introduction preventatively or as soon as the first aphids are detected in the crop. Introduction rates typically range from 100-600 pupae per ha/ release. Releases should be repeated a number of times. The Marmalade hoverfly is most effective between 15 and 23°C. High humidity is favourable for larval development and hatching of pupae. Adult hoverflies feed on pollen and nectar. Ensure flowering plants are present for optimal establishment.

Feltiella
Predatory Midge

Botanical name
Feltiella acarisuga

Class
Predators

English name
Feltiella acarisuga predatory midge

Names in other languages
Feltiella acarisuga predatory midge (En). Feltiella acarisuga cécidomyie prédatrices (Fr). Feltiella acarisuga räuberischen Mücke (De). Feltiella acarisuga roofmug (Nl).

Description
Feltiella is a species of beneficial midge native to much of the world. The larvae are voracious predators of many spider mite species including the destructive carmine mite. The Feltiella females deposit eggs near prey mites. The eggs hatch within two days and the larvae begin to feed right away. All stages of spider mites are consumed by Feltiella. Larvae forage on leaves for prey. The four larval stages last around a week. After which, a cocoon is spun. This cocoon is attached to leaves, often against a leaf vein. One adult will emerge from each cocoon. Adult females will lay close to 30 eggs over a five day time span. The entire life cycle last between two to four weeks.

Feltiella acarisuga

Used on Vegetables
Feltiella acarisuga can be used to manage spider mite populations in a variety of greenhouse and field crops. Artichoke, Carrot, Courgette, Cucumber, Eggplant, Green Bean, Common Bean, Melon Pepper, Bell Pepper, Pumpkin, Tomatoes.

Used for
The Feltiella larvae are voracious predators of many spider mite species. Tomato Russet Mite, Red Spider Mite, Two-spotted Mite.

How to use
Depending depending on the temperature, humidity, and abundance of spider mite,. purchase and release Feltiella.

Fern

Dryopteris filix-mas

Botanical name
Dryopteris filix-mas, Pteridium aquilinum

Class
Repellent

English name
Male fern, Bracken

Names in other languages
Fern (En). Fougères (Fr). Farn (De). Varen (Nl).

Description
The male fern (*Dryopteris filix-mas*) has semi-evergreen leaves with an upright habit and reach a maximum length of 150 cm (59 in), with a single crown on each rootstock. The bipinnate leaves consist of 20–35 pinnae on each side of the rachis. The leaves taper at both ends, with the basal pinnae about half the length of the middle pinnae. The pinules are rather blunt and equally lobed all around. The stalks are covered with orange-brown scales. On the abaxial surface of the mature blade 5 to 6 sori develop in two rows. When the spores ripen in August to November, the indusium starts to shrivel, leading to the release of the spores. *Pteridium aquilinum* (bracken, brake or common bracken), also known as eagle fern, and Eastern brakenfern. Common bracken is a herbaceous perennial plant, deciduous in winter. The large, roughly triangular fronds are produced singly, arising upwards from an underground rhizome, and grow to 0.3–1 m (1–3ft) tall; the main stem, or stipe, is up to 1 cm (0.4 in) diameter at the base. It dies back to ground level in autumn.

Propagation
The quickest way to grow more ferns is through division, preferably in spring.

Treatment name
Fern decoction

Names in other languages
Fern decoction (En). Décoction de fougères (Fr). Farn Pflanzenabsuds (De). Varen decoctie (Nl).

Used on Vegetables
Beetroot, Beet, Celeriac, Celery, Chard, Cucumber, Lettuce, Peas, Rutabaga, Spinach.

Used for
Fern decoction, undiluted, is used against shell-less snails (every time needed): Slug and Snail. Garden Slug. Loach. Little Grey Slug. Vine Snail. White Garden Snail.

Preparation
Collect the whole plant, without the roots. Chop the leaves in very small pieces. For 1 litre of water. Use non-chlorinated water like rainwater. Use 100 grams of fresh ferns or 10 grams of dried plants. Bring to a boil, cover and let simmer for 30 minutes. Let cool down covered. Let Macerate for 12 to 24 hours. Filter the liquid through a sieve. The undiluted decoction can be stored for a few weeks, in a cool and dark place, preferable in glass or plastic containers. Preparation time: Two days.

How to use
Use as a spray on plants and soil. Diluted or not diluted depending on target, prior to utilisation at 10 or 20%. Apply every 6 to 7 days, repeat, if necessary.

Treatment name
Liquid manure of fern

Names in other languages
Liquid manure of fern (EN), Purin de fougère (FR), Varengier (NL), Farnjauche (DE).

Used on Vegetables
Artichoke, Asparagus, Beetroot, Beet, Broad Bean, Broccoli, Brussels Sprout, Cabbage, Carrot, Cauliflower, Celeriac, Celery, Chard, Citrus, Courgette, Cucumber, Eggplant, Fennel, Garlic, Green Bean, Common Bean, Kohlrabi, Lamb's Lettuce, Leek, Lettuce, Melon, Napa/Chinese Cabbage, Onion, Parsnip, Peas, Pepper, Bell Pepper, Potato, Pumpkin, Radish, Romanesco Broccoli, Rutabaga, Spinach, Sweet Corn, Tomatoes, Turnip.

Used foe
The fern preparation is a repellent for aphids and mites. It can be used combined with nettle or horsetails preparations: Tomato Russet Mite, Thistle Aphid, Onion and Leek Rust, Rust, Cabbage Aphid, Lettuce Root Aphid, Click Beetle. Striped Elaterid Beetle, Wireworms, Powdery Mildew, Bean Aphids. Black Dolphin Aphids, Green Peach Aphid, Potato Aphid, Cotton Aphid, Grain Aphid, Slug and Snail. Garden Slug. Loach. Little Grey Slug. Vine Snail. White Garden Snail Hawthorn Aphids, Onion Maggot Red Spider Mite, Two-spotted Mite, March Crane Fly.

Preparation
Use the whole plant, without the roots, broken or chopped into small bits. For 1 litre of water. Use non-chlorinated water like rainwater. Use 100 grams of fresh ferns or 10 grams of dried plants. Macerate for one to two weeks. By preference use plastic or wooden recipients. Stir or shake the mixture regularly. Strain after fermentation is complete or no air bubbles form. The undiluted manure can be stored for a few weeks, in a cool and dark place, preferable in glass or plastic containers. Preparation time: Two weeks.

How to use
Spray on plants and soil. Use diluted at 10% as repellent for insects. Non diluted as repellent for fungi and non diluted for deficiencies. Repeat, if necessary, every 3 to 4 days.

Freeze Seeds

Class
Cultural control practices

English name
Freeze seeds

Names in other languages
Freeze seeds (En). Congeler les graines (Fr). Einfrieren Saatgut (De). Ingevroren zaadgoed (Nl).

Description
Freeze grains for at least 1 week or store permanently in the freezer to kill any eggs of beetles.

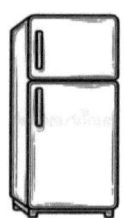

Freeze seeds

Used on Vegetables
Broad Bean, Green Bean, Common Bean, Peas.

Used for
Bean Beetle, Pea beetle.

How to use
Prepare storage zip bags or cans by writing the name of the seed and the date on the outside. Fill the zip bag and zip the bag shut, squeezing out as much air as possible. Place the bag with the seeds into the freezer until you're ready to use them.

French Marigolds

Botanical name
Tagetes patula

Class
Repellent

English name
French marigolds

Names in other languages
French marigolds (En), Œillets d'Inde, Tagète, Tagette (Fr), Niedrige Studentenblume (De), Afrikaantjes (Nl).

Description
French marigolds (*Tagetes patula)* is a compact bushy annual to 30 cm tall and wide with aromatic, deeply-divided leaves and single or double flowerheads in shades of yellow, orange, red or brown from summer into early autumn.

Propagation
Propagate by seed. Grow in moderately fertile, well-drained soil in full sun.

Tagetes patula

Treatment name
French marigolds infusion

Names in other languages
French marigolds infusion (En). Infusion de tagète (Fr). Tagetes infusion (De). Afrikaantjes infusie (Nl).

Used on Vegetables
Asparagus, Broad bean, Cabbage, Carrot, Cauliflower, Celeriac, Celery, Eggplant, Garlic, Bean, Lettuce, Napa, Onion, Peas, Pepper, Potato, Tomatoes, Turnip.

Used for
French marigolds ((Tagetes patula) infusion is used as repellent against aphids, whiteflies and especially nematodes. Stem and bulb nematodes, Potato tuber nematodes, Carrot root nematodes, Pea root nematodes, Cabbage and cauliflower cyst nematodes, Glasshouse whitefly.

Preparation
Use the whole plant, without the roots, chop into small pieces. Use about 25 grams of dried marigolds or 250 grams of fresh marigolds for one liter of water, best rainwater. Bring to a boil and cut the heat, Filter the liquid through a sieve. Let cool down and infuse for 12 hours.

How to use
To spry on plants diluted prior to utilization at 10 %. Keep in a cold place and utilise before it starts to ferment.

Garlic

Botanical nameå
Allium sativum

Class
Repellent

English name
Garlic

Names in other languages
Garlic (En). Ail (Fr). Knoblauch (De). Knoflook (Nl).

Description
Garlic (*Allium sativum*) is a bulbous plant. Garlic is a herbaceous, perennial plant producing 6 to 12 leaves, from 15 to 60 cm long and at flowering stage up to 80 cm tall.

Propagation
Garlic is grown as an annual. The individual cloves being planted in early winter or spring and the bulbs being harvested in the summer.

Allium sativum

Treatment name
Garlic Decoction

Names in other languages
Garlic decoction (En). Décoction de l'ail (Fr). Knoblauch Pflanzenabsuds (De). Knoflook decoctie (Nl).

Used on Vegetables
Artichoke, Asparagus, Beetroot. Beet, Broad Bean, Broccoli, Brussels Sprout, Cabbage, Carrot, Cauliflower, Celeriac, Celery, Chard, Citrus, Courgette, Cucumber, Eggplant, Fennel, Garlic, Green Bean. Common Bean, Kohlrabi, Lamb's Lettuce, Leek, Lettuce, Melon, Napa/Chinese Cabbage, Onion, Parsnip, Peas, Pepper. Bell Pepper, Potato, Pumpkin, Radish, Romanesco Broccoli, Rutabaga, Spinach, Sweet Corn , Tomatoes, Turnip.

Used for
Garlic decoction is a repellent for fungi like mold, mildew, oidium, rust and some insects like mites and aphids: Gray Mold. Grey Mould. Botrytis Blight, Early Blight of Potato/Tomato. Damping Off, Anthracnose Fruit Rot, Onion and Leek Rust, Downy Mildew of Alliums, Rust, Cabbage Stem Flea Beetle, Cabbage Aphid, Downy Mildew of Crucifers, Powdery Mildew, Red Spider Mite. Two-spotted Mite, Cabbage Bug. Rape Bug. Crucifer Shield Bug. Brassica Bug.

Preparation
Use the whole plant or cloves. Shop the garlic cloves. For 1 litre of water. Use non-chlorinated water like rainwater. Use 100 grams of fresh garlic or 10 grams of dried plants. Bring to a boil, reduce heat, cover and simmer for 15 minutes. Let cool down covered. Let macerate for 10 to 12 hours. Filter the liquid through a sieve. The garlic decoction can not be stored. Preparation time:

One day.

How to use
Spray on plants and soil. Not diluted. Every 3 to 4 days, repeat, if necessary.

Treatment name
Garlic macerate oil

Names in other languages
Garlic macerate oil (En). Macérât de l'ail (Fr). Mazerat Knoblauch (De). Knoflookolie-maceraat (Nl).

Used on Vegetables
Artichoke. Asparagus. Beetroot. Beet Cabbage Carrot. Courgette. Cucumber, Eggplant, Green Bean, Common Bean, Kohlrabi, Leek, Lettuce, Melon, Onion, Peaches, Pears, Peas, Pepper, Bell Pepper, Potato, Pumpkin, Radish, Rutabaga, Spinach, Tomatoes, Turnip.

Used for
Glasshouse Whitefly, Greenhouse Whitefly, Southern Green Stink bug, Tomato Russet Mite, Thistle Aphid, Green Peach Aphid, Potato Aphid, Cotton Aphid, Onion Thrips, Thrips, Cabbage Bug, Rape Bug, Crucifer Shield Bug, Brassica Bug.

Preparation
Use cloves and olive oil. For 1 litre of olive oil use 100 grams of fresh garlic cloves or 10 grams dried garlic. Use a garlic press to crush the cloves. Maceration is carried out by chopping or crushing garlic cloves and steeping them in oil. The garlic is left in the oil for a minimum of 24 hours, before the oil is strained and the garlic discarded. Preparation time: Two days. The undiluted oil can be stored for a few weeks, in a cool and dark place, preferable in glass bottles.

How to use
Spray on plants. Diluted prior to utilisation at 5%. Adding some small quantity of black soap in the garlic oil when spraying, as repellent. provide more efficiency. Apply every 3 to 4 days. Repeat if necessary.

Green Manure

Class
Cultural control practices

English name
Green manure

Names in other languages
Green manure (En). Engrais vert (Fr). Gründüngung (De). Groen bemesting (Nl).

Description
Green manure is a type of crop grown mainly to add nutrients to the soil and improve its health. It involves growing plants and then incorporating them back into the soil, which enhances soil fertility and structure. The primary goal of green manuring is to improve soil health. When green manure crops are turned into the soil, they add nutrients that are essential for plant growth. This method can increase soil organic matter, improve soil structure, and enhance moisture retention. Another goal is to manage weeds by suppressing their growth during the green manure crop's growing season. Green manuring can also reduce soil erosion by providing ground cover. Additionally, it can help break disease cycles by rotating crops that are not hosts to particular pests or diseases, making it a valuable tool in sustainable agriculture practices.

Used on Vegetables
Potato

Used for
Potato scab

How to use
Utilizing a disease suppressive rotation with green manures, such as buckwheat, canola, oat, rye or millet can inhibit *Streptomyces scabies*.

Hansfordia pulvinata

Botanical name
Hansfordia pulvinata

Class
Biopesticide

English name
Hansfordia pulvinata

Names in other languages
Hansfordia pulvinata (En). Idem (Fr). Idem (De). Idem (Nl).

Description
Hansfordia pulvinata is a mycoparasitical species could be used as a biological control agent against cladosporiosis of tomato in glass house cultures.

Used on Vegetables
Tomatoes.

Used for
Leaf Mould, Cladosporiosis of Tomato.

How to use
Further studies are required to assess the biocontrol efficacy.

Heterorhabditis Nematode

Botanical name
Heterorhabditis bacteriophora

Class
Predators

English name
Heterorhabditis bacteriophora nematode

Names in other languages
Heterorhabditis bacteriophora nematode (En).
Heterorhabditis bacteriophora nématode (Fr).
Heterorhabditis bacteriophora Nematoden (De).
Heterorhabditis bacteriophora Aaltjes (Nl).

Description
Entomopathogenic nematodes, such as *Heterorhabditis bacteriophora*, occur naturally in the environment as parasites of many insect larvae. The mass release of these nematodes provides an efficient and curative control of key insect pests in a wide range of crops. Once released, nematodes actively seek out their insect hosts. When a host has been located, the nematodes penetrate the insect through body openings and release symbiotic bacteria that multiply and rapidly kill the insect. Subsequently, nematodes feed upon the host and mature into adults, which mate and produce the next generation. The life cycle is completed within a few weeks and hundreds of thousands of nematodes emerge in search of new hosts.

Used on Vegetables
Asparagus, Beetroot, Beet, Broad Bean, Broccoli, Brussels Sprout, Cabbage, Carrot, Cauliflower, Chard, Cucumber, Eggplant, Green Bean, Common Bean, Kohlrabi, Leek, Lettuce, Napa/Chinese Cabbage, Onion, Peas, Potato, Radish, Romanesco Broccoli, Rutabaga, Spinach, Sweet Corn, Tomatoes, Turnip.

Used for
Heterorhabditis bacteriophora nematodes are most effective against Japanese beetles, European chafers and other grubs that are pests. Asparagus Beetle, Twelve-spotted Asparagus Beetle, Asparagus Fly, Asparagus Maggot, Colorado Potato Beetle, Dark Sword-grass Moth, Black cutworm, Greasy cutworm, June Beetles, May Beetles, Cabbage Stem Flea Beetle, Click Beetle, Striped Elaterid Beetle, Wireworms, Pea Weevil, Pea and Bean Weevil, Turnip Gall Weevil, Asparagus Moth.

How to use
They can be applied a number of different ways, through manually and automated equipment. They can be put through just about any irrigation setup or using buckets, watering cans, or sprayers.

Hirsutella thompsonii

Botanical name
Hirsutella thompsonii

Class
Biopesticide

English name
Hirsutella thompsonii fungus

Names in other languages
Hirsutella thompsonii fungus (En). Hirsutella thompsonii champignon (Fr). Hirsutella thompsonii Pilz (De). Hirsutella thompsonii schimmel (Nl).

Description
Hirsutella is a genus of asexually reproducing fungi this genus includes species that are pathogens of insects, mites and nematodes; there is interest in the use of these fungi as biological controls of insect and nematode pests.

Used on Vegetables
Artichoke, Carrot, Courgette, Cucumber, Eggplant, Green Bean, Common Bean, Melon, Pepper. Bell Pepper, Pumpkin, Tomatoes.

Used for
Hirsutella thompsonii is a fungus who can be applied on vegetables. It targets especially mites. Red Spider Mite. Two-spotted Mite

How to use
Use as a foliar spray against mite in standing crop at the time of mite appearance. Follow 2-3 foliar spray in the morning time by using high volume spray to cover both side of leaves at 15 days interval to control the mites.

Horsetail

Botanical name
Equisetum arvense, Equisetum telmateia

Class
Repellent

English name
Horsetail

Names in other languages
Horsetail (En). Prèles (Fr). Schachtelhalm (De).
Paardestaart (Nl).

Description
Horsetail (*Equisetum arvense* and or *Equisetum telmateia*) is a perennial plant growing everywhere in Europe on waste grounds, along the roads, and in dunes. *Equisetum arvense* creeps extensively with its slender and felted rhizomes that freely fork and bear tubers. The erect or prostrate sterile stems are 10–90 cm (3.9–35.4 in) tall and 3–5 mm (0.12–0.20 in) diameter, with jointed segments around 2–5 cm (0.79–1.97 in) long with whorls of side shoots at the segment joints; the side shoots have a diameter of about 1 mm (0.039 in). Some stems can have as many as 20 segments. The solid and simple branches are ascending or spreading, with sheaths that bear attenuate teeth. The off-white fertile stems are of a succulent texture, 10–25 cm (3.9–9.8 in) tall and 3–5 mm (0.12–0.20 in) diameter, with 4–8 whorls of brown scale leaves and an apical brown spore cone. The cone is 10–40 mm (0.39–1.57 in) long and 4–9 mm (0.16–0.35 in) broad.The fertile stems are typically precocious and appear in early spring. It absorbs silicon from the soil, which is rare among herbs.

Equisetum arvense

Treatment name
Horsetail decoction

Names in other languages
Horsetail decoction (En). Décoction prèles (Fr).
Schachtelhalm Pflanzenabsuds (De). Paardestaart decoctie (Nl).

Used on Vegetables
Artichoke, Asparagus. Beetroot, Beet. Broad Bean. Broccoli, Brussels Sprout, Cabbage. Carrot, Cauliflower, Celeriac, Celery, Chard, Courgette, Cucumber, Eggplant, Fennel, Garlic, Green Bean, Common Bean, Kohlrabi, Lamb's Lettuce, Leek, Lettuce, Melon, Napa/Chinese Cabbage, Onion, Parsnip, Peas, Pepper. Bell Pepper, Potato, Pumpkin, Radish, Romanesco Broccoli, Rutabaga, Spinach, Sweet Corn, Tomatoes, Turnip.

Used for
Gray Mold, Grey Mould, Botrytis Blight, Early Blight of Potato/Tomato, Damping Off, Anthracnose Fruit Rot, Bacterial Spot, Bacterial Canker of Tomato, Thistle Aphid, Onion and Leek Rust, White Rot. White Mold. Sclerotinia Wilt, Downy Mildew of Alliums. Rust, Verticillium Wilt, Downy Mildew of Crucifers, Celery Late Blight , Powdery Mildew, Anthracnose of Cucurbits, Scab of Cucurbits, Green Peach Aphid, Potato Aphid, Cotton Aphid, Red Spider Mite. Two-spotted Mite, Botrytis Rot. Neckrot

Preparation
Collect the whole plant. For 1 litre of water. Preferably rainwater. Use 100 grams of fresh horsetail or 25 grams of dried horsetail. Bring to a boil, reduce heat, cover and simmer for 30 minutes. Allow to cool and let infuse for about 12 hours. Filter the liquid through a sieve. The undiluted decoction can be stored for a few

weeks, in a cool and dark place, preferable in glass containers. Preparation time: One day.

How to use
Apply from early spring at bud break. By preference in the morning. Spray on plants. Diluted prior to utilisation. 1:20.

Treatment name
Liquid manure of horsetail

Names in other languages
Liquid manure of horsetail (EN), Purin de prêle (FR), Paardestaartgier (NL), Schachtelhalmjauche (DE).

Used on Vegetables
Artichoke, Asparagus. Beetroot, Beet. Broad Bean. Broccoli, Brussels Sprout, Cabbage. Carrot, Cauliflower, Celeriac, Celery, Chard, Citrus, Courgette, Cucumber, Eggplant, Fennel, Garlic, Green Bean, Common Bean, Kohlrabi, Lamb's Lettuce, Leek, Lettuce, Melon, Napa/Chinese Cabbage, Onion, Parsnip, Peas, Pepper. Bell Pepper, Potato, Pumpkin, Radish, Romanesco Broccoli, Rutabaga, Spinach, Tomatoes, Turnip.

Used for
Gray Mold, Grey Mould, Botrytis Blight, Damping Off, Onion and Leek Rust, Leek Moth, Onion Moth, Downy Mildew of Alliums, Rust, Downy Mildew of Crucifers, Powdery Mildew, Botrytis Rot, Neckrot.

Preparation
Commercially processed horsetail decoction can be purchased in garden centres, online or you can brew your own. Collect the whole plant, without the roots, broken or chopped into small bits. For 1 litre of water. Use non-chlorinated water like rainwater. Use 100 grams of fresh horsetail or 10 grams dried plants. Macerate for one to two weeks. Vigorously stir the mixture one or two times a day in order to guarantee a complete fermentation. Strain after fermentation is complete or no air bubbles form. The undiluted manure can be stored for a few weeks, in a cool and dark place, preferable in glass or plastic containers. Preparation time: Two weeks.

How to use
Spray on plants and soil. Diluted prior to utilisation at 20%. Repeat every 3 to 4 days, if necessary.

Hot Water Treatment of Seeds

Class
Cultural control practices

English name
Hot water treatment of seeds

Names in other languages
Hot water treatment of seeds (En). Traitement des semences à l'eau chaude (Fr). Heißwasserbehandlung die Samen (De). Heet water behandeling van zaden (Nl).

Description
Hot water seed treatment is a cheap and effective way to penetrate the seed and kill pathogens that might be present. The temperature of water for treating seed varies from 45 to 50°C (115 to 125°F), depending on the crop, and the treatment period varies from 10 to 60 minutes. It is important to use the appropriate protocol for each crop to control pathogens without damaging the seed.

Used on Vegetables
Asparagus, Celeriac, Celery, Lamb's Lettuce, Tomatoes

Used for
Phoma, Celery Root Rot.

How to use
Protocols are described and you can find hot-water treatment temperatures and timings per crop on the internet.

Insect-proof Net

Class
Cultural control practices

English name
Insect-proof net, Insect net, Mesh crop cover.

Names in other languages
Mesh Crop Cover (En). Filets anti-insectes (Fr). Insektendichten Netzen (De). Insectenwerend gaasafdekking (Nl).

Description
Insect-proof nets provides protection against insects as well as birds and hail. It can be used as floating row crop covers or hoop netting. Can be purchased from your garden centre or online or home made from your old net curtains.

Used on Vegetables
Beetroot, Beet. Broccoli, Brussels Sprout, Cabbage. Carrot, Cauliflower, Celeriac, Celery, Chard, Courgette, Eggplant, Fennel, Garlic, Green Bean, Common Bean, Kohlrabi, Lamb's Lettuce, Leek, Napa/Chinese Cabbage, Onion, Parsnip, Peas, Pepper. Bell Pepper, Potato, Radish, Romanesco Broccoli, Rutabaga, Spinach, Sweet Corn, Tomatoes, Turnip.

Used for
Seedcorn Maggot. Bean Seed Fly, Southern Green Stink bug, Tomato Leaf Miner, Onion Fly, Leek Moth, Onion Moth, Brachyserus of Garlic, Beet Fly, Mangold Fly, Cabbage Maggot, Cabbage Stem Flea Beetle, Carrot Fly, Celery Fly, Onion Maggot, Itersonilia Canker, Parsnip Canker, Pea Midge, Pea Moth, Mosaic Virus on Pepper. TMV. CMV, Turnip Maggot, Turnip Root Fly, Cabbage Fly, Cabbage Root Fly, Green Pentatomid Bug, Green Shield Bug, Green Stink Bug, Diamond-back Moth.

How to use
The key point to remember with insect barriers, mesh netting or otherwise, is to ensure that they cover the whole crop from top to bottom. Insects, even butterflies, will find any gap however small. The most common point of entry is where the mesh rests on the ground. If the mesh is wide enough the edges which touch the ground can be buried in soil but this makes removing the netting, for weeding etc., time consuming. Various pegs are sold to hold the netting in place on the ground but the best method is thin planks of wood laid onto flat ground, bricks also work well if you have enough of them.

Insectary Plants

Class
Cultural control practices

English name
Insectary plants

Names in other languages
Insectary plants (En). Plantes attractif a insectes (Fr). Pflanzen attraktive fur Insekten (De). Planten aantrekkelijk voor insecten (Nl).

Description
Insectary plants are those grown to attract, feed, and shelter insect parasites (parasitoids) and predators to enhance biological control. Insectary plants can provide an energy source and protein to naturally occurring beneficial insects, which help growers by attacking the pests that are attacking their crops. These plants flower quickly, giving the beneficial predators a food source throughout the season.

Insectary plants

Used on Vegetables
All

Used for
Insects

How to Use
Herbs like coriander, dill, lavender, fenne, lemon balm, parsley and spearmint attract natural enemies like green lacewings, lady beetles, flower flies, pirate bugs, damsel bugs, big eyed bugs and tachnid flies.

306

Install Insect Hotels

Class
Cultural control practices

English name
Install Insect hotels, Bug hotels or Insect houses.

Names in other languages
Insectary plants (En). Plantes attractif a insectes (Fr). Pflanzen attraktive fur Insekten (De). Planten aantrekkelijk voor insecten (Nl).

Description
An insect hotel, also known as a bug hotel or insect house, is a manmade structure created to provide shelter for insects. There are a number of good guides online written by entomologists and wild bee experts.

Install insect hotels

Used on Vegetables
Asparagus, Beetroot, Beet. Broccoli, Broad Bean, Cabbage. Carrot, Cauliflower, Chard, Cucumber, Eggplant, Garlic, Green Bean, Common Bean, Kohlrabi, Leek, Lettuce, Onion, Peas, Pepper. Bell Pepper, Potato, Radish, Rutabaga, Spinach, Tomatoes, Turnip.

Used for
Onion Fly, Asparagus Beetle, Twelve-spotted Asparagus Beetle, Green Artichoke Aphid, Beet Fly, Mangold Fly, Lettuce Root Aphid, Bean Aphids, Black Dolphin Aphids, Asparagus Aphid, Green Artichoke Aphid, Turnip Maggot, Turnip Root Fly, Cabbage Bug, Rape Bug, Crucifer Shield Bug, Brassica Bug, Lettuce Aphid, Current-lettuce Aphid, Potato Tuberworm, Potato Split-worm, Potato Tuber Moth, Cotton Worm, African Cotton Leafworm.

How to use
There is no standard design for an insect hotel. Just design with your available materials.

Iron Phosphate Granules

Class
Insecticide

English name
Iron Phosphate Granules. Ferric Phosphate Pellets

Names in other languages
Iron phosphate, also ferric phosphate (En). Phosphate de fer (Fr). Eisenphosphat (De). Ijzerfosfaat (Nl).

Description
iron phosphate is used in controlling snails and slugs on food crops and ornamentals at outdoor and indoor sites. Iron phosphate is a common chemical with a variety of uses, including as a human nutritional supplement and as an ingredient in fertiliser. The substance is not harmful to humans, to other not target organisms, or to the environment. It is an alternative to a more toxic chemical that has been used for controlling snails and slugs.

Used on Vegetables
Beetroot, Beet, Celeriac, Celery, Chard, Cucumber, Lettuce, Peas, Rutabaga, Spinach.

Used for:
Slug and Snail, Garden Slug, Loach, Little Grey Slug, Vine Snail, White Garden Snail.

How to use
Pellets are broadcast to the soil at planting time, and reapplied as needed.

Kaolin Clay Spray

Class
Cultural control practices

English name
Kaolin clay spray

Names in other languages
Kaolin clay spray (En). L'argile au kaolin pesticide (Fr). Kaolin Blattspritzung (De). Kaolien klei spuitmiddel (Nl).

Description
Kaolin clay repels pests by making the vegetable plant or fruit tree an unsuitable environment for certain insects to land, feed and lay eggs. The tiny clay particles serve to disguise the target fruit and can clog the eyes, ears and reproductive organs of many common pest insects like Colorado potato beetles, Cucumber beetles, Squash bugs, Flea beetles, Japanese Beetles, Codling Moths, Stink Bugs.

Used on Vegetables
Broad Bean, Cabbage, Cauliflower, Courgette, Cucumber, Eggplant, Green Bean. Common Bean, Leek, Onion, Peas, Pepper, Bell Pepper, Pumpkin, Tomatoes, Turnip.

Used for
Southern Green Stink bug, Onion Thrips, Thrips, Pea Thrips, Turnip Flea Beetle, Large Striped Flea Beetle, Striped Turnip Flea Beetle.

How to use
Mix in between 30 to 50 grams of kaolin clay with 1 litre of water. Reapply Kaolin clay for plants every 7 to 21 days for at least four weeks. Kaolin clay insect control should occur within three applications as long as sufficient and uniform spray has been achieved.

Lacewings
Predators

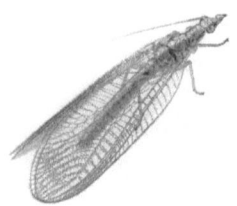

Botanical name
Chrysoperla carnea, Chrysoperla rufilabris

Class
Predators

English name
Lacewings

Names in other languages
Lacewings, Common green lacewing (En).
Chrysopes, Chrysope verte, Demoiselle aux yeux
d'or (Fr). Florfliegen (Chrysoperla) (De).
Gaasvliegen (Nl).

Description
The Lacewings (*Chrysoperla spp.)* larvae prey on
aphids, mites, scales, small caterpillars, thrips and
other soft-bodied insects as well as insect eggs.
Chrysoperla carnea (common green lacewing) is
an aphids predator very common in nature. Only
the larval stages can feed on aphids, while the
adult usually feeds on nectar, honeydew and other
sugar sources. The adult female lay eggs right in
the middle of an aphid colony, the larvae are pale
brown or grey and start preying after emergence.
The range of preys is very large and among them
mites, thrips, mealybugs, moth eggs and larvae
are the most common. A developing larva can
destroy more than 200 aphids. At 26°C constant it
takes about 20-25 days from egg to adult but
remarkably *C. carnea* shows a good flexibility to
temperature fluctuations even in field condition.
Even if the temperature reaches very low levels for
few hours, the larva can survive and start again
feeding as soon as a suitable condition returns.
They offer season on season benefits and work
well with most beneficial insects. Combine
lacewing releases with companion planting and
cover cropping to help keep adults around to lay
eggs for coming seasons.

Chrysoperla carnea

Used on Vegetables
Artichoke, Carrot, Courgette, Cucumber,
Eggplant, Green Bean, Common Bean, Leek,
Lettuce, Melon, Onion, Peas, Pepper, Bell Pepper,
Potato, Pumpkin, Spinach, Sweet Corn,
Tomatoes.

Used for
Tomato Russet Mite, Grain Aphid, Onion Thrips,
Thrips, Red Spider Mite, Two-spotted Mite,
European Red Mite.

How to use:
Depending on infestation of your plants chose
control systems by eggs, larvae or adults. If you
want to establish Green lacewing at the beginning
of the season or have a limited infestation, order
the appropriate numbers of eggs for your garden
or greenhouse. If you have a more severe
infestation, consider to order the larval stadium.
They provide the quickest means to control
unwanted pests with the larvae arriving ready to
feed. If you are treating a large area and want to
create standing populations, order adult lacewing.

Ladybird Predatory Beetle

Botanical name
Adalia bipunctata

Class
Predators

English name
Ladybird

Names in other languages
Ladybird (En). Coccinelle (Fr). Marienkäfer (De). Lieveheersbeestje (Nl).

Description
The two-spotted ladybirds *Adalia bipunctata* is a coccinellid beetle very common in nature and very efficient in aphids predation. *Adalia bipunctata* can be found with two main colour varieties. Most are red with two black spots but some are black with red spots. Egg to adult development takes place in around 3 weeks at 20-25°C in which 4 larval stages with different size and predation capacity can be found. L3 and L4 larvae can feed upon high quantities of prey but also adults are able to eat over 100 aphids.Adult females lay their eggs in a small bunch very close to aphid colonies so the newly hatched larvae can found enough food very easily. In the beginning small preys are preferred but later on predation of larger sizes and movement to a larger distance increase.

Adalia bipunctata

Used on Vegetables
Artichoke, Beetroot, Beet, Cabbage, Carrot, Courgette, Cucumber, Eggplant, Lettuce, Melon, Peas, Pepper, Bell Pepper, Potato, Pumpkin, Spinach, Sweet Corn, Tomatoes.

Used for
Thistle Aphid, Potato Aphid, Cotton Aphid, Grain Aphid, Cotton Whitefly, Tobacco Whitefly, Green Artichoke Aphid, Green Pentatomid Bug. Green Shield Bug. Green Stink Bug, Cotton Worm, African Cotton Leafworm.

How to use
Release adult ladybirds and larvae late spring or early summer on infested "hot spots" in your garden. Far more beneficial than purchasing lady beetles can be steps taken to conserve and enhance the activity of native species. Ladybugs eat two things: insect pests and pollen. They need both to survive and when these things are in abundance, ladybugs will happily relocate to your garden.

Lavender

Botanical name
Lavandula angustifolia (formerly named *L. officinalis*)

Class
Repellent

English name
Lavender

Names in other languages
Lavender (En). Lavande (Fr). Lavendel (De). Lavender (Nl).

Description
Lavender *(Lavandula angustifolia)* is a genus of 47 known species of flowering plants in the mint family, Lamiaceae. Leaf shape is diverse across the genus. They are simple in some commonly cultivated species; in other species they are pinnately toothed, or pinnate, sometimes multiple pinnate and dissected. In most species the leaves are covered in fine hairs or indumentum, which normally contain the essential oils. Flowers are borne in whorls, held on spikes rising above the foliage, the spikes being branched in some species. Some species produce coloured bracts at the apices. The flowers may be blue, violet or lilac in the wild species, occasionally blackish purple. The calyx is tubular. The corolla is also tubular, usually with five lobes (the upper lip often cleft, and the lower lip has two clefts).

Propagation
Lavender roots easily from stem cuttings. Layering and division of plants is easier than propagation by seeds.

Lavandula angustifolia

Treatment name
Lavender infusion

Names in other languages
Lavender infusion (En). Infusion lavande (Fr). Lavendel Pflanzenabsuds (De). Lavender infusie (Nl).

Used on Vegetables
Carrot, Celeriac, Fennel, Garlic, Leek, Onion, Parsnip.

Used for
The infusion made with lavender is used as repellent against ants, aphids and flies: Onion Fly, Carrot Fly.

Preparation
Collect the whole plant, without the roots. Chop the plant in very small pieces. For 1 litre of water. Use non-chlorinated water like rainwater. Use 100 grams of fresh lavender or 10 grams dried plants. Bring to a boil and cut the heat. Let cool down and infuse for 24 hours. Filter the liquid through a sieve. Decoction has to be used before it starts to ferment. Preparation time: Two days.

How to use
Spray on plants. Not diluted. Repeat every 6 to 7 days, if necessary.

Treatment name
Liquid manure of lavender

Names in other languages
Liquid manure of lavender (EN), Purin de lavende
(FR), Lavendelgier (NL), Lavendeljauche (DE).

Used on Vegetables
Carrot, Celeriac, Celery, Fennel, Parsnip.

Used for
The liquid manure made with lavender is used as
repellent against ants, aphids and fly: Carrot Fly,
Celery Fly.

Preparation
Collect the whole plant, without the roots, broken
or chopped into small bits. For 1 litre of water. Use
non-chlorinated water like rainwater. Use 100
grams of fresh lavender or 10 grams of dried
plants. Let macerate for one to two weeks. Stir or
shake the mixture regularly. Filter the liquid
through a sieve. Preparation time: Two weeks. The
undiluted manure can be stored for a few weeks,
in a cool and dark place, preferable in glass or
plastic containers.

How to use
Spray on plants. Diluted prior to utilisation at 20%.
Every 8 to 10 days, repeat , if necessary.

Lecanicillium muscarium

Botanical name
Lecanicillium muscarius *muscarium/Akanthomyces*

Class
Biopesticide

English name
Lecanicillium muscarium beneficial fungi/ Akanthomyces muscarius beneficial fungi

Names in other languages:
Lecanicillium muscarium/Akanthomyces muscarius. Beneficial fungi (En). Lecanicillium muscarium/Akanthomyces muscarius. Champignons bénéfiques (Fr). Lecanicillium muscarium/Akanthomyces muscarius. Nützliche Pilze (De). Lecanicillium muscarium/ Akanthomyces muscarius. Nuttige schimmels. (Nl).

Description
This fungus is known for its effectiveness in controlling various insect pests, including whitefly, aphids and thrips. *Lecanicillium muscarium* infects its target pests by penetrating their bodies through natural openings or by direct contact. Once inside the pest, the fungus grows and proliferates, ultimately leading to the death of the insect host. This process is often facilitated by the production of enzymes and toxins by the fungus, which weaken the pest's immune system and disrupt its normal physiological functions.

Used on Vegetables
Bean, Eggplant, Common bean, Peas, Tomatoes.

Used for
Pea thrips, Glasshouse whitefly

How to use
The efficacy of Lecanicillium depends on temperature and relative humidity conditions inside the crop canopy and the timing of application. The following conditions are required: It requires sufficient humidity inside the crop canopy for several hours after application for the spores to germinate and infest the pest. Spray at late afternoon and/or early evening.

Light Trap

Light trap

Class
Cultural control practices

English name
Light trap

Names in other languages
Light trap (En). Pièges lumineux (Fr). Lichtfallen (De). Lichtvallen (Nl).

Description
Light traps are widely used to survey nocturnal moths. Light traps can be purchased or locally made. To make a light trap use a jar or a bucket and place a white light at the top of the container with an inch or two of vegetable oil or a soap solution at the bottom of the jar or bucket. The container should be open so that the insects can fly in towards the light. They will fall into the oil or solution below and be unable to fly away again. Light traps are not selective of insects and hence may harm the advantageous insects too. Usually used on nocturnal insects.

Used on Vegetables
Beetroot. Beet, Lettuce, Potato, Spinach, Sweet Corn.

Used for
June Beetles, May Beetles, Green Pentatomid Bug. Green Shield Bug. Green Stink Bug.

How to use
Usually 5 to 10 light traps per hectare, or 2 to 4 traps per acre.

Lithothamnion Algae

Class
Cultural control practices

English name
Lithothamnion algae. Calcified Seaweed. Maerl

Names in other languages
Lithothamnium algae (En). Lithothamne. Maërl (Fr). Kalkalgen (De). Kalkwier (Nl).

Description
Lithothamnion calcareum or maerl or calcified seaweed consists of about 50% calcium, 5-10% magnesium carbonate and a wide range of beneficial trace elements: Zinc, Copper, Sulphur, Iron, Manganese, Cobalt, Boron, which may be lacking in some soils. It can be incorporated into the compost or used directly on acidic soils or used as powder application to improve the development of the plant and its self-defence capabilities. The lithotamnion dust on the plant creates a thin layer of limestone particles which is an obstacle for the mouthparts of insects that feed on the green parts of the plant and for the penetration of pathogens. Maerl should be considered as a non-renewable resource.

Used on Vegetables
Artichoke, Beetroot. Beet, Broad Bean, Broccoli, Brussels Sprout, Cabbage, Carrot, Cauliflower, Celeriac, Celery, Chard, Courgette, Cucumber, Eggplant, Fennel, Garlic, Green Bean, Common Bean, Kohlrabi, Lamb's Lettuce, Leek, Lettuce, Melon, Napa/Chinese Cabbage, Onion, Parsnip, Peas, Potato, Pumpkin, Radish, Romanesco Broccoli, Rutabaga, Spinach, Tomatoes, Turnip.

Used for
Damping Off, Ascochyta Rot, Black Rot, Leaf Spot, Powdery Mildew, Boron Deficiency, Molybdenum Deficiency, Whiptail.

How to use
Dust the plants 2 or 3 times with Maerl powder. As soil improver use about 25 kg per 1000 square meter, avoid using it on alkalic soils (pH > 7).

Warning
Do not apply lithothamnion on windy days.

Long Rotation Crop Rotation

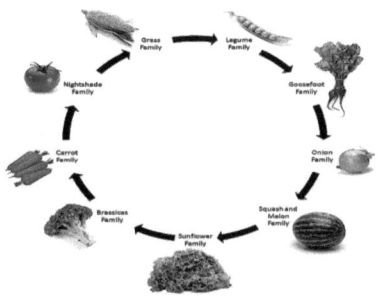

Crop Rotation

Class
Cultural control practices

English name
Long Rotation. Crop Rotation

Names in other languages
Crop Rotation (En). Rotation des cultures (Fr). Fruchtfolge (De). Vruchtwisseling (Nl).

Description
Crop Rotation is the practice of growing specific groups of vegetables on a different part of the garden each year. This helps to reduce a build-up of crop-specific pest and disease problems. Carefully selected rotations, can greatly assist control of plant diseases and nematodes. Many pests and diseases are plant family specific. By rotating crops between sites these pests tend to decline in the period when their host plants are absent which helps reduce build-up of damaging populations of spores, eggs and pests.

Used on Vegetables
All

Used for
Anthracnose Fruit Rot, Bacterial Spot, Onion Fly, White Rot, White Mold, Sclerotinia Wilt, Basal Rot, Stem Nematode, Bulb and Stem Nematode, Beet Fly, Mangold Fly, Cabbage Club Root, Violet Root Rot, Click Beetle. Striped Elaterid Beetle. Wireworms, Celery Late Blight, Powdery Mildew, Fusarium Wilt, Anthracnose of Cucurbits, Scab of Cucurbits, Maize Smut, Corn Smut, Cercosporosa Leaf Spot, Phoma, Onion Maggot, Bean Yellow Mosaic Virus. BYMV, Bacterial Brown Spot, Botrytis Rot, Neckrot, Onion Smut, Smut of Onion, Itersonilia Canker, Parsnip Canker, Black Scurf, Rhizoctonia Canker, Stem Canker, Potato Tuber Nematode, Potato Cyst Nematode, Fusarium Root Rot, Potato Scab, Strawberry Root Weevils, Carrot Root Nematode, Carrot Cyst Nematode, Pea Root Nematode, Pea Cyst Nematode, Cabbage and Cauliflower Cyst Nematode. Brassica Cyst Nematode, Potato Tuberworm, Potato, Split-worm, Potato Tuber Moth, Turnip Flea Beetle, Large Striped Flea Beetle, Striped Turnip Flea Beetle, Diamond-back Moth, Black Rot of Cabbage, Leaf Blight of Maize, Soft rot, White Rot on Carrot, Cottony rot, White Root-rot, Bacterial Blight, Pea Bacterial Blight, Lettuce bacterial rot.

How to use
Do not plant the same vegetables in the same place year after year.

Macrolophus Predatory Bug

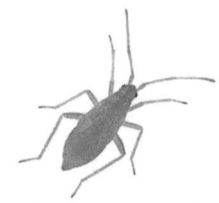

Botanical name
Macrolophus pygmaeus/Macrolophus caliginosus

Class
Predators

English name
Macrolophus   caliginosus/M.   pygmaeus.
Predatory bug

Names in other languages
Macrolophus predatory bug (En). Macrolophus punaises prédatrices (Fr). Macrolophus Raubwanze (De). Macrolophus roofwantsen (Nl).

Description
Macrolophus pygmaeus (formerly known as M. caliginosus) is a predatory mirid bug very common in the Mediterranean Basin in which it can overwinter. All stages are very mobile and can prey on different whiteflies. All different stages of the pest are a good food source for larvae and adults. The adults are pale green with a whitish hairiness while larvae are completely green with red eyes. Macrolophus survives even with low food available and once established can resist to bad conditions and is capable to prey even with fluctuation of high and low temperature. Other food sources like aphids, mites, leafminer and moth eggs could be very important for its development. The development of young stages could take a very long time in unsuitable conditions. While at 25°C, 30 days are needed to complete egg to adult development, at 15° C it takes more than 90 days.

Macrolophus pygmaeus

Used on Vegetables
Artichoke, Asparagus, Beetroot, Beet, Broccoli, Brussels Sprout, Cabbage, Carrot, Cauliflower, Celeriac, Celery, Courgette, Cucumber, Eggplant, Fennel, Green Bean. Common Bean, Kohlrabi, Leek, Lettuce, Melon, Napa/Chinese Cabbage, Onion, Peas, Pepper, Bell Pepper, Potato, Pumpkin, Radish, Romanesco Broccoli, Rutabaga, Spinach, Sweet Corn , Tomatoes, Turnip.

Used for
Macrolophus caliginosus is a highly polyphagous predatory bug, which has proven to be effective in controlling many insect pests of greenhouse vegetables especially whiteflies, aphids, and thrips. Glasshouse Whitefly. Greenhouse Whitefly, Tomato Leaf Miner, Thistle Aphid, Cabbage Aphid, Green Peach Aphid, Potato Aphid, Cotton Aphid, Grain Aphid, Hawthorn Aphids, Onion Thrips. Thrips

How to use
Macrolophus predatory bug should be introduced very early in the season even with low or no whitefly detection. A multiple introduction (1 to 3 individuals per square metre are recommended) could help to get a good population density.

Manage Soil Conditions

Class
Cultural control practices

English name
Manage soil conditions

Names in other languages
Manage soil conditions (En). Gérer les conditions du sol (Fr). Bodenbedingungen verwalten (De). Bodemomstandigheden beheren (Nl).

Description
Creating an healthy environment for your plants. By environment, we mean the chemical, physical, and biological components of your soil and increasing soil health. The pH level of your soil. Soil organic carbon. Nutrient availability. Microbial activity. Water holding capacity. Cation exchange capacity. Soil texture and structure If properly cared for, your soil can create an environment that is non-conducive to pathogen growth. Without a conducive environment, plant disease less probable.

Used on Vegetables
All

Used for
Soil borne diseases

How to use
Avoid working wet soil, limit compaction from equipment, and incorporate cover crops with fibrous root systems to maintain an healthy environment for your plants.

Micronised Sulphur

Class
Fungicide

English name
Micronised Sulphur

Names in other languages
Micronized sulphur (En). Soufre micronisé (Fr). Mikronisierten Schwefel (De). Gemicroniseerde zwavel (Nl).

Description
Micronised sulphur is a micronised dust that can be applied dry or mixed with water for a wet application. Dusting sulphur is applied to crops with a sulphur duster. See also wettable sulphur, who is the commercial name for dusting sulfur formulated with additional ingredients to make it water miscible.

Used on Vegetables
Asparagus, Beetroot, Beet, Carrot, Celeriac, Celery, Chard, Green Bean, Common Bean, Leek, Lettuce, Melon, Pepper, Bell Pepper, Potato, Sweet Corn, Tomatoes.

Used for
Cercosporosa Leaf Spot

How to use
Always follow label instructions and take steps to avoid exposure.

Milky Spore

Botanical name
Paenibacillus popilliae

Class
Biopesticide

English name
Milky spore bacterium

Names in other languages
Milky spore bacterium (En). Milky spore bactérie (Fr). Milky spore Bakterie (De). Milky spore bacterie (Nl).

Description
Paenibacillus popilliae (formerly Bacillus popilliae) is a soil-dwelling bacterium. It is responsible for a disease commonly called milky spore of the white grubs of Japanese beetles.

Used on Vegetables
Beetroot, Beet, Lettuce, Potato, Spinach, Sweet Corn

Used for
June Beetles, May Beetles, Japanese Beetle Grubs (Popillia japonica)

How to use
The best time of year to use the product is fall, when the grubs are feeding aggressively. Although the grubs are in the soil year round, it only works when they are actively feeding. Apply milky spore correctly is important for effective control. Place a teaspoon of milky spore powder on the lawn, spacing the applications about four feet apart to form a grid. Don't spread or spray the powder. Water it in with a gentle spray from a hose for about 15 minutes. Once the powder is watered in, you can safely mow or walk on the lawn. One application is all it takes.

Nesidiocoris Predatory Bug

Botanical name
Nesidiocoris tenuis

Class
Predators

English name
Nesidiocoris tenuis predatory bug

Names in other languages
Nesidiocoris tenuis predatory bug (En). Punaises prédatrices Nesidiocoris tenuis (Fr). Nesidiocoris tenuis Raubwanze (De). Nesidiocoris tenuis roofwantsen (Nl).

Nesidiocoris tenuis

Used on Vegetables
Eggplant, Pepper, Bell Pepper, Tomatoes.

Description
Nesidiocoris tenuis predatory bug is closely related to *Macrolophus pygmaeus* and shares similar behaviour and prey range. Both adults and nymphs have a large appetite and feed on several species of insects and mites. The eggs and larvae of whitefly are its primary prey, but it also feeds on the eggs of the South American leafminer *Tuta absoluta*. Once its population is at full strength, it turns into a highly efficient predator, safeguarding the crop against unexpected infestations.

Used for
The predatory bug (Nesidiocoris tenuis) develop rapidly on whitefly and Tomato leaf miner. It also feeds on spider mite, moth eggs and thrips and, to a lesser extent, aphids and leaf miner larvae. Tomato Leaf Miner

How to use
In order to optimise control of whitefly, a combined release with whitefly parasitoids is the best strategy.

Nettle

Botanical name
Urtica dioica

Class
Repellent

English name
Common nettle, Stinging nettle

Names in other languages
Nettle (En). Ortie (Fr). Brennnessel (De). Brandnetel Nl).

Description
Urtica dioica is a dioecious, herbaceous, perennial plant, 1 to 2 m (3 to 7 ft) tall in the summer and dying down to the ground in winter. It has widely spreading rhizomes and stolons, which are bright yellow, as are the roots. The soft, green leaves are 3 to 15 cm (1 to 6 in) long and are borne oppositely on an erect, wiry, green stem. The leaves have a strongly serrated margin, a cordate base, and an acuminate tip with a terminal leaf tooth longer than adjacent laterals. It bears small, greenish or brownish, numerous flowers in dense axillary inflorescences. The leaves and stems are very hairy with non-stinging hairs, and many stinging hairs, whose tips come off when touched, transforming the hair into a needle that can inject several chemicals causing a painful sting.

Propagation
Nettle can be propagated by seeds or vegetatively by divisions.

Urtica dioica

Treatment name
Nettle infusion

Names in other languages
Nettle infusion (En). Infusion de l'ortie (Fr). Brennnessel infusion (De). Brandnetel infusie (Nl)..

Used on Vegetables
Artichoke, Beetroot. Beet, Cabbage, Carrot, Courgette, Cucumber, Eggplant, Green Bean. Common Bean, Lettuce, Melon, Peas, Pepper. Bell Pepper, Potato, Pumpkin, Spinach, Tomatoes.

Used for
The common nettle or stinging nettle infusion is a repellent against mites and aphids. Tomato Russet Mite, Thistle Aphid, Green Peach Aphid, Potato Aphid, Cotton Aphid, Red Spider Mite, Two-spotted Mite.

Preparation
Collect the whole plant, without the roots, broken or chopped into small bits. For 1 litre of water. Use non-chlorinated water like rainwater. Use 100 grams of fresh nettles. or 10 grams dried plants. Bring to a boil and cut the heat. Let cool down and infuse for 24 hours. Filter the liquid through a sieve. Nettle infusion has to be used before it starts to ferment. Preparation time: Two days.

How to use
As a spray on plants and soil. Diluted prior to utilisation in between 10 to 20%. Repeat every 6 to 7 days, if necessary.

Treatment name
Liquid manure of nettle

Names in other languages
Liquid manure of nettle (EN), Purin de l'ortie (FR), Brandnetelgier (NL), Brennesseljauche (DE).

Used on Vegetables
Artichoke, Asparagus, Beetroot. Beet, Broad Bean, Broccoli, Brussels Sprout, Cabbage, Carrot, Cauliflower, Celeriac, Celery, Chard, Courgette, Cucumber, Eggplant, Fennel, Garlic, Green Bean. Common Bean, Kohlrabi, Lamb's Lettuce, Leek, Lettuce, Melon, Napa/Chinese Cabbage, Onion, Parsnip, Peas, Pepper. Bell Pepper, Potato, Pumpkin, Radish, Romanesco Broccoli, Rutabaga, Spinach, Sweet Corn , Tomatoes, Turnip

Used for
Liquid manure of nettle is used for deficiency of oligo-elements repellent of whitefly, aphids and fungi: Chlorosis, Damping Off, Anthracnose Fruit Rot, Glasshouse Whitefly. Greenhouse Whitefly, Verticillium Wilt, Cabbage Stem Flea Beetle, Cabbage Aphid, Powdery Mildew, Boron Deficiency, Scab of Cucurbits, Cladosporium Leaf Spot

Preparation
Collect the whole plant, without the roots, broken or chopped into small bits. For 10 litre of water. Use non-chlorinated water like rainwater. Use 1 kg of fresh nettles or 100 to 200 g of dried nettles. Let macerate for 2-4 weeks. Stir the mixture well at least once a day. Strain to remove the small fibres. The undiluted manure can be stored for a few weeks, in a cool and dark place, preferable in glass or plastic containers. Preparation time: 2–4 weeks

How to use
Liquid manure of nettle can be sprayed directly onto the leaves of plants as repellent or on the ground around the plants as liquid fertiliser. 10%–20% dilution. Repeat every 6 to 7 days, if necessary.

No-Till

Class
Cultural control practices

English name
No-till

Names in other languages
No-till (En). Sans labour (Fr). Direktsaat (De).
Zonder grondbewerking (Nl).

Description
Increased tillage is associated with increased
numbers of bean seed fly larvae and minimum
tillage may help to manage the pest. Furthermore,
there is some evidence that leaving a period of at
least seven days between latest cultivation and
drilling may help to reduce levels of damage
caused by larvae.

Used on Vegetables
Green bean, Common bean, Lamb's lettuce.
Spinach, Sweet corn, Tomatoes.

Used for
Seedcorn Maggot. Bean Seed Fly.

How to use
Avoid planting for at least two weeks after fresh
organic materials have been incorporated into
soil.

Orius Pirate Bug

Botanical name
Orius insidiosus

Class
Predators

English name
Orius insidiosus pirate bug

Names in other languages
Orius insidiosus pirate bug (En). Orius insidiosus punaise prédatrice (Fr). Orius insidiosus Raubwanze (De). Orius insidiosus roofwants (Nl).

Description
Orius insidiosus, common name the insidious flower bug, is a species of minute pirate bug, a predatory insect. They are considered beneficial, as they feed on small pest arthropods and their eggs. They are mass-reared for use in the biological control of thrips. The predator can be purchased in garden centres or online and released in- or outdoors.

Orius insidiosus

Used on Vegetables
Artichoke, Broad Bean, Courgette, Cucumber, Eggplant, Green Bean, Common Bean, Leek, Onion, Peas, Pumpkin, Tomatoes.

Used for
Onion Thrips. Thrips, Green Artichoke Aphid, Pea Thrips.

How to use
For maintenance, release 1 to 2 Orius per plant in greenhouses or 1 to 4 Orius per plant in hot spot areas outdoors. For treatment a serious infection by whitefly, aphid, thrips or other pest infestation, releasing up to 500 Orius per 250 sq. ft. area. For field crops, releasing between 100 and 2,000 Orius per acre, depending on the level of infestation.

Pachycrepoideus Parasitic Wasp

Botanical name
Pachycrepoideus vindemmiae

Class
Predators

English name
Pachycrepoideus vindemmiae parasitic wasps

Names in other languages
Pachycrepoideus vindemmiae parasitic wasps (EN), *Pachycrepoideus vindemmiae* guêpes parasites (FR), *Pachycrepoideus vindemmiae* sluipwesp (NL), *Pachycrepoideus vindemmiae* parasitische Wespe (DE).

Description
Pachycrepoideus vindemmiae is an insect of the family of bees and wasps used against Drosophila suzukii the spotted wing drosophila, a fruit fly.

Pachycrepoideus vindemmiae

Used on Vegetables
Cabbage, Radish, Turnip.

Used for
Cabbage Fly. Cabbage Root Fly

How to use
See instructions of provider.

Phasmarhabditis Nematode

Botanical name
Phasmarhabditis hermaphrodita

Class
Predators

English name
Phasmarhabditis hermaphrodita Nematode

Names in other languages
Phasmarhabditis hermaphrodita Nematode (En).
Nématode Phasmarhabditis hermaphrodita (Fr).
Phasmarhabditis hermaphrodita Nematode (De).
Phasmarhabditis hermaphrodita aaltjes (Nl).

Description
Phasmarhabditis hermaphrodita nematode was developed into a natural molluscicide to prevent crop damage from horticultural slug pests. *Phasmarhabditis hermaphrodita* nematodes enters the slug while it's below ground. The slug stops eating within a few days, and dies within a week. The nematodes feed off the decomposing slug and reproduce, creating a new generation to move on and infect more slugs.

Used on Vegetables
Beetroot, Beet, Celeriac, Celery, Chard, Cucumber, Lettuce, Peas, Rutabaga, Spinach.

Used for
Slug and Snail. Garden Slug. Loach. Little Grey Slug. Vine Snail. White Garden Snail

How to use
The nematodes are sold as infective juveniles approximately 1 mm long, which can be just seen with the naked eye. The infective juveniles are formulated onto clays or gels that can be added to water and applied with conventional spray equipment.

Warning
It only kill slugs and snails and does not harm non-target organisms like earthworms, insects & acarids.

Pheromone Traps

Class
Cultural control practices

English name
Pheromone traps

Names in other languages
Pheromone traps (En). Pièges à phéromones (Fr). Pheromonfallen (De). Feromoonvallen (Nl).

Description
A pheromone trap consists of a small glue trap that is impregnated with sex pheromone or it comes with a small vial of sex pheromone that will be placed on the trap. Sex pheromones are hormones scents that are emitted by the female insect. Male pests are attracted to the trap for the purpose of mating and are then caught. There are many different traps on the market, each geared toward specific pests. Pheromones are frequently used to monitor and control lepidopteran and coleopteran species, with many available commercially.

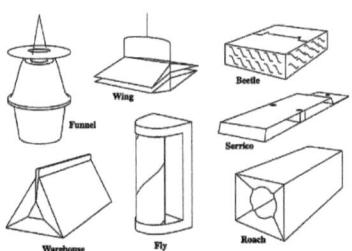

Pheromone traps

Used on Vegetables
Artichoke, Asparagus, Beetroot, Beet, Broad Bean, Broccoli, Brussels Sprout, Cabbage, Carrot, Cauliflower, Celery, Eggplant, Green Bean. Common Bean, Kohlrabi, Leek, Lettuce, Napa/Chinese Cabbage, Onion, Peas, Pepper, Bell Pepper, Potato, Radish, Romanesco Broccoli, Rutabaga, Spinach, Sweet Corn , Tomatoes, Turnip.

Used for
Artichoke Moth. Artichoke Plume Moth, Tomato Fruitworm. Old World Bollworm, Cabbage Maggot, Click Beetle. Striped Elaterid Beetle. Wireworms, Bean Beetle. Pea beetle, Pea Weevil. Pea and Bean Weevil, Pea Moth, Dark Sword-grass Moth. Black cutworm. Greasy cutworm, Silver-Y moth, Common Silver-Y moth, Cabbage Army Moth. Potato Tuberworm, Potato Split-worm. Potato Tuber Moth, Beet Armyworm, Diamond-back Moth, Bright-line Brown-eyes Moth, Cotton Worm. African Cotton Leafworm.

How to use
Follow instructions of manufacturer.

Physical Barriers

Class
Cultural control practices

English name
Physical barriers

Names in other languages
Physical barriers (En). Barrières physiques (Fr).
Physische Barrieren (De). Fysieke barrières (Nl).

Description
Create barriers with slug collars, grit, wool pellets, and cloches made from plastic bottles. Granular barriers – you may see recommendations to use various materials like diatomaceous earth, sawdust, powdered lime, crushed eggshells and wood ash. In our experience these are not very effective. To have any chance of working the material needs to be applied as a continuous thick band around a plant and be kept dry in order to protect plants. Even in these conditions we've often seen snails slide right over the material. Lastly while salt will kill them it is also bad for soil health and should not be used.

Used on Vegetables
Beetroot, Celeriac, Celery, Chard, Cucumber, Lettuce, Peas, Rutabaga, Spinach.

Used for
Slug and Snail.

How to use
Barriers of dry diatomaceous earth, heaped in a band 1 inch high and 3 inches wide around the garden, can also be effective. However, these barriers lose their effectiveness after becoming damp, making them difficult to maintain and not very useful in most garden situations. Crushed egg shells or coffee grounds have not been shown to be effective deterrents.

Phytoseiulus Predatory Mite

Botanical name
Phytoseiulus persimilis

Class
Predators

English name
Phytoseiulus persimilis predatory mite

Names in other languages
Phytoseiulus persimilis predatory mite (En).
Phytoseiulus persimilis acariens prédateurs (Fr).
Phytoseiulus persimilis Raubmilben (De).
Phytoseiulus persimilis roofmijt (Nl).

Description
The predatory mite (*Phytoseiulus persimilis*) is commonly used for pest control of red spider mite. Adult predatory mites and nymphs search actively for their prey and suck them dry. The Phytoseiulus adult females with the typical pear-shaped body are shiny orange, very mobile and slightly bigger than a red spider mite. Development of young stages is very quick and at 20°C takes less than 10 days while in the same conditions the pest needs almost 18 days to reach the adult stage. The predator has a good searching capability and walk rapidly especially when food is scarce even if the plant canopy could influence its action and walking speed.

Phytoseiulus persimilis

Used on Vegetables
Artichoke, Carrot, Courgette, Cucumber, Eggplant, Green Bean, Common Bean, Melon, Pepper, Bell Pepper, Pumpkin, Tomatoes.

Used for
Phytoseiulus persimilis is a predatory mite for the control of the Red Spider Mite in a wide range of protected and open field crops. Red Spider Mite, Two-spotted Mite, Rust Mite.

How to use
Phytoseiulus is dispatched as nymphs and adults which should be released in sheltered positions on infested plants. It is recommended to start the release programme very early when the first signs of infestation are detected.

Pseudomonas chlororaphis

Botanical name
Pseudomonas chlororaphis

Class
Biopesticide

English name
Pseudomonas chlororaphis Beneficial bacteria

Names in other languages
Pseudomonas chlororaphis Beneficial bacteria (En). Pseudomonas chlororaphis Bactéries bénéfiques (Fr). Pseudomonas chlororaphis Nützliche Bakterien (De). Pseudomonas chlororaphis Nuttige bacteriën (Nl).

Description
Beneficial bacteria. Biological seed dressing to control seed-borne fungal diseases in vegetable crops (carrots, peas, spinach, arugula, dill, parsley, red cabbage, white cabbage, turnip) against seed-borne fungal diseases; fusarium wilt (Fusarium spp.), grey mold (Botrytis spp.), blight (Ascochyta pisi). Controls also Acrothecium rot (Pseudocercosporidium carotea).

Used on Vegetables
Artichoke. Broccoli, Brussels Sprout, Cabbage, Cauliflower, Courgette, Cucumber, Eggplant, Green bean, Common bean, Kohlrabi, Lamb'slettuce, Lettuce, Melon, Napa, Peas, Pepper, Potato, Pumpkin, Rutabaga, Tomatoes, Turnip.

Used for
Grey Mold, Botrytis Blight

How to use
Pseudomonas chlororaphis is effective under a wide range of conditions, including cold environments, and is easy to use, being compatible with existing seed-treatment equipment. With its targeted approach, Pseudomonas chlororaphis is a future-proof solution against seed-borne diseases, offering reliable protection for many crops.

Pyrethrum Insecticide

Botanical name:
Tanacetum cinerariifolium

Class
Insecticide

English name
Insecticide based on pyrethrum

Names in other languages
Insecticide based on pyrethrum (En). Insecticide à base de pyrèthre (Fr). Pyrethrum Insektizide (De). Insecticide pyrethrum (Nl).

Description
Pyrethrin naturally occurs in chrysanthemum flowers (*Chrysanthemum cinerariifolium/ Tanacetum cinerariifolium*), since it is directly extracted from a plant, and since it is considered nontoxic to humans, pyrethrum is approved for use on organic farms, or at least when it is not combined with piperonyl butoxide or other synthetic adjuvants. Pyrethrum is highly toxic to most insects. This means that it's effective against the pests, but it's also deadly to the beneficial insects that pollinate your vegetables and help out by eating those pests.

Used on Vegetables
Artichoke, Asparagus, Beetroot, Beet, Broad Bean, Broccoli, Brussels Sprout, Cabbage, Carrot, Cauliflower, Celeriac, Celery, Chard, Courgette, Cucumber, Eggplant, Fennel, Garlic, Green Bean, Common Bean, Kohlrabi, Leek, Lettuce, Melon, Napa/Chinese Cabbage, Onion, Peas, Pepper, Bell Pepper, Potato, Pumpkin, Radish, Romanesco Broccoli, Rutabaga, Spinach, Sweet Corn , Tomatoes, Turnip.

Used for
Glasshouse Whitefly. Greenhouse Whitefly, Thistle Aphid, Leek Moth, Onion Moth, Asparagus Beetle, Twelve-spotted Asparagus Beetle, Green Artichoke Aphid, Colorado Potato Beetle, Cabbage Maggot, Cabbage Stem Flea Beetle, Cabbage Aphid, Bean Aphids, Black Dolphin Aphids, Green Peach Aphid, Potato Aphid, Cotton Aphid, Grain Aphid, Onion Thrips, Thrips, Onion Maggot, Pea Midge, Pea Moth, Cabbageworm, Imported Cabbage Worms, Beet Armyworm, Bean Bruchid, Pea Aphid. Green Pea Louse, Asparagus Aphid, Turnip Maggot, Turnip Root Fly, Pea Thrips, Tomato Fruitworm, Old World Bollworm, Celery Miner Fly, American Serpentine

Tanacetum cinerariifolium

Leaf Miner, Lettuce Aphid, Current-lettuce Aphid, Potato Tuberworm, Potato Split-worm, Potato Tuber Moth, Beet Moth, Turnip Moth.

How to use
Follow label instructions during the application, wear gloves and protective coverings, and repeat applications as needed. In the presence of sunlight, pyrethrins breaks down rapidly in water and on soil and plant surfaces.

Warning
Pyrethrins are practically non-toxic to birds but highly toxic to honey bees. Pyrethrins are highly to very highly toxic to fish. They are also very highly toxic to lobster, shrimp, oysters, and aquatic insects.

Pyrethrum Plant

Botanical name
Tanacetum   cinerariifolium/Chrysanthemum cinerariifolium/Chrysanthemum coccineum

Class
Repellent

English name
Pyrethrum

Names in other languages
Pyrethrum (EN), Pyrèthre (FR), Pyrethrum (NL), Pyrethrum (DE)

Description
Pyrethrum continues to be used as a common name for *Tanacetum cinerariifolium*. It is a species of flowering plant in the aster family, Asteraceae. It is called the Dalmatian chrysanthemum, denoting its origin in that region of the Balkans (Dalmatia). It looks more like the common daisy than other pyrethrums do. Its flowers, typically white with yellow centres, grow from numerous fairly rigid stems. Plants have blue-green leaves and grow to 45 to 100 cm (18 to 39 in) in height. The plant is economically important as a natural source of an insecticide called "pyrethrum." The flowers are pulverised and the active components, called pyrethrins, contained in the seed cases, are extracted and sold in the form of an oleoresin. This is applied as a suspension in water or oil, or as a powder. Pyrethrins attack the nervous systems of all insects, and inhibit female mosquitoes from biting. When present in amounts less than those fatal to insects, they still appear to have an insect repellent effect. They are harmful to fish, but are far less toxic to mammals and birds than many synthetic insecticides and are not persistent, being biodegradable and also decompose easily on exposure to light. They are considered to be amongst the safest insecticides for use around food.

Tanacetum cinerariifolium

Treatment name
Liquid manure of pyrethrum

Names in other languages
Liquid manure of pyrethrum (EN), Purin de pyrèthre   (FR),   Pyrethrumgier   (NL), Pyrethrumjauche (DE).

Used on Vegetables
Asparagus, Carrot, Celeriac, Eggplant, Fennel, Parsnip, Pepper. Bell Pepper, Tomatoes.

Used for
Glasshouse Whitefly, Greenhouse Whitefly, Tomato Russet Mite, Carrot Fly.

Preparation
Collect the flowers. For 1 litre of water. Use non-chlorinated water like rainwater. Use 100 grams of fresh flowers or 7 to 10 grams of dried flowers. Macerate for one to two weeks. Stir or shake the mixture regularly. Strain after fermentation is complete or no air bubbles form. The undiluted manure can be stored for a few weeks, in a cool and dark place, preferable in glass or plastic containers. Preparation time: Two weeks.

How to use
Spray on plants. Diluted prior to utilisation at 20%. Every 3 to 4 days. Repeat if necessary.

Warning
Not to be ingested. Wear gloves, mask and protective clothing.

Ramial
Chipped Wood

Class
Cultural control practices

English name
R.C.W (Ramial Chipped Wood)

Names in other languages
R.C.W (Ramial Chipped Wood) (En). Bois raméal fragmenté (BRF) (Fr). Holzhackgut (De). Houtsnippers (Nl).

Description
Adding Ramial chipped wood (R.C.W.) to the soil and as mulch seems to increase yield, water availability, pest and disease control, as well as frost and drought resistance.

Used on Vegetables
Asparagus

Used for
Violet Root-rot of Asparagus

How to use
Spread the ramial chipped wood in a layer, 2 to 5 cm thick, atop your soils.

Raise Soil pH

Class
Cultural control practices

English name
Raise your soil pH

Names in other languages
Raise your soil pH (En). Augmenter le pH du sol (Fr). Erhöhen des pH Boden (De). Verhoog pH bodem (Nl).

Description
Raise your soil's pH to a more alkaline 7.2 pH by mixing oyster shell or dolomite lime into your garden in the fall. Simple and affordable soil test kits are available to check pH often.

Used on Vegetables
Broccoli, Brussels Sprout, Cabbage, Cauliflower, Kohlrabi, Napa/Chinese Cabbage, Romanesco Broccoli, Rutabaga, Turnip.

Used for
Cabbage Club Root

How to use
Ground agricultural limestone is used to raise the soil pH, or wood ashes can be used to raise the soil pH.

Remove Ants

Class
Cultural control practices

English name
Remove ants

Names in other languages
Remove ants (En). Eliminer les fourmis (Fr). Vernichten Ameisen (De). Verwijder mieren (Nl).

Description
Anytime you see a large number of ants on a tree or plant, it is likely you have a large infestation of aphids. Managing ants is one way of controlling the aphid population. Aphids are sucking insects that are common on both outdoor and indoor plants. They feed on the sap of plants and secrete a substance called honeydew. This sticky resin is a favorite food of ants, who actually "milk" the aphids for it by stroking their abdomen. The relationship between aphids and ants is symbiotic in that both receive some benefit from the arrangement. Ants protect the aphids from predators, such as lacewings and ladybugs.

Remove ants

Used on Vegetables
Artichoke, Carrot, Celeriac, Celery, Fennel, Green Bean. Common Bean, Lettuce.

Used for
Lettuce Root Aphid.

How to use
Ant bait stations are effective because the ants take the bait and bring it back to the main colony or wrap the plant or tree with sticky tape or netting.

Remove Aphids

Class
Cultural control practices

English name
Remove aphids

Names in other languages
Remove aphids (En). Détruire les pucerons (Fr). Vernichten Blattläuse (De). Verwijder bladluizen (NI).

Description
The majority of viruses infecting plants are spread by insects, and aphids are the most common group of virus vectors or carriers.

Remove aphids

Used on Vegetables
Artichoke, Beetroot, Beet, Celeriac, Celery, Chard, Courgette, Cucumber, Eggplant, Green Bean, Common Bean, Lettuce, Melon, Peas, Pepper, Bell Pepper, Potato, Pumpkin, Spinach, Sweet Corn, Tomatoes.

Used for
Tomato Chlorosis Crinivirus. ToCV, Tobacco Mosaic Virus. TMV, Cucumber Mosaic Virus. CMV, Beet Curly Top Virus. BCTV, Bean Yellow Mosaic Virus. BYMV, Mosaic Virus on Pepper. TMV. CMV, Potato Leaf-drop Streak. Potato Virus Y, Potato Leaf Roll Virus, Pea Seed-borne Mosaic Virus, Lettuce mosaic virus, Eyespot of maize.

How to use
See section in pests on aphids.

Remove Fallen Leaves and Dead Material

Class
Cultural control practices

English name
Remove fallen leaves and dead material

Names in other languages
Remove fallen leaves and dead material (En). Ramasser et detruire les feuilles tombées ou malades (Fr). Entfernen Sie das Laub und abgestorbene Pflanzenteile (De). Verwijder afgevallen bladeren, plantenwortels en dood hout. (Nl).

Description
To help reduce disease pressure remove leaves in the fall. During the dormant season rake up and destroy fallen leaves and prune out and destroy dead branches.

Used on Vegetables
Garlic, Onion, Peas.

Used for
Basal Rot, Pea Downy Mildew

How to use
Check stored onions and garlic and remove any rotting bulbs immediately. For pea downy mildew remove the plants and clean up all of the fallen leaves. These should be bagged and disposed of in the trash as they can serve as a source of further infection.

Remove Infested Plants Parts

Class
Cultural control practices

English name
Remove infested plants parts

Names in other languages
Remove infested plants parts (En). Retirer et détruire les plantes ou parts atteintes. (Fr). Entfernung der befallenen Pflanzen (De). Aangetaste planten of delen worden verwijderd. (Nl).

Description
Prune out and destroy infested plant parts. Sick plants and infested leaves or branches should be removed and destroyed. By removing these infested plant parts (whether infested by insect pests or diseases), the source for further spreading is taken away.

Used on Vegetables
Cabbage, Lettuce, Potato, Radish, Sweet Corn, Tomatoes, Turnip

Used for
Cabbage Fly. Cabbage Root Fly, Root rot, Verticillium Wilt, Leaf Blight of Maize, Lettuce drop, Tomato Corky Root, Lettuce bacterial rot, Potato Leaf Roll Virus, Tuber Rot, Ring Spot on Lettuce. Anthracnose, Lettuce mosaic virus

How to use
Plants that are severely infested should be discarded. Leaves and stems that are infested are best pruned away and discarded.

Remove Manually Pests

Class
Cultural control practices

English name
Remove manually pests

Names in other languages
Remove manually pests (EN), Supprimer manuellement les insects (FR), Verwijderen handmatig insecten (NL). Hand entfernt (DE).

Description
Handpicking is an excellent method of controlling pests especially when only a few plants are infested. It is the easiest and direct way to kill the visible and slowly moving pests. By handpicking the adults before they have the chance to lay their eggs and by crashing the eggs before they hatch prevent the pests' build-up and the resulting damage. Some insects can be removed with a hand vacuum cleaner.

Used on Vegetables
Artichoke, Asparagus, Beetroot, Beet, Broad Bean, Broccoli, Brussels Sprout, Cabbage, Carrot, Cauliflower, Celery, Cucumber, Eggplant, Fennel, Garlic, Green Bean. Common Bean, Kohlrabi, Lettuce, Napa/Chinese Cabbage, Onion, Parsnip, Peas, Pepper, Bell Pepper, Potato, Radish, Romanesco Broccoli, Rutabaga, Spinach, Sweet Corn , Tomatoes, Turnip.

Used for
Glasshouse Whitefly. Greenhouse Whitefly, Southern Green Stink bug, Asparagus Beetle, Twelve-spotted Asparagus Beetle, Brachyserus of Garlic, Green Artichoke Aphid, Colorado Potato Beetle, June Beetles, May Beetles, Lettuce Root Aphid, Bean Beetle. Pea beetle, Onion Smut. Smut of Onion, Itersonilia Canker. Parsnip Canker, Cabbageworm. Imported Cabbage Worms, Late Blight. Potato and Tomato Late Blight, Beet Armyworm,Green June Beetle. June Bug. June Beetle Cabbage Bug. Rape Bug. Crucifer Shield Bug. Brassica Bug, Asparagus Moth.

How to use
Most medium sized to larger insects can be picked up by hand. and disposed off. Various tweezers exists to help handle smaller specimens. To pick up small specimens without touching them, an aspirator is ideal. Tiny insect and mite specimens can be collected using a fine paint brush or cotton swab. Early removal of diseased leaves is also helpful to prevent disease transmission to the rests of the plants.

Remove White Fly

Class
Cultural control practices

English name
Remove white fly

Names in other languages
Remove white fly (En). Supprimer mouche blanche (Fr). Entfernen weiße Fliege (De). Bestrijd Witte vlieg (Nl).

Description
Whiteflies (Trialeurodes vaporariorum) is a sap-sucking insect, that look like small white moths. They group and breed in large numbers on the undersides of leaves. The nymphs and adults damage plants directly by sucking the sap and by transmitting viruses. Easily identified when infested plants are disturbed, great clouds of the winged adults fly into the air.

Remove white fly

Used on Vegetables
Tomatoes.

Used for
White fly who transmit Tomato Chlorosis Crinivirus. ToCV.

How to use
See White fly in section pests.

Repellent Plants

Class
Cultural control practices

English name
Repellent plants. Companion plants

Names in other languages
Repellent plants (En). Plantes répulsif (Fr). Abstoßend Pflanzen (De). Afstotende planten (Nl).

Description
Companion plants is a gardening technique that involves planting two or more plants near each other to derive some type of benefit. That benefit could be more vigorous growth, higher yield, repelling pests or attracting predators of common pests. A long list of companion plant is available on the internet. Pest-repelling plants includes plants used for their ability to repel insects, nematodes, and other pests.

Used on Vegetables
Broad Bean, Cabbage, Carrot, Cauliflower, Garlic, Green Bean. Common Bean Onion Peas, Turnip.

Used for
Stem Nematode, Bulb and Stem Nematode, Carrot Root Nematode, Carrot Cyst Nematode, Pea Root Nematode, Pea Cyst Nematode, Cabbage and Cauliflower Cyst Nematode, Brassica Cyst Nematode.

How to use
Example given: French Marigold (*Tagetes patula*) kills nematodes when used as a green manure. Other plants like: Dahlia, Castor Bean (*Ricinus communis*), Partridge Pea (*Chamaecrista fasciculata*), Rapeseed (*Brassica napus subsp. napus*), Showy Crotalaria (*Crotalaria spectabilis*), Velvet Bean (*Mucuna pruriens)* may repel several types of nematodes.

Review
Irrigation

Class
Cultural control practices

English name
Review irrigation. Watering

Names in other languages
Review irrigation. Watering (En). Revoir l'irrigation et de distribution d'eau (Fr). Überprüfung Bewässerungssysteme (De). Herzie de bewatering of irrigatie (Nl).

Description
An efficient watering system applies the right amount of water to the right parts of the garden at the right time. This conserves water and helps plants stay healthy to resist pests and diseases. Use a low-flow system like drip, with schedules matched to the plant needs, soil type, weather, and season. Avoid runoff so sidewalks, driveways, and other non-target areas stay dry. Employ other sustainable practices such as mulching to retain soil moisture, water-wise plant selection, and use of alternative water supplies like collected rainwater or greywater.

Used on Vegetables
Artichoke, Beetroot, Beet, Broad Bean, Broccoli, Brussels Sprout, Cabbage, Carrot, Cauliflower, Celeriac, Celery, Chard, Eggplant, Fennel, Garlic, Green Bean, Common Bean, Kohlrabi, Lamb's Lettuce, Leek, Lettuce, Melon, Napa/Chinese Cabbage, Onion, Parsnip, Peas, Pepper, Bell Pepper, Potato, Pumpkin, Radish, Romanesco Broccoli, Rutabaga, Spinach, Tomatoes, Turnip.

Used for
Gray Mold, Grey Mould, Botrytis Blight, Early Blight of Potato/Tomato, Damping Off, White Rot, White Mold, Sclerotinia Wilt, Basal Rot, Powdery Mildew, Red Spider Mite, Two-spotted Mite, Bacterial Brown Spot, Black Rot of Cabbage, Bacterial Blight, Pea Bacterial Blight, Lettuce bacterial rot, Collar Rot. Ink Disease, Pea Downy Mildew, Ring Spot on Lettuce, Anthracnose, Leaf Mould. Cladosporiosis of Tomato.

How to use
Try out micro-irrigation or drip irrigation.

Reynoutria Extract

Botanical name
Reynoutria sachalinensis

Class
Biopesticide

English name
Reynoutria sachalinensis extract. Giant Knotweed

Names in other languages
Reynoutria sachalinensis extract (En). Reynoutria sachalinensis extrait (Fr). Reynoutria sachalinensis extracten (De). Reynoutria sachalinensis aftreksel (Nl).

Description
Extract of Giant Knotweed (Reynoutria sachalinensis) is recommended as a spray on greenhouse grown plants for the purpose of boosting their natural defence mechanisms against certain fungal diseases. The product should be used as a preventive application mainly for the control of powdery mildew and is used for vegetable and fruit plants for outdoor/greenhouse cultures.The extract is prepared by mixing the dried and ground plant material with ethanol.

Reynoutria sachalinensis

Used on Vegetables
Artichoke, Asparagus, Beetroot, Beet, Broccoli, Brussels Sprout, Cabbage, Carrot, Cauliflower, Celeriac, Celery, Chard, Courgette, Cucumber, Eggplant, Garlic, Green Bean. Common Bean, Kohlrabi, Leek, Lettuce, Melon, Napa/Chinese Cabbage, Onion, Parsnip, Peas, Pepper, Bell Pepper, Potato, Pumpkin, Radish, Romanesco Broccoli, Rutabaga, Spinach, Sweet Corn , Tomatoes, Turnip.

Used for
Bacterial Spot, Bacterial Canker of Tomato, White Rot. White Mold. Sclerotinia Wilt, Bacterial Blight of Garlic, Downy Mildew of Alliums, Downy Mildew of Crucifers, Scab of Cucurbits, Cercosporosa Leaf Spot, Cladosporium Leaf Spot, Bacterial Brown Spot , Late Blight. Potato and Tomato Late Blight, Powdery Mildew, Soft rot. White Rot on Carrot, Cottony rot, Lettuce drop, Downy mildew of Cucurbits, Bacterial Blight. Pea Bacterial Blight, Lettuce bacterial rot, Downy mildew, Spinach Downy Mildew, Bleu Mold, Pea Downy Mildew.

How to use
In the case of giant knotweed, organic farmers and gardeners can harvest wild plants and easily produce aqueous extracts to protect crops. Most producers, how-ever, will probably buy commercially available extracts.

Rhubarb

Rheum × hybridum

Botanical name
Rheum × hybridum

Class
Repellent

English name
Rhubarb

Names in other languages
Rhubarb (EN), Rhubarbe (FR), Rabarber (NL), Rhubarb (DE).

Description
Rhubarb is a cultivated plant in the genus Rheum in the family Polygonaceae. It is a herbaceous perennial growing from short, thick rhizomes. The large, triangular leaves contain high levels of oxalic acid, making them inedible. The reddish leaf stalks contains less toxin and are edible. The small flowers are grouped in large compound leafy greenish-white to rose-red inflorescences.

Propagation
Rhubarb is propagated by dividing rhizomes.

Warning
Rhubarb leaves are poisonous, take care when preparing and handling. Do not use on food bearing plants.

Treatment name
Liquid manure of rhubarb

Names in other languages
Liquid manure of rhubarb (EN), Purin de rhubarbe (FR), Rabarbergier (NL), Rhubarbjauche (DE).

Used on Vegetables
Eggplant, Pepper, Bell Pepper, Tomatoes.

Used for
Liquid manure of rhubarb is used as repellent against: Tomato Leaf Miner.

Preparation
Collect the leaves. For 1 litre of water. Use non-chlorinated water like rainwater. Use 150 grams of fresh chopped leaves or 15 grams of dried chopped leaves. Macerate for 72 hours. Filter the liquid through a sieve. The undiluted manure can be stored for a few weeks, in a cool and dark place, preferable in glass containers. Preparation time: Two days.

How to use
Spray on plants. Diluted prior to utilisation at 5%. Repeat every 6 to 7 days, if necessary.

Warning
This plant is toxic. Children and pregnant women avoid handling this produce.

Sanitation

Class
Cultural control practices

English name
Sanitation

Names in other languages
Sanitation (En). Assainissement (Fr). Hygiene (De). Sanitatie (Nl).

Description
Sanitation is one of the most crucial methods for managing pests and diseases. Clearing up crop residues as soon as possible after harvest is one of the best things growers can do. Sanitation is a crucial component of integrated pest management and should be regarded as an effective preventative measure against many pest and disease issues that affect crops. Sanitation refers to any practice that aims to prevent the spread of pathogens by removing diseased and asymptomatic infected material, as well as decontaminating tools, equipment and washing hands.

Used on Vegetables
Eggplant, Pepper, Tomato

Used for
Bacterial Canker of Tomato

How to use
Sanitize benches, tools, and equipment with 10% bleach (1 part bleach to 9 parts water), or other ecological disinfectants.

Soil Solarization

Class
Cultural control practices

English name:
Soil solarisation

Names in other languages
Soil solarization (En). Solarisation du sol (Fr). Solarisation die Boden (De). Solarisatie van de bodem (Nl).

Description
Soil solarisation heats up the top 15 cm (6 inches) or so of soil to temperatures high enough to kill some fungus. Prepare the soil by tilling or digging and then wetting it down. Cover the area with a clear plastic tarp and bury the edges under a few inches of soil to hold it in place and keep the heat in. It takes three to five weeks of bright sunlight and warm temperatures for the soil to heat up enough to kill the fungus.

Used on Vegetables
Artichoke, Asparagus, Beetroot, Beet, Broad Bean, Brussels Sprout, Cabbage, Carrot, Cauliflower, Celeriac, Celery, Courgette, Cucumber, Eggplant, Garlic, Green Bean. Common Bean, Melon, Onion, Peas, Pepper, Bell Pepper, Potato, Pumpkin, Spinach, Tomatoes, Turnip.

Used for
Basal Rot, Verticillium Wilt, Fusarium Wilt, Potato Tuber Nematode, Potato Cyst Nematode, Fusarium Root Rot, Carrot Root Nematode, Carrot Cyst Nematode, Cabbage and Cauliflower Cyst Nematode, Brassica Cyst Nematode.

How to use
To solarise your soil: Clear the area of plants and debris. Water the soil deeply until it is wet or wait for a rainy period. Cover the area with clear plastic. Bury the plastic edges in the soil to trap the heat. Leave the plastic in place for at least 4 weeks in the hottest part of the summer. Remove the plastic. Soil solarisation works best on heavy soils—those containing clay, loam, or mixtures of them. They can hold more water than can light soils, long enough to produce steam every day. Steam is needed to kill nematodes, weed seeds, and insect eggs in the soil. Solarisation may be less effective on sandy soil, which drains faster and produces less steam. To maximise the benefit of solarisation in sandy soils, lay drip irrigation lines under the clear plastic cover and add water regularly.

Spinosad

Botanical name
Saccharopolyspora spinosa

Class
Biopesticide

English name
Insecticide based on spinosad

Names in other languages
Insecticide based on spinosad (En). Spinosad insecticide (Fr). Spinosad Insektizid (De). Spinosad insecticide (Nl).

Description
This product's active ingredient, spinosad, is biologically derived from the fermentation of *Saccharopolyspora spinosa*, a naturally occurring soil organism. Control of Ants, Caterpillars, Colorado Potato Beetle, Corn Earworms, Flea Beetle, Leafminers, Loopers, Mites, Thrips. Spinosad is a broad-spectrum, organic insecticide. The term "broad-spectrum" means that it is toxic to a wide variety of insects. It is, however, relatively non-toxic to mammals and beneficial insects.

Used on Vegetables
Artichoke, Asparagus, Beetroot, Beet, Broad Bean, Broccoli, Brussels Sprout, Cabbage, Cauliflower, Celery, Eggplant, Garlic, Green Bean, Common Bean, Kohlrabi, Leek, Lettuce, Melon, Napa/Chinese Cabbage, Onion, Peas, Pepper, Bell Pepper, Potato, Radish, Romanesco Broccoli, Rutabaga, Spinach, Turnip.

Used for
Artichoke Moth, Artichoke Plume Moth, Colorado Potato Beetle, Dark Sword-grass Moth, Black cutworm, Greasy cutworm, Onion Maggot, Pea Moth, Silver-Y moth, Common Silver-Y moth, Cabbage Army Moth, Tent Caterpillars, Pea Thrips, Frosted Orange Moth. Artichoke Moth, Celery Miner Fly, Lettuce Aphid, Current-lettuce Aphid, Artichoke Root Aphid, Daisy-root Aphid.

How to use
Follow label instructions for use. Spinosad has a period of residual protection effectiveness from pests for five to seven days. Spinosad breaks down in sunlight, so late-day applications will better expose insects to the toxins.

Warning
Spinosad can kill bees and other beneficial insects along with pests. So use it sparingly, only when you think you have to.

Steinernema Nematodes

Botanical name
Steinernema carpocapsae, Steinernema feltae

Class
Predators

English name
Steinernema carpocapsae. Steinernema feltae nematodes

Names in other languages
Steinernema Nematodes (En). Steinernema Nématodes (Fr). Steinernema Nematoden (De). Steinernema Aaltjes (Nl).

Description
Steinernema carpocapsae is an entomopathogenic nematode and a member of the family Steinernematidae. It is a parasitic roundworm that has evolved an insect-killing symbiosis with bacteria, and kills its hosts within a few days of infection. This parasite releases its bacterial symbiont along with a variety of proteins into the host after infection, and together the bacteria and nematode overcome host immunity and kill the host quickly. As a consequence, *S. carpocapsae* has been widely adapted for use as a biological control agent in agriculture and pest control.

Used on Vegetables
Artichoke, Asparagus, Beetroot, Beet, Broccoli, Brussels Sprout, Cabbage, Carrot, Cauliflower, Celery, Eggplant, Garlic, Kohlrabi, Leek, Lettuce, Napa/Chinese Cabbage, Onion, Peas, Pepper, Bell Pepper, Potato, Radish, Romanesco Broccoli, Rutabaga, Spinach, Sweet Corn, Tomatoes, Turnip.

Used for
Nematode species including *Steinernema carpocapsae* and others beneficial nematodes have shown a very high efficacy against adult, larval and pre-pupal stages of Colorado potato beetles. Artichoke Moth, Artichoke Plume Moth, Onion Fly, Asparagus Beetle, Twelve-spotted Asparagus Beetle, Colorado Potato Beetle, Dark Sword-grass Moth, Black cutworm, Greasy cutworm, June Beetles, May Beetles, Cabbage Maggot,Click Beetle, Striped Elaterid Beetle, Wireworms, European Corn Borer, Maize Pyralid, Cabbageworm, Imported Cabbage Worms, March Crane Fly, Beet Armyworm.

How to use
Distribute the nematodes over the infested area, then water. Optimally, nematodes should be applied at sunset to protect them against sunlight. Repeat weekly for a minimum of three weeks. To control boring insects, prepare a water suspension, then inject or spray the solution into the burrows. Repeat weekly for a minimum of three weeks. Nematodes do not prey on ladybugs, earthworms or most other beneficial insects. They are harmless to plants and humans as is the bacterium they produce.

Streptomyces lydicus

Botanical name
Streptomyces lydicus

Class
Biopesticide

English name
Streptomyces lydicus bacterium

Names in other languages
Streptomyces avermitilis (En). Streptomyces avermitilis. Bactéries bénéfiques (Fr). Streptomyces avermitilis (De). Streptomyces avermitilis (Nl).

Description
Streptomyces lydicus is a ubiquitous, naturally occurring bacterium that is commonly found in soil. The isolate WYEC 108 has been commercialised as an antifungal agent for greenhouse, nursery, turf, and agricultural uses. It colonises plant roots, competing with root pathogens for physical space and nutrients exuded by the roots. The commercial product is a soluble powder that contains *Streptomyces lydicus* spores and proprietary inert ingredients.

Used on Vegetables
Artichoke, Asparagus, Beetroot, Beet,, Broccoli, Brussels Sprout, Cabbage, Carrot, Cauliflower, Celeriac, Celery, Courgette, Cucumber, Eggplant, Garlic, Green Bean, Common Bean, Kohlrabi, Lamb's Lettuce, Leek, Lettuce, Melon, Napa/Chinese Cabbage, Onion, Parsnip, Peas, Pepper, Bell Pepper, Potato, Pumpkin, Radish, Romanesco Broccoli, Rutabaga, Spinach, Tomatoes, Turnip.

Used for
Early Blight of Potato/Tomato, Damping Off, White Rot, White Mold, Sclerotinia Wilt, Basal Rot, Downy Mildew of Alliums, Violet Root-rot of Asparagus, Verticillium Wilt, Downy Mildew of Crucifers, Violet Root Rot, Fusarium Wilt, Botrytis Rot. Neckrot, Black Scurf. Rhizoctonia Canker. Stem Canker, Fusarium Root Rot, Late Blight. Potato and Tomato Late Blight, Root rot, Verticillium Wilt, Soft rot. White Rot on Carrot, Cottony rot, Lettuce drop, Tomato Corky Root, Collar Rot. Ink Disease, Celery Root Rot

How to use
This organism is sold as a powder that is soluble in water. You can apply it to turf grass or potted and greenhouse plants as a drench or mixed in with soil. You can also spray *Streptomyces lydicus* on the leaves of your plants every 7-14 days depending on how severely your plants are infected. Apply several times at lower rates rather than making one application at high rates. UV light degrades the bacteria, so it's best to apply them in the evening or morning or on cloudy days.

Tansy

Tanacetum vulgare

Botanical name
Tanacetum vulgare

Class
Repellent

English name
Tansy, Common tansy, Bitter buttons, Cow bitter, or Golden buttons.

Names in other languages
Tansy (En). Tanaisie (Fr). Rainfarn (De). Boerenwormkruid Nl).

Description
Tansy (*Tanacetum vulgare*) is a perennial, herbaceous flowering plant of the aster family. Tansy is a plant with finely divided compound leaves and yellow, button-like flowers. It has a stout, somewhat reddish, erect stem, usually smooth, 50–150 cm (20–59 in) tall, and branching near the top. The leaves are alternate, 10–15 cm (3.9–5.9 in) long and are pinnately lobed, divided almost to the centre into about seven pairs of segments, or lobes, which are again divided into smaller lobes having saw-toothed edges, giving the leaf a somewhat fern-like appearance. The roundish, flat-topped, button-like, yellow flower heads are produced in terminal clusters from mid-to-late summer. The scent is similar to that of camphor with hints of rosemary. The leaves and flowers are toxic if consumed in large quantities; the volatile oil contains toxic compounds including thujone, which can cause convulsions and liver and brain damage.

Cultivation
Easily grown in average, dry to medium, well-drained soils in full sun to part shade. Appreciates some afternoon shade in hot summer climates. Prefers moist, humus soils where it can rapidly spread by rhizomes, but tolerates a wide variety of soils including poor, dry soils where its spreading habit is more restrained. Tansy can be multiplied by sowing in spring or autumn or by dividing plants. Tansy seeds are believed to be viable for just one season. The germination rates increase if the seeds are planted in the spring but they will still need cold stratification. Tansy is planted as companion plant and insect repellent.

Treatment name
Tansy infusion

Class
Repellent

Names in other languages
Tansy infusion (En). Infusion de tanaisie (Fr). Rainfarn infusion (De). Boerenwormkruid infusie (Nl).

Used on Vegetables
Artichoke, Asparagus, Broccoli, Brussels Sprout, Cabbage, Carrot, Cauliflower, Courgette, Cucumber, Eggplant, Green Bean. Common Bean, Kohlrabi, Melon, Napa/Chinese Cabbage, Pepper. Bell Pepper, Pumpkin, Radish, Romanesco Broccoli, Rutabaga, Tomatoes, Turnip.

Used for
Asparagus fly, Cabbage aphid, Red spider mite, Turnip gall weevil, Cabbage worm.

How to prepare
Use leaves, stems and flowers. For 1 litre of water. Use non-chlorinated water like rainwater use 300 grams of fresh plant or 30 grams of dried plant. Bring to a boil and cut the heat. Let cool down covered. Filter the liquid through a sieve. Preparation time: One hour. Conservation: Infusion has to be used before it starts to ferment.

Use
As a spray on plants. Diluted prior to utilisation at 20%. Repeat every 4 to 4 days, if necessary.

Warning
Do not add tansy to the compost heap.

Treatment name
Tansy decoction

Class
Repellent

Names in other languages
Tansy decoction (En). Décoction de tanaisie (Fr). Rainfarn Pflanzenabsuds (De). Boerenwormkruid afkooksel (Nl).

Used on Vegetables
Artichoke, Beetroot. Beet, Broccoli, Brussels Sprout, Cabbage, Carrot, Cauliflower, Celeriac, Chard, Cucumber, Eggplant, Fennel, Garlic, Green Bean. Common Bean, Kohlrabi, Leek, Lettuce, Napa/Chinese Cabbage, Onion, Parsnip, Potato, Radish, Romanesco Broccoli, Rutabaga, Spinach, Tomatoes, Turnip

Used for
Tansy decoction is used as repellent for Artichoke pear-shaped weevil, Artichoke moth, Leek moth, Onion moth, Dark sword-grass moth, Cabbage stem flea beetle, Carrot fly, Lettuce root aphid, Silver-Y moth.

How to prepare
Use the whole plant, without the roots, broken or chopped into small bits. For 1 litre of water. Use non-chlorinated water like rainwater take 30 grams of fresh plant or 3 grams of dried plant. Bring to a boil, reduce heat, cover and let simmer for 20 minutes. Let cool down and macerated for 12 to 24 hours. Filter the liquid through a sieve before use. Preparation time: Two days.

Use
As a spray on plants, not diluted. Repeat, if necessary, every 6 to 7 days.

Warning
Do not add tansy to the compost heap.

Treatment name
Liquid manure of tansy

Names in other languages
Liquid manure of tansy (EN), Purin de tanaisie (FR), Boerenwormkruidgier (NL), Rainfarnjauche (DE).

Used on Vegetables
Asparagus, Broad Bean, Carrot Celeriac, Celery, Chard, Green Bean, Common Bean, Parsnip, Rutabaga.

Used for

Liquid manure of tansy is used as repellent for fungi: Rust

How to prepare
Collect leaves, stems and flowers. Chop in small pieces. For 1 litre of water. Use non-chlorinated water like rainwater. Use 200 grams of fresh tansy or 20 grams of dried tansy. Macerate for one to two weeks. By preference use plastic or wooden recipients. Stir or shake the mixture regularly. Strain after fermentation is complete or no air bubbles form. The undiluted manure can be stored for a few weeks, in a cool and dark place, preferable in glass or plastic containers. Preparation time: Two weeks.

Use
Spray on plants. Diluted prior to utilisation at 20%. Repeat every 6 to 7 days, if necessary.

Warning
Do not add tansy to the compost heap.

Tomato

Botanical name
Solanum lycopersicum

Class
Repellent

English name
Tomato

Names in other languages
Tomato (EN), Tomate (FR), Tomaten (NL), Tomaten (DE).

Description
Tomato plants are vines, initially decumbent, typically growing 180 cm (6 ft) or more above the ground if supported, although erect bush varieties have been bred, generally 100 cm (3 ft) tall or shorter. Indeterminate types are "tender" perennials, dying annually in temperate climates (they are originally native to tropical highlands), although they can live up to three years in a greenhouse in some cases. Tomato vines are typically pubescent, meaning covered with fine short hairs. These hairs facilitate the vining process, turning into roots wherever the plant is in contact with the ground and moisture, especially if the vine's connection to its original root has been damaged or severed. The leaves are 10–25 cm (4–10 in) long, odd pinnate, with five to 9 leaflets on petioles, each leaflet up to 8 cm (3 in) long, with a serrated margin; both the stem and leaves are densely glandular-hairy. Flowers in domestic cultivars can be self-fertilising. The flowers are 1–2 cm (0.4–0.8 in) across, yellow, with five pointed lobes on the corolla; they are borne in a cyme of three to 12 together. Although in culinary terms, tomato is regarded as a vegetable, its fruit is classified botanically as a berry. As a true fruit, it develops from the ovary of the plant after fertilisation, its flesh comprising the pericarp walls. The fruit contains hollow spaces full of seeds and moisture, called locular cavities.]

Propagation
Mostly by seeds. The seeds need to come from a mature fruit, and be dried or fermented before germination.

Solanum lycopersicum

Treatment name
Liquid manure or maceration of tomato

Names in other languages
Liquid manure or maceration of tomato (EN), Purin de tomate (FR), Tomatengier (NL), Tomatenjauche (DE).

Use on Vegetables
Asparagus, Beetroot, Beet, Broccoli, Brussels Sprout, Cabbage, Cauliflower, Chard, Cucumber, Garlic, Kohlrabi, Leek, Napa/Chinese Cabbage, Onion, Potato, Radish, Romanesco Broccoli, Rutabaga, Tomatoes, Turnip.

Use for
Liquid manure of tomato is an efficient repellent to ward of many phytophagous insects: Leek Moth, Onion Moth, Asparagus Fly, Asparagus Maggot, Cabbage Stem Flea Beetle, Cabbageworm, Imported Cabbage Worms.

Preparation
Collect leaves, stems and flowers. Chop in small pieces. For 1 litre of water. Use non-chlorinated water like rainwater. Use 100—200 grams of fresh tomato plants. Macerate for 24 to 48 hours. Stir or shake the mixture regularly. By preference use plastic or wooden recipients. Strain after fermenting and before use. The undiluted manure can be stored for a few weeks, in a cool and dark place, preferable in glass or plastic containers. Preparation time: Two to tree days.

How to use: Spray on plants. Not diluted. Repeat every 3 to 4 days, if necessary.

Transseius montdorensis

Botanical name
Transeius montdorensis

Class
Predators

English name
Transeius montdorensis Predatory mite

Names in other languages
Transeius montdorensis Predatory mite (En).
Transeius montdorensis Acarien prédateur (Fr).
Transeius montdorensis Raubmilbe (De).
Transeius montdorensis Roofmijt (Nl).

Description
Transeius montdorensis is an active predatory mite that contributes to the control and management of thrips, whitefly and molluscum mites, among others. Transeius montdorensis controls both the first and second larval stages of thrips, and eggs and larvae of whitefly. Adults (females) lay single eggs on leaf hairs. After 1 to 2 days, the eggs hatch into larvae. This is followed by two more nymphal stages until the adult stage is reached. From the first stage, the mites are predatory. The predatory mite is resistant to high temperatures and dry conditions, and is also active at lower temperatures and low light in winter.

Transeius montdorensis

Used on Vegetables
Bean, Courgette, Cucumber, Eggplant, Common bean, Leek, Onion, Peas, Pepper, Pumpkin, Tomatoes.

Used for
Onion thrips, Tomato Russet Mite, Pea Thrips, Glasshouse whitefly.

How to use
The predatory mite is active from 10 °C. The optimum is 25 °C. The predatory mite actively searches for prey and sucks it empty. The predatory mite can then eat about 10 thrips larvae per day. Hatching Thrips eggs are also eaten by the predatory mite. The predatory mites must be used in the crop as soon as possible after delivery.

Trap Cropping

Class
Cultural control practices

English name
Trap cropping

Names in other languages
Trap cropping (En). Cultures-pièges (Fr). Fallen bau (De). Valkuil gewassen (Nl).

Description
Trap cropping, in which attractive plant species are planted near the main crop to draw the pest away.

Used on Vegetables
Cabbage, Cauliflower, Cucumber, Eggplant, Green Bean, Common Bean, Pepper, Bell Pepper, Tomatoes, Turnip

Used for
Southern Green Stink bug, Turnip Flea Beetle. Large Striped Flea Beetle, Striped Turnip Flea Beetle

How to use
Example given. Trap crops, such as mustard and radish, can be planted near garden areas to draw flea beetle away.

Trichoderma Fungus

Botanical name
Trichoderma virens/Gliocladium virens

Class
Biopesticide

English name
Trichoderma fungus

Names in other languages
Trichoderma fungus (En). Trichoderma fungi (Fr). Trichoderma Pilz (De). Trichoderma schimmel (Nl).

Description
Trichoderma is a free-living fungus which is common in soil and root ecosystems.

Used on Vegetables
Artichoke, Asparagus, Beetroot, Beet, Broccoli, Brussels Sprout, Cabbage, Carrot, Cauliflower, Chard, Celeriac, Celery, Courgette, Cucumber, Eggplant, Garlic, Green Bean, Common Bean, Kohlrabi, Lamb's Lettuce, Leek, Lettuce, Melon, Napa/Chinese Cabbage, Onion, Parsnip, Peas, Pepper, Bell Pepper, Potato, Pumpkin, Radish, Romanesco Broccoli, Rutabaga, Spinach, Tomatoes, Turnip.

Used for
Trichoderma is a potent biocontrol agent and used extensively for soil born diseases. It has been used successfully against pathogenic fungi belonging to Fusarium, Phytopthora, Scelerotia, Damping Off, Ascochyta Rot, Black Rot, Leaf Spot, White Rot, White Mold, Sclerotinia Wilt, Basal Rot, Downy Mildew of Alliums, Violet Root-rot of Asparagus, Violet Root Rot, Fusarium Wilt, Black Scurf, Rhizoctonia Canker, Stem Canker, Late Blight, Potato and Tomato Late Blight, Soft rot, White Rot on Carrot, Cottony rot, Lettuce drop, Collar Rot, Ink Disease, Celery Root Rot, Brown Rot Gummosis, Foot Rot.

How to use
The Trichoderma fungus can be added straight to compost piles, potting soils or planting holes three days before planting. Or used as a spray.

Trichogramma Predatory Wasp

Botanical name
Trichogramma ostriniae

Class
Predators

English name
Trichogramma predatory wasps

Names in other languages
Trichogramme   predatory   wasps   (En).
Trichogrammes   guêpes   parasites   (Fr).
Trichogramma   parasitische   Wespe   (De).
Trichogramma sluipwesp (Nl).

Description
Trichogramma is a genus of minute polyphagous wasps that are endoparasitoids of insect eggs. Trichogramma is one of around 80 genera from the family Trichogrammatidae, with over 200 species worldwide. Trichogramma wasps are specifically selected for maximum results in suppressing European corn borer eggs in sweet corn, sweet and hot peppers. The adults are tiny, measuring less than 1 mm. The trichogramma larvae develop and feed on the pest embryo.

Trichogramma ostriniae

Used on Vegetables
Beetroot, Beet, Broccoli, Brussels Sprout, Cabbage, Cauliflower, Kohlrabi, Leek, Lettuce, Napa/Chinese Cabbage. Onion, Potato, Radish, Romanesco Broccoli, Rutabaga, Spinach, Sweet Corn, Turnip.

Used for
European Corn Borer, Maize Pyralid,

How to use
Trichogramma prefer to attack freshly deposited moth eggs (up to 4 days old), the time to release Trichogramma is when moths are flying and laying eggs. Begin releases as early in the season as field and row crops provide shade for the parasites. Trichogramma can be released as larvae or as adults, many commercial formats are on the market.

Trissolcus basalis
Predatory wasp

Botanical name
Trissolcus basalis

Class
Predators

English name
Trissolcus basalis Predatory wasp

Names in other languages
Trissolcus basalis Predatory wasp (En). Trissolcus basalis Guêpe prédatrice (Fr). Trissolcus basalis Raubwespe (De). Trissolcus basalis Roofwesp (Nl).

Description
Trissolcus basalis is a solitary parasitoid of stinkbug eggs. The female stalks adult stinkbugs to lay an egg inside their recently laid eggs; the entire egg mass can be parasitized. After three instars, the Trissolcus larva undergoes metamorphosis and reaches the adult stage. Parasitization becomes evident after a few days due to the change in color of the eggs, which become grayish. Each female lives for about two weeks, during which time she lays up to 250 eggs. At the optimal temperature of 27°C, the cycle takes about ten days.

Used on Vegetables
Cucumber, Eggplant, Common bean, Pepper, Tomatoes.

Used for
Southern Green Stink Bug.

How to use
Introduction rates. Preventive: 10 000 wasps/ha, light curative: 30 000 wasps/ha, heavy curative: 60 000 wasps/ha, hot spot treatment: 100 000 wasps/ha for at least 3-4 weeks. Releases should be repeated at weekly intervals throughout the season or until control is achieved.

Resistant Varieties

Class
Cultural control practices

English name
Use resistant varieties/cultivars

Names in other languages
Use resistant varieties/cultivars (En). Utilisation de variétés résistantes. (Fr). Verwenden resistente Sorten (De). Maak gebruik van resistente rassen (Nl).

Description
The cheapest, easiest and most efficient way for gardeners to reduce losses from diseases is to plant resistance varieties. Many seed companies, offer seeds that are resistant to certain common pathogens.

Used on Vegetables
All

Used for
Early Blight of Potato/Tomato, Downy Mildew of Alliums, Rust, Tobacco Mosaic Virus. TMV, Cabbage Club Root, Fusarium Wilt, Scab of Cucurbits, Maize Smut. Corn Smut, Bacterial Brown Spot, Itersonilia Canker. Parsnip Canker, Mosaic Virus on Pepper. TMV. CMV, Potato Tuber Nematode. Potato Cyst Nematode, Fusarium Root Rot, Late Blight. Potato and Tomato Late Blight, Carrot Root Nematode. Carrot Cyst Nematode, Pea Root Nematode. Pea Cyst Nematode, Potato Tuberworm. Potato Split-worm. Potato Tuber Moth, Black Rot of Cabbage, Verticillium Wilt, Leaf Blight of Maize, Tomato Corky Root, Downy mildew of Cucurbits, Potato Leaf-drop Streak. Potato Virus Y, Potato Leaf Roll Virus, Potato Virus A, Potato Virus X, Collar Rot. Ink Disease, Downy mildew. Spinach Downy Mildew. Bleu Mold, Pea Seed-borne Mosaic Virus, Ring Spot on Lettuce. Anthracnose, Lettuce mosaic virus, Eyespot of maize

How to use
Lists of recommended vegetables cultivars for your region are often available on the internet.

Verticillium Fungus

Botanical name
Verticillium lecanii

Class
Biopesticide

English name
Verticillium lecanii fungus

Names in other languages
Verticillium lecanii fungus (En). Verticillium lecanii fungi (Fr). Verticillium lecanii pilz (De). Verticillium lecanii schimmel (Nl).

Description
Verticillium is a biological insecticide that contains spores of *Verticillium lecanii*, a naturally occurring entomopathogenic fungus that infects targeted sucking insect groups (aphids). The spore of this fungus come in contact with the skin or the insect and grows directly through the skin to the inner both of the host. The fungus proliferates throughout the whole insect body draining out the vital nutrients eventually killing it in about 48-72 hours after spray.

Used on Vegetables
Tomatoes.

Used for
Aphids bearing Tomato Chlorosis Crinivirus. ToCV.

How to use
As a spray.

Watering at the Root

Class
Cultural control practices

English name
Watering only at the root

Names in other languages
Watering only at the root (En). Arroser seulement aux racines (Fr). Bewässern Wurzelzone (De). Water geven aan de wortels alleen (Nl).

Description
Avoiding water on the foliage will prevent diseases from forming. Watering just the soil around the plants. Think of watering cans and hoses who can be replaced by drip or trickle irrigation systems.

Used on Vegetables
Artichoke, Asparagus, Beetroot, Beet, Broad Bean, Carrot, Celeriac, Celery, Chard, Courgette, Cucumber, Eggplant, Fennel, Green Bean, Common Bean, Lamb's Lettuce, Leek, Lettuce, Melon, Onion, Parsnip, Peas, Potato, Pumpkin, Radish, Rutabaga, Spinach,Tomatoes

Used for
Rust, Powdery Mildew

How to use
Avoid watering plants from overhead in order to reduce relative humidity.

Weed Control

Class
Cultural control practices

English name
Weed control

Names in other languages
Weed control (En). Contrôle des mauvaises herbes (Fr). Unkrautbekämpfung (De). Onkruidbestrijding (Nl).

Description
Weeds along ditch banks, roads, in farm yards, and other noncultivated areas contribute directly to the aphid problem on potatoes. Malva, tumble mustard (Sisymbrium altissimum), penny cress (Thlaspi arvense), and other mustards (Brassica spp.) serve as early season host plants where aphid populations increase before spreading to other host plants, including commercial potatoes.

Used on Vegetables
Beetroot, Cabbage, Cucumber, Eggplant, Lettuce, Peas, Pepper, Potato, Tomatoes.

Used for
Potato Aphid.

How to use
To assist controlling potato aphids is to remove nearby plants that might harbor these pests. This means keeping weeds away from potato patch. Malva, penny cress, and various mustards, in particular, can act as early season host plants for this pest.

Wettable Sulphur

Class
Fungicide

English name
Wettable sulphur

Names in other languages
Wettable sulphur (En). Soufre mouillables (Fr). Netzschwefel (De). Spuitzwavel (Nl).

Description
Wettable Sulphur is a fungicide and insecticide suitable to be used in organic gardens and has an exceptionally low level of toxicity. It is used to control mites and a range of fungal disorders including powdery mildew, rust, and brown rot.

Used on Vegetables
Artichoke, Asparagus, Beetroot, Beet, Broad Bean, Broccoli, Brussels Sprout, Cabbage, Carrot, Cauliflower, Celeriac, Celery, Chard, Courgette, Cucumber, Eggplant, Fennel, Garlic, Green Bean. Common Bean, Kohlrabi, Lamb's Lettuce, Lettuce, Melon, Napa/Chinese Cabbage, Onion, Parsnip, Pepper, Bell Pepper, Potato, Pumpkin, Radish, Romanesco Broccoli, Rutabaga, Spinach, Sweet Corn , Tomatoes, Turnip.

Used for
Damping Off, Anthracnose Fruit Rot, Tomato Russet Mite, Onion and Leek Rust, Violet Root-rot of Asparagus, Rust, Downy Mildew of Crucifers, Violet Root Rot, Powdery Mildew, Anthracnose of Cucurbits, Cercosporosa Leaf Spot, Red Spider Mite. Two-spotted Mite, Mealybugs, Rust Mite, European Red Mite, Powdery Mildew, Ring Spot on Lettuce. Anthracnose.

How to use
Refer to product label for detailed instructions.

Whitefly Traps

Class
Cultural control practices

English name
Whitefly traps

Names in other languages
Whitefly traps (En). Pièges aleurode (Fr). Fallen Weißen Fliegen (De). Gele signaalplaten voor wittevlieg (Nl).

Description
Whitefly traps are small squares of yellow cardboard with sticky glue on them, see also chromatic traps. Whiteflies are attracted by the yellow or orange colour and attach to the trap and can't fly away. You can purchase them from garden centres, online or make them yourself. Procure a can of sticky glue coating, apply the coating to a yellow paper and your trap is ready for use.

Used on Vegetables
Asparagus, Eggplant, Tomatoes

Used for
Glasshouse Whitefly. Greenhouse Whitefly

How to use
For use indoors and outdoors. Attach the traps to your houseplants or hang discreetly in your kitchen or garden area. For badly infested plants, place the trap in the plant and then gently shake, causing the insects to swarm and stick into the trap.

Wood Ash

Class
Cultural control practices

English name
Wood ash

Names in other languages
Wood ash (En). Cendre de bois (Fr). Holzasche (De). Houtas (Nl).

Description
Wood ash, charcoal dust, charcoal left overs can be used as borders around the plants. This works well in dry conditions. Wood ash is best used either lightly scattered or by first being composted along with the rest of your compost. This is because wood ash will produce lye and salts if it gets wet. In small quantities, the lye and salt will not cause problems, but in larger amounts, the lye and salt may burn your plants. Composting fireplace ashes allows the lye and salt to be leached away. Not all wood ash are the same. If the fireplace ashes in your compost are made primarily from hardwoods, like oak and maple, the nutrients and minerals in your wood ash will be much higher. If the fireplace ashes in your compost are made mostly by burning softwoods like pine or firs, there will be fewer nutrients and minerals in the ash.

Used on Vegetables
Beetroot. Beet, Broccoli,,Brussels Sprout, Cabbage, Cauliflower, Chard, Cucumber, Kohlrabi, Napa/Chinese Cabbage, Potato, Radish, Romanesco Broccoli, Rutabaga, Tomatoes, Turnip

Used for
Cabbage Stem Flea Beetle, Snails and slugs.

How to use
To use wood ash for pest control, simply sprinkle it around the base of plants being attacked by soft bodied pests. If the ash gets wet, you'll need to refresh the wood ashes as the water will leach away the salt that makes wood ashes an effective pest control.

Wormwood

Artemisia absinthium

Botanical name
Artemisia absinthium

English name
Wormwood

Names in other languages
Wormwood (En). Absinthe (Fr). Wermutpflanze (De). Alsem (Nl).

Description
Artemisia absinthium is a herbaceous perennial plant with fibrous roots. The stems are straight, growing to 0.8–1.2 metres (2 ft 7 in–3 ft 11 in) tall, grooved, branched, and silvery-green. The leaves are spirally arranged, greenish-grey above and white below, covered with silky silvery-white trichomes, and bearing minute oil-producing glands. the basal leaves are up to 250 mm (9.8 in) long, bipinnate to tripinnate with long petioles, with those on the stem smaller, 50–100 mm (2.0–3.9 in) long, less divided, and with short petioles. The uppermost leaves can be both simple and sessile (without a petiole). Its flowers are pale yellow, tubular, and clustered in spherical bent-down heads (capitula), which are in turn clustered in leafy and branched panicles. Flowering is from early summer to early autumn. Pollination is by wind. The fruit is a small achene. The seed dispersal is by gravity.

Cultivation
It grows naturally on uncultivated arid ground, on rocky slopes, and at the edge of footpaths and fields. The plant can easily be cultivated in dry soil. It should be planted under bright exposure in fertile, mid-weight soil. It prefers soil rich in nitrogen. It can be propagated by ripened cuttings taken in spring or autumn in temperate climates, or by seeds in nursery beds. A common consideration applies to growing the plant with others as it tends to stunt their growth; accordingly it is not considered to be a good companion plant. *A. absinthium* also self-seeds generously.

Treatment name
Wormwood infusion

Class
Repellent

Names in other languages
Wormwood infusion (En). Infusion de absinthe (Fr). Wermutpflanze infusion (De). Alsem infusie (Nl).

Use on Vegetables
Artichoke, Beetroot. Beet, Broccoli, Brussels Sprout, Cabbage, Cauliflower, Celeriac, Celery, Chard, Cucumber, Green Bean. Common Bean, Kohlrabi, Lamb's Lettuce, Lettuce, Napa/Chinese Cabbage, Peas, Radish, Romanesco Broccoli, Rutabaga, Spinach, Sweet Corn, Tomatoes, Turnip.

Use for
Wormwood infusion can be used as a natural repellent against aphids and caterpillars.

How to prepare
Take leaves, stems and flowers. Use 300 grams of fresh plant or 30 grams of dried plant for 1 litre of water. Use non-chlorinated water like rainwater. Bring to a boil and cut the heat. Let cool down and infuse for 15 minutes. Filter the liquid through a sieve. The infusion has to be used before it starts to ferment. Preparation time one hour.

Use
As a spry on plants. Diluted prior to utilisation at 20%. Repeat if necessary every 3 to 4 days.

Warning
This plant is toxic. Children and pregnant women avoid handling this produce.

Treatment name
Wormwood decoction

Names in other languages
Wormwood decoction (En). Décoction absinthe (Fr). Wermutpflanze Pflanzenabsuds (De). Alsem afkkoksel (Nl).

Use on
Artichoke, Eggplant, Spinach

Use for
Wormwood decoction is used against the caterpillars of Artichoke moth and Silver-Y moth.

How to prepare
Cut leaves, stems and flowers. Use 30 grams of fresh plant or 3 grams of dried plant for 1 litre of water. Use non-chlorinated water like rainwater. Bring to a boil, cover and let simmer for 30 minutes. Let cool down covered. Macerate for 24 hours. Filter the liquid through a sieve. Preparation time: Two days.

Use
As a spray on plants. Not diluted. Repeat if necessary every 8 to 10 days.

Warning
This plant is toxic. Children and pregnant women avoid handling this produce.

Index

Annex

Further readings
Handbook of pest management in organic farming, V. Vacante, S. Kreiter, CABI.

Websites
http://ephytia.inra.fr

Credits
American Serpentine Leaf Miner © https://www.biosecurity.govt.nz. Anthracnose of Cucurbits © https://tse4.mm.bing.net. Anthracnose © https://tse1.explicit.bing.net. Artichoke Moth © https://ffnaturesearch.org. Artichoke Pear-shaped Weevil © https://tse4.mm.bing.net. Ascochyta Foot-rot © https://s3.amazonaws.com. Asparagus Beetles © https:/tse1.mm.bing.net. Asparagus Fly © https://diptera.info. Asparagus Moth © https://www.lepiforum.de/bh/personen/egbert_friedrich. Bacterial Blight of Garlic © https://tse4.mm.bing.net. Bacterial Blight of Pea © https://www.plantdiseases.org. Bacterial Brown Spot © https://extension.usu.edu. Bacterial Canker of Tomato © https://bpb-us-e1.wpmucdn.com. Bacterial Spot © https://bugwoodcloud.org. Basal Rot © https://swettlab.faculty.ucdavis.edu. Bean Aphids. © https://www.futurity.org. Bean Beetle © https://c1.staticflickr.com. Bean Yellow Mosaic Virus © https://d3qz1qhhp9wxfa.cloudfront.net. Beet Armyworm © https://extension.usu.edu. Beet Curly Top Virus © https://bugwoodcloud.org. Beet Fly © https://tse3.mm.bing.net. Beet Moth © https://agroflora.ru. Black Leg © https://tse1.explicit.bing.net. Black Rot of Cabbage © https://bpb-us-e1.wpmucdn.com/blogs.cornell.edu. Black Scurf © https://tse2.mm.bing.net. Boron Deficiency © https://content.ces.ncsu.edu. Botrytis Rot © https://extension.usu.edu. Brachyserus of Garlic © https://orchidee-poitou-charentes.org. Bright-line Brown-eyes © Moth https://live.staticflickr.com. Cabbage Aphid © https://tse2.mm.bing.net. Cabbage Bug © https://tse2.mm.bing.net. Cabbage Club Root © https://media.licdn.com. Cabbage Fly © https://www.lovethegarden.com. Cabbage Stem Flea Beetle © https://warehouse1.indicia.org.uk. Cabbageworm © R. Lemmens. Carrot Fly © https://www.nature-and-garden.com. Carrot Root Nematode © https://ag.purdue.edu.Celery Fly © https://www.naturspaziergang.de. Celery Late Blight © https://sites.science.oregonstate.edu. Celery Miner Fly © https://www.agrolink.com.br. Celery Root Rot © https://tse2.mm.bing.net. Cercosporosa Leaf Spot © https://tse2.mm.bing.net. Chlorosis © https://tse2.mm.bing.net. Cladosporiosis of Tomato © https://tse3.mm.bing.net. Cladosporium Leaf Spot © https://bugwoodcloud.org. Click Beetle © https://inaturalist-open-data.s3.amazonaws.com. Colorado Potato Beetle © https://extension.entm.purdue.edu/publications. Common Swift Moth © https://bugguide.ne. Cotton Aphid © https://tse4.mm.bing.net. Cotton Whitefly © https://tse4.mm.bing.net. Cotton Worm © https://bugwoodcloud.org. Cucumber Mosaic Virus Cucumber © https://gardenandhappy.com. Damping Off © https://bugwoodcloud.org. Dark Sword-grass Moth © https://insecta.pro. Diamond-back Moth © https:/alchetron.com. Downy Mildew of Crucifers © https://s3-us-west-1.amazonaws.com. Downy mildew of Cucurbits © https://bpb-us-e1.wpmucdn.com.Early Blight of Potato © https://apps.lucidcentral.org. European Corn Borer © https://www.ukmoths.org.uk. Eyespot of Maize © https://d3mdtxxgfz6upn.cloudfront.net. Frosted Orange Moth © https://www.suffolkmoths.co.uk. Fusarium Root Rot © https://backyardgardenersnetwork.org. Fusarium Wilt © https://eu-images.contentstack.com. Garden Dart Moth © https://www.westmidlandsmoths.co.uk. Glasshouse Potato Foxglove Aphid © https://bugguide.net. Grain Aphid © https://www.jic.ac.uk. Green Artichoke Aphid © https://bugwoodcloud.org. Green Tortoise Beetle © https://www.learnaboutnature.com. itersonilia-canker © https://extension.usu.edu. June Beetles © https://bugguide.net. Late blight © https://cropscience.bayer.co.uk. Leaf Blight of Maize © https://apps.lucidcentral.org. Leaf Mould © https://ag.purdue.edu. Leek Moth © https://tse2.mm.bing.net. ettuce Bacterial Rot © https://eorganic.org. Lettuce Root Aphid © https://tse1.mm.bing.net. maize-smut © https://plantwiseplusknowledgebank.org. March Crane Fly © https://bugguide.net. Molybdenum deficiency © https://cropaia.com. Mosaic Virus on Pepper © https://tse1.explicit.bing.net. Oignon Smut © https://bugwoodcloud.org. Onion and Leek Rust © https://www.learn-how-to-garden.co. Onion Fly © https://www.iriisphytoprotection.qc.ca. Onion Thrips © https://tse2.mm.bing.net.